GIRLIE

TONY SHILLITOE

Copyright © 2024 Tony Shillitoe
All rights reserved.

Cover design by TS

ISBN: 978-1-7637241-1-2

"Life wasn't about becoming, was it? It was about being."
Kate Atkinson, *Life After Life*.

1944

"As soon as this one's born, let's have another kid. I'd hate to think of a guy growing up without brothers."
Albert Leo 'Al' Sullivan

Two things astonished her: bright red blood pooling on the concrete pavement beneath the green bus stop bench, and the soldier's indifference to it. Eileen stared at the dark stain spreading through the man's khaki shirt, blood ebbing over his fingers as he clasped his stomach, wondering if he was feeling the throbbing pain she felt when she cut her finger with the kitchen knife. Sharp sunlight glittered on his silver wristwatch; a warm breeze stirred blond hairs on his arm. A fly crawled across his shoulder. February afternoon heat pressed down.

And then she remembered where she was.

She turned to her brothers and ordered, 'Fetch Mum!' When neither boy responded, transfixed by their morbid fascination for blood, she yelled, 'Now!'

Peter grabbed Ian's bony arm and pulled his little brother after him, the gangly schoolboys running across The Broadway, bewildered by their big sister's anger and the vision of the stabbed soldier.

Eileen recognised the soldier – Mister Whitehead. He lived in number thirty-four. Before he joined the army, he was a painter in white overalls spattered with rainbow colours, but he was away at the war a very long time. His wife, Missus Whitehead, shopped at Sendy's store, and she sometimes said hello to Eileen's mother. She wore her dark blond hair like Claudette Colbert in a curly bob, and she was always smartly dressed in bright floral frocks and wide-brimmed sailor hats. When she smiled, her teeth were perfect, like a movie star.

Eileen whispered, 'Mister Whitehead?' and waited for him to look up, but his head hung forward, his oily blond fringe dangling languidly, his shadow hunched in the gutter.

'Girlie!' The sharp cry brought Eileen around to her mother gesticulating frantically as she hurried across the street in her emerald dress and bare feet. 'Away from there!'

A maroon Ford coupe slowed on The Broadway, brakes squeaking as it stopped, and a stocky man in grey woollen vest, white shirt and grey trousers, climbed out and stood on the road with the driver's door open. He tilted his hat and scratched his sparse greying hair, and called, 'Everything all right, Clarice?'

Eileen thought she knew the driver, but her mother was talking frantically, Mister Whitehead was bleeding, the sun was unbearably hot, and she couldn't think clearly. The world was out of kilter and unrecognisable.

'Girlie!' Go inside and look after the children!' Clarice ordered.

'Will he die?' Eileen asked.

Clarice assessed the soldier on the bench, and muttered, 'Oh, Good Lord,' before she turned on her daughter, and barked, 'Girlie Bonney, do as I say! Go home and look after your brothers and sisters!'

Eileen knew better than to dither when her mother was angry. She crossed The Broadway, acutely conscious of her four siblings' faces pressed against the parlour windowpane, squinting against the late afternoon glare. She passed the corrugated iron Anderson shelter in the narrow front yard, opened the green house door, entered the cream hallway and turned right, into the parlour, where her brothers and sisters were crowded at the window.

Josie, curly brunette hair and pale cheeks, waved cheerily, happy to see her big sister, until Eileen ordered, 'Away from there!' Startled by their sister's ferocity, Judy and Josie retreated to stand beside the polished mahogany coffee table, and Ian stepped back from the window, but Peter stayed, nose smudging the windowpane.

'Will the man die?' Judy piped.

Eileen put her hands on her sister's bony shoulders, looked into her steel blue eyes, and said, 'No. Mister Whitehead isn't dying. He will be all right.'

'Doesn't look all right to me,' Peter countered, voice echoing off the glass.

'Peter Bonney!' Eileen barked. 'Mum said you are to go to the back yard and wait.'

'Mum's across the road, so she hasn't said anything to me,' Peter retorted. 'She's talking to Mister Chapman.'

'Peter!' Eileen snapped. 'Get away from that window or there'll be trouble!' She turned to Ian. 'Take your sisters out the back.'

'I don't want to go out the back,' Ian complained.

'Do as you are told!' Eileen snarled, her bright blue eyes glittering with anger.

Ian recoiled from his sister's glare, pulled Judy's arm, and ushered Josie into the hall. Eileen whirled to deal with Peter, but he was retreating from the window, warning, 'Mum's coming,' and he judiciously followed in his brother and sisters' wake.

As Eileen entered the hall, the children's footsteps pattering towards the kitchen, Clarice hurried through the front door and reached for the wall phone. 'Where are the children?' she asked, as she unhitched the ebony receiver.

'Outside,' Eileen replied. 'I thought it was best they weren't being nosey parkers.'

'Good,' Clarice agreed. She spun the silver dialler across the numbers, the phone mechanism whirring busily, and said, 'Put the kettle on, please.'

Brown school shoes clomping on the floorboards where the brown and black hall runner ended, Eileen passed through multi-blue patterned curtains beneath the gothic arch dividing the front of the house from the rear and headed for the kitchen. She skirted the painted green table where the family gathered to eat in the evenings to retrieve a box of Redhead matches from the mantlepiece over the Metters stove. She checked for kindling in the burner and stuffed newspaper between the wood to light it, but she remained attentive to her mother's voice on the phone as the odours of burning paper and wood filled the kitchen.

'Clarice Bonney – Yes – Yes, Bonney – That's correct – There's been a terrible accident – Yes, a man is injured, a soldier – Stabbing, I believe – No – I don't know – On the corner of Partridge and The Broadway – Yes, Glenelg – Yes, I do – Ron Whitehead – A soldier – Yes, I will – Robert Chapman is with him – Yes – Yes, I will – Thank you.'

Eileen was numb from the shock of finding the man bleeding on the bench. That kind of violence was the province of movies and the war, and far removed from her life, and she couldn't understand how or why it came so rudely into their street. She poured water from a dented metal bucket into the smoke-smeared silver kettle, wondering what would happen to Mister Whitehead and who would come to help him, and her hands shook as she placed the kettle on the stove. When her mother entered the kitchen, she asked, 'Will Mister Whitehead be all right?'

'They are sending an ambulance,' Clarice replied. She reached for the Royal Albert teacups and saucers on the tall wooden sideboard.

'But what happened to him?' Eileen asked.

'I don't know,' Clarice replied. She placed three cups and saucers on the table. 'I expect the Military Police will find that out. They will be here shortly. Be on your best behaviour. They will want to talk to you.'

'Why me?' Eileen blurted.

'You saw poor Mister Whitehead first.'

'Peter saw him first,' Eileen disputed. 'We were coming home from school and Peter and Ian spotted him. I only went to shoo the boys away.'

'Shush!' Clarice warned, as she arranged teaspoons on the saucers. 'The police will not want to talk to a small boy.'

Eileen noticed the discoloration on her mother's dress. 'There's blood on your sleeve.'

Clarice looked at Eileen for an explanation, realised what was said, saw the stain, and gasped. 'Oh, my goodness. That won't do,' she muttered, before she retreated to the bathroom.

Eileen attended to her tea-making task. She didn't want to talk to the Military Police. She didn't know what she could say. She was confused as to why anyone would want to hurt Mister Whitehead. He was a good man and a soldier. He was fighting the Japanese. Why would anyone want to hurt him at home while he was on leave? Why did she have to talk to the Military Police?

When Clarice returned, Eileen was pouring boiled water into the teapot, steam wrapping her in humid warmth as it settled on her arms and face.

Peter stuck his curly head through the back door and asked, 'Is he dead?'

'Peter Bonney!' Clarice cautioned.

'Only asking,' Peter replied. He brushed leaves and flecks of dry grass from his grey school cardigan, and asked, 'Is he?'

'Did you wipe your shoes?' Clarice challenged. Peter scuffed his grubby brown shoes on the threadbare floor mat. 'Where are the girls?' Clarice asked.

'In the fig tree with Ian,' Peter replied.

'Then see if your little brother is asleep,' Clarice ordered.

'You didn't answer my question,' Peter complained, but seeing his mother's rising anger he headed for the boys' bedroom.

'Watch your manners, young man,' Clarice warned in his wake.

From the hallway, Peter yelled, 'Father!'

Eileen looked to Clarice, surprised that her father was home – he was meant to be on duty at the Loveday Italian Prisoner-of-war camp near Barmera – but before Clarice could explain Peter bounced out of the hall leading a tall, thin man with neatly combed, wispy brown hair in a khaki Military Police uniform, cap in hand.

'Donald,' Clarice said in greeting, and she embraced her husband, the pair pausing for a polite kiss.

Peter burst out the back door, calling 'Father's home!'

'I thought you were away?' Eileen queried, her voice quavering with pleasure at her father's unheralded appearance.

'Hello, Girlie,' Donald acknowledged.

'Your father was at the barracks when I rang,' Clarice explained. 'He was back on leave.'

'Yes,' Donald agreed, winking at Clarice. 'Very lucky timing.'

'Are you here about Mister Whitehead?' Eileen asked.

Donald nodded sombrely. 'I hear you found him.'

Eileen wanted to refute her priority in the discovery of the crime, but before she could clarify the sequence of events her brothers and sisters burst through the back door to mob their father. The noisy chaos stirred the youngest child, Wally.

'Excuse me, Donald,' Clarice said above the clamour, and she headed for the hallway.

'That's enough hilarity,' Donald told the children, disengaging from their embraces and straightening his posture. 'I have a colleague waiting outside, so you all must go into the backyard until we finish the vital business at hand. Does everyone understand?'

The children stepped back obediently, nodding, and responding, 'Yes.' Donald singled out Peter. 'Go to the front door and escort Corporal Matheson into the parlour. Tell him I will join him shortly.' Pleased to be assigned an important task, Peter scampered into the hall. 'Everyone else outside,' Donald added.

'Can we go to the beach, Father?' Ian asked.

'Please?' Judy chimed in.

'Please?' Josie echoed.

'I think I said you were to wait out the back,' Donald reminded them.

'Yes, Father,' the trio muttered in disappointed unison, and they withdrew.

Donald turned to Eileen. 'Come with me, Girlie. You can tell us what you saw.'

'What about Mum?' Eileen asked. 'She was there, too.'

Donald touched the side of his nose, his family signal for secrecy, and said, 'Official business, Girlie. We will talk to each of you, one at a time. But you, young lady, are first.'

When she sat on the parlour armchair, Eileen crossed her ankles and placed her hands neatly in her lap, as was appropriate for formal situations, and waited for her father to begin his questions. Donald stood by the window, his imperious khaki clad figure exuding military authority, and the seated dark-haired, moustached Corporal Matheson held a cigarette between the fingers of his left hand, smoke twirling towards the ceiling as he leaned forward to scribble notes in his brown leather diary. Eileen shifted uncomfortably, conscious of the chair fabric against her legs.

'Nothing to be afraid of, Girlie,' Donald assured her, as a way of opening his questions. 'Simply tell us what you saw.'

Eileen had little to share. 'I brought the children straight home from school, like every day. Mister Whitehead was already on the bench when I saw him. Peter and Ian saw him first. You should talk to them,' she said hopefully.

'I am not sure two young boys would have much to tell us,' Donald replied dismissively. 'Did Corporal Whitehead speak to you?'

Eileen recalled the image of the young man hunched on the bus stop seat and her stomach churned. She shook her head.

'Was anyone else with him?'

'No,' Eileen replied. 'He was alone.'

'Anyone else in the street?'

'I didn't see anyone coming or going along the street.'

'Did you see the knife?'

Eileen shivered at the thought that she might have seen such a thing. 'I didn't see a knife.'

'Did you touch anything?'

'No,' she replied. 'I left when Mum came.'

Donald drew a deep breath. 'All right, Girlie. I think that will do. Do you have any questions, Matheson?'

'No, sir,' Matheson replied, without looking up from his scribbling.

'I think we will talk to your mother, now,' Donald said. 'Can you fetch tea for the Corporal and myself, Girlie?'

'What will happen to Mister Whitehead?' Eileen asked.

'Hospital,' Donald replied curtly. 'Then back to the war, I expect.'

'So, he won't die?'

Donald and Corporal Matheson grinned at each other, before Donald said, 'He'll be fine, Girlie. His wound isn't serious. When you go to the kitchen, ask Mother to join us.'

Relieved to leave the parlour and the interview, heart racing and hands shaking, Eileen found Clarice rocking Wally to sleep in the kitchen. Her brother was growing, almost too big to be nursed. 'Do you want me to take him?' Eileen offered.

'No,' Clarice replied. 'I will pop him back in bed.'

'Father said he wants to talk to you now. He wants me to make tea.'

Clarice hefted Wally onto her chest and shoulder as she rose, saying. 'I better go, then. You get on with making the tea. It will be plenty strong enough by now. It might need more hot water.'

Eileen's nerves settled as she prepared the tea. Black. No sugar. Rationing prohibited luxuries like milk and sugar. Three china cups artfully arranged on saucers on a silver tray, she headed to the parlour, careful not to trip on the runner. The adults ceased talking when she entered, and they waited for her to place the tray on the coffee table and withdraw before they resumed their conversation.

From the hall, Eileen overheard her mother say, 'Poor man. Goes through all that trouble over there, only to come back here to be stabbed in his own home.'

'Most unfortunate,' Corporal Matheson agreed. 'Seems Missus Whitehead was being somewhat indiscrete.'

With the word 'indiscrete' and its adult associations echoing in her mind, Eileen crept into the boys' bedroom where Wally was sleeping and she watched his chest rise and fall, his fist curled against his cheek. 'I hope the world is a peaceful place when you grow up,' she whispered, and she touched his hand softly before she retreated into the hall.

Long late afternoon shadows filled the backyard, spreading from the corrugated iron washhouse to the broad fig tree at the centre and the outside dunny in the corner of the yard. Heat lingering on metal and stone made the air mellow and thick.

'Up here!' called a shrill voice.

Spying the three smaller children nestled in the lower fig tree limbs, Eileen tucked up her skirt and climbed onto an adjoining branch, smooth wood pressing against her skin. The fig tree was getting too small for her, but it remained a haven for the children.

'Tell us what happened,' Judy urged.

'What did Father say?' Josie asked. 'Was he angry?'

'Where's Peter?' Eileen queried, noting his absence and instantly feeling responsible for his whereabouts.

'Over the fence,' Ian replied. 'What did they ask you?'

'Father will be furious,' Eileen warned, annoyed how Peter hardly ever did as he was told anymore. A year younger than Eileen, already twelve, he was establishing an attitude of disrespect for anything she or her mother said to him, and it worried her, in case he went wild and ran away like her older brother Clive. Clive was absent from home since before Christmas and Eileen knew her mother was worried sick for her son. He was mischievous and funny, and Eileen missed him. She asked, 'What is he doing?'

'He's talking to Clive,' Ian confessed.

Startled by the serendipitous mention of the wayward older brother, Eileen peered in the direction of the corrugated iron fence separating the house yard from the adjacent vacant block on the street corner where local families collectively grew vegetables. 'When did Clive come back?' she asked.

'Just now,' said Judy. 'He stuck his head over the fence and called us when we came out here.'

'Did he say where he's been?'

'No,' the children chorused.

'You haven't told us what happened,' Judy complained. 'Tell us.'

'There's not much to tell,' Eileen replied. 'They asked questions about what we found, and I told them what I saw.'

'But do they know what happened to Mister Whitehead?' Josie asked. 'Why did someone hurt him?'

'They don't know,' Eileen answered, deciding her little sister didn't need to know about adult indiscretions. 'They don't know any more than we do.'

'They're lying.'

The children turned to the intruding voice to find Clive climbing over the fence, trailed by Peter. Shabby and dirty, his blue shirt tattered, his khaki shorts oversized and grimy with oil and grease stains, Clive's dark dishevelled hair had a precocious lock hanging across his forehead and his mouth was fixed in a crooked grin.

Eileen slid out of the tree to confront her older brother, and demanded, 'Where have you been?'

'Steady on, Girlie, you're not my mother,' Clive retorted, his skinny arms akimbo. 'I don't have to answer to you.'

'If Father finds out-' Eileen began.

'But the old man won't find out, will he, Miss?' Clive taunted.

Of all names, Eileen hated being called 'Miss', the name her father reserved for when he was annoyed or angry. Clive was defying her, teasing her, but she wasn't taking his bait, not this time. 'You said they were lying,' she reminded him, redirecting the interchange.

'They are,' Clive asserted.

'How do you know?'

'Because we've been talking to Bob,' Peter interjected as he joined Clive under the tree canopy, and the pair chuckled conspiratorially.

'Bob was there when they took old Whitehead away,' Clive explained.

'The bloke that stopped in the Ford,' Peter added. 'You saw him.'

Eileen remembered why the man was familiar: Bob – Mister Robert Chapman – the Brighton Road shopkeeper who sometimes delivered goods along the street. 'Go on,' she prompted.

Clive relaxed against the tree trunk. 'It turns out old Whitehead was back on leave, looking to get some knee trembling with his wife-'

'Don't be crass in front of the children!' Eileen warned.

Clive sniggered and ruffled Peter's hair, replying, 'Didn't mean to corrupt minors, Girlie.'

'You're a minor!' Judy countered.

'I'm sixteen!' Clive proudly reminded her.

'Can't drink, can't vote, still a minor until you're twenty-one,' Peter cheekily taunted. Clive cuffed his brother's head.

'Get on with the story,' Eileen urged.

'Anyway,' said Clive, clearing his throat, 'seems old Whitehead walked in on Missus Whitehead having her own recreational leave with Lenny, the barber's son.'

'Len Carter?' Eileen gasped. Len was handsome, perhaps eighteen or nineteen. She had a crush on him when he was at school, but he was much older, and he left.

'Yeah,' Peter confirmed. 'Him.'

'Isn't he the boy you keep perving on over the fence?' Ian queried.

'I don't perve on anyone!' Eileen objected, colour rising in her cheeks.

'Yes, you do,' said Judy from the branch above Eileen. 'I've seen you do it. You wave to all the drivers and the boys going past!'

'Ew!' Josie complained.

'That's enough!' Eileen cautioned, glaring at Judy, before she looked at Clive to ask, 'How do you know what happened?'

'Bob saw the coppers hauling Lenny away, after the Army ambulance carted off Whitehead,' Clive said. 'I spoke to him.'

'That doesn't prove he did anything,' Eileen argued.

'Yeah, but Bob heard the coppers charging him,' Clive told her. 'And he said they found a bloody kitchen knife in the Whitehead's place. Adds up. Lenny's definitely going to the slammer.'

'Poor Mister Whitehead,' Judy said. 'That was mean of Lenny to hurt him.'

'Where have you been, Clive?' Eileen asked. 'Mum's been worried sick.'

'On the rattler,' Clive replied evasively. 'Working. Travelling. Keeping as far as I bloody well can away from this joint.'

'Mind your language,' Eileen warned. 'You know Mum doesn't like you talking like that.'

'Oops, excuse me. Bloody sorry,' Clive taunted.

Eileen glared, and asked, 'Why have you come back today?'

'Thought it was time to make an appearance,' Clive replied, 'but it looks like my timing is shitty.'

'Clive!' Eileen chastised.

'Sorry, Miss,' Clive replied.

'And don't call me that! You know I don't like it!'

Clive smirked and nodded. 'Yeah. I'm sorry, Girlie. He gets to you, too, doesn't he? Mean, cheating, conniving bastard.'

'Clive!' Eileen remonstrated again, glancing at the children who were grinning.

'I know, mind my language,' Clive said. 'Anyway, I'm not staying, not while he's here, so you won't have to worry about my bad manners.'

'You'll eat something?' Eileen pleaded. 'At least say hello to Mum?'

The creaking back door turned the children's heads to where their father stood in the doorway, his eyes fixed on Clive. Before Eileen could speak, Clive bolted for the fence with Donald in pursuit and Clarice screaming, 'No!' from the kitchen. Clive hurdled the fence, Donald clambered over after him, and the children in the tree shouted encouragement to both parties. Eileen ran to the fence and she peered over in time to see her father's lean khaki figure vanish at full tilt around the corner of the neighbouring house on Partridge Street.

*

'Now, Girlie, you know what to do,' Clarice said, while she applied rouge to her cheeks. 'Wally is asleep. There's broth for tea. You can let the others listen to the radio until seven-thirty, but make sure they go to bed straight after that. No horsing around.'

'What time will you be home?' Eileen asked.

'The usual.'

'I'll wait up.'

'You have school tomorrow morning. Don't wait up.'

'I will have a cup of tea ready,' Eileen promised.

'Tomorrow night, your father will be here with his army friends. Make sure the parlour is clean,' Clarice instructed. She adjusted the back of her grey snood, collected her dark grey overcoat and headed for the front door. Late afternoon light spilled across the runner and the polished floorboards. 'Missus Drake is next door if you need. Missus Nicholls is also home.'

'We will be fine,' Eileen reassured her mother. 'We always are.'

Clarice leaned forward to kiss Eileen on the forehead, and Eileen smelt the soft lavender scent of her mother's powder as she said, 'I won't be late.'

Clarice walked past the Anderson shelter, with its bedraggled coat of sandbags and weeds, opened the gate, and onto The Broadway, where she waited for a maroon and cream double decker bus proclaiming 'Crompton's Bunyip Soap' on its advertising banner to roar past before crossing the street. On the far side, she paused to wave, and headed for Partridge Street.

Eileen watched her mother walk out of sight towards Jetty Road where she would take the tram into the city to play piano for the radio show. As unhappy as she was being left with the household responsibilities every time her mother went into the city to perform or work at the Cheer-up hut, she was glad to see her mother go because Clarice was happiest when she was playing the piano.

Eileen closed the front door and walked along the hall to the rear of the house to find the children. Josie sat on the floor in the girls' bedroom, playing with her broken baby doll, so intent on telling the doll how to talk nicely to other dolls that she didn't see her big sister observing her. Eileen envied how Josie had time to play, time to live in a child's world where the presence of the war and the lack of rations were less important than teaching a doll manners.

Outside, Judy was perched in the fig tree, singing 'Old Mother Hubbard' to a black and white piping shrike that tilted its head to listen to the melody. Eileen watched the child and bird interaction, enjoying the treasurable moment, until she realised Peter and Ian were conspicuously absent. 'Where are the boys?' she asked. The piping shrike took flight and Judy complained at the interruption before she pointed to the adjoining vacant block.

Over the iron fence, Eileen spotted Peter backing towards her and Ian was crouched in the far corner of the garden block. 'What are you doing?' she asked. Peter turned quickly with his index finger to his lips. 'Why do I need to be quiet?' she queried.

Ignoring Eileen's question, Peter beckoned to Ian, and as Ian trotted towards them Peter crept closer to Eileen to say, 'Grab this.' He handed Eileen the end of a shabby piece of yellow twine before he mounted the fence.

'What on earth?' Eileen asked. 'Peter, what is this for?' Ian climbed into the yard and the boys giggled uncontrollably. 'What are you two up to?' Eileen insisted.

'Pull!' Peter urged.

'No,' Eileen refused, and she dropped the twine.

Peter snatched it up, and said, 'Watch this.' The boys peeped over the rim of the fence and Peter tightened the twine. When the twine lifted out of the hotchpotch mass of vegetables and yellow late summer grass, Eileen saw that the line ran to the neighbouring house and disappeared around the corner. A bell tinkled. The boys collapsed in laughter.

'What's so funny?' Eileen asked.

Peter reached for the fence lip, peered over, pulled the twine again, and again a distant bell tinkled, which made Ian snort and double-up, clutching his stomach. 'Watch,' Peter urged as he yanked the twine a third time. Apart from the vibrating twine, there was nothing untoward to see. And then the twine went limp. Disappointed, Peter tugged to see if the twine would regain tension. 'It broke,' he announced.

'I don't think it broke,' Eileen corrected, as she squatted beside Ian. 'Mister Cooper came around the side of the house.'

Peter dropped the string and bolted for the back door. Perplexed by his brother's abrupt departure, Ian asked, 'What happened?' before he sprinted after Peter, leaving Eileen crouching behind the fence, wondering what to do as she comprehended the prank her brothers were staging. She peeped over the fence. Mister Cooper was gone. The sun's waning heat prickled her skin.

'Are they in trouble?' Judy asked from her perch. 'Mister Cooper looked terribly angry.'

'I think they are in very big trouble,' Eileen told her, as she approached the base of the tree. 'You best come inside too. It's tea-time.'

Peter and Ian hid in the boys' bedroom, while Eileen organised dinner with Judy's help, heating a potato and leek broth. As she stirred the broth, savouring the warm aroma, she wondered how many more years of war lay ahead and what more rations would be imposed. Last year, there was meat to mix in the broth, but Government-enforced meat rationing in the new year meant there was much less meat available to anyone, and no meat that night to add to the soup. She was eight when Prime Minister Menzies announced Australia was going to war. She never heard the radio announcement – it was broadcast late one September evening when she was asleep – but she knew it began with the words, "It is my melancholy duty," because all the adults quoted the phrase thereafter. 1939. She was eight. The family lived in Black Forest, her father's building business was flourishing, Wally was a new baby, and Lady, the family's red setter, made everyone laugh with her clever antics. There was no rationing. The troubles in Europe and Asia were far away. Everyone was happy.

'Is it ready?' Josie asked from the doorway. Her bedraggled, one-armed doll hung limply in her left hand. 'It smells very tasty.'

Eileen smiled. They had the same soup the night before, but Josie always complimented the smell of cooking. 'Almost ready,' Eileen told her. 'Can you ask the boys to come to the table please?'

Josie disappeared, calling her brothers, and Eileen mused on how her little sister parroted their mother's adamant tone and phrases. Clarice insisted they all practise elocution and learn the correct enunciation of words and phrases. 'There is no place for vulgarity in this house,' Clarice told them. 'One's level of education and civilisation is evident in the manner by which one uses the King's English. Never stoop to gutter talk. It betrays a base upbringing.' Their mother never swore. Neither had she ever heard their father swear. And if any of the children used bad language, there remained the ever-present threat of soap to wash the filth from their mouths.

Judy pitched in to help Eileen prepare the evening meal by laying out the bowls before the children gathered at the table to eat in the yellow glow of the electric lamp as the evening darkened outside the kitchen window. 'Where is Walter Graham?' Eileen asked, using Wally's formal name as she ladled soup into the bowls.

'Sleeping again,' Ian replied. 'Shall I wake him?'

Eileen hesitated, before replying, 'No. I'll put some soup aside for him.'

'Soup again?' Peter complained.

'You can go without, if you want,' Eileen warned, and she stopped ladling the steaming liquid into his bowl.

'No. I'm hungry,' Peter told her. 'Is there any bread?'

'Did you eat the middle out of this one?' Eileen teased, raising an eyebrow as she reminded her brother how Ian and he were sent to Lovell's Brighton Road bakery the previous year to fetch bread for the family but chose to eat the centre out of the loaf on their homeward walk.

Peter grinned and replied, 'Not this time.'

'Mum says you were selfish for doing that,' Judy accused.

'Eat your soup, Miriam Judith, or I'll eat it for you,' Peter warned. Judy poked out her tongue defiantly, but she wrapped her hands protectively around her bowl in case Peter carried out his threat. The chatter stopped. Bowls clattered with spoons.

'Is Mum playing on the radio tonight?' Ian asked between mouthfuls.

'She is,' Eileen confirmed.

'Can we listen?' Judy asked.

'Please?' Josie chimed in.

'Of course,' Eileen replied, 'but then it's straight to bed, and no shenanigans from anyone. Promise?' The children promised in unison. 'And you must be in your pyjamas before the show starts.'

'We will be,' Judy vowed.

Eileen dipped her spoon in her soup, but she put it aside when she heard stirring in the boys' bedroom and she went to check on Wally. She turned on the hall light and crept into the bedroom, to find Wally sitting up, rubbing his eyes. 'Hungry?' Eileen asked, squatting beside the bed.

'I want to sleep,' Wally grizzled, and he lay down again, closing his eyes.

'You should eat,' Eileen whispered, but Wally squeezed his eyelids tighter, so she patted her little brother's shoulder and rose, deciding she would let him sleep. She glanced along the hall towards the kitchen, where the children were chatting and laughing, before she walked to her mother's bedroom, switched on the green shrouded dresser lamp and regarded the mantlepiece where her mother kept her collection of framed family photographs.

Eileen loved the instances frozen in black and white and grey. Wrapped in the competing miasma of her mother's cheap perfume her father bought on the black market and the odour of naphthalene mothballs stashed in drawers to keep bugs from eating precious fabric, she studied the images of her mother's family, grandparents and great-grandparents dressed in Sunday finery for the photographer to record.

Her father and mother's wedding photo took central position; Clarice Stephens, professional musician, already twenty-nine by the time she was engaged to the tall, handsome builder, Donald Bonney. In the post-wedding thirteen years, Clarice bore nine children, Wally being the last. Eileen wondered how her mother made the transition from one life to another, why she would choose to leave a musician's career to be a stay-at-home mother, why she exchanged Miss Clarice Stephens for Missus Clarice Bonney, but she understood, from everything she learned and observed, that it was an expectation of all women to marry and bear children. At age twenty-nine, with the spectre of spinsterhood looming, despite her musical talent and independence, her mother chose to conform to social expectation.

Next to the wedding portrait was a photo of her eldest brother, Bruce, taken before he was shipped to an RAAF base in Queensland. In his blue uniform, forage cap jauntily askew, he was handsome, the epitome of a romantic Hollywood star. More than her father, or the other brothers, Bruce was her male role model and idol, the big brother who taught and teased her and made her laugh. She missed him deeply, and she prayed every night for his safe return.

Beside Bruce's portrait sat a smaller picture of the third eldest, John. A year older than Eileen, he lived with Uncle Spot and Auntie Fay in Kurralta Park because he was considered the brightest of the children. He was learning piano, and Auntie Fay was paying for him to attend Adelaide High School, and eventually college, an educational opportunity reserved for families much better off than Eileen's family and a privilege Eileen knew her parents could never afford to give their children. She missed John as well, although she saw him on Sundays when he joined Eileen in the choir at Saint Martin's.

A picture nestled in the collection was taken of the first seven children before Josie and Wally were born. Clive leaned forward in the photo, a cheeky grin splitting his face, as if he knew at twelve that he would mock the world and its expectations. Eileen was solemn in the group, as if she realised being the eldest daughter meant she was the one expected to do the housework and look after the younger children. Her three siblings – Peter, Ian and Judy – grinned awkwardly, little children curious about the world but unprepared for a war and its ramifications.

'It's almost seven!' Peter called from the hallway. 'Everyone's in their pyjamas!'

Eileen switched off the lamp and closed the bedroom door. She frowned at her brother, and said, 'Fetch the others, and be quiet for Wally's sake.'

The children crowded into the small room halfway along the hallway reserved for the radio, and Eileen drew the navy curtains at the window. Peter switched on the tall corner lamp before joining his brother on the dark blue floormat, while Josie and Judy perched on high-backed wooden chairs, snuggling against the purple cushions for comfort. 'Are we ready?' Eileen asked.

'Yes!' the girls chorused. Peter begged Eileen to hurry. Eileen turned the brown Bakelite knob, and the soft golden backlight, as the radio warmed up and the radio show began.

'Is Mum playing?' Josie asked.

'Of course she is,' Judy returned. 'Can't you hear the piano?'

'Shush,' Eileen urged softly. 'I will close the parlour curtains and come back.'

Eileen hurried into the parlour, but as she drew the heavy curtains her eyes moved to the dark upright Steinway piano against the wall. The piano was the family heart, the place where the children, and sometimes their father, spent afternoons and evenings singing popular songs, or listened in wonder to musical phrases Clarice conjured on the keys. Eileen knew only a little of the tale of how her concert-trained mother, a woman who could play Rachmaninoff's "Concerto Number Three" without the score, travelled to South Australian country cinemas in the State's south-east accompanying silent movies on piano before she settled to marry. It was a romantic memory, a side to her mother Eileen treasured because her mother was an adventurous and free-spirited young woman.

She sighed. She tried to learn the piano, but her efforts were wooden, as if her fingers understood nothing more than the mechanics of the keys and their notes. Her mother was an accomplished pianist, and John was learning to play like Clarice, but the black and white keys kept their mystery locked from Eileen's fingers, allowing her only to doggedly imitate pieces. 'Your heart doesn't find the notes,' Clarice told her when she was eight. 'Only your fingers do.' Eileen was devastated by her mother's assessment, because she wanted to emulate her mother's talent and musical prowess, but Clarice gave Eileen another outlet. 'You may not have the touch of a Stephens on an instrument, but you are blessed with a voice like your father. I will ask if you can join the choir.' So, Eileen sang. Sunday choir gave her opportunities to use her voice to explore the scales within the sacred hymns, and for that she was grateful, but she loved listening to popular radio songs, and she practised them every day, honing her voice to imitate singers like Martha Tilton and Helen Forrest, secretly wishing she could sing with a swing band. 'One day,' she murmured. She closed the parlour door and hurried to the radio nook.

As she entered, Judy asked, 'Who's that singing?'

'The announcer said it was Brian Coleman,' Peter explained.

'And Mum on piano,' Josie squeaked, and the children laughed.

'It's called "In the Blue of the Evening",' Eileen informed them.

'We know it,' Peter replied. 'We've sung it here, with Father. It's Frank Sinatra.'

'No,' said Josie, imperiously correcting her brother. 'It's Brian Coleman.' The older children laughed, and Judy pushed Josie's shoulder playfully, leaving the seven-year-old bewildered by her siblings' amusement.

Eileen listened to the pitch and fall of the strains in each song, immersing herself in the chorus and rhythms, imagining how the composer created the piece and how the musicians interpreted it, especially the singer. *How will I sing that song*? she mused, rehearsing the lyrics silently.

The show compere announced it was seven-thirty, the band struck up the closing theme, and Eileen ushered her brothers and sisters to the bathroom to wash their faces and hands. Judy kept vigil over Josie, ensuring her little sister cleaned everything and made no fuss as the girls retired to their room. When Eileen checked Peter and Ian were in their beds, Peter asked, 'Did Father say anything more about Mister Whitehead?'

'No,' Eileen replied.

'I think he died,' Ian said.

'Father said his wounds weren't serious,' Eileen contradicted. 'He will be back on duty soon.'

'Has Father gone back to Loveday?' Peter asked.

'No,' Eileen said. 'He'll be here tomorrow night with his friends.'

'Will they get drunk and sing all night?' whined Ian.

'Father doesn't drink,' Eileen reminded him.

'I bet he does,' Peter asserted. 'He just doesn't do it around Mum.'

'They're allowed to have fun,' Eileen remonstrated. 'It's wartime, and they don't get many opportunities to relax. But you do. It's time to be quiet. Light's out.' She flicked the switch and pulled the door.

'Don't close it!' Ian begged. Eileen left the door ajar to placate her little brother.

Back in the radio nook, she turned off the lamp to let darkness dominate and listened to the chilling tale of Old Nancy and her black cat, Satan, revelling in enveloping fear as "The Witch's Tale" whispered across the airwaves. Imagination sparked by the tale of horror and evil, Eileen retreated from the reality of the interminable war raging across the world. In Europe, in the Middle East and in Asia, people's lives were torn apart, people were dying in battle after battle after battle, but the radio shows carried on as if tomorrow everything would be like it was before Manchuria was annexed or Poland invaded, or Darwin bombed. Radio serials allowed her to escape from the heroic acts and atrocities. Radio brought order and fantasy to the chaotic reality.

"The Witch's Tale" over, Eileen turned off the radio and tip-toed along the hallway, pausing to check the bedrooms to ensure everyone was asleep, before she gravitated to the kitchen to boil the kettle and prepare to make a cup of tea for her mother. She sat beside the wood stove, staring at the tiny flames, and pondered what might have happened to poor Mister Whitehead and Missus Whitehead and Lenny. She wanted to ask her mother to give her the facts, but "Children should be seen and not heard" replayed in her head, reminding her it would be rude to ask for details. The Whiteheads' fate was doomed to remain an adult mystery. Life was full of adult mysteries and Eileen was keen to be an adult so she could be privy to that secretive world.

*

'Where's that beautiful young girl who does the best boot shine in the world?'

Hearing her father's strident voice echoing in the hallway, Eileen came from the kitchen to find Donald at the archway curtains, holding his military boots and white leggings towards her.

'There she is!' he declared. 'A little Cinderella in the kitchen, but always a princess to me.'

Eileen eagerly received the dusty brown boots and leggings and retreated through the back door to the wash house, her appointed mission clear. She soaked the leggings in a bucket of tepid water, before fossicking on the shelf for the Kiwi brown boot polish and polishing brushes. If her father did one thing to make her feel special since the war began, it was to let her polish his boots and wash his leggings in readiness for his return to active duty. He taught her what to do, how to use spit and polish to bring out the brightest shine, and she was proud of her work. The polishing ritual gave her connection with him. 'No one else dares to touch my boots, Girlie,' he told her. 'Only you. When I look at how my boots shine, I think of you and how good you are, and it makes me happy.'

The day fading into evening, Eileen switched on the light to continue her work, enjoying the polish's aromatic aura, and ignored calls from her sisters to join them in the fig tree. Judy teased her with, 'Hurry! It's Tim from Mister Sendy's shop. We know you like him.'

Ian stuck his head in to offer judgement. 'I think you missed a bit around the left heel,' he taunted, and retreated before Eileen could cuff his curly head.

Eileen polished until she could see her face reflected in the boot tips, and then she tidied her workspace, smoothed her dress, and proudly carried the gleaming boots into the house. 'Where's Father?' she asked when she encountered Peter at the entrance to the hall.

'Right here, Girlie,' Donald answered. He stood before the stove, a green apron wrapped around his waist, wooden spatula in hand, a pot bubbling on the burner. 'Show me.'

Eileen dutifully approached and held up the boots for inspection.

'Magnificent!' Donald exclaimed, bending his tall frame to study the shine. 'Truly magnificent, young lady. Major General Blamey would be impressed. Well done! You know where to put them.'

Eileen carried her prize past Peter, along the hallway to the front bedroom, and placed the boots neatly inside the doorway by the wooden Cheval dress mirror. She couldn't be happier. Her father was pleased with her.

Hearing voices in the adjoining parlour, she poked her head through the doorway to discover her mother seated in the company of three men wearing the same khaki uniform as her father. 'You all know our eldest daughter,' Clarice said, waving for Eileen to enter.

'The famous polisher of boots,' one beefy, florid-faced man commented, grinning beneath his black moustache. 'Your reputation precedes you, young lady.'

'The child is as beautiful as her mother,' another man remarked, causing Eileen and Clarice to blush.

'Best help your father,' Clarice recommended.

When Eileen re-entered the kitchen, the savour of meat and pastry tantalised her nostrils and made her mouth water. Before he became a military policeman, her father was an army cook when the war broke out, abandoning his building business and joining the forces to serve the nation. Sometimes he brought home fresh produce grown by the Italian prisoners, but he must have obtained the meat and other scarce goods via the black market because of the rationing laws. If the children queried how he came by hard-to-get foodstuff and condiments, he would touch the side of his nose and say, 'No questions asked, none need to be answered.' 'Now, Girlie, you can get five plates ready for the adults,' Donald said, spying his daughter. 'And when these are served, you can share the leftovers with the children, so you better have bowls ready for them.'

Eileen organised the crockery and cutlery and watched her father prepare the adult serves: a dollop of stewed meat, a vegetable pasty, a scoop of spinach, a slice of buttered bread. He filled a small white ceramic jug with steaming, thick brown gravy. 'Take these plates to the parlour and give one to each person, beginning with Mother. Come back for the gravy after you deliver the plates.'

Eileen ferried the food to the parlour, serving her mother and her father's three friends, and by the time she completed her task her stomach was churning with anticipation of eating her father's offering. She loved his ability to conjure tasty food when meals were mostly austere and inadequate. 'Share what remains with the children,' Donald reiterated. 'Make sure everyone finishes their meal and goes to bed. Peter can help you wash up. Fetch the dishes from the parlour when you are called. No one else is allowed past the hallway curtain. Understood, Girlie?' Eileen nodded. 'Good,' Donald said, and he strode out of the kitchen carrying a baked sultana cake that Eileen hadn't noticed, but the cake explained the kitchen's lingering sweet aroma.

Discovering that her father made exactly one pasty for each child, Eileen put the leftover food portions into bowls, laid a warm pasty on each, and placed the bowls on the table, before she went to the back door and called into the evening, 'Teatime!'

Squeals of delight from her sisters trailed the three eager boys into the kitchen. The children scrambled into their chairs, smiles and noses delighting in the uncommon fare. 'Pasties!' Judy chortled, clapping her hands.

'Father's pasties!' Ian emphasised.

'The best!' Peter declared.

'Now, you know the rules,' Eileen began, but she was interrupted by Peter's recitation.

'Say Grace, eat our dinner, wash our face and hands, and go to our rooms.'

Eileen glared at Peter, but she acknowledged him with, 'Precisely.'

'I'm saying Grace!' Josie asserted.

'It's my turn,' Ian protested.

'No, it's mine!' Josie insisted, her lip quivering.

'Let Josie say it,' Peter urged, nudging Ian. 'I'm hungry.'

Josie clasped her tiny hands in prayer, squeezed her eyes tight, and began, 'Two, four, six-'

'I beg your pardon?' Eileen interrupted. 'Say it properly. Where did you learn that?' Josie pointed at Peter, who grinned mischievously when Eileen looked to him for an explanation. 'If you're going to say Grace, you have to say it properly,' Eileen repeated.

Josie resumed her pious pose, hands clasped in prayer, and recited in her piping voice, 'Dear God, for what we are about to receive may we be truly grateful. In Jesus' name, amen.'

'Amen!' the children chorused.

'Very good,' Eileen said. 'Now we can eat.'

'Peter started before Josie finished Grace,' Judy pointed out.

'Did not, dibber-dobber,' Peter denied, tell-tale pastry crumbs adorning his lips.

'Eat and be grateful,' Eileen warned. She waited for her siblings to begin eating before she started, wondering if she was as annoying to her mother when she was younger as they sometimes were to her. *Most likely*, she decided, and set to eating.

Meal enjoyed, faces and hands washed and bedclothes on, dishes collected and cleaned, children in their beds, Eileen entered the parlour to collect the adults' crockery and cutlery. Her mother was seated at the piano, talking to one man while her father was busy filling glasses with a clear liquid – she assumed water since her parents never drank alcohol in the house. 'You are a perfect hostess, Girlie,' Donald said, as Eileen balanced the plates. 'Leave the cake. We may have more after with tea.' Eileen carted her load to the kitchen to wash and dry them.

By the time she finished her chores, the parlour echoed to piano chords and melodies accompanying a choir of male voices. Eileen undressed and crept into her bed beside where Judy and Josie were snuggled.

'It's fun, isn't it?' Judy whispered. 'They sound so grand.'

Eileen smiled in the dark, hearing the familiar strains of "As Time Goes By" reach the final notes. 'Our own private concert,' she said. She settled into her pillow, pulled the quilted blanket made by her Auntie Fay up to her chin, and listened as her mother's fingers caressed the keyboard into the opening melody of the next tune. A solitary tenor took up the lyrics of Vera Lynn's "The White Cliffs of Dover" and Eileen immersed herself in the extraordinary quality of the man's voice as it transported her across the oceans to a distant land. *Even in a world of war*, she decided, *there is always music*.

*

Eileen waited at the school gate, arms crossed, and when her sisters arrived she demanded, 'Where are your brothers?'

'I don't know,' Josie piped tremulously, tugging at her grey school skirt.

'There's Ian!' Judy declared, pointing at a solitary boy emerging from the red brick building.

'Hurry up!' Eileen called. 'I'll be late if you don't hurry.' Ian trotted towards his sisters and halted dutifully in front of Eileen. 'What took you so long?' she asked.

Ian held up his chalk-dusted hands. 'Miss Bowker made me stay behind to clean the board.'

'And why was that?'

Ian looked sheepishly at the accusing stares of his younger sisters, before he confessed, 'I was flicking paper at Ron.'

'You know better,' Eileen said, the corners of her mouth twitching as she held back her amusement. 'Where's Peter?'

'I don't know. Maybe he's tending his vegie patch,' Ian suggested. 'Or playing in the trenches.'

Eileen harrumphed. 'I can't be late. Missus Higgins will have a fit.' She searched the school grounds, until she spotted a boy from Peter's class appear from behind a garden shed. 'Wait here,' she said, but as she headed for the shed another boy darted from the side of the main building and vanished behind the shed, and Peter stepped into view, brushing down the back of his dark grey shorts. Eileen spied a wisp of smoke hovering above the shed. 'You've been smoking,' she accused.

'No, I haven't,' Peter refuted. 'I was keeping my friends company.'

'Likely story,' Eileen declared, imitating the phrase her father used when he suspected lying. 'You're making me late for work. And I'm telling Mum. And you stink of smoke.'

'I wasn't smoking,' Peter denied. 'No need to dob.'

'I don't have time to argue,' Eileen said. 'Hurry up.' Peter lagged as Eileen led him to the other children, and when they reached the gates Eileen saw Mister McInerny emerge from the school administration and stride towards the shed. She turned to Peter, pointing towards the teacher, and said, 'And you were very, very lucky, Peter Bonney.' Boys scattered from behind the shed as Mister McInerny arrived.

'You stink,' Josie complained with disgust, wrinkling her nose at Peter.

'You were caught smoking,' Judy taunted, and she poked out her tongue. Peter made a swipe at the back of her head, intentionally missing, but Judy stepped onto the road to avoid being hit and a car horn blared.

'That's enough!' Eileen warned, as Judy skipped onto the footpath and the grey Austin puttered past. Eileen made the children stop. 'You know the rules,' she said firmly. 'Brighton Road is dangerous, and you have to be careful walking along every road. No more dawdling or mucking around. We have to get home quickly.'

'I'm tired,' Josie complained.

'And I'm hungry,' said Ian.

'And both those problems will be solved when we get home,' Eileen replied irritably, 'so let's hurry.'

'There's that boy you like,' Judy announced, pointing at a group of Sacred Heart students sidling along the opposite footpath, heading for Jetty Road and the shops.

'Don't point,' Eileen remonstrated. 'It's rude,' but she glanced across the road to discover the blond boy looking in her direction. Embarrassed, she turned and ushered the gaggle of children on. Her obligations frustrated her. If she tarried to talk to the older boys, which is what she wanted to do, everyone would tease her, and she would be late for work. It wasn't fair having to be responsible for her siblings every day. 'Come on,' she urged. 'Home.' She desperately wanted to drag the cohort along, but she ended up driving them from behind as she nearly always did.

At home, Eileen changed out of her school clothes into a grey dress and a grey knitted vest over a white blouse and hurried along Partridge Street to Jetty Road. She was late for work. She was nearly always late to the Bon Marche millinery because she was compelled to herd her brothers and sisters to and from school every day. Eileen felt her mother should do that task, but Clarice was unwell lately and seemed unable to do the jobs Eileen believed her mother ought to do. No one knew what was wrong. Clarice stopped travelling into the city to play on the radio shows and she stopped playing piano at home in the evenings. She suffered headaches almost every day, but she never went to the doctor.

Eileen strode along Jetty Road, weaving between pedestrians and ignoring the window displays. The tram screeched to a stop and disgorged people onto the footpath, blocking Eileen's way, but she waited until the shop doorway cleared before she entered.

'Late again, Miss Bonney,' Missus Higgins, the shop manager noted.

'Sorry, Missus Higgins,' Eileen apologised, wilting under the manager's sharp dark-eyed glare. 'I was–'

'None of your lame excuses, girl,' Higgins interrupted. 'Out the back.

You can unbox the new stock. And handle the hats carefully. I don't need them soiled with dirty fingerprints.'

'Yes, Missus Higgins,' Eileen said. She hurried through the shop and into the rear storeroom, glad to be out of Missus Higgins' way. The store manager set exacting standards and she expected everyone to meet them. She preferred her dresses tight, with a belt to accentuate her waist and full bosom, and she always wore a fashionable hat to promote her products. She was a stickler for punctuality and neatness.

Eileen knew she was lucky to work at Bon Marche, thanks to her Auntie Fay being acquainted with the shop owner, and she was grateful for the part-time work to help the family income. Every afternoon, after school, she worked from four to six o'clock sweeping, unpacking boxes, washing windows. The work was menial, but she was working in a fashion store and that was exciting. The millinery's kaleidoscopic colours and chemical and cloth aromas and myriad fashions made her head swirl and, while she laboured, she dreamed of soirees and romances in exotic and plush cities, dressed in satin and silk. She longed to take home a Parisienne bonnet for her mother, although she personally much preferred the snappy berets that were becoming fashionable. She sighed and set to carefully unboxing the newly arrived millinery.

That evening, as the children settled with Eileen in the radio nook to listen to a mystery serial, she was startled by knocking on the front door. 'Stay here,' she instructed. At the front door, she asked warily, 'Who is it?'

'Sergeant Fenwick,' a deep voice answered. 'May I come in?'

Eileen knew the Sergeant, the local policeman who always cheerily greeted her mother in the street, but the police didn't normally visit people after hours unless something was terribly wrong.

Sergeant Fenwick bowed his head in the light spilling from the doorway, and asked, 'Is your mother in?'

'She's not well,' Eileen replied.

'Oh,' Sergeant Fenwick said, his smile evaporating beneath his bushy moustache. 'I'm sorry to hear that.'

'I am right here,' said Clarice. Eileen turned to find her mother, dishevelled hair, eyes puffy and red, standing in the bedroom doorway in her maroon dressing gown.

Sergeant Fenwick bowed his head again, removed his blue policeman's cap to reveal his neatly parted and oiled fair hair, and said, 'Good evening, Missus Bonney. I'm sorry to get you out of bed.'

'I was getting up to make a cup of tea,' Clarice said. 'Would you like one, Sergeant?'

'I wouldn't want to impose,' Sergeant Fenwick answered politely.

'A cup of tea is not imposing. Let the Sergeant in, Girlie.'

Eileen stepped aside to allow Sergeant Fenwick to follow her mother through the hall curtain to the kitchen. The children's heads peered around the radio nook doorway. 'What does the copper want?' Peter whispered.

'None of your business,' Eileen replied. 'Are we listening to the rest of the show, or is it bedtime?'

'I thought Mum was too sick to get up,' said Judy.

Eileen shuffled her brothers and sisters into the radio nook and closed the door. 'The show's finished,' Ian complained.

'Well, we can listen to one more,' Eileen suggested, 'or we can go to bed.'

'One more!' Josie and Ian chorused.

Eileen turned the radio dial, searching for another fifteen-minute serial to keep the children amused to give her mother privacy to talk to the Sergeant, and when she found the station she closed the door.

As the show reached its climactic moment, dramatic music swelling to a crescendo, the door opened and Sergeant Fenwick appeared, framed by the hall light, his face solemn. He stared at Peter and Ian, and said sternly, 'Mind if I have a word with you two boys?' Peter glanced at Ian and Eileen before he sheepishly led his brother into the hall. Fenwick closed the door.

'Are they in trouble?' Josie asked.

'Of course they're in trouble,' said Judy.

'Why do you say that?' Eileen asked, one ear cocked towards the door in case she could overhear the conversation beyond it.

'Because they keep teasing Mister and Missus Cooper with their string trick on the door knocker,' Judy explained.

'I asked them to stop doing that,' Eileen said.

Judy raised an eyebrow, replying haughtily, 'As if they listen to you.'

Eileen told Judy to be quiet, but she couldn't hear what was being said beyond the door. When it opened again, Peter and Ian wore contrite expressions on reddened faces, and Fenwick asked, 'I gather you know what this is about, Eileen?'

'I told them not to be mean to Mister and Missus Cooper,' Eileen explained quickly, feeling guilt for her brothers' behaviour.

'I'm sure you did,' said Fenwick. 'The boys admitted as much, but boys will be boys, even when they're given wise advice.' He glowered at Peter and Ian before saying to Eileen, 'Tomorrow morning being Saturday, would you mind escorting these two young men around the corner to apologise to Mister and Missus Cooper?'

'I will,' Eileen promised.

'And then they have a small civic duty to complete,' Fenwick continued. He looked grimly at Peter and Ian again, prompting them with, 'Haven't you, boys?'

'Yes, Sergeant Fenwick,' they replied in unison.

'They will weed the vegetable plot next door and clean up the area. Isn't that correct, boys?' he prompted again.

'Yes, Sergeant Fenwick,' they chorused.

'And I will drop by tomorrow afternoon to inspect the garden,' Fenwick concluded.

'I think you two can get ready for bed,' Eileen told Peter and Ian, and to the girls and Wally she added, 'In fact, it's time everyone went to bed.'

'That's not fair,' Judy complained, but she submissively followed Peter and Ian out of the parlour, with Josie and Wally in her wake.

'You're a busy girl,' Fenwick observed.

'It's to help Mum out,' Eileen replied.

'May I speak to you outside?'

Surprised by the policeman's request, Eileen stepped into the front yard with Sergeant Fenwick. The streetlights glowed between the pine trees and a bus rumbled by. The Anderson shelter entrance yawned black by the brief stone path.

'I wanted to say if there's anything I can do to help, in any way,' Fenwick said, 'call the station or drop in.'

The Sergeant's offer caught Eileen unawares and, unsure what to say, she mumbled, 'I think we're all right, thank you.'

'Being brave's one thing, young lady, and I'm impressed by how you're holding up, but I know what's happening,' Fenwick said. 'Oh, and I'll drop by occasionally. I think your mother appreciates the company.'

'Thank you, Sergeant Fenwick,' Eileen said.

Fenwick smiled, nodded, donned his cap, and mounted his bicycle.

Eileen waited until the Sergeant rode away before she went inside and closed the door on the night, pondering Fenwick's offer. She was perplexed by his statement that he knew what was happening. Nothing in particular was happening, that she knew of, apart from what was happening to everyone because of the war and the rationing. She made sure the children were in bed before she went to the kitchen to talk to Clarice, but her mother wasn't there. Eileen padded up the hall and peered into her mother's bedroom to find a lamp glowing on the dresser and Clarice curled under her blanket. 'Mum?' Eileen whispered.

'I'm tired, Girlie,' Clarice murmured.

Eileen reached for the lamp and switched it off. 'Goodnight,' she whispered. She stood in the hallway shadows, wondering why her mother was keeping to herself, why she seemed so melancholy, what Sergeant Fenwick knew that she didn't, why adult secrets were so hard to grasp or decipher.

Back in the kitchen, she poured herself a cup of tea from the warm teapot and returned to the radio nook, closed the door, and settled in to enjoy the music, quietly singing along, pretending she was a vocal star with the band. *That would be grand*, she thought, *to be a singer. That would be truly wonderful.*

*

'It's absolutely true,' the tall lady with her hair tied tightly in a bun on top of her head confirmed. 'It's started.'

'What's started?' asked the stout woman in the khaki blouse.

'We're fighting back!' the young red-haired woman proudly asserted. 'We're taking Europe back!'

Eileen paused from washing the shop window to listen to the

conversation.

'I heard it on the radio last night,' the tall lady said. 'They're calling it Operation Overlord.'

'Well, that's a silly name,' scoffed the stout woman. 'Why Overlord?'

'It doesn't matter,' the redhead replied. 'We're finally giving Mister Hitler some of his own back!'

'What are you gawking at, young miss?'

Eileen dropped her yellow washcloth and turned from the window to face the shop manager who was frowning from under her mauve Pompadour hat. 'I'm sorry, Missus Higgins,' Eileen simpered. 'I was interested in what the ladies were saying. About the war.'

'I don't pay you to eavesdrop on customers, young lady. I pay you to clean windows, sort merchandise and have some common decency,' Missus Higgins warned. 'About your work!'

Eileen fumbled to retrieve her cloth and returned to polishing the window, cleaning away smudges, moving carefully between the colourful collection of bonnets, chaplets, cloche hats and turbans perched on stands and faux ceramic heads. As she buffed the glass, she became aware of two young men on the footpath staring at her, one in military uniform, grinning broadly; the other in a dark grey suit and matching tie, his light brown Homburg hat tilted cheerfully on his blond hair. She pretended not to notice, but when the men didn't move she lifted her head, caught the sparkling eyes of the young man in the suit, blushed and looked away.

'Excuse me,' a woman interrupted. 'Would you pass that hat please? The green one?'

Eileen looked over the customer's shoulder to see Missus Higgins nodding approval. 'Yes, Ma'am,' Eileen replied. She carefully lifted the green cartwheel hat with a flourish of lace from its stand and handed it reverently to the young woman, determined not to be distracted by the men outside.

'It's Miss, actually,' the woman said as she accepted the hat. 'Thank you.'

Eileen watched the customer try on the hat, flouncing her brunette curls and tilting the hat back so the brim revealed her fringe for effect. When she returned to her window duty, circumspectly looking under her brow for the men outside, to her disappointment she discovered they had moved on. She sighed and settled into her tasks. She was grateful to have the job because the money helped her mother make ends meet, but she wished her father was home more often. A young man in a grey baker boy cap glanced at her and smiled coyly before he walked on. She wished she had a boyfriend.

*

The evening purple sky was brooding over Saint Vincent's Gulf with incoming rain as Eileen walked home along Partridge Street. Some house lights revealed people settling into their evenings, but most homes were dark and quiet, reminding her that the war was ever-present. Car headlights threw strips of yellow light along the road and footpath, swinging tree shadows in arcs as they passed, and on the opposite footpath a white terrier trotted off leash towards Jetty Road pursued by a woman hunched in a black overcoat. Thunder boomed like distant artillery in the north and rolled over her, heading for Seacliff and the southern coast and the Great Southern Ocean beyond. She stopped to watch lightning flash in the dark northern sky, counting methodically in her mind, like her father taught, to measure the distance as she waited for the next rolling wave of thunder. And a voice behind her said, 'And six and seven and eight-' Eileen spun to face the intruding voice, ready to slap or run from an attacker.

'Easy, Girlie,' the shadowy figure coaxed. Lightning revealed a gaunt youth with large dark eyes, shaggy hair and a craggy supercilious grin.

'Clive!' Eileen gasped.

'Guilty as charged,' Clive replied, holding up his hands in mock surrender.

When Eileen hugged her brother, she was surprised at how wiry and tall he'd become. 'You scared the life out of me,' she confessed, and followed with, 'Where have you been? Mum's worried sick.'

Clive eased out of Eileen's embrace and replied enigmatically, 'Around and about. Seen some places and found some more places.'

'Riding trains again,' Eileen accused, slapping her brother's bony chest.

'Too right I've been on the bloody rattlers. They go to amazing places, Girlie, places we'd never get to see otherwise.'

'You'll get caught one day, and then what?'

'Too quick and too smart to get caught,' Clive bragged. 'Besides, I'm a kid. What are they going to do with me, eh?'

'You're sixteen.'

'Still can't do anything,' Clive retorted.

'Put you in a home,' Eileen warned. 'They can do that.'

'They have to catch me first.'

Thunder rumbled across the rooftops. A large raindrop splashed against Girlie's hand. 'Are you coming home?' she asked.

'Is he there?'

'Father?' Eileen shook her head. 'He went back to Loveday three weeks ago.' Rain spotted the street, heavy drops clunked on corrugated iron roofs. 'Come on. It's going to bucket down,' she urged.

Brother and sister jogged towards The Broadway as the rain thickened and thunder rolled over, halting at the intersection to let two blurred shapes behind headlights cross. Eileen's heart pounded. She was excited to have Clive with her because she was eager to learn about his adventures and keen to know if he was going to stay a while.

They reached the front door, soaked from the rain, and laughed while Eileen fumbled in her purse for her house key. 'Mum?' she called, as she led Clive into the hallway. 'Mum? Clive's home!' The kitchen light threw its earthy glow along the hall runner and under the dividing curtain. 'They must be eating tea,' Eileen said. 'Come on. You look like you haven't eaten in days.' She ushered Clive forward, anticipating the children's excitement. Her brother's back stiffened when a soldier appeared in the kitchen doorway. Clive pivoted and scrambled for the front door, but a figure burst from the bedroom and slammed into him, driving Clive sideways into the parlour. Eileen screamed.

'Rod!' Donald yelled from the parlour. 'In God's name, Rod! Help me!'

The soldier from the kitchen pushed Eileen aside and hurried into the parlour, trailed by the children streaming up the hall, as grunts and swearing intensified and furniture thudded and crashed. Eileen peered around the doorway and saw the coffee table overturned, a chair tipped sideways, and a tangle of struggling arms and legs. Clive swore profusely as he struggled to break free.

'Hold him!' Donald yelled. 'Stand the little bastard up!' he growled, and the men hauled Clive to his feet. 'This way!' Donald ordered. 'Clear the hallway! Everyone! Now!'

Eileen stepped into the entrance of her mother's room and the children retreated into the bedroom as the men half-marched, half-dragged Clive through the curtains and along the hall to the back bedroom. Feeling a presence, Eileen turned her head as her mother put a hand on her shoulders. Tears scored streaks through Clarice's rouge and foundation. 'My poor little boy,' she whispered, and soft sobs escaped her chest. 'My poor little boy.'

Peter materialised in the doorway, with Ian, Judy, Josie and Wally pressed close behind. 'What's Father going to do to Clive?' Peter asked.

'Hush,' Clarice said. 'Back to your rooms.'

'But we didn't finish tea,' Josie complained.

Eileen broke from her mother's embrace and said to the children, 'Come on. Back to our rooms.'

'You're all wet,' Peter complained, when Eileen gently ushered him through the curtains and into the boys' bedroom, with Ian and Wally obediently following. 'What's Father going to do with Clive?' Peter repeated.

'None of our business,' Eileen told him. 'And don't be nosey.'

'It is our business!' Peter retorted angrily. 'Clive's our brother!'

'I want Mum!' Wally demanded.

'She will be here in a moment,' Eileen reassured him. She looked at Peter, pleading to her brother with her eyes. 'Play a game.'

'What game?' Peter asked.

'Marbles,' Ian suggested.

Eileen squeezed Ian's arm affectionately and went to the girls' room to check on Judy and Josie. 'How long do we have to stay in here?' Judy asked, irritably.

'Until Mum or Father say otherwise,' Eileen replied.

'What do you think Father is doing with Clive?' Josie asked.

'I don't know,' Eileen said. 'Play with the dolls while I get out of these wet clothes.' Thunder rolled across the roof.

Eileen was buttoning her lilac blouse when the bedroom door opened, and her mother's head appeared. 'You can finish your tea now, girls. But you must be very quiet.'

The remnants of their meal – sausages and mashed potato – waited on the plates, and Clarice placed a fresh plate in front of Eileen as the other children ate. The rain beat solidly against the iron roof. 'Where's Father?' Ian asked between mouthfuls.

'With Rod – with Mister Edmund in the parlour,' Clarice said.

'And Clive?' Eileen asked.

'In his room.'

'Can we say hello to him?' Peter asked.

'No!' Clarice said sharply. 'Your father strictly forbids it. No one is to go in that room. Do you hear?'

'Yes, Mum,' Ian and Judy said. The others nodded silently.

Eileen glanced at the closed dark blue door adjoining the kitchen that led into the rear bedroom of the house. The two eldest boys shared the room before Bruce joined the RAAF. They had a bunk each, and storage and privacy from the younger children. Clive had the room to himself for a handful of months after Bruce joined up. Before he started disappearing. Eileen wished she knew why her brother ran away, why her father was so angry with him.

'Penny for your thoughts?' Clarice asked.

'I thought Father was in Barmera,' Eileen said, as she cut a slice of sausage.

'As did I,' Clarice replied. She sat at the table with a cup of freshly brewed tea. 'Seems he was back on special orders. Something happened. He would not tell me what.'

'How long is he here?'

'A couple of days. He goes back the day after tomorrow.'

'Can I take Clive something to eat? He's so skinny.'

Clarice hesitated, looked Eileen squarely in the eye, but lowered her head and cup, and said, 'No.'

'But he must be hungry,' Eileen insisted.

'I will feed him after you are in bed,' Clarice said. 'That is the end of it.'

'Can we listen to the radio?' Judy asked.

'Not tonight,' Clarice told her. 'Everyone to bed early. School tomorrow morning.'

Eileen ushered the younger ones to bed, the boys protesting as always, before she helped her mother clean the kitchen. When the cleaning was done, Clarice said, 'You can prepare a pot of coffee for the men and take it to them.' Seeing Eileen's perplexed expression, Clarice pointed to a grey cannister on the sideboard. 'Your father brought coffee this time. Best not ask where it came from.'

Alone in the kitchen, Eileen prepared the coffee, savouring the enticing, robust, nutty flavour when she opened the tin. She heated the kettle, poured the water on the coffee granules in a small silver pot and placed the pot and cups on a tray to take to the parlour. She paused by the bedroom door to listen for Clive, hoping to hear him stir, but her brother was silent.

Eileen entered the parlour and placed the tray on the table, noting the table was unsteady on one leg after the melee. 'Thank you, Girlie,' Donald said, as she straightened.

'I'm sorry there's no sugar or milk,' Eileen apologised.

'We are used to it that way,' said Mister Edmund.

'How long has he been here?' Donald asked.

Eileen's heart pounded. 'Tonight,' she replied. 'He met me in the street.' Her father's accusing stare made her lower her eyes. 'Just tonight,' she repeated.

'Did he tell you where he's been?'

'No.'

'Nothing at all?'

Donald's stern question forced Eileen to look at her father's steel blue eyes. She thought them handsome, except when he was angry. Then they were cold, cruel eyes promising pain. 'Nothing, Father,' she said quietly. 'We didn't have time to talk.'

'All right, Girlie. You may go.'

Her father's dismissal sent Eileen scurrying to the kitchen to continue cleaning, but she crept to the hallway and listened in on the adults when she was finished. The men were talking in the parlour about war events and their work. In breaks in their conversation, she heard Clarice crooning to Wally in the boys' bedroom.

Satisfied the adults were engrossed in their worlds, Eileen crept to the back bedroom blue door and quietly opened it. To her horror, she discovered her brother handcuffed to the lower bunk. Dried blood stained his forehead, left eye and cheek. She hurried to the kitchen sink, moistened a cloth, and returned to the bedroom, pausing at the hallway to be sure no one was coming. Trembling, she knelt beside her brother, and whispered, 'Oh, Clive.' She dabbed at his forehead to clean away the blood, conscious of puffiness and bruising emerging on his face. She couldn't believe her father would hurt her brother so much.

'Don't,' Clive complained.

'You're hurt,' she argued.

'If that bastard catches you in here-'

'He's busy in the parlour,' Eileen told him. 'Keep still.' She continued to wipe away the crusty blood, finding a small cut and a bruise on her brother's forehead. 'Why do you always run away?' she asked as she sat back.

'You don't want to know,' Clive whispered angrily.

'I do want to know.'

'No, you bloody don't!' he retorted. 'One day you'll find out, but not from me.'

'It can't be that bad,' Eileen said.

'Girlie!' Clarice whispered harshly. Eileen rose and retreated into the kitchen, avoiding her mother's gaze. 'You're lucky it was me and not your father,' Clarice said, closing the door and following her.

'I wanted to make sure Clive was all right,' Eileen explained.

'Your father's word is law. You know that,' Clarice reminded her. 'Go to your room, and do not dare to come down here again.'

Eileen withdrew, but she glimpsed tears welling in her mother's eyes and the vision troubled her as she settled into bed. 'What's happening?' Judy whispered in the dark.

'Go to sleep!' Eileen hissed. She lay on her pillow, listening between bursts of rain against the iron roof to the murmuring voices at the front of the house, the men joined by her mother, although she heard mainly the burr of men. She was confused as to why her father was being so cruel to Clive, why Clive hated their father, why Clive stayed away from home. She had no answers, no clues, but the conundrum cycled through her mind until she slept.

As the first early light peeped through the curtains, Eileen woke and listened to the sounds of sleeping: her brothers and sisters snuffling in their beds, her father snoring at the front of the house, the house creaking as stone, iron and wood woke to the rising sun's warm caress. Confident everyone was asleep, her feet bristling as they pressed against the icy floorboards, she crept along the hall to the rear bedroom.

The dark blue door was ajar. She listened, wary that someone was in the room with Clive. She never heard Mister Edmund leave last night. When she gathered the courage to peer around the door, the room was empty. Open handcuffs hung against the bunk. Clive was gone.

1945

"There's great beauty on this world if you just have the eyes to see it."
Henry Travers

Wrapped in the radio valve glow and lounging in the armchair, Eileen listened to "Martin's Corner," a rare privilege. With new gas and electricity restrictions, the war in Europe closing in on Hitler's Germany, the battles in the Pacific raging against Japan, the Government's call for citizens to do their part through greater sacrifice reached deeper into everyone's lives, and Eileen was pleased to give what little she earned to help her family get by. "Martin's Corner" and fifteen minutes of privacy was her reward.

Wally's head popped around the corner as the closing theme music rose to a crescendo. 'Come on,' Eileen invited, and Wally climbed eagerly onto the chair, squishing beside his big sister. Josie entered next, carrying her doll, and squatted on the floor. Judy and Ian arrived as the "Dad and Dave" show theme began. 'Where's Peter?' Eileen asked.

'He has to help Mum because he spat out his broccoli,' Josie said, relishing her brother's punishment.

'Mustn't waste food,' Eileen recited.

'They're still gross,' Ian said. Eileen tickled him, until he giggled, and then she shushed him as the radio serial began in earnest.

Peter arrived as the show ended, annoyed to miss it, but he dutifully led the younger children to their bedroom, leaving Eileen to listen to the news update. There was a tragedy involving a United States aircraft carrier off the Japanese mainland, but the more important news was that the Allies were driving the Japanese back to their homeland. The famous big band leader, Glenn Miller, was still missing, his plane lost over the English

Channel on a flight to Paris before Christmas. The news upset Clarice and she played a tribute to Miller at the family Christmas singsong around the piano. Big tragedies, small tragedies, some hope: the news was light and dark. Eileen was glad when the music swelled for "Lorna Doone", and she settled into the Seventeenth Century tale of romance, intrigue and adventure.

Fifteen minutes later, she emerged from the nook and checked on the bedrooms. Judy and Josie were asleep, but she caught Peter whispering to Ian in the darkness. 'You should be asleep,' she cautioned, and she waited until she was convinced the boys were being obedient before she closed the door and walked to the kitchen. Her mother sat at the table, head in hands. 'Mum?' she asked. 'What's wrong?'

Clarice lifted her head, her eyes red-rimmed, wiped her tears with the backs of her hands, and shook her head, mumbling, 'It doesn't matter.'

Eileen took her mother's hand. 'Something is wrong. Is it-?' She hesitated, before asking timorously, 'Is it Bruce?'

'Oh, good Lord, no, Girlie! God protect your brother from any harm.'

'Then what is it?' Eileen asked.

'No,' Clarice said. 'I am all right. Just something silly.' She stood and pushed her chair in. 'Are the others in bed?'

'Wally and the girls are asleep, but I think Peter and Ian are still awake.'

'Boys are always awake,' Clarice replied. 'I will clean up, and then I will come to the parlour and play piano. You can listen to the radio until I come.'

'I can help here,' Eileen offered.

Clarice took Eileen's hand in her own. 'You are a good girl. Go listen to the radio, Girlie. Pick a song from the music you like to sing, and I will play it when I am done here. I would like to hear you sing.'

In the parlour, sidelamp on, Eileen searched through her mother's sheet music stored in the piano stool, chose "We'll meet Again" and placed the score on the music rack. Singing in the church choir was always fun, but singing in the parlour, with her mother playing piano, was her favourite.

She wished she knew what was ailing her mother. Clarice was spending most evenings in her bedroom lately, and she was detached from ordinary housework during the days, so much so that Eileen was taking responsibility for organising and feeding the children and cleaning and washing. And it was tiring her out. Something was terribly wrong, she knew it, but no one was telling her what it was. If her father was home, he would sort it out, but he was too often away. She wished the war would end and her father could come home. She sat in an armchair with the music score to wait for her mother, letting tiredness pull on her eyelids.

Eileen jerked awake. The white face and black hands of the mantlepiece clock showed it was after nine. She looked around the semi-lit parlour and realised her mother had not come as promised. She rose and stepped into the hallway.

The kitchen was dark, the house quiet. A soft sob came from behind her mother's bedroom door. When another sob broke the silence, Eileen gently opened the door, and she was enveloped by the jarring scent of lavender and mothballs. Clarice was hunched on the end of the bed, her head in her hands in the same way Eileen found her in the kitchen. The bedside lamp threw awkward shadows across the walls and curtains. 'Mum,' Eileen whispered. 'Are you all right?'

'I can't do this,' Clarice sobbed. 'I can't keep doing this.'

'Can't do what?' Eileen asked as she sat on the bed.

Clarice looked up, eyes redder than before, her hair bedraggled, her cheeks stained with tears. 'Oh,' she sobbed. 'Oh, you poor child.'

'What?' Eileen asked, unsettled by her mother's irrational gaze.

'Your father,' Clarice said hesitantly. 'He's been misbehaving.'

Bewildered by the confession, Eileen asked, 'What do you mean?'

Clarice grasped Eileen's hand and squeezed it. 'He's seeing another woman.'

Eileen heard the words, but they didn't render understanding. Searching for a question that made sense to her, she asked, 'Who told you this?'

'Ethel. She saw him with her.'

'When?'

'Last year. And, again, two weeks ago.'

'Don't take any notice of Auntie Ethel,' Eileen advised, remembering how she overheard relatives say her mother's younger sister was a notorious family gossip. 'She's saying that because Father is away so much.'

'She saw him, Girlie,' Clarice repeated and sobbed. 'She even told me where the woman lives. He goes to see her when he is on leave.'

'But he comes here when he's not at Loveday,' Eileen argued.

'Oh, we are so naïve,' Clarice muttered, and she sobbed uncontrollably.

'Mum,' Eileen crooned. 'Mum, it's not true. He wouldn't do that sort of thing.' She held her mother's heaving shoulders, afraid and unsure of what was really happening.

'I want to drown myself!' Clarice sobbed. 'I want all this to end!'

'Hush!' Eileen urged, fear rising in her gut. 'Don't say those terrible things, Mum.'

'I want it to be over.'

'Mum!' Eileen begged. 'Please!' She held her mother close, feeling her sobs subside and her breathing ease between sniffles. 'I'll fetch a hankie,' she offered, and she eased off the bed to open the dresser, wood grating against wood as she slid the drawer open. She handed Clarice a white laced handkerchief and waited for her to calm.

'I am sorry,' Clarice finally said, sniffing. 'I need to pull myself together. It's not right that I should tell you these things.'

'It's all right,' Eileen reassured her, but she was battling confusion, coming to terms with her mother's accusation of her father. 'What will we do?'

'I've made up my mind,' Clarice announced. 'I am going to go see the woman.'

'Why?' Eileen asked, dumbfounded by her mother's assertion. 'How will that help?'

'She needs to know Donald has a wife and family. She needs to know what she is really doing,' Clarice said resolutely. 'She needs to know the truth.'

*

The maroon and gold tram rattled along the Glenelg-to-City line, swaying and rocking in the late March mid-morning heat, the bell clanging at each stop and intersection, the passengers lurching with the brakes. The clattering carriage where Eileen sat on hard red leather seats with her mother was almost empty, the rush hour workers long gone to work. Two days earlier, the family gathered at the kitchen table to sing 'Happy birthday' to her – fourteen years old – and the world was happy and held promise, but now she was on the tram with her mother, full of trepidation, heading for an appointment with the awful, impossible truth about her father's infidelity. She loved him, for all his moods. He was taciturn, but kind. She didn't believe he could do what her Auntie Ethel claimed he was doing. Against all evidence, she hoped this journey would vindicate her father.

The night Clarice made her awful confession, Eileen struggled to sleep, her mind besieged by all the possibilities of what it meant for her father to be 'misbehaving.' She imagined her father the victim of a stabbing, like Mister Whitehead, or worse. Why would her father want to be with another woman? None of it made sense. Her dreams were confusing images of her father not being her father. When she was little, the world was ordered and happy. Everything was in its place, and everyone was who they were meant to be. But the war sent the world askew, and every year it was becoming more and more fractured, tilted off-centre and falling apart – Bruce joining up, John moving out, Clive running away, her mother unwell, and now her father 'misbehaving.' The adult world she depended on was fragmenting and she could do nothing except cling to the pieces in her reach.

She couldn't concentrate the next few days at school, thinking over and over about why her parents were not happy with each other and what that really meant for them, for everyone. Her teacher, Missus Farnham, scolded her for inattentiveness and sat her outside. Her classmates stared at her, but she didn't care. She offered to go with her mother to visit the woman her father was apparently seeing, because she wanted to protect her mother. She wasn't sure from what.

She watched her mother methodically dress. Clarice put on her best dress – a high-waisted dark blue cotton floral afternoon dress and white belt – and over it she wore a light grey capelet despite the sun's impending warmth. She applied a light layer of demure mauve lipstick and damped powder across her cheeks, as if she was determined to show the 'other woman' she was still attractive and desirable. She tucked her greying hair under a snug-fitting cloche hat, highlighted with a pink cloth rose, and slid into her best brown shoes, the ones she wore to play piano for the radio shows. She stowed light blue gloves in her belt. Everything was done with military precision, a warrior preparing for battle, and Eileen was in awe of her mother's meticulous preparation.

Eileen chose her green dress with the white buttoned bodice and the brown shoes she wore to school last year. Her hair was down, and she had no make-up. Lipstick was banned by her parents, a sign, her father warned her, of a girl with 'loose morals.' If her father was cheating on her mother, she wondered if he wasn't being a hypocrite. But she thought through the whole situation, and she didn't accept her mother's accusation. The trip to Port Adelaide, she believed, would vindicate her father.

Mother and daughter alighted from the tram in King William Street and walked through the bustling crowds to the bus stop on North Terrace where they waited until the bus to Port Adelaide halted with a screech of brakes in a cloud of hot air. Eileen followed her mother aboard, shuffling to take a warm seat halfway along the aisle, and a cocktail of cigarette smoke and sweat assaulted her as the bus lurched onto Port Road.

Uncomfortable in the close atmosphere, Eileen studied the passengers, the scattering of men and women in uniform, young mothers with small children, older men in jackets and hats and caps, and she wondered where they came from, where they were headed, what hopes and secrets they carried. Her gaze settled on two young women, she guessed weren't much older than herself, smiling and laughing as they chatted, their shoulder-length hair curled and topped with the highly fashionable Victory Roll, the style Eileen wanted to wear. They seemed blithe, happy, free, and she wanted to be like them. She was fourteen. Why couldn't she be older? Why did growing up take so long?

Clarice ushered Eileen off the bus at a stop in front of an engineering factory and led her away from the multi-lane expanse of Port Road, walking slowly in her low heels along a suburban street. Eileen peered at the front gardens of the bungalows and asked, 'Where are we?'

'Allenby Gardens,' Clarice muttered and trudged on.

The day's heat was aggressive, but the sun was dissolving behind a layer of dull grey cloud and the rising humidity portended rain. Eileen wiped perspiration from her brow and hoped the rain arrived soon. *Getting wet will be worth it*, she decided, conscious of the sweat staining her dress.

At an intersection, Clarice turned west, saying, 'This is the street.'

'Which house?' Eileen asked.

'Number eight.'

Eileen trailed a step behind, until Clarice stopped at a symmetrical bungalow with an open front yard, a wide porch, dark green wooden door and leadlight windows. A chain link fence defined the footpath boundary. 'Is this it?' Eileen asked, but she spotted the number eight on the letterbox. 'Do you think she's home?' When Clarice stayed silently staring at the house, Eileen asked, 'Are we going to knock?' Her mother did not answer. 'Mum?' Eileen prompted. 'Shall I knock?'

'No,' Clarice mumbled.

'But I thought-' Eileen began, until she realised her mother wasn't listening. She fell silent and stood beside her mother on the pavement. A ginger cat slouched along the porch and sat to lick itself. Three brown and grey sparrows flitted under the eaves and vanished over the neighbour's fence. The humidity was stifling.

'Come on,' Clarice said, and she turned to retrace her steps towards Port Road. Eileen dutifully followed, but with a nagging sense that, as she turned away, there was movement behind the rose print curtain in the window. She looked back, but the curtain was drawn.

Soft rain was settling in when they arrived home, the humidity as intense as Eileen's emotions. Whatever intention possessed her mother to travel the entire journey to the woman's house to confront her must have evaporated in the street when they stood outside the house. Eileen ached to know on the return trip why her mother changed her mind, but Clarice was silent, twisting the handle of her lilac purse while she stared impassively through the bus and tram windows at the factories and shops, the houses and flats that defined the lives of others. When they walked from Jetty Road, Clarice seemed oblivious to the drizzle, and she only spoke to Eileen when she reached the front door. 'Fetch Wally from

Missus Nicholls. He stayed home from school today because of his cold. And change your clothes when you come back in.'

Eileen walked to the Nicholls' house and knocked politely on the black door with its polished brass fittings. Her mind was in turmoil, trying to guess what her mother felt and why she was so stolid in her manner after being so determined and focussed when they left in the morning.

Missus Nicholls opened the door and looked aghast. 'Come out of the rain, young lady!' she urged, stepping aside. 'You'll catch your death!' Eileen waited in the hall while Missus Nicholls headed deeper into the house and returned with a grey bath towel. 'Dry yourself,' she ordered, thrusting the towel into Eileen's hands. 'What have you been doing?'

'Shopping in the city,' Eileen lied. 'Mum sent me to collect my brother.'

'Of course she has,' said Missus Nicholls, 'but first you must dry yourself and have a warm cup of tea.'

'Oh no, I can't, Missus Nicholls,' Eileen protested. 'Mum is expecting me to come back quickly.'

Missus Nicholls raised her pencil-lined eyebrow, an action Eileen herself learned to imitate from the movies whenever she doubted a comment. 'Yes, of course she is,' Missus Nicholls said. 'I'll fetch your brother.' She entered a room along the hall where Eileen heard her speaking low, although she couldn't discern the words, but Missus Nicholls reappeared leading Wally, who was rubbing his eyes sleepily. 'I feel so mean,' said Missus Nicholls.

'Was he good for you?'

'Bless the little man, yes he was,' Missus Nicholls affirmed. 'Make sure your mother hears that. He's still snuffly, so it was good he stayed home in this weather.'

'I'll tell her,' Eileen promised.

'Is your mother playing on the radio this week?' Missus Nicholls asked.

'I don't think so,' Eileen replied.

'Shame,' said Missus Nicholls. 'I like listening to the orchestra and her piano.' She pulled a dark blue umbrella from the hat stand by the front door. 'Take this.'

'It's only a few steps,' Eileen said.

'Don't be silly!' Missus Nicholls remonstrated. 'It's for both of you. No need to get wet, even for a few steps.'

Eileen took her little brother's hand, enjoying the warm contact. Missus Nicholls opened the door, unlocked the umbrella, and handed it to Eileen as she stepped into the drizzle. 'Thank you,' Eileen said.

'Tell your mother she can leave the boy with me whenever she needs. All right?'

'Thank you, Missus Nicholls,' Eileen reiterated, and she led Wally through the rain.

Inside her home, Eileen ushered Wally to the kitchen. Her brothers and sisters would be home from school shortly, bringing their chaos and demands for biscuits and cordial, and then it would be time to organise tea. Her mother wasn't in the kitchen, so Eileen lifted Wally onto a chair, poured him a glass of water and fetched a biscuit from the Arnott's tin, reminding herself to return the tin to Mr Sendy to help the war effort. 'Wait here while I fetch Mum,' she said.

She headed outside to search the wash house and the toilet, but her mother wasn't inside either building. Eileen re-entered and reassured herself Wally was occupied before she walked along the hall, peering in the rooms as she passed. Her mother's bedroom door was closed. The room was silent. Eileen knocked gently. When no one answered, she opened the door and found Clarice lying on the bed, still dressed in her good clothes. 'Mum?' Eileen whispered.

'Go away,' Clarice replied, voice muffled by her arms and the pillows.

'Can I help?' Eileen asked.

'Go away!' her mother repeated.

Eileen paused before leaving, closing the door quietly, but Peter opened the front door, startling her. 'What are you doing?' Eileen asked.

'Coming home from school,' he replied. 'Is Mum all right?'

'She's sleeping,' Eileen replied. 'Where are the others?'

Peter grinned. 'At Mister Sendy's shop.'

'It's raining,' Eileen said.

'Not anymore,' Peter told her.

'What are they doing at the shop?' Eileen asked.

'Buying bullseyes.'

'Where did they get the money?'

'Auntie Fay picked us up from school in her car,' Peter explained. 'She gave us each a half-penny.' He held up a brown bag. 'Want one?'
Eileen wanted to say no, but lollies were hard come by, so she reached in and drew out a black and white candy and rolled it in her fingers, saying, 'Thank you.'

'And here they are!' Peter announced, as he opened the door to let Ian lead Judy and Josie into the house.

'I'll make tea soon,' Eileen told them. 'You can play in your rooms, or out the back if it's not too wet. Mum is sleeping, so be very quiet.'

'We could go to the beach,' Ian suggested eagerly.

'I don't think so,' Eileen said.

'Come on,' Peter said to the others. 'We'll play Snap.'

'Again?' Ian complained.

'I want to play with my doll,' Josie said.

'Play with your doll,' Ian retorted. Josie poked out her tongue.

'No need to be rude,' Eileen warned her.

'He was rude first,' Josie squeaked, and she kicked at Ian's leg, but the older boys skipped away down the hall.

'Sh!' Eileen urged as they disappeared through the curtain.

While the children played, Eileen orchestrated a meal from bread, potatoes, cabbage and beans and, when the plates were ready, she called the children to the kitchen table and set them to eating, making Judy sit beside Wally to supervise him. 'Is this it?' Peter queried, examining the mashed potato surrounded by greens.

'Be thankful you have anything at all,' Eileen warned.

'I thought you and Mum went shopping today.'

'Not for food,' Eileen replied. 'Not enough coupons left.'

'Is Mum still sleeping?' Judy asked.

'Yes,' Eileen said.

'Can I go see her?'

'She's sleeping,' Eileen reminded Judy.

'She's always sleeping,' Judy remarked disdainfully.

'I will see if she wants something to eat,' said Josie.

'You will stay right there and finish your meal,' Eileen told her. 'I'll take something to Mum afterwards.'

'Bet she doesn't want this,' Peter grumbled.

'Don't be so ungrateful,' Josie scolded, and the older children grinned. 'What's so funny?' Josie asked.

'You,' Peter said. 'You sound like Mum with a squeaky voice.'

'Peter,' Eileen warned.

'No, she really is funny,' Peter argued, smiling.

Eileen shook her head. 'I'm going to check on Mum,' she said. 'Ian can be in charge of the dishes.'

'Why me?' Ian asked.

'Because you're not me,' Peter told him gleefully.

Freed from the children's bickering, Eileen listened at her mother's bedroom door, opened it, and found Clarice face-down on the bed. She crept in, sat beside her mother and stroked her hair. Clarice sighed and asked, 'Where are the children?'

'Eating tea,' Eileen replied.

Clarice sighed again and was quiet. After a few moments, face still buried in the pillow, she drew a deep breath and said, 'I can't do this.'

'Can't do what?' Eileen asked.

'Your father,' Clarice cryptically replied. 'I can't do it.'

'What do you have to do?' Eileen asked, confused, the day's journey weighing on her.

'Never mind.'

'Can I help?' Eileen asked.

'You already are,' Clarice said. 'Get the children to bed after a radio show.'

'Do you want me to bring food?'

'No. I'm not hungry.'

'You haven't eaten all day,' Eileen reminded her.

'I'm not hungry,' Clarice repeated. 'Let me sleep.'

As Eileen waited for her mother to fall asleep, she tried to imagine her mother's pain, but she couldn't. She knew it was caused by her father, or the gossip about him, but having never had a boyfriend she couldn't delve into past pain to make an association. Her parents loved each other. She saw them laugh and smile together, and hug and kiss, although the kissing was always polite, brief pecks in front of the children. It made no sense that they might not still love each other. Her memories were full of joyful family times, the familiarity and comfort of her father smelling of sawdust, her mother all lavender and music, and a room full of children. *Is this what happened between Mister and Missus Whitehead,* she wondered? *Can people fall so far out of love that they are willing to hurt each other*? She shuddered at the thought. She would never be like that. When she found the man of her dreams, she would be devoted to him and he would be devoted to her, and their love would be eternal. That's how it was meant to be.

She rose from her sleeping mother's side and ventured into the hall to discover Ian waiting. 'Are the dishes washed and put away?' she asked.

'It's almost time for the radio show,' Ian complained.

'All right,' Eileen conceded. 'If you get everyone else into the nook, and go to bed when I ask, I will do the dishes.'

Ian grinned at the offer, returned to the kitchen, and organised the children to wash their hands. Judy steered Wally into the bathroom, Josie following, and Ian and Peter headed for the radio nook.

Eileen cleaned the table and stoked the embers in the wood stove to boil water for the dishes. She noted the wood box was empty. That meant a walk to Saint Leonards with the wheelbarrow tomorrow to fetch wood. The housework was endless. She waited for the water to boil, wondering how long it would be before her mother wasn't sick and could do her share. It was as if her life was filled with waiting – waiting for the children, waiting for her mother, waiting for kettles to boil and food to cook, waiting – she winced as a sharp pain twinged a tooth. That was another complication. 'So many problems,' she whispered to the tea towel.

The children obediently went to their bedrooms after the serial ended and Eileen bade them goodnight after tucking in Wally. She left the boys' bedroom door ajar and tiptoed down the hall to her mother's bedroom. Clarice was asleep on the bed in a foetal position. She watched her mother's chest rise and fall, glad her mother was finally resting.

In the radio nook, she tuned the radio to "The Shadow" serial and let the world of horror and intrigue swallow her emotion. She didn't want to keep thinking about what was consuming her mother, why her father could be so cruel to her, or why the world was such a dark and callous place for so many people, why the war never seemed to end. She only wanted her mother to be happy again. She wanted her family to be happy again. She wanted to be happy again.

*

Missus Higgins, green pillbox hat fixed askew to her hair with bobby pins, belt snug around her waist, met Eileen at the shop entrance. 'Morning, Missus Higgins,' Eileen said politely.

'And what time do you call this?' Missus Higgins asked brusquely.

'I'm sorry I'm late,' Eileen replied, blushing. 'Mum is unwell, and I had to get the children to school.'

'No excuses,' Missus Higgins said. 'Last year, you were late because you were taking children home from school and I accepted that, although you know I do not brook tardiness. This year, I give you fulltime employment, and you still can't be dependable. I really shouldn't have taken you on. There are plenty of girls who would die to work in this shop. Apparently, you're not one of them.'

Fear swelling in her throat, Eileen drew her breath and stammered, 'I really am sorry, Missus Higgins. I do want to work here.' She noticed an older woman watching and felt the world closing in.

'You spend too much time gawking out the window at boys, your work is shoddy, you're unreliable, and you are late again,' said Missus Higgins. 'You are no longer required.'

'But Missus Higgins -' Eileen protested.

'Do not come in this shop again,' Missus Higgins concluded.

'My family needs the money,' Eileen argued, tears welling.

'Everybody's family needs the money,' Missus Higgins retorted. 'It seems you don't need it enough. Please leave at once, and do not make an embarrassing scene.'

'What about my pay for this week?'

'Tsh!' Missus Higgins snorted. 'You weren't here enough to earn it. Now get going, or I will call the police.'

The older woman was still staring as Eileen pulled on her brown coat and retreated from the shop. Distraught, Eileen buttoned her coat against the cold and stood on the footpath, gazing through tear-blurred eyes at the hat display. People shuffled dispassionately around her. Trucks, trams, buses and cars clattered and rumbled along Jetty Road. A woman in a green spotted dress asked if she was all right. 'Yes,' Eileen sniffed. 'Sorry. I'm fine,' she replied. The woman walked on. Eileen was numb, paralysed, until she saw Missus Higgins glaring through the window. She wiped her face and moved away.

The journey home was slow and eerie. The world was upside down again. Last year, she hurried home from school every afternoon to change and jog to Jetty Road to arrive at work on time because her pay went to her mother to bolster the war coupons for groceries and shoes and clothing and supplement the money her father brought in. She had frantic purpose. She finished her Progress Certificate in August with a score of eighty-four out of one hundred and was proud of her achievement. School had been fun, and she enjoyed laughing and learning with her friends, Joyce Fielder and Lena Stronghurst, but by October she was missing more and more school days to help her mother when children were sick, or when her mother was busy with volunteering at the Cheerio hut or sick herself. In November, the Headmaster called her father in to tell him his daughter was a lazy, unreliable student who disappointed the school with her behaviour. She never found out what her father told the Headmaster, but she didn't go back to school after that interview. Instead, she worked full-time at Bon Marche, cleaning the shop, and learning the millinery craft. At least, she did. Now, everything was crashing down around her.

When she reached the front gate under a cloudy mid-morning sky, she hesitated. Her mother would not be expecting her home so early, and she would have to explain that she lost her job. Her mother might be angry, but more likely she would collapse in tears and Eileen would be left with the household duties again. She didn't need another emotional roller-coaster this morning.

A dark blue Humber ambled by, distracting Eileen, and she glimpsed a naval uniform on the passenger. The war was rolling to a close. Hitler committed suicide more than a month ago and people celebrated Victory in Europe not long after, ending almost a year of fighting since the Allied forces stormed the beaches of Normandy, and six years since the war began. The war in the Pacific was keeping Australian forces occupied, but radio reports confirmed that the Japanese were being systematically driven from their island strongholds and the US Airforce was bombing cities in Japan. Her father would be released from his duties overseeing the remaining prisoners in Loveday and Bruce would come home. The world would be back in order.

But not yet.

Her job was gone.

And her tooth was aching worse than ever.

Going home wasn't an option. She needed to consider how to break the news gently to her mother.

Instead of opening the gate, she headed for the Esplanade, passing familiar shops and houses and Mister Allen's Broadway Hotel, avoiding eye contact in case someone recognised her and wanted to know what she was doing.

On the foreshore, she sat in the dunes and gazed at the cold metal ocean hunkered beneath the grey clouds. Rain moved along the invisible York Peninsula shoreline across the Gulf, and a brisk breeze flicked white tufts from the rolling waves before they unfolded against the shore. The high tide pressed against the dunes, sucked at the sand, and slapped against the bathing sheds. The kiosk, closed for winter, hunched on the foreshore as if anticipating the coming rain. A gull swept low across the waves, chased by two more, all three buffeted by the capricious breeze that was determined to dunk them in the water. A solitary soldier walked the water's edge towards Glenelg where the jetty strode into the water, its long arm bulging in the middle at the aquarium before stretching out to the three-storey pavilion squatting at the seaward end.

Eileen pulled her coat collar up to her cheeks and hugged her knees against her chest. It was easier being in school. As taxing as the lessons were, at least for a part of the week she was a child whose only responsibility was to learn and behave. She spent recess and lunch breaks with her friends, chatting about fashion and music and boys. Her family tasks huddled around the school day perimeter, and they could not intrude. But, this year, too much was being expected of her, especially with her mother's illness worsening since she learned her husband was unfaithful. Clarice stayed in her room, sleeping, crying, leaving Eileen to go to work to provide money, and come home to cook meals and do the housework her mother was letting go. It wasn't fair. Now, her one respite, time at the millinery shop, was taken away. Life wasn't meant to treat her like this.

She removed her shoes and walked to the shoreline, the gritty sand scrubbing her soles, and at the water's edge she let the dying waves chilling wash thrill her toes, sharpening her senses. The sensation temporarily distracted her from the persistent twinges in her tooth. The throbbing made sleep difficult, and she knew she would have to visit the dentist to find out what could be done. The problem was, without a job, how could she afford to go?

She sauntered southward between waves and dunes, past Somerton Park, towards the shadow of Brighton jetty, her mind rolling a cinematic collage of her life as she walked: chasey around the big old house in Black Forest, her father cupping a strawberry blond red setter puppy, winning the essay prize after the school trip to Humbug Scrub, singing with her family in the parlour on Sunday afternoons, her mother's fingers caressing the ivory keys, her father's tenor voice rising in lead with the children's backing vocals, dancing to Swing music in the kitchen with Bruce, polishing her father's boots, listening to the radio horror serials and swimming at the beach in summer. Happy times, times when the family was the best place to be, when life was full and rich.

But darker shadows skulked in her memories and intruded: the war breaking out, her father joining the army, Bruce joining the navy and then the army, John living away from the family with Auntie Fay, Clive running away for no known reason, the drudgery of being eldest sister and helping raise the younger siblings, leaving school, the lies about her father's infidelity, her mother's illness from the enveloping sadness, the job loss.

The whipping wind flattened Eileen's tears as they rolled onto her cheek and the swirling sand stung her ankles, and she realised she had walked all the way along the beach to Brighton, lost in her thoughts. A curtain of rain swept across the brittle grey ocean from the southwest, bearing down on her, so she walked briskly to the stairs and up to the road – another Jetty Road, this one at Brighton – and took shelter beneath the

Grosvenor Hotel veranda as the rain flowed across the beach and onto the Esplanade. The deluge liquefied the world, blurring the landscape as it cascaded from veranda gutters and downpipes onto the road before sluicing towards the foreshore. A black De Soto ploughed through the rain, tyres shearing through puddles and showering sheets of water onto the footpath, windscreen wiper furiously trying to make sense of the watery chaos for the driver. Her life was dissolving in the same way, running out of control, and like the driver she was struggling to make sense of it. Eileen clutched her coat and hugged herself to keep the cold at bay. There was no going home in the downpour.

*

Damp and shivering, Eileen hurried along The Broadway in the fading light and chill air. She pushed through the gate, opened the front door, and was astonished to discover her father standing in the hall. 'You're wet through,' he observed in his peremptory military tone as he pulled the bedroom door closed behind him. 'Get dry clothes on, Miss, and make sure the children stay in the kitchen.'

'Yes, Father,' Eileen stammered, clasping her coat to her body to minimise the droplets spilling to the floor. He called her 'Miss', not 'Girlie', she realised, and that meant he was in a foul mood. She eased through the hallway curtains and into her room to change her clothes. As she donned her grey A-line skirt and khaki woollen jumper, she heard the rise and fall of voices through the wall, her father and her mother, sharp tones, angry tones, hysterical tones, distressed battling words that frightened her. She crept to the kitchen and opened the door where Peter, Ian, Judy, Josie and Wally were gathered at the table, the four older children playing cards. The wood stove was alight, and the room was stiflingly warm.

'They still at it?' Peter asked, looking up.

Eileen closed the kitchen door.

'They've been at it since we got home,' Peter continued. 'Do you know what's going on?'

Eileen shook her head.

'Mum is really upset,' Judy said. 'I think that's why she's been crying so much.'

'I don't like it,' said Josie, tears glittering.

Eileen squatted and put an arm around Josie, crooning, 'It's all right. Sometimes adults have to talk about things.'

'But they're shouting at each other,' Josie protested. 'Mum says we shouldn't shout at each other. It's not nice.'

'I guess they will sort that out,' Eileen replied. 'What are we playing?'

'Snap,' Ian explained. 'Playing?'

Eileen glanced at the wood stove and benches. 'I should start making tea.'

'Play!' Peter urged. 'We're not hungry yet, are we?'

'I am,' Josie said.

'Me too,' Wally agreed.

'Come on,' Peter said. 'We can play a couple more games.'

Eileen shrugged and declared, 'I'm in.' She sat between Josie and Wally and waited for Peter to shuffle and deal the cards. The adult voices echoed along the hall, muffled enough to be a distracting background.

'Your turn,' Ian said to Eileen's right.

Eileen listened to the muted argument grow quiet, become silent, and she wondered if her mother was confronting her father over the rumours; or maybe the argument was about something entirely different.

'Your turn,' Ian prompted, pulling Eileen from her contemplation.

As she played her card, the hall door opened, and Donald entered, his face red. 'Girlie,' he said gruffly. 'Go to your mother. The rest of you off to your rooms while I make tea.'

'What are you making?' Ian asked eagerly.

'Pasties,' Donald announced to the children's delight. 'Now wash and wait in your rooms.' Her siblings raced for the bathroom, and Eileen went to guide Wally in the wake of the others, but Donald said, 'Leave him. Judy can get him ready. Go to your mother.'

Sharply aware of her father's simmering anger, Eileen obediently walked along the hallway and opened the bedroom door to find Clarice studying herself in the dress mirror. 'Father said you wanted me,' Eileen quietly announced.

When Clarice turned, Eileen saw the tear stains down her mother's cheeks and her puffy eyes. She looked haggard and deeply sad. 'I am sorry,' Clarice said. 'I did not want this to happen.'

'What to happen?' Eileen asked.

'I have asked your father to leave.'

Shocked, Eileen blurted, 'Why?'

'You know why, Girlie,' Clarice replied. 'I will not have him living under this roof again, not after that.'

Her father was hardly ever home in recent months, but a world in which he was no longer an integral part was unimaginable. Eileen wanted to protest, but she faltered, and meekly asked, 'Where will he go?'

'Where he already is,' Clarice said. 'He has been living with that woman.'

'When?' Eileen asked, bewildered. 'He's been at Loveday.'

'Oh, Eileen,' Clarice said and sighed. 'He was discharged from the army months ago. He was lying about where he was all the time.' She burst into tears and sank to the floor. 'All these years I looked after his kids, and what has he done to me? I want to die,' she sobbed.

Eileen crouched beside her mother. 'Don't say that!' she pleaded.

'I want to throw myself in the ocean and drown,' Clarice moaned.

'Mum!' Eileen implored. 'Stop it!' She grabbed her mother's shoulders and she wondered at the cruel oddities of life that her mother was bawling in the bedroom while her father, the cause of her pain, was blithely cooking tea in the kitchen as if nothing was changed.

*

'It will have to come out,' Doctor Henty announced, leaning back from inspecting Eileen's teeth. 'If it stays in your mouth, the germs will fester, and they will infect every other tooth. Bad teeth don't belong.'

'When will you take it out?' Eileen asked.

'Now,' Henty replied. 'It doesn't take long. Going on the state of the rest of your teeth, young lady, you'll be back for more extractions. Wait here. I will talk to your mother first.' The dentist put down his instruments and left the room, leaving Eileen to stare at the array of shiny metal tools methodically arranged on the dentist's tray, tools for poking and cutting and scraping, implements that would as easily be found in a slaughterhouse or torture chamber, she surmised, her imagination racing to the radio serials. Apart from the red leather padding, everything around the dental chair was chromium and metallic. Eileen caught the eye of the brunette dental nurse, and asked, 'What will he do?'

The dental nurse, in her crisp white apron, blue blouse and white cap, said reassuringly, 'It's a simple procedure. But let's wait to see what Doctor Henty has to say after talking with your mother, shall we?'

The nurse smiled and Eileen admired her perfect white teeth. 'I wish I had good teeth like yours,' she said.

'You can,' the nurse replied.

'But my teeth are all terrible.'

'So were mine. I had them replaced with dentures last year.'

'You had all your teeth out?'

'Yes,' said the nurse. 'Lots of people do. Teeth are so bothersome, so dangerous. They get infected, they rot, they make us sick, and toothache is so horrible, as you well know. Now, I don't have to worry about any of that. I clean them every night in vinegar and water, and pop them in every morning, and they're perfect.' She smiled to show off her faultless dentures.

'That must have hurt,' Eileen said, wincing.

'It wasn't so bad,' the nurse said. 'You go to sleep and when you wake up it's done. I admit it's sore for a few days, and you do have to get used to your new set of teeth, but it's definitely worth it.'

Eileen was about to ask how much the full extraction and dentures cost, but Doctor Henty returned. 'I talked to your mother. She said we can take out the tooth that's giving you so much pain, and the one beside it that's been infected,' he announced.

'Will I have to have all my teeth out?' Eileen asked.

'I certainly hope not,' Henty said, 'but, as I said before, you will need more work later. Do you brush your teeth?'

'When I remember,' Eileen admitted.

'If you want to save the teeth you can save, I suggest you brush them every day, young lady,' Henty advised. 'For now, I will take out the ones giving you grief and we will see how you go.'

Eileen nodded.

'Good,' said Henty. 'I'm going to ask you to take a sedative and sit for a little while, and then we'll give you some laughing gas and get on with the task at hand. We should have you out of here in good time.' He smiled reassuringly, and turned away to say, 'Nurse Brady? The sedative for Miss Bonney, if you will.'

Eileen took the sedative and lay back on the dental chair. The idea of having all her teeth out was very strange, although she realised the women she envied obviously had dentures because their teeth were so perfect, like Nurse Brady's teeth. *How will we pay for this dental work*, she wondered?

*

Morning sunlight angling through the window sparkled on metal and threw elongated shadows across the commuters who pressed together in the aisles, swaying erratically, lurching back and forth as the tram stopped and started at each station. Sandwiched between a large woman in her blue WAAF uniform, buttons and back shoes polished like Eileen prepared her father's boots, and another woman in a dark green tailored suit, wearing a matching pillbox hat perched jauntily on her head, arms bunched against arms, the edge of the larger woman's breast occasionally pushing against her, Eileen was self-conscious of her green knitted sweater and second-hand grey skirt. And she was nervous. Today was her first morning at Ingerson's Tailors for Men on King William Street.

On a Saturday afternoon, a fortnight after the dreadful night when her mother told her father to never return, Donald Bonney appeared on the doorstep and asked for Eileen. Surprised to see him, but secretly glad, Eileen greeted her father politely. 'I hear you need a job,' Donald said, without pleasantries. 'Well, I found you one. 'He handed Eileen a hand-written note. 'The foreman is a mate from the army, and he says he'll take you on, providing you are punctual, and you work without gossiping or fooling around. You start Monday morning.' He tipped his cap and walked towards a black car, but he looked back to say, 'You're one of the family breadwinners, now, Girlie. Time to grow up.' And he drove away, leaving

Eileen bewildered because he didn't stay, and elated because he found her a job.

On Sunday morning, after singing in Saint Martin's choir, Eileen and Clarice accompanied Auntie Fay and brother John to Fay's house in Kurralta Park. 'Come for a cup of tea,' Auntie Fay invited. 'I have carrot cake.'

Tea and cake consumed, the sisters turned to chat, and Eileen retreated to the parlour to listen to her brother practise piano, as he was required to do every Sunday. His elegant fingers stroked the keys with finesse, but not yet with the nuances or passion their mother evoked when she immersed herself in the music and became the piano. When John finished a run of Mozart, Eileen asked, 'Do you like the school you're attending?'

'It's full of boys,' John said, winking. 'What's not to like?' He laughed and added, 'All the business and accountancy practice is a total bore, the teachers are horrid, and old Cummins my form master is an absolute shit.'

'John!' Eileen gasped, astonished by his blunt swearing.

'It's just a word, Girlie,' John admonished. 'I'm sure you say it all the time.'

'Father would wash my mouth out with soap if I said anything like that.'

'Well, he isn't around to do that, is he?' John retorted. 'And that's because he's been a right shit too.'

'What do you mean by that?' Eileen asked.

'You know exactly what I mean, Girlie. He isn't doing the right thing by Mother, he keeps trying to lock up Clive, and he didn't want me around the house.'

'How do you know what he's been doing?' Eileen demanded.

'Girlie Bonney,' John scoffed. 'Don't think the rest of the family doesn't know what goes on.'

'It's gossip,' Eileen argued.

'Gossip stems from a seed of truth,' John retorted. 'Anyway, enough about that. How about a tune?'

'Can you play anything modern?'

'I beg your pardon?' John sneered, and he broke into a boogie riff, rattling the piano keys with extraordinary flair. 'Name your tune,' he challenged.

"Moonlight Becomes You," Eileen said.

John's fingers rolled across the keys, straying into the named melody, and Eileen took the key to break into voice. She relished the chance to sing accompanied instead of singing alone in the house, and she swept through the melody, smiling when John embellished phrases on the piano.

As they finished their duet, clapping resounded from the parlour doorway, and Eileen blushed at the sight of her mother and Auntie Fay applauding. 'Very impressive,' Clarice offered. 'Beautiful, in fact.'

'You are a natural singer!' Fay declared, smiling at Eileen. 'However, I am not sure that is exactly the kind of music I am paying good tuition fees to hear from you, Jonathon Bonney,' she noted mockingly. 'Your tutor would be horrified.'

'Old Banks is a leech,' John retorted tartly. 'He's probably never even heard of Bing Crosby.'

'Mind your manners, young man,' Clarice warned. 'You are a very privileged boy. Act like you understand that.' Girlie suppressed her grin and nudged John's shoulder. 'It is time to go,' Clarice continued. 'Please thank Fay, Girlie. She gave us a set of clothes you can wear to your new job tomorrow morning.'

Eileen fingered the cuff of her knitted sweater as the tram lumbered through the south parklands. Auntie Fay's gift was generous, but dowdy and oversized, and Eileen felt like a small child in an adult's outfit. She wished she could wear clothes like the Hollywood actors she idolised, but she wasn't even allowed to wear makeup. 'Don't ever let me catch you with lipstick on,' her father warned. 'It's the badge of harlots.' War-time austerity accounted for part of his ban, but she felt if she was going to have to be the grown-up of the family makeup was surely part of her new responsibility. Her father and mother thought otherwise.

The tram disgorged passengers along King William Street and Victoria Square, and Eileen climbed down into the morning crowd hurrying to work. She crossed the road to the footpath and unfurled the note her father gave her, reading "Ingerson's, 78 King William Street." A quick search revealed the building, and she hastily fixed her hair and clothes as she entered the foyer, where a fresh-faced young woman at a counter asked, 'Yes, miss?'

Eileen replied, 'I'm to start work here today.'

The receptionist raised a querying eyebrow. 'Is that so? And your name?'

'Eileen Bonney.'

The receptionist opened a register to peruse a page, nodded and said, 'Ah yes, upstairs. First floor. Ask for Mister Herriman.'

Eileen thanked the receptionist and hurried up the flight of stairs, arriving at a landing and a dimple glass wooden door. She entered a workshop humming with industrial sewing machines. A tall imperious clean-shaven man in a dark blue suit studied her. 'Mister Herriman?' Eileen asked.

'That is me, young lady,' he said authoritatively. 'And you are?'

'Eileen Bonney.'

Mister Herriman nodded approvingly. 'Donald Bonney's offspring. Your father's a good man. I served with him.' He pointed to a workspace in the middle of the room. 'Buttons girl,' he announced. 'Mary will show you what to do. Pay attention. Learn quick. Be efficient.' He glanced at his fob watch. 'And be here fifteen minutes earlier in future.'

'Thank you, Mister Herriman,' Eileen said respectfully. She weaved through the sewing and cutting benches with their yards of light and dark grey and charcoal and blue and black cloth to the buttons section and approached the woman who was fossicking in a jar of blue buttons. 'Hello,' Eileen said. 'My name is Eileen. Mister Herriman said I was to work here.'

The woman scrutinised the thin teenager, before she stood and held out a hand to shake. 'I'm Mary,' she said. 'Pleased to meet you. Take a seat and I'll show you how to sort.'

Eileen shook Mary's hand, and sat, excited to be accepted.

*

'It's horrible what happened,' said the brunette, who was wearing a blue bouquet on her navy tunic. 'All those poor people, gone in an instant.'

'One bomb,' said the redhead in the green beret. 'Those poor people.'

'I know,' the brunette acknowledged. 'They say no one will be able to go near those places for years.'

'Why?' asked the redhead.

'Radiation,' the brunette explained. 'They're calling it atomic warfare, the war of the future.'

Standing in the crowded aisle, clinging to the overhead leather strap, her back against a soldier in his khaki kit, trying not to brush against his behind, tempting as it was, Eileen listened to the women discussing the horrific war events of the preceding week as the tram lurched across South Terrace. The concept that a plane could destroy an entire city with one bomb was inconceivable, and yet the women were discussing news that Hiroshima and Nagasaki were vaporised in exactly that manner. She hoped they were wrong, and that the news was distorted because a future where a single bomb could be so destructive sounded horrible.

The women alighted near the Law Courts. Released from their conversation, Eileen focussed on arriving at work. The passing weeks at Ingerson's were gratifying, once she accepted Mister Herriman's officious nature and expectations and the workshop's relentless pace. In a short space of time, she learned how to select, match, and attach buttons to coats and trousers, operate the industrial Singer sewing machines and fold the finished suits artfully to highlight their thread and quality. The workshop women were friendly, and travelling to and from the city each day on the tram made her feel grown up and independent. The wage she brought home contributed to paying the rent and feeding the family. She felt worthwhile, purposeful.

The bell dinged, the tram halted at her stop, and she climbed down amid the crush of people and headed for work. A car horn blared brassily near North Terrace as she entered Ingerson's, creating an unexpected raucous clamour for the morning, but, tempted as she was to see if the offending car came along King William Street, she hurried upstairs to the first floor. Mister Herriman did not tolerate tardiness.

Susan at the coats bench, laying out the first tweed jacket for the morning, chirped, 'Well, who looks pretty this morning?'

Eileen blushed, pleased Susan noticed the curl at the edge of her brunette hair that she laboured overnight to put in place. 'Do you like it?'

'Of course I like it,' Susan replied. 'It makes you look older.'

The car with the honking horn turned onto King William Street and was crawling along, its piercing cry persistent and pervasive, and people in the street shouted and cheered. 'What on earth is going on?' asked Chloe, an older woman who worked an industrial sewing machine.

'Not our concern. Work to be done,' Mister Herriman reminded the women.

As he moved to the window to glance sideways into the street, a bus horn hooted below, the workroom door swung open and Grace the seamstress cried exultantly, 'It's over! The war! It's over!' Astonishment flashed across the room, chased by realisation and joy.

'What do you mean?' a woman yelled.

Tears streaming, Grace declared, 'Mister Chifley announced it ten minutes ago on the radio! He said, "Fellow citizens, the war is over." It's over! Our boys are coming home! They're coming home!'

Overwhelmed by a surge of unbridled relief, Eileen cheered 'Hooray!' in unison with the other women, and the workshop erupted in excited voices.

'That will do, ladies!' Mister Herriman bellowed imperiously, and he waited for silence against a street background of shouting and cheering and beeping horns. 'It is indeed wonderful news, and we should all be very grateful,' he said, 'but we have important work to do and customers who will be expecting our finest wares to be ready on time. War or no war, business is still business. So, very good news, but let's get on with our jobs, shall we? I'm sure there will be plenty of time for celebration after work.' A ragged rendition of "The White Cliffs of Dover" rose over his voice from the rowdy chaos in the street.

Eileen battled her urge to run out of the workroom and into the street in defiance of Mister Herriman. The war had been going on forever. She was eight when it started, and she was already fourteen. Her father was a builder before the war, but it seemed to her like he was in uniform most of his life. Brother Bruce was nineteen. The fortunate part was that, of immediate relatives, only one cousin was lost in the years of conflict, Robert Ash, a gunner aboard a bomber over Europe. But the war was finally over. The anxiety, the austerity, the making do was ending. The world would be better. Life would be like it was when she was younger.

She looked up at Susan who was grinning as she worked on the jacket.

'It's really over,' Susan whispered. 'My Lionel will be coming home.'

'You must be so excited,' Eileen said.

'More than you can ever imagine,' Susan replied, her grin widening, tears forming in her eyes. 'I'm so happy!'

The hullabaloo outside swelled to a crescendo. 'Mister Herriman, please?' a young woman near the window pleaded.

'In good time,' Mister Herriman replied, but he was already distracted by the festivities and kept staring out the window.

Shadows moved across the workshop glass door, it swung open, and Mister Cole, the company manager, resplendent in his grey suit, white hair neatly combed, entered and yelled, 'Work's done for today, ladies! The war is over! Time to celebrate!' The room echoed with euphoric shouts as women and girls dropped their tools and tasks and pushed eagerly towards the stairwell, following Mister Cole down and into King William Street.

Eileen let the surging bodies carry her into the cacophony of horns and whistles, and shouting and singing, and her spirit exploded with joy. Strangers linked arms. Hats of all shapes and kinds rose and fell as people tossed them high in fits of ecstasy, and people climbed onto car roofs and truck trays and danced and sang a mad discordance of tunes. The crowd parted for a man cartwheeling through the throng and parted again as three soldiers aboard a BSA motorcycle weaved through the mob.

'Eileen!' Susan yelled, and she grabbed Eileen's arm and dragged her through the cram, until they reached a group of young men and women. 'This is Eileen! She works with me!' Susan yelled.

Before Eileen could respond, they swept her into their midst and started singing 'Let's all go down the Strand', enthusiastically and out of tune. Paper confetti rained from a first storey window.

'It's a damned fine party!' declared a young man to Eileen's right. 'I'm Bob!' Eileen flinched as Bob slid his arm through hers, but he laughed and put his arm around Susan, yelling, 'Let's march on boldly to victory!' The threesome lurched forward, drawing others in their wake, until they were caught in the press outside the Adelaide Town Hall where more paper swirled in the air, and hats erupted, and people sang and gambolled. 'Back to Rundle Street!' Bob yelled, and he steered the women haphazardly through the crowd.

Susan stopped Bob and handed a small golden cylinder to Eileen. 'Lipstick!' she yelled. 'Put it on!'

'I'm not allowed!' Eileen yelled, shaking her head, and handing the lipstick back.

'Don't be such a dag!' Susan yelled. 'Put it on! It's a whole new world! We can do anything!' Eileen pasted the lipstick onto her lips, struggling against the bodies moving around her, laughing as she slipped and smeared a stripe across her cheek. 'There!' Susan shouted. 'You look like a real woman!'

'Bloody gorgeous sheila!' Bob chimed in and he leaned forward to kiss Eileen, but she shrieked and pulled away, leaving everyone laughing hysterically.

'Back up, mate!' a young man chided. 'That filly is a wee bit skittish, eh.'

'I'm so sorry,' Eileen apologised, embarrassed.

'Don't apologise to that leech,' Susan said, pushing Bob in the chest. 'He tries it on with every girl he sees.'

'And what's wrong with that?' Bob asked, feigning chastened disbelief.

'Cop this!' a stranger in a khaki shirt interrupted as he shoved a brace of beer bottles in Bob's hands. 'Bottoms up!'

'Where did you pinch this from?' Bob asked, admiring the Cooper's labels.

The beer-giver touched the side of his nose in the same manner Eileen's father did as he said, 'Mum's the word!' and disappeared into the crowd.

Susan grabbed a brown bottle and took a hefty swig, before she thrust it at Eileen, who hesitated. 'Oh, Eileen!' Susan complained. 'Not a wowser too?'

Eileen grabbed the bottle and hoisted it to her lips, gulping a mouthful of the bitter liquid before the taste made her gag. She wiped her mouth, smearing the ill-applied lipstick, and handed the bottle to another man in the group.

'Watch out!' a lad warned.

Two police grey horses pressed through the heaving mob, the riders resplendent in dark blue military-style uniforms and white pith helmets. 'Hooray for the men in uniform!' Susan yelled, and the mob cheered the policemen.

'I love those horses!' Eileen said.

'I love those men!' Susan replied in a hungry, sultry voice, and the young women laughed.

Eileen pushed towards the police horse, and, with Susan's bright red lipstick, she drew a big V for 'Victory' on the horse's speckled grey and white flank, the horse's flank twitching. Her action evoked a riotous cheer from the crowd and a camera flashlight popped. Eileen retreated to her new-found friends who slapped her on the shoulder and back, and a young lad with bright blond hair and buck teeth separated by a gap remarked, 'You really are a cheeky sheila, eh?'

'I couldn't resist it,' Eileen replied.

'I'm Stephen,' the lad said.

'Eileen!' she replied, but Stephen was absorbed into the throng, and arms linked through hers again as a new parade of people began marching and singing. Overwhelming excitement and hope surrounded her. The war was over. All the pieces torn apart would come back together.

*

'Where have you been?' Clarice demanded when Eileen pushed the front door open.

'Everyone's celebrating!' Eileen explained as she embraced her startled mother. 'Everywhere, Mum. In the streets. On the tram. Bruce will be coming home!'

Clarice pushed her daughter to arm's length and scolded her. 'You smell of beer and smoke, and there is lipstick smeared all over your face! When your father sees this, you will get a hiding!'

'Oh, Mum! Don't be such a dag!' Eileen chided, grinning.

'And do not use that vulgar language in this house!' Clarice warned.

Giggling, Eileen pushed passed her mother and headed for the kitchen, calling in her wake, 'Besides, Father doesn't live here anymore!'

'No. I don't,' Donald said. He loomed in the kitchen doorway, a tall thin figure backlit by the early evening light filtering through the rear screen door, halting Eileen in her tracks. 'But I am still your father.'

'I didn't know,' Eileen stammered, terror rising in her throat.

'There are a lot of things you don't know, Miss,' Donald said in a threatening tone. 'You have a great deal to learn. Now, get in the bathroom and wash that filthy mess off your face.'

Eileen eased past her father, in case he smacked her backside like he sometimes did when she was younger, and she stumbled into the bathroom, aware her siblings at the kitchen table were staring. In the mirror, she saw her dishevelled hair, the lipstick smudged around her mouth from kissing boys and men in the revelry, and she was subsumed by shame and bewilderment. Of all the days so many people longed for, the day when the war was done and things could be set right, when things could be happy again, she was caught twixt disgrace and fear. She washed her face, wiped away the lipstick stains, rinsed the taste of cigarettes and beer from her mouth, and brushed her hair into a semblance of order, all the while straining to hear the curt conversation taking place between her parents in the hall. And she wondered why her father was in the house, hoping there was reconciliation – that, like the war ending, the family would be what it was before the war began.

Refreshed, Eileen tiptoed into the kitchen, casting a glance at her brothers and sisters. Peter and Ian were grinning, but the other three were watching in curious anticipation. She averted her eyes and continued up the hall, stopping when her mother emerged from the parlour, crying. 'Mum?' Eileen asked, but Clarice ignored her as she rushed into the front bedroom and closed the door. Eileen's dread rose.

Her father stood by the coffee table as if he was on military parade, hands clasped behind his back. 'Come in, Miss,' he ordered curtly. Eileen noted he wore a crisp light grey shirt and dark pressed trousers and jacket. The military boots she devotedly polished were replaced with black shoes. She stood before him obediently. 'What exactly do you think you are playing at?' he asked.

'I,' she began, hesitated, and said, 'The war is over.'

'I know the war is over,' Donald said. 'I asked you, what do you think you are playing at?'

'Everyone was so happy,' Eileen explained. 'We all went into the streets, and everyone was singing and dancing -'

'And you thought you could be a little whore, and paint and flaunt yourself, and drink, and do who knows what else,' her father interrupted sharply. 'You are fourteen, Miss. Fourteen. A child. You know there is to be no lipstick until you are old enough to wear it, but you wore it. No drinking until you are twenty-one, and yet you drank.' He glared, daring her to argue, but she lacked the courage to defy him. 'There are rules for this family, and you know them. You disgraced your family today.' Donald held up a newspaper in his left hand, the evening copy, and turned to the third page. Amid the photos of revellers and party scenes in the city, a black and white photo of a police horse with a large V in lipstick and two laughing girls accused her. 'This,' Donald said with rising anger, 'this makes a mockery of your mother and me and your whole family. How dare you!' Eileen never saw his hand rise, but the sharp smack across her cheek shocked her. Tears welled as she stumbled back. 'Into your room!' her father ordered. 'Now! There will be no more working in the city!'

Eileen retreated down the hall, through the curtains, and into her bedroom. Her father never hit her like that. A pat on the bottom for misbehaving was one thing, but he never raised his hand. Paralysed by her stinging cheek, she stood in the room fighting to stifle her sobs before she flung herself onto her bed and wept. Everyone was celebrating the end of years of war, and she was ordered to her room in tears. It was wrong. It was all so wrong.

1946

"Strange, isn't it? Each man's life touches so many other lives. When he isn't around, he leaves an awful hole, doesn't he?"
Clarence

Eileen hungrily eyed the bright blue Saint Vincent's Gulf water shimmering in the mid-afternoon heat. Wednesday morning's radio show announcer warned it was the start of another heat wave, like the sweltering heat of Christmas Day when everyone stayed indoors for lunch and the beach was packed in the afternoon until well after sunset. Still, a heat wave meant more time at the beach, and Eileen relished that outcome.

'Come on, Girlie!' Peter yelled from the Esplanade. The lanky youth scrambled onto the sand and sprinted for the water, eagerly chased by Ian and Judy.

'It's too hot,' Josie whined, clinging to Eileen's arm. Wally trotted after his brothers and sister, and Eileen marvelled how quickly he had grown into a gangly seven-year-old boy.

'Let's go,' Eileen said, urging Josie forward. 'The water will be beautiful and cool.' She led her sister across the short strip of warm sand to the cool water where Wally was dabbling his feet. Peter, Ian and Judy were already waist deep and bobbing with the placid waves. 'You know the rules!' Eileen yelled. 'Not too deep!'

Peter duck-dived into a low wave and emerged, laughing, sweeping his hands through his sodden curls, and Ian started splashing him. Experience warning her, Judy moved away from the boys, knowing she could quickly become the target for their amusement, but Josie clung to Eileen's arm, as she tentatively tested the water, and complained, 'It's cold.'

'It's meant to be,' Eileen chided, and she reached for Wally as he began to move forward. 'Waist-deep only, mister,' she warned.

'I can swim fine,' Wally said, pulling his arm free and diving into the water.

I'd love to throw myself in and roll in the waves and feel the cool freshness on my skin like that, Eileen reflected and sighed. 'But I'm the responsible one,' she murmured.

'What did you say?' Josie asked.

Eileen looked down at her brunette sister in her frilled grey knitted bathing suit. 'I said we are so lucky to be here.'

'Why?' Josie asked.

'Because it's hot and we can get cool,' Eileen answered. 'Go on. Get in the water.' Shrieking from the water's first touch, Josie waded up to her knees and stopped to watch her siblings play.

Satisfied the children were safe, Eileen strode forward and sank into the cool water, letting it soothe her, glad to have the freedom to enjoy the ocean in the summer heat. The beach was a haven, like the radio nook when a serial was playing, a place where cares dissolved. She bobbed in the waves, letting the water wrap her in its embrace, and she sank beneath the surface and opened her eyes in the green underwater light and silence. Corrugated sand at her feet glowed and flashes of silver darted across her vision between dark flecks and strands of drifting seaweed. She focussed on holding her breath, isolated, alone, content, and imagined she was a mermaid. The world was flickering light and peace. She could stay in a place like this forever.

When the daylight waned, Eileen herded her sun-burned coterie along The Broadway, but she stopped at the front of their house to watch the boiling sun melt into the ocean, the sky awash in apricot and gold and soft blue. A horn tooted as a dark blue Vauxhall passed, and Ian waved excitedly, saying, 'That's Conroy. He's in my class.'

'All right,' Eileen said. 'Everyone inside. Wipe your feet. No sand in the house. Straight to the laundry and change. Wash your hands and faces for tea.'

'What's for tea?' Ian asked.

'Surprise,' Eileen replied. 'Off and change.'

'Can we play outside while you cook?' Judy asked.

'No,' Eileen said. 'Play in your rooms,' but seeing their disappointment, and remembering her mother was in bed, she relented. 'All right, you can play in the backyard, but you have to wash your hands again when I call you in.' The children disappeared through the hall curtain.

Eileen peered into her mother's bedroom. The curtain was closed, but Clarice was sitting up in bed in the gloom. 'Are you all right?' Eileen asked.

'Yes, Girlie, thank you,' Clarice replied.

Eileen sat on the bed. 'What did Doctor Musgrave say?'

'What he always says. Rest.'

'But did he say what's wrong?'

Clarice's smile faded. 'He says I'm having the change of life.'

'What's that?'

'It's when a woman stops being a woman,' Clarice explained, and her face sagged into sadness.

'What does that mean?'

'You'll learn one day when your turn comes.' Clarice rolled onto her side, face away from Eileen.

Eileen waited for further explanation, but Clarice was silent, so she asked, 'Can I fetch you anything?'

'No,' her mother muttered.

'I'll bring tea down when it's ready.'

'I'm not hungry.'

'You have to eat, Mum. Doctor Musgrave would surely say that. I'll bring something after the others are in the parlour.' Clarice didn't answer, so Eileen tiptoed from the bedroom and closed the door.

Eileen opened the groceries cupboard and surveyed the meagre store of tins and packets. The ice box had three sausages in a bowl. The loaf in the bread bin was stale. A wilted cabbage sat on the bench beside an onion and three carrots. She would improvise and make a casserole. Tomorrow, she would go shopping for what she could procure. The war was over, and yet the Government was persisting with austerity measures and rationing. Magazine advertisements promoted recipes requiring minimal or substitute ingredients and produce like tea and butter and sugar remained hard to come by at the shops. Gathering the scant food to create the casserole, Eileen pondered the phrase 'change of life' and wondered what her mother meant when she said it was when a woman stopped being a woman. How could that even be possible? She wondered if it was tied to the things that made her a woman in her thirteenth year; breasts, bleeding, hair. What was happening to her mother? What new and unfathomable adult mystery did her mother's illness hide?

*

Eileen stared at the ceiling where the choir voices congregated before rolling across the assembled host. Light filtered through the stained-glass windows depicting Christ's story, reminding her of the sanctity of Palm Sunday and her role in helping parishioners celebrate the days of the Holy Week leading to the crucifixion and resurrection. Eileen licked her dry lips, took a deep breath in anticipation of the organ's chords, and joined with the choir in the opening lines of "How Great Thou Art". She revelled in singing the hymns, exploring notes and their shape and tenor in her throat and mouth and on her lips. Hymns, like "Holy, Holy, Holy" and "How Firm a Foundation" were easy, written to be sung in unison by the congregations, while others, like "Amazing Grace" and "Be Thou My Vision," were technically difficult, but she tackled them with gusto to master their notation and harmonies.

She listened to Father Cavanaugh's sermon, and took communion when it was offered, but her thoughts circled back to the issue of the family budget and feeding everyone within the limitations of rationing coupons and no steady source of income. She would find work if her mother wasn't so reliant on her to maintain the home and childcare responsibilities, but her mother was struggling with her father's infidelity and her change of life, and Clarice couldn't manage the family alone.

At the close of service, the choir sang "At the Cross" while the small congregation filed out, until Eileen's family and a handful of people remained. The organ's last chord fading, Eileen joined her brother, John, and they walked down the aisle to where grey-haired Father Cavanaugh, in his white cassock-alb and green chasuble, was talking to Clarice. Father Cavanaugh took Clarice's hand between his and pressed firmly. 'It's good to see you,' he said in his polished pseudo-English accent. 'And your beautiful children,' he added. 'Eileen and John are wonderful additions to the choir.'

'Thank you for an inspiring Holy Eucharist, Father,' Clarice responded.

'Thank you, Father,' said a woman in a dark blue overcoat as she squeezed past the children.

'Blessings on you, Missus Cunningham,' Father Cavanaugh offered, but he retained a firm grasp of Clarice's hand and returned his attention to her, asking, 'Is everything well with your family?'

Clarice blushed and replied, 'Yes, Father, of course.'

'I listened to your recitals on the radio when I could,' Father Cavanaugh said. 'Of course, I am also often with parishioners, so I didn't get to hear you play as often as I would have liked.'

'I have not played for a while,' Clarice confided.

'Can we go?' Peter interjected impatiently.

Father Cavanaugh laughed, and said to Peter, 'I was impatient when I was your age, especially when having to wait for adults to finish their conversations.' He patted Clarice's hand as he released it, saying, 'I will drop by during the week, if I may.'

'That would be lovely,' Clarice said. 'I will have a pot of tea ready.'

'That would be very kind,' Father Cavanaugh replied, smiling.

Clarice and Eileen herded the children along Hastings Road and onto The Broadway where John farewelled the group at the house before he headed for Jetty Road to catch a tram. 'He could have visited,' Ian griped.

'Perhaps he's had enough of whinging little brothers,' Peter teased.

'You're his little brother,' Ian retorted. 'I heard you whinging in the church.'

'Enough!' Clarice warned. 'I have a job in mind for both of you when we get inside.'

'And you both have homework to finish before school tomorrow,' Eileen reminded them. Peter laughed and Ian poked out his tongue.

'The cat will take that one day,' Eileen warned.

'We don't have a cat,' Ian retorted.

'Can we get a cat?' Judy asked.

GIRLIE

*

The jangling phone woke Eileen from her nap in the kitchen and she hurried down the hall to answer it. As she lifted the black receiver, her mother appeared in the bedroom doorway, face ashen and drawn, wrapped in her maroon dressing gown. 'Hello?' Eileen asked.

'Who is it?' Clarice asked.

Eileen put her finger to her lips. 'Yes. This is Eileen. Who's speaking?' she asked.

The voice responded, and Eileen's stomach churned, her hands shook, and tears welled. 'Bruce!' she screamed. 'Bruce!'

Clarice sagged to the floor.

'Oh, Bruce,' Eileen said, caught between joy to hear her brother's voice and her mother's collapse. 'Wait. Mum's fallen.' She knelt, stretching the phone cord taut, touching Clarice's arm. 'Mum?' she asked. 'Mum, are you all right?'

'Is it really Bruce?' Clarice whispered.

'Yes,' Eileen said to the voice in the receiver. 'She's all right. She's just so, so overwhelmed.' She listened to the response before passing the receiver to her mother who was seated against the wall. 'Bruce wants to talk to you.'

'Oh, my darling boy!' Clarice said as she clutched the receiver to her ear. 'My darling, darling boy!'

Eileen couldn't contain her elation and wrung her hands as she listened to her mother. Her big brother's voice thrilled her, filled her with joy.

'Yes,' Clarice, tears trickling down her cheeks. 'Yes, we will be home – Of course you can come – Oh, Bruce, we can't wait to see you.'

Clarice handed the receiver to Eileen who lifted it to her ear, but Bruce was gone, so she hung the receiver and bent to help her mother. 'When is he coming?' she asked eagerly.

Clarice clutched Eileen's hand and said, 'Saturday. He will be here Saturday. Oh, it has been so long. So long.'

Eileen guided her mother to bed, pulling back the sheet and fluffing the pillows, but Clarice sat on the edge and said, 'We need to shop.' Her face creased into a broad smile. 'We need to cook.' She looked around the bedroom. 'We need to tidy everything up. Oh, there is so much to do.'

'You need to rest,' Eileen reminded her.

'Tosh!' Clarice replied dismissively. 'There is too much to do. I need to wash and do my hair. Fetch my blue dress. Has it stopped raining?'

'Yes,' Eileen replied.

'What time is it?'

'Almost eleven,' Eileen said, glancing at the clock on her mother's mantlepiece.

'See what we need in the kitchen and make a list while I get ready. You can get my purse from the top drawer,' Clarice instructed.

Eileen measured the food and household goods, making a list on a small yellow note pad kept on the sideboard for exactly that task. A quart of milk, and a tiny noggin of butter crouching on a green glass butter dish, sat in the refrigerator. There was no meat. Eileen listened to the regular radio announcements designed to remind Australians of the importance of Australian goods being sent to war-ravaged England to help alleviate suffering as the reason for rationing continuing, and she took comfort that people like her family were contributing to a better world by sharing, but it would be nice to have a little extra butter and meat and eggs to celebrate Bruce's homecoming. List complete, Eileen returned to her mother's bedroom where Clarice was adjusting her dress in the mirror. 'Coupons are under the purse,' Clarice said as Eileen opened the drawer.

Eileen retrieved the black purse and the orange ration coupons, but when she opened the purse she was disappointed to find a meagre scattering of coins. 'I think there's four shillings and sixpence, no, eight pence,' Eileen said, sifting through the coins.

'We will make do,' her mother replied. 'We can get vegetables from the plot next door, but we will walk to Lovell's for fresh bread first.'

'Bruce will be here for my birthday!' Eileen chortled.

'Yes, he will,' Clarice replied. She turned, inspected Eileen, and said quietly, 'My big girl is almost fifteen.' Eileen blushed. 'I need to put on a hat,' Clarice continued. She reached into her closet and pulled out a small black hat with netting that covered her forehead and eyes and used a long bobby pin with an imitation pearl head to secure it. 'What do you think?' she asked, turning from the mirror to Eileen.

'You look beautiful,' Eileen remarked, pleased to see life and energy sparkling in her mother's eyes.

'Let the adventure begin!' Clarice declared.

Despite overnight rain, the late morning was warm, and the blue sky was reflected in puddles as Eileen accompanied her mother along The Broadway and onto Brighton Road. The news that Bruce was coming home after so long away at the war, and her mother's willingness to rise from her bed and go walking, buoyed Eileen's spirits. She was tired after endless weeks at home, escorting her siblings to and from school, cleaning the house, shopping and caring for her ill mother. She missed the tram rides into the city, the independence, the comradery and responsibility that employment at Ingerson's gave her, but she was tied to the house by her mother's lethargy and headaches and sorrow, and her absent father's unfair rules. Eileen hoped Bruce's return would bring a much-needed change in her mother's health and happiness.

Fresh bread bought at the bakery, the pair retraced their steps along Brighton Road. The pervasive March heat was making Eileen perspire, and she was glad when they reached the halfway mark on the return journey. And that's when she heard her mother's steps falter. She turned to ask, 'Are you all right?'

Clarice swayed and stopped, her left hand resting against a wire fence. 'I feel dizzy,' she rasped, and she sank to the pavement.

Eileen squatted, fighting anxiety. 'It will be all right, Mum,' she said. 'Have a rest. There's no hurry. When you are ready, we can walk slowly home. I'll finish the shopping.'

'I was a silly thinking I could do this,' Clarice rebuked herself.

'Not at all,' Eileen reassured her. 'This was good. You needed to get out and get fresh air. It's only because you're not used to walking so far lately.'

A car engine decelerated, brakes squeaked, and a green Oldsmobile stopped at the kerb. The passenger door opened, and a soldier in a creased khaki uniform with dishevelled blond hair stepped out, and asked, 'Are you ladies all right?'

'Mum's a little tired,' Eileen explained.

The soldier squatted beside Eileen to assess Clarice. 'It's getting hot,' he said. 'We'll give you a lift.' He lightly tapped his temple with his fingers in an informal salute, saying, 'Captain Ashby, by the way.'

Wary of a stranger's offer, Eileen said, 'Thank you. We will be all right,' although she appreciated the Captain's handsome profile, sharp nose, full lips and clean-shaven cheeks.

The driver emerged from the car to join the scene, and inquired, 'Everything all right, Captain?'

'I think we need to lend these ladies a hand,' Ashby replied.

'Come on, Missus,' the driver urged, holding his hand towards Clarice. 'Warrant Officer Bob Miller, at your service,' he said jovially. 'I believe the Captain's already introduced himself.'

Eileen's mother accepted Bob's proffered hand and, as he helped her to her feet, she replied, 'Clarice Bonney.'

Eileen stood without taking the Captain's hand. 'And you are?' Ashby asked, eyebrow raised.

'Eileen,' she answered, blushing.

Captain Ashby opened the car's rear door and bowed as Bob guided Clarice to enter. He skirted the rear of the car and waited for a clanking Dodge truck to roll by in a blue cloud of diesel fumes before he opened the door for Eileen.

Eileen was grateful that the soldiers stopped, although the combination of men's cologne and cigarette smoke threatened to overpower her when she eased into the brown leather seat. The men clambered into the front, closed the doors firmly, and Bob turned to ask, 'Where to, ladies?'

'Turn left into The Broadway,' Clarice advised. 'Number seventy. First house on the left after Partridge Street.'

'At your service,' said Ashby, grinning. Bob eased the car into gear and pulled away from the kerb.

Eileen took her mother's hand and smiled at Clarice, but within she was concerned that her mother was struggling with what should have been a simple walk to the shops, even in the warm weather.

At the house, Ashby leapt out of the passenger side to open the door for Clarice, and Bob reciprocated for Eileen. 'Shade and water,' Ashby advised as Clarice and Eileen stood at the gate. 'Surprising how quickly a little heat can get to you.'

'Would you like a cup of tea?' Clarice offered.

Ashby winked at Bob, saying, 'Thanks, Missus, but I think we're headed for a watering hole down the Bay.' He waved congenially, and the men climbed into the car, did a U-turn on The Broadway, and headed north along Partridge Street.

Eileen seated her mother in the kitchen with a freshly brewed tea before she walked to the grocery store and on to the butcher. Between coupons and the meagre cash, she procured sausages, a small chunk of lamb, two rabbits and ham slices from the butcher, and a small serve of butter and various goods from the greengrocer. The newspaper stand advertised a DC3 plane crash in Hobart, Tasmania, killing twenty-five passengers, and Eileen wondered at the irony of a world where a war could end but random tragedies still happen; how sad the families of the plane passengers would be. She headed home, excited she would be preparing a meal on Saturday for her eldest brother.

*

Hands trembling, speechless, Eileen stared at the fine-looking man in the blue RAAF uniform standing in the doorway, swag over his shoulder, cap tilted jauntily to the right. 'Well?' Bruce asked with a grin. 'Do I get a hug?' Released by his invitation, Eileen launched at her brother and embraced him, holding him like she never intended to let him go. 'Woah!' Bruce said, laughing and pushing his sister back a step. 'Ease up, Girlie.'

'It's really you,' Eileen stammered.

'It sure is,' Bruce said, giving Eileen a cursory examination. 'And look at you. Strewth, Girlie! You are a young woman.'

'Bruce!' Peter yelled from behind Eileen, and he led a stampede of brothers and sisters to encircle and embrace the man in the doorway.

'You've all grown so much!' Bruce exclaimed, as he hoisted Josie. 'You, young lady, I wouldn't have recognised.' He put her down and took Wally by the chin. 'You were a baby when I left,' he said. 'Now look at you.'

Wally broke free, swatting Bruce's hand, and everyone laughed. 'You best come in,' Eileen invited.

'Where's Mother?' Bruce asked, as he doffed his cap.

'In the kitchen, waiting for you,' Eileen said.

'Come with us!' Judy yelled. She grabbed Bruce's hand and led him through the curtains and down the hall ahead of the throng.

Following in the wake of the family procession, Eileen heard her mother's joyful cry as her eldest son entered the kitchen. Everyone crowded around Bruce, asking questions, telling him stories, until Clarice declared, 'Time to eat!'

'It's a feast!' Peter declared, his eyes wide at the table display.

'You might like to add this,' Bruce said, lifting his swag. He pulled on the drawstring and out tumbled a block of butter, four Hershey chocolate bars, a bag of sugar and three tins of tea. Judy grabbed a chocolate bar and eagerly exhibited it to the others.

'Wow!' Ian exclaimed. 'Real chocolate!'

Clarice scooped up a tea tin, examining the Bushell's label, and exclaimed, 'Oh my goodness! Real tea!' She looked at Bruce, and asked, 'Where did you get this?'

'Through a couple of mates.'

'It's not black market?' Clarice asked, putting down the tin.

Eileen snatched up the tin and headed for the stove, saying, 'Oh Mum, don't be so silly. I'm making a brew.'

Bruce took his mother's hand and said, 'It's all fair and square and legit, Mother. I brought it home for you. Some of this clobber I got from the Yanks in ration exchanges, and the rest came from different places I stopped on the way home.'

Clarice hugged her son and told him to take a seat at the head of the table. She waited for Eileen to pour hot water from the kettle into the teapot and join the family at the table before putting her hands together in prayer, closing her eyes and saying, 'Dear Lord, thank you for bringing us together today. Thank you, especially, for bringing home my precious, precious Bruce.' Eileen opened one eye to peek at her brother and Bruce winked. 'Thank you also for this bounteous offer of food, Lord,' Clarice continued. 'For what we are about to receive, may we be eternally grateful. Amen.'

As the children chorused 'Amen,' Peter's hand snaked towards the cold meat cuts that Eileen begged from the butcher.

'Bruce first!' Clarice snapped, smacking Peter's hand.

'Ladies first,' Bruce responded, and he lifted the cold meat platter towards Clarice.

'I'm a lady!' Judy declared.

'And you will get your turn,' Bruce promised, proffering the meat to Eileen.

'And me!' Josie cried eagerly.

'There's enough for everyone,' Bruce told her.

'Did you kill any Japs?' Peter asked between mouthfuls of bread and ham.

'Don't be rude at the table,' Clarice warned.

Bruce laughed and replied, 'No, Peter. I didn't kill anyone.'

'But it was a war,' Peter complained. 'Lots of people were killed.'

'And there are a lot of jobs in a war that don't involve killing people,' Bruce said.

'Like what?' Ian asked.

'I was an LAC,' Bruce said. 'Leading Aircraftman. Do you know what that is?' Ian shook his head. 'My job was to make sure things were done properly.'

'So, you didn't have a gun,' Peter said, dissatisfied.

'We all had guns. I was lucky I never had to use mine.'

'Where did you go?' Judy asked.

'Borneo, then Hiroshima,' Bruce replied.

'You were in Japan?' Josie asked.

'Where they dropped the atomic bomb?' Peter added.

'After it was safe to be there, yes,' Bruce replied.

'Did you fly planes?' Ian asked.

Bruce laughed. 'No. But I got to ride in a few. We had Kittyhawks at Cloncurry and Mitchell bombers. I flew in a Liberator to Labuan, then on to the Philippines, Okinawa and into Hiroshima aboard a DC3.'

'That must have been exciting!' Peter exclaimed.

'It had its moments,' Bruce replied.

Eileen listened attentively to the children interrogate their big brother, although she noticed he was circumspect with his answers, especially when Peter pressed him about what it was like in Hiroshima.

'It was messy,' he said, when Peter asked if there were bodies all over Hiroshima. 'The whole city was flattened. I was mainly involved on seeing supplies ferried in.' But something darker lay beneath his tone, a warning that he witnessed far worse things than he was going to tell his little brother. Eileen wondered if he might share that part of his experiences with her, later, privately. Maybe. Clarice asked if he was home for good. 'Two months leave, Mum. I go back to Japan in June,' he confided.

'Why?' Eileen asked, unable to mask her disappointment.

'I'm still enlisted, Girlie, and there's still plenty to do over there. But it won't be for long this time.'

Meal finished, Bruce suggested the family join him in a walk to the Esplanade because he hadn't strolled along the Glenelg beach for a long time. Clarice said she would stay to clean the table and wash the dishes, but Bruce insisted she walk with the family. At Mister Sendy's shop, Bruce bought ice-cream cones for everyone, and the children devoured the treat as they walked towards the beach. Clarice sauntered beside her son, smiling, chatting to him, and Eileen was happy because her mother's tired eyes were filled with joy.

*

'She's only fifteen,' Clarice argued.

'And that's why she needs to go to dancing lessons,' Bruce asserted. 'She needs to learn how to be a young lady. I'll be her chaperone and dancing partner, and she can learn good manners.'

'Please, Mother?' Eileen begged.

Clarice looked at Eileen, and then back at Bruce who had an eyebrow raised, before she sighed and relented. 'All right. She can go.'

'Thank you!' Eileen cried, and she hugged her mother excitedly.

Clarice pushed Eileen away, protesting, and said, 'But abide by the rules of decency. Be home by ten o'clock. Stay with your brother. And no dancing with other men.'

Bruce sustained his serious tone, assuring Clarice, 'No one else will dare look at my little sister.'

'I'll get changed!' Eileen declared, and she headed for the bedroom.

'Make sure you wear the grey dress,' Clarice warned. 'Nothing inappropriate. No skin and no cleavage. And no make-up.'

Eileen opened her wardrobe and flicked through her meagre choice of clothes. One day, she would have enough money to have a dress in every colour and style, and she would go dancing every night. She put on the demure grey dress her mother ordained and grabbed a black bag.

Bruce whistled when Eileen entered the parlour and Eileen blushed. Clarice scolded him for being lewd, and told Eileen, 'Be polite. Always remember your manners. Don't act badly in front of anyone.'

'I won't,' Eileen promised.

'What's in the bag?' Clarice asked.

'A shawl, in case it gets cold, and a handkerchief,' Eileen said, as she swept out the front door ahead of Bruce.

A black Vauxhall sedan sat at the kerb and a red-headed woman leaned out the passenger's window and called, 'Come on, Brucie!'

The driver jumped out and announced himself as, 'Warrant Officer Brian Samuels,' as he opened the back door for Eileen.

'He's Rabbits to everyone else,' Bruce said, pushing Brian's arm as he walked to the opposite side. A truck roared past.

'Why Rabbits?' Eileen asked.

'Farm boy from Yorke Peninsula,' Bruce said climbing into the car.

Eileen settled into the seat beside Bruce, excited that they were going to the dance in a car, and Brian returned to the driver's seat. 'I thought petrol was still rationed,' Eileen said.

'It is,' replied Bruce. 'It's who you know. And I might know some people.'

'Let's get this show on the road,' Brian announced. He crunched the gears and drove away from the kerb.

'You can collect those on the way back,' Bruce teased.

'I'm Lorna,' said the red-haired woman as she turned to Eileen and held out her hand to shake. 'And you're Girlie, right? Brucie told us all about you.'

Eileen shook Lorna's hand, enviously noticing her Victory roll red hair, lipstick and soft rouge and nail polish. 'Where are we going?' Eileen asked.

'The Argosy,' Brian replied. 'That right, Bonney?'

'That's right,' Bruce replied. 'Seacliff esplanade.'

'I thought we were going to the dance class at the Glenelg Town Hall?' Eileen queried.

Brian and Lorna laughed, and Bruce said, 'Best way to learn to dance is to go dancing. You don't mind, do you Girlie?'

'Not at all!' Eileen declared.

'I didn't think so,' said Bruce. 'So, let's go!'

Eileen gazed at the vestiges of amber light gracing the line of the western horizon as the Vauxhall cruised along the Glenelg South Esplanade, the sun long sunk, the day's warmth dissolved into cooling evening air, stars glittering in the berry sky. Brian turned sharp left, the ocean swung away to the rear, and the car's dull yellow headlights arced across sand dunes, open paddocks and shadowy buildings, before he turned onto Brighton Road, and cruised south. He turned and headed down the steep incline of Wheatland Street to Seacliff beach and the corner of the Esplanade by the Hotel Australia, led by The Argosy Palais lights, and parked among the collection of bicycles, motorcycles and cars.

As Bruce opened the car door for Eileen, she announced, 'I have to change.'

'Why?' Bruce asked.

'I don't want to be seen dead in this drab dress. I brought another one in here.' She raised the black bag.

'Come on,' Lorna pressed, overhearing the conversation. 'I'll help you bring out that beauty,' and she steered Eileen towards the Palais side entrance.

'We'll wait inside,' said Brian. 'Might be some sheilas to ogle before the girls get back.' He winked at Bruce and the young men headed for the main doors.

Lorna led Eileen into the women's toilets where she said, 'Let's see the dress.' Eileen removed a bright blue garment from her bag and held it up for Lorna to inspect. Gathered at the waist and fitted with a dark blue collar, Lorna pronounced it, 'Serviceable, if a bit demure. Put it on.' She helped Eileen tweak the fitting and, when the dress was buttoned, she asked, 'Did you bring make-up?'

'I'm not allowed,' Eileen replied.

'Oh, fiddlesticks,' Lorna said scornfully. 'Here.' She fossicked in her dark green purse and extracted a silver lipstick tube and a round compact. 'Stand still and close your eyes.' Lorna patted a layer of powder onto Eileen's cheeks and smoothed it in to create a foundation. 'Some Maybelline on your eyelids. Don't open your eyes yet.' Lorna applied the product and smoothed it across Eileen's nose and cheeks. 'Now your lips.'

'I can do it,' Eileen said, as two women entered the toilet.

'Use the mirror,' Lorna advised. Eileen leaned over the basin and tentatively applied the red lipstick, like she sometimes did secretly at home when her mother was asleep. 'Smack your lips together and roll them, like this,' Lorna instructed, mimicking applying lipstick. Eileen copied her. 'See?' Lorna said, turning Eileen to the mirror. 'A butterfly has emerged.'

Eileen studied her face in the reflection, quietly amazed and proud of how mature makeup made her appear. 'Wow,' she breathed.

'If I'd known, we could have brought cold cream and also done something with your hair,' Lorna remarked, 'but next time. Let me look at you.' Eileen turned and smiled. 'You look more beautiful already,' Lorna said, grinning. 'All right, Cinderella, time to wow the princes.'

Lorna guided Eileen along the hallway, the melody of a swing band and a female singer intensifying as they approached the auditorium. Eileen felt she was rising from the ocean, muted sound becoming loud and embracing beneath the sparkling lights of the arched ceiling, and the Palais dance floor was bursting with couples swinging to "The Boogie Woogie Bugle Boy." Lorna tapped Eileen's shoulder and pointed to where Bruce and Brian were waving and, as Eileen reached Bruce, he exclaimed, 'Is that my little sister?' He spun her by the hand as the band finished the final strains. 'You look all grown up!'

Eileen smiled awkwardly, replying 'Of course, it's me.'

'Where did you get the lippy?'

'Lorna,' Eileen told him, but she dropped her voice and whispered conspiratorially, 'Don't tell Mum. I'll wipe it off before we go home.'

The band broke into "In the Mood", the crowd cheered, and Bruce grabbed Eileen's arm, saying, 'Okay, Girlie, let's dance!'

Eileen let her brother drag her into the fray where she was swept up in the frenetic music, swinging to the rhythm, the euphoric atmosphere washing through her soul, shifting beat and mood with each change in the band's repertoire. She revelled in the movement, the freedom, the absence of responsibility, the fun, remembering the dance steps she copied from films and practised in the parlour.

When Bruce announced he wanted a break to catch his breath, and headed for the door, Eileen withdrew to find Lorna in a small group of young women near a side entrance. 'This is Girlie!' Lorna announced. 'Brucie's little sister. And this is Jenny, Elaine, Helen, Patty and Doris.' The women greeted Eileen, smiling. 'Come on,' Lorna said, taking Eileen's arm. 'We're getting some fresh air.'

'But Bruce–' Eileen began to protest.

'He's a big boy,' Lorna interrupted. 'He'll be here when we come back in.' She steered Eileen through the side door, and into the cool night, where the susurration of waves rolling onto Seacliff Beach filled the air and a cream half-moon hung over the dark ocean and flowed across the corrugated water in a rippling line to the shore.

The girls produced cigarettes and Lorna retrieved a gold lighter from her purse. Doris passed a cigarette to Eileen, but Eileen shook her head, saying, 'I don't smoke.'

'You do now,' Doris replied, and she thrust the glowing cigarette into Eileen's mouth. Eileen pulled it out in disgust and the girls laughed.

'Bet she won't do the drawback,' said Patty.

'That's because you don't,' Lorna rebutted.

'Who's up?' Elaine asked, raising a silver hip flask.

'I am!' Lorna shouted. She snatched the flask, unscrewed the cap, swigged, gasped, and grinned before handing it back, saying, 'That hit the spot!'

'Unlike your Brian,' Doris quipped.

'Who's going to buy a bikini?' Patty asked.

'A what?' Jenny queried.

'Oh, Jenny!' Lorna scolded. 'Keep up with the times! They're selling them in Paris.'

'What?' Jenny persisted.

'Two-piece bathing suits that expose your tummy,' Patty explained.

'Can you imagine the boys?' Doris wolf-whistled and the girls laughed.

Eileen held her cigarette to her lips and pretended to inhale, not quite understanding the banter between the girls about bikinis and boyfriends, although she guessed it had to do with kissing and canoodling and similar fascinating matters around sex, things she hadn't experienced but dreamed of when she watched the boys over the fence and in the street. She took a fake swig from the flask each time it came around to her, testing the fiery liquid on her lips and the tip of her tongue. Whatever the girls were drinking, it was stronger than any alcohol she previously tasted, which was altar wine and beer. Her father and mother would be mortified if they knew she was imbibing the evil liquid.

'All right,' said Lorna. 'We better go back in.' The young women dropped their cigarettes and stubbed them out with their toes, sparks flashing, and Eileen mimicked them to give the impression she was experienced. The flask was stowed, and the girls adjusted their hair. 'Here's a Mintie,' Lorna said, shoving a wrapped candy into Eileen's palm. Eileen unwrapped the gift as she followed the girls into the dance hall and put the hard, white lolly in her mouth, sucking to soften it. She shuffled between onlookers, searching the room, until she spotted Bruce dancing with a short, big-bosomed brunette with blood red lipstick and ruby rouge cheeks. Disappointment flooded her.

'Guess you better dance with someone else,' said a person to her left. Eileen turned to a young man with dark, dazzling eyes and a cheeky grin. 'May I?' he asked, offering his hand.

'Do I know you?' Eileen asked.

'You should,' he replied, holding his hand steady.

Amused, Eileen accepted the hand and allowed the stranger to usher her onto the floor and take the lead in a Foxtrot as the band played, "They're Either Too Young or Too Old." 'I'm not very good at this dance,' Eileen apologised.

'I'll teach you,' the young man offered, and he guided her through the two steps and side-step motion. 'See? Easy.'

Eileen said, 'You're a good dancer.'

'I come here every week I can,' he replied. 'Oh, and my name's Dudley. What's yours?'

'Eileen,' she replied.

'Eileen it is,' Dudley said, and he grinned as he steered Eileen between the dancers.

Eileen felt the warmth of his left hand enfolding hers and the pressure of his right hand in the small of her back. He was lithe, strong, and wore an intoxicating fragrance that tantalised her senses. His lips were neither thin, nor too full, and his charming smile captured her. He was her height, a good height that allowed her to look into his deep brown eyes, although she tried not to, afraid she would be drawn in and he would be embarrassed by her stare.

When the song finished, the band leader announced, 'Let's liven this show up!' The drummer broke into a rapid staccato beat, a roll, the singer began with the dramatic cry of 'Undecided!' and the band launched into "One Girl and Two Boys" to a raucous cheer. Couples broke apart and swung to the rhythm.

'Are you ready?' Dudley asked, grinning.

'No,' Eileen protested, but she was pulled by one arm into a swing motion and let herself be absorbed in the dance. *How many times*, she thought, *have I imagined this moment when we danced at home*? She let Dudley pull and push and swing and turn her, and she improvised her moves as she watched for cues of what to do from other girls on the dance floor. By the time the dance was over, she was perspiring and laughing and happy. 'Wow!' she gasped as she leaned on Dudley's shoulder.

'You learn quickly,' he complimented. 'I bet you've been out dancing plenty of times.'

Before Eileen could deny his assertion, she felt a hand on her arm and Bruce said, 'That's all we have time for, Girlie.'

'But I was just starting to have fun,' she protested.

Bruce met Dudley's inquiring gaze, and said, 'I made a promise to have you home on time. Let's not make a mess of it on the first night.'

'I have to go,' Eileen told Dudley.

'I understand,' he replied, smiling warmly, and he respectfully nodded to Bruce, adding, 'If I was your brother, I would do exactly the same.'

Eileen dutifully followed Bruce from the dance floor, glancing back at Dudley who waved nonchalantly before he merged into the crowd.

The night was colder, invisible waves crashed with greater intensity on the beach and the southerly wind ruffled Eileen's hair. Brian and Lorna were waiting in the car, engine running and headlights on, and when Eileen settled into the backseat Lorna turned and passed a handkerchief and another Mintie, saying, 'Best turn Cinderella back into a drudge.'

'But it will mess up your handkerchief,' Eileen protested.

'I have another,' Lorna answered. 'You can wash that one and give it back to me next time.'

'Who was that girl you were dancing with?' Eileen asked as Bruce settled into the car seat beside her.

'Oh, her? An acquaintance,' Bruce replied.

'Brucie has plenty of acquaintances,' Lorna said from the front seat.

'And who was the soldier I saw you with?' Bruce asked.

'I didn't know he was a soldier,' Eileen replied. 'His name is Dudley.'

'Well, best keep Dudley out of conversation at home,' Bruce advised. 'Mother expects me to keep you safe from men like that. I'll lose my job if it gets out my little sister was dancing with a soldier boy.'

Outside her home, as Brian and Lorna drove away, Eileen hugged Bruce and asked, 'Do I smell of anything?'

Bruce laughed and replied, 'You smell of fun.' He looked at her in the streetlight, wiped a lingering patch of rouge from her cheek, and asked, 'Did you enjoy tonight?'

'It was grand!' Eileen replied.

'Good. Then we'll do it again.'

She hugged Bruce again, saying, 'You're the best.'

'I know,' he replied, as he broke the embrace, and they laughed.

Clarice met Eileen and Bruce at the front door with her finger to her lips to warn them not to wake the children. 'Straight to bed,' she ordered Eileen. 'Want a cup of tea, Bruce?' she invited.

'Another time, Mum,' Bruce replied. 'I best get back to Uncle Spot's.'

Eileen tiptoe-waltzed down the hall to the bathroom, washed her face and checked she had no tell-tale signs of the night before she crept into the bedroom. As she undressed in the dark, a tiny voice asked, 'Was it fun?'

'You are meant to be asleep,' Eileen cautioned.

'Did you dance with any boys?' Judy asked.

'Maybe,' Eileen teased, suppressing her glowing delight at how the evening transpired. 'Now, back to sleep.'

'Did you kiss any boys?' Judy asked.

'Miriam Judith Bonney, you are a rude little girl!' Eileen scolded. 'Go to sleep or I'll tell Mum you're awake.'

Eileen waited, anticipating another comment, but Judy stayed silent. Eileen slid into her nightdress, climbed into bed and pulled the blankets close. The scent of Dudley's cologne lingered, as did the sensation of his hands in her hand and on her waist, and she could see his enchanting grin and glittering brown eyes, his soft lips, hear his invitation to dance and his cultured voice. She curled up in her memory and relived the night, consumed by the reminiscences of new and invigorating sensations before sleep wrapped her tight.

*

Heavy knocking brought Eileen in through the back door from the wash house, and Clarice was opening the front door when Eileen came through the curtains. Two burly men with navy flat caps and sweat-stained khaki shirts stood in the front yard. Parked behind them was a battered khaki Chevrolet flatbed truck with a business name, *Ron May Removals*, stencilled in white across the door. The August sky threatened rain. 'Yes?' Clarice asked.

One man handed Clarice a piece of paper, saying, 'Morning, Missus. We're here to collect the piano listed on that pick-up order.'

'I never sold it,' Clarice said.

'Your husband sold it, Missus,' the removalist said. 'Says so on the order.'

'It's not his piano to sell!' Clarice protested.

'He's your husband, isn't he?' the removalist asked rhetorically. 'Mind if we get on with our job, Missus?' Clarice hesitated, crushing the note in her hand, indicating residual defiance was pumping through her veins, but she stepped aside and allowed the men to enter the parlour.

'Mum?' Eileen inquired.

Clarice steered Eileen through the hall curtain, saying, 'Come away,' and she started crying as they reached the kitchen.

Eileen heard the men shifting the piano, grunting as they manoeuvred it through the door, the casters scraping the floorboards. 'Mum,' Eileen said. 'They can't take the piano. It's yours.'

'Your father sold it,' Clarice said. 'He didn't even ask.'

'Why?' Eileen asked.

'To pay the rent.'

'But I thought he was meant to pay the rent,' Eileen argued.

'He doesn't have a job anymore,' Clarice explained. 'He's been demobbed. With the war over, they don't need men like him to look after prisoners of war or hunt down AWOL men. He has to go back to his building trade, only there's hardly any work, not with the rationing and austerity and no one with money.'

'Then he'll have to find any kind of job to earn money and he can pay with that,' Eileen argued. 'It's not fair that he sells the piano. It's yours, isn't it?'

'Too late,' Clarice said, throwing the receipt onto the table. 'It's done,' and she sank onto a kitchen chair, put her head in her hands, and cried quietly.

Eileen rubbed her weeping mother's shoulders, confused as to why her father would sell her mother's treasured possession. What right did he have to do it? Why did her mother have no say? She sighed and pressed her mother's shoulder, before she walked to the stove to put the kettle on to boil.

'There's no tea left,' Clarice said.

'I'll get some from Sendy's,' Eileen offered.

'I don't have a coupon for it this week,' Clarice told her.

'I'll ask Mister Sendy anyway,' Eileen said. She kissed her mother on the top of her head as she left the kitchen and grabbed her dark grey coat from the hall hooks on her way to the front door. The removalist truck was gone when she emerged, and a strong wind pushed along The Broadway from the Esplanade, carrying the tang of seaweed and ocean, and paper fragments skipped and tumbled along the road. A man in grey overalls stepped out of a cream van and scrambled into the haven of The

Broadway pub. Eileen pulled up her collar and walked briskly to the corner store.

The bell tinkled when she entered. As she shut the door in her wake, forcing the wind to whistle under the doorsill, an elderly woman at the counter, grey hair in a tight bun, looked up, hitched her shopping bag and headed for the door. Behind the counter, a cherub-faced, balding man with a jaunty moustache and bright smile greeted her. 'Good morning, Miss Bonney. What can I get for you?'

Eileen waited for the older woman to leave before she approached the counter to ask timorously, 'Mister Sendy, do you have any tea?'

'Of course,' he replied. 'The usual amount?'

Eileen sighed and said, 'I don't have a coupon, Mister Sendy.'

'Did you forget it?'

'I,' she began, halted, and said quietly, 'We ran out.'

Mister Sendy raised an eyebrow. 'That presents a problem.'

'Is there any chance I can borrow some tea?'

Mister Sendy chuckled. 'This is a shop. We don't give things away.'

'But you have a tab, don't you?'

Mister Sendy nodded. 'Yes. There is a tab for those who need it.'

'Can we have some tea on a tab?' Eileen asked.

Mister Sendy shook his head. 'You already have a tab and it's full.'

'Full?' Eileen asked.

'Your mother has quite a few items to pay for.'

'How much?' Eileen asked.

'That would be improper for me to share.'

'Sorry,' Eileen apologised. 'I only wanted to make Mum a cup of tea to cheer her up. I'll go.'

She turned and headed for the shop door, but as she reached for the handle Mister Sendy called her back. 'Here,' he said, handing Eileen a small brown paper bag.

'But we can't afford it,' Eileen reminded him.

'This one's from a neighbour to another,' Mister Sendy said. 'Now, off you go and make that cup of tea for Clarice.'

'Thank you, Mister Sendy,' Eileen said. 'I will pay you back.'

'Never mind with that,' Mister Sendy said, waving Eileen away.

GIRLIE

Eileen stepped into the windy street, clutching the bag beneath her coat, grateful for Mister Sendy's generosity. The world was a strange place where the local shopkeeper could break the rules and extend generosity and yet her father could callously sell the family piano without discussing it with her mother.

*

'Bruce? Why don't you have a girlfriend?'

Bruce raised an eyebrow at Eileen's question, and answered, 'I do.'

'Who?' Eileen asked, dabbing foundation on her chin as the car trundled along the Esplanade. 'I haven't seen her.'

'Who do you think I was dancing with last week when I wasn't dancing with you?' Bruce replied, chuckling.

'I didn't see you dancing with anyone,' Eileen said, handing the foundation container across the seat shoulder to Lorna.

'I think you were too interested in your new friend,' Bruce teased. 'You've danced with him every Saturday night for the past four weeks.'

Eileen blushed, but as Brian parked the car outside The Argosy she asked, 'What's your girlfriend's name?'

'What's your boyfriend's name?' Bruce countered. 'Dudley, isn't it?'

'He's not my boyfriend,' Eileen replied brusquely.

'Come on!' Lorna urged from the front seat as she opened her door. 'We have dancing to do!'

In the crush of people, as the band played a waltz melody, Eileen searched for the one who owned her dreams and was disappointed not to find Dudley. 'Hey! Girlie!' Lorna called. 'Come over here!' Eileen followed Lorna along the edge of the crowd to where Bruce was talking with a petite, dark-haired girl among a larger group.

'My sister,' Bruce announced when Eileen reached him.

'Eve,' the young woman said. 'Pleased to meet you.'

'And this is Lawrie,' Lorna said, introducing another young man.

'Hello,' Lawrie said. Tall and angular, his eyes dark like his hair, he had a crooked grin and a small scar on his jaw. Eileen smiled in reply. 'Dance?' Lawrie asked.

'Go on,' Lorna urged, pushing Eileen's arm.

Eileen acquiesced and followed Lawrie onto the dance floor, conscious of the height difference when he took her hand and put his right hand on her waist. Her brothers were tall, but Lawrie was taller still, and awkward in his grip, and she was staring at his chest and the buttons of his white shirt. 'Sorry,' he said as he steered Eileen back a couple of steps. 'I'm not the best dancer.'

'It's all right,' Eileen replied. 'I'm still learning too.' She let him lead her through the waltz, but at every opportunity she searched the passing throng and other dancers for Dudley's face. She smiled at Lorna, who was dancing with Brian, and Bruce and Eve swirled past.

'What do you do?' Lawrie asked.

'I help Mum at home.' Eileen replied. 'And you?'

'I'm a painter,' he said.

Eileen knew she should ask more questions, be polite, make Lawrie feel comfortable, but she wasn't interested in him: a nice enough boy, just not her type. When the band ended the waltz, Eileen smiled and said, 'Thank you.'

'Would you like to dance again?' Lawrie asked hopefully.

'Perhaps later,' Eileen said, retreating to the margins. 'I need to catch my breath.'

'Ladies and gentlemen,' the band leader began. 'We're in a bit of a bind this evening. Our regular singer, Lottie Winters, couldn't make it, and we couldn't contact her usual stand-in. Is there anyone here, tonight, who would grace us with their voice? We would be delighted to take a volunteer.'

Eileen stopped to watch how the dilemma would unfold, realising she didn't notice the singer's absence during the instrumental waltz. The band leader's invitation was the stuff of her dreams. She dreamed of singing with a big band when she sang in the choir and at home, and fantasised that one night exactly what was happening would happen. Several women and men were encouraged to step up on the bandstand, but they emphatically declined. Then, to Eileen's horror, above the hubbub, Bruce yelled, 'My sister! She can sing!' and he pointed towards her. Faces turned and her heart raced. 'Come on, Girlie!' Bruce urged. 'Sing for us!'

Before Eileen could decline, the band leader announced, 'Ladies and gentlemen! Put your hands together for our new voice!'

Flushed, terrified, her mind blank, trapped by the smiling faces, encouraging applause and the band leader's welcome, Eileen reluctantly allowed Bruce's guiding arm to conduct her to the stage. She almost didn't hear the band leader say, 'I'm Max Williams,' as he offered Eileen his hand to ascend the steps. 'And you are?'

'Eileen Bonney,' she answered, trembling.

Max introduced the band members, naming the saxophonist and piano player, before asking, 'We were going to play "Dream." Do you know it?'

'The Pied Pipers?' Eileen asked. 'I love that song.'

'Then let's get these people dancing!' Max declared. He turned to the microphone, grinning broadly as he announced, 'Ladies and gentlemen, Eileen Bonney and "Dream!"' He gestured to the band, the crowd applauded again, and the saxophonist and bass player began the introductory melody.

Eileen wrestled with the words in her head as she stepped up to the microphone, afraid she would hit the wrong notes and the words would dissolve on her tongue. At home, she imitated June Hutton's voice, but she wasn't June Hutton, and the saxophone was not a clarinet. Everything was different. And she had to sing because everyone expected it. The dancers were swaying into a slow waltz. Bruce was urging her on with his smile and a nod. The pianist ran a brief trill across the keys, Eileen drew a breath, and sang as the melody opened for the vocalist, 'Dream, when you're feeling blue.' She was startled by the spontaneous applause that greeted her opening line and reddened as she continued. Bruce clapped enthusiastically and Lorna's face was drawn in wonder before she clapped with the others. As the song drew to the final notes, the band members singing background harmonies, Eileen's confidence rose, and she was disappointed when the last 'dream' left her lips and the saxophone sighed, but the moment was consumed in a burst of applause.

'Wow!' Max said to Eileen, taking her arm. 'You really can sing. Where have you been hiding?'

'I-' Eileen stuttered, but she had no answer and smiled shyly, trembling. Max turned to the band, exchanged a few words, and turned back to

Eileen to ask, 'How about "Boogie Woogie Bugle Boy"? Can you sing it?'

'I can try,' Eileen replied. 'It would be better if there was three of me.'

Max laughed and nodded to the band, before announcing to the hall, 'Let's liven this joint up a notch! Hit it, boys!'

The saxophonist replaced his saxophone with a horn and broke into the opening faux reveille riff, followed by the rhythmic bass and drum. The dancers gyrated into swing, the Palais writhed with excitement, and Eileen launched into the lyrics.

When the song ended, Eileen realised she was perspiring under the lights. Max took her arm again. 'You are really good! Grab a drink while we do "Sing, Sing, Sing" to keep these kids going, and then do you know "Always"?'

'I do,' Eileen replied.

'Great!' Max said. 'We'll do that one to calm them down for a couple of slower numbers. See you back here!' He turned and pointed to the drummer who thumped the rhythmic intro to "Sing, Sing, Sing," while Eileen retreated into the crowd, where Bruce was waiting.

'Told you, you could do it,' he said.

'You were amazing!' Eve declared, as Lorna and her friends pressed around.

'You didn't say you were a singer!' Lorna scolded.

'I'm not,' Eileen said. 'I just like singing.'

'She sings with the church choir,' Bruce told the group.

'Voice of an angel,' one of Lorna's male friends stated. 'I could fall in love with that voice.' His comment drew a mock slap from Lorna, who winked at Eileen, and said, 'Let's go celebrate outside and get some fresh air.'

'I can't,' Eileen replied. 'I have to go up there again.'

'Then we'll have one for you,' Lorna said, 'and we'll be back in time for the next song.' Lorna's companions followed her out of the hall, leaving Eileen standing among strangers.

Two men asked her to dance, but she declined, choosing to listen to the band as she rehearsed the lines of the song she promised to sing. She searched again for Dudley, but he obviously hadn't come, and she was so lost in her thoughts she only realised it was time for her to re-join the band when the bandmaster announced, 'Ladies and gentlemen, let's get Eileen up on stage again!' Hands ushered her forward and she stepped up beside Max. 'Are you ready?' he asked. 'We'll do this nice and slow.'

'I'm ready,' Eileen replied, battling her nerves.

'Okay, lovers!' Max declared. 'Find your partners and hold them close for a slow waltz to that all-time favourite "Always"! Take it away band!'

The clarinet lilted through the opening melody, and Eileen broke into song, enjoying the luminary moment of living a childhood dream. Only when she started into the second verse did she recognise the man beyond the dancers, and she almost faltered, aware how keenly he was watching her, but she took heart and sang to him over the heads of the slow-moving couples. She imagined more than saw the smile bloom on his face, and during the brief orchestral interlude, before the final verse, she looked shyly at her feet, wondering if he liked her singing to him, hoping she wasn't embarrassing herself.

Again, the crowd applauded as Eileen and the band finished, and Eileen saw Dudley approaching. 'They love you,' Max said. 'You're a natural. If you're looking to do this regularly, we'd love to have you sing with us. How about another one now?'

'Thank you,' Eileen said, 'but I promised someone a dance.'

Max looked down at Dudley and chuckled as he turned to Eileen. 'You kids go and dance,' he said. 'And we'll have you back on stage here any time. You've got a talent, kid.' Eileen thanked Max before she stepped down from the stage.

'I couldn't believe my eyes when I saw it was you up there!' Dudley declared. 'Where did you learn to sing like that?'

'Church,' Eileen replied, 'and around home.'

'Well, you can sing, that's for sure,' he said. He took Eileen's hand and led her to the middle of the floor as the band began another slow melody. 'May I?' he asked charmingly.

'Of course you may,' she replied, and she flowed into the dance, happier than she could ever remember.

*

Valiantly trying to control her frustration, Eileen said, 'But Mum, it's to the Botanic Gardens. Everyone will be there.'

'That is not the point,' Clarice responded, lowering her mixing bowl. 'A girl your age is not gallivanting around the countryside with a young man unchaperoned. I will not countenance it. Especially a young man you have only dated – what? How long?'

'Months, Mum! I've known Dudley for months!'

'And have you brought him home to meet me?'

'Bruce knows him,' Eileen affirmed, hoping her mother would acquiesce at the mention of her favourite son.

'But I don't,' Clarice bluntly responded.

Flummoxed by her mother's cold reply, Eileen stammered, 'Well, no, but that's because we only see each other at the dances.'

'Exactly my point. You hardly know the boy.'

'But what if someone else was going?' Eileen argued.

Clarice sighed and recommenced stirring the pastry mixture. 'That might be a different matter.'

'Dudley's friend is going with us,' Eileen said.

'And who is this Dudley's friend?'

'Frank Evansley.'

'Good Lord!' Clarice exclaimed, lowering the bowl. 'A fifteen-year-old girl gadding about with two young men? What kind of scandal are you trying to bring on this house? Has this Frank a girlfriend?'

'Yes,' Eileen replied. 'Her name is Joan.'

'Not that it matters,' Clarice said, shaking her head. 'You are definitely not going.'

'Mum!'

'How old is this Dudley?'

'He's nineteen,' Eileen lied, because she knew admitting her beau was twenty-four would end all hope of going out with him.

'And he is in the army.'

'Yes.'

'All the more reason,' Clarice concluded.

'What is that supposed to mean?'

'Don't be so naïve, Girlie.'

'What if one of my friends can go?' Eileen asked hopefully.

'I might reconsider,' Clarice said, adding, 'but that is not at all a promise.'

Possibilities uplifted, Eileen hurried to the hall telephone but, when she lifted the receiver, the line was dead. She repeated the process without success. Puzzled, she returned to the kitchen to ask, 'What's wrong with the phone?'

Clarice turned, lowering her bowl again, and said, 'It's been disconnected.'

'Why?' Eileen asked, but she guessed the answer before Clarice could respond, and declared, 'I'm walking to Joyce's.'

'Whatever for?'

'She might be able to go to the Botanic Gardens,' Eileen explained, turning to walk along the hall. 'Will that help?'

'Don't be too long,' Clarice said. 'School's almost out and it's starting to rain.'

'I'll be on Brighton Road, Mum,' Eileen replied as she reached the front door. 'I'll meet the children after school.'

'Take an umbrella!'

'I am!' Eileen replied, and she grabbed a black umbrella from the hallway stand before she closed the door.

Umbrella open, rain pattering on the cloth, Eileen strolled along The Broadway, stepping over puddles, enjoying the gloomy afternoon light and steady drizzle, her thoughts filled with Dudley and dancing and singing at The Argosy. She longed to press her lips against Dudley's, wanted to feel what it was like to be kissed and cuddled by a man. The idea made her tingle with pleasure.

She headed north on Brighton Road, crossed the Diagonal Road intersection and entered a green picket fence gateway. When she knocked on a dark brown wooden door, an older woman in a mauve dressing gown, with straggly black, grey-streaked hair, no make-up, and a cigarette hanging from the corner of her mouth opened the door and scrutinized her, before saying, 'Bonney, isn't it? You haven't been around in ages.'

'I've been looking after my Mum, Missus Fielder,' Eileen said. 'Is Joyce in?'

'Joycie!' the woman screeched into the house. She turned to Eileen to say, 'You're lucky. She should be at work, but she's unwell today.' She sucked in a lungful of smoke and turned her head into the house again to repeat, 'Joycie!'

'Coming!' a shrill voice replied.

'I'll leave you girls to it, then,' Joyce's mother said, and she shuffled down the hallway as Joyce arrived.

'Bonney!' Joyce exclaimed and she eagerly embraced her former school friend.

'I thought you might be at school,' Eileen said.

'Come inside,' Joyce urged. She ushered Eileen into the parlour and invited Eileen to sit on a threadbare light green couch beside her. Beaming, she took Eileen's hands, and said, 'I've missed you.'

'I've missed you, too,' Eileen replied.

'School wasn't the same after you left. I left at the end of the year.'

'I thought you were going on to High School,' Eileen said.

Joyce grinned sheepishly and patted her tummy, as she replied, 'I did, until I met a Yank.'

Unable to hide her surprise, Eileen blurted, 'You're not!'

'Yes,' Joyce replied, nodding gleefully. 'I am.'

'Are you getting married?'

Joyce laughed. 'Hardly, Bonney. I'm sixteen. And he's long gone home.'

'Oh my gosh!' Eileen remarked. 'How long?'

'Four months.'

'How?'

Joyce laughed again. 'I think you know how.'

'No,' Eileen corrected herself and blushed. 'I mean, how did you meet him?'

'Dancing at the Town Hall. He was there with two friends, and Lena, Margot and I lied to get in. They asked us to dance, he offered to drive me home, and then one thing led to another.'

'In his car?' Eileen asked. Joyce wrinkled her nose, grinning. 'Joyce Fielder!' Eileen gasped. 'What did your father say?'

'Dad still doesn't talk to me,' Joyce said. 'He was going to kick me out, but Mum and my sister Gwyneth stopped him. He wanted to find Mike and shoot him. Mum wanted to send me to a convent. My Auntie Beth offered for me to stay on the farm down in Penola. Everyone wants to fix the problem. I just want to have my baby.'

'You're happy?'

'Of course!' Joyce said. 'Why wouldn't I be?' She looked defiantly at Eileen, but Eileen smiled, and Joyce laughed. 'It's so good to see you again. We had such good times at school.'

'We did,' Eileen agreed.

Joyce leaned forward and asked, 'So why have you come by?'

*

'Are you all right?'

Eileen stared into Dudley's languid brown eyes. 'I'm very happy.'

'But you were elsewhere.'

'I was remembering how I had to convince Mum to let me come along,' Eileen explained, squeezing his hand. 'Lucky Joyce could come.'

'Joyce?' Dudley asked, perplexed.

Eileen grinned. 'Joyce,' she repeated. 'The girl in the green dress who waved to us at the tram stop on King William Street. Mum thinks she's with us.'

'Oh,' Dudley said, and chuckled. 'You are a devious one. Should I be trusting you?'

Eileen blushed. 'Don't be silly.'

Dudley slid his arm through the crook in her elbow and said, 'I'm surprised you didn't bring your brother. What's his name?'

'Bruce,' Eileen said. 'He's heading back to Japan this week.'

Dudley sighed. 'Ah, yes. We ship off, too.'

'Oh? When?'

'One more week.'

Eileen clutched Dudley's arm, protesting, 'That's not fair!'

He patted her hand gently. 'It's for six months. That right, Frank?'

Frank turned from studying the glass panels in the Palm House and replied, 'Yep. New Guinea for us, mate. Back around March next year, I heard. Maybe a Christmas furlough, if we're lucky.'

'You can bring us a present from New Guinea,' Frank's girlfriend, Joan, prompted, fluffing out her curled brown hair.

'Would you like a shrunken head or a blowpipe?' Dudley asked.

'I was thinking silk stockings, actually,' Joan pouted, accentuating her bright red lips. 'A girl finds them hard to come by.'

'I'll see what I can get,' Frank said, and he wrapped his arms around Joan's waist from behind and whispered in her ear which made Joan giggle and blush.

'Let's go see the Sunken Garden,' Eileen suggested.

The overcast sky threatened rain, but Eileen's heart was light as she hung on Dudley's arm. The tranquillity of the trees and plants, the freshness and vitality in the air, Dudley's cologne and his warm presence pressed against her arm, made her giddy with happiness.

She chatted with Joan as they walked, about new shoes and hats, and the latest styles and music. In her fluffy light green sweater under her woollen dark green trench coat, and a long green plaid skirt, her hair curled under and full, Joan seemed less attached to Frank than Eileen expected, and she had an enviable air of confidence and maturity. She wasn't so much pretty as handsome, but she laughed and smiled so broadly that she was strong and beautiful to look at, like a film heroine.

In contrast, with her borrowed dark grey Reefer coat, and grey beret, her brunette hair hand-curled at the tips, Eileen felt dun and boring alongside Joan. She wore a modicum of makeup stolen from her mother's case, lipstick, and a touch of liner, which she hurriedly applied after she left home on the walk to the Jetty Road tram stop where she met Joyce to begin the adventure. She was concerned the lipstick might not be red enough, and that her mother would discover the theft and be waiting for her return, and she was saddened by her inability to push her guilt aside.

'This is swell,' Dudley remarked, admiring the blooms and the rough stone border when they reached the garden.

'Established in 1939,' Joan announced. 'Obviously built below the natural landscape level to retain the water.'

'How do you know that?' Frank asked, gaping at her quizzically for an explanation.

Joan laughed and pointed to a plaque. 'I can read, Mister Evansley.'

Frank tilted his brown Fedora and remarked, 'The wonders of modern civilisation!'

'That women can read?' Dudley asked.

Joan glared with sharp green eyes at Dudley, and winked at Eileen as she replied, 'One of the sexes has to be literate if we're to progress, Mister Wright. Isn't that correct, Eileen?'

'I believe so,' Eileen replied, feigning an air of superiority until she couldn't contain her giggles.

A flash of lightning followed by a sharp thunderous crack startled the group and Eileen gripped Dudley's arm. 'I think we're for it,' Frank said, looking up.

'Shelter it is,' Dudley agreed.

The foursome retreated to the cover of a broad tree canopy as rain dissolved the city and inundated the gardens. Dudley enfolded Eileen protectively in his arms and she snuggled against his shoulder for warmth and security, her head pressed against his. When she looked across at Frank and Joan, they were locked in a lingering kiss, Joan's face tilted up to Frank's face, lips pressed, eyes closed, and the thought of kissing like that made Eileen long for such a moment.

'Eileen,' Dudley murmured. Hearing her name, Eileen's gaze shifted to meet Dudley's meltingly warm brown eyes, and when she realised that he was leaning towards her, lips parted, she closed her eyes and waited for his lips to brush against hers, emotions swirling as she tingled from his touch, oddly conscious of the cigarette odour on his breath and in his hair. His hand pressed against the middle of her back to bring her closer and she let his warm mouth envelop her lips. And then he was leaning away, easing his pressure on her back, and he was smiling.

'What is it?' she asked.

'You've never kissed anyone before, have you?'

Not expecting the question, she blushed and said warily, 'Not like that.' She glanced at Frank and Joan, but they were busy in their embrace beneath the dripping tree, oblivious to the rain and their companions.

'Then we best practise,' Dudley whispered. 'The first thing to do is let your lips part slightly and relax, let them be soft.'

Eileen took in Dudley's advice, begging her desire to master her nerves, and closed her eyes as Dudley leaned in again.

*

Mister McMahon stood in the doorway in his tie-less grey suit, stout, clean-shaven and smelling of cheap talcum powder, his grey Homburg not quite fitting his head, a letter in his hand. 'Is your mother home?' he asked, peering into the hallway past Eileen's shoulder.

'She's in the kitchen,' Eileen told him. 'Is it about the rent?'

'I'd prefer to talk to your mother,' McMahon said haughtily. 'Would you mind?'

He went to step over the threshold, but Eileen stopped him by saying, 'If you please, Mister McMahon, wait here. I'll tell Mum you are here.' She saw him twitch around his small mouth with its narrow lips, but he stayed put, so Eileen turned and headed through the hallway curtain. 'Mum,' she said, as she entered the kitchen. 'Mister McMahon is at the door.'

Clarice handed a red checked tea towel to Eileen, after she wiped her hands, and told her, 'Finish cutting the carrots. I'll see to him.'

Eileen continued chopping the carrots into the bowl, but she attuned her listening to the conversation at the end of the hall. The voices were muffled by the curtain, until she heard her mother's voice rise sharply. 'That is simply not possible, Mister McMahon!'

McMahon's reply was inaudible, but Eileen heard the front door slam, so she put down the peeling knife and found her mother slumped against the door, crying, the letter lying on the floor. She put a hand on Clarice's shoulder and asked, 'What happened?'

Clarice thrust Eileen aside, pushed to her feet and retreated into her bedroom, collapsing on the bed. 'Oh,' she sobbed repeatedly. When Eileen sat beside her, Clarice stammered, 'What are we going to do?'

'Mum,' Eileen urged. 'What happened?'

'I can't pay the rent. We can't stay here,' she confessed, and her sobs grew longer and deeper.

'How much is it?' Eileen asked.

'More than we have,' Clarice answered.

'I can find another job,' Eileen said. 'I should be working.'

'It's too late. Can't you see that? It's too late.'

'Why is it too late?'

'It's in that horrible letter. Mister McMahon has evicted us.'

Eileen knew the word, but it was alien, something that happened in Dickensian stories but not to real people. She retrieved the letter her mother dropped in the hall and opened it to read the eviction notice. They had five days to be out of the house or the police would be called to remove them, by force if necessary. Her heart sank. The offending letter shook in her hand, but she neatly folded it and placed it in the envelope before returning to her mother. 'What will we do?' Eileen whispered.

*

Eileen hurried through the dunes, carrying a newspaper bundle of fish and chips to the huddle of tents on Brighton beach. A woman, drying her young son after washing him outside their tent, nodded as Eileen passed, and a man in a shabby military uniform beside another tent stopped shaving to wave.

Four days earlier, the police came to the house and ordered the family to leave. Bruce arrived and argued for leniency, but the police were steadfast, and two officers escorted Bruce from the scene, respectfully recognising his service record when his temper boiled over. Eileen led Wally and Josie down the street to Missus Nicholls who was willing to take the younger ones in until the matter was resolved, while Clarice organised Peter, Ian and Judy to fill two old suitcases, a duffle bag and a portmanteau with clothes and assorted personal goods. Eileen had no idea what her mother was planning, even as the family traipsed south along the beach. 'It will be like a picnic, a camping holiday,' Clarice said as she ushered everyone towards the dunes, and only then did Eileen understand that they were going to sleep among the poor and homeless scattered along the Brighton and Seacliff foreshore. She always felt sorry for people who couldn't afford a home, soldiers returning from the war without homes to go to, and men and women who lost jobs as the war industry wound down, but she never imagined her family would be thrust into their ranks. Now, they were homeless and struggling, all because her father failed to be a good husband.

Eileen squatted and lifted the canvas tent flap, the sun illuminating a triangular patch on the red and black tartan blanket serving for flooring. She passed the warm bundle to Peter before kneeling beside Clarice, who was lying on her side wrapped in a grey army blanket. 'How long are we staying here?' Peter asked, sitting with his arms wrapped around his knees. Ian leaned against him, staring with wide dark eyes, a second army blanket pulled over his head into a hood.

'Until we find another house,' Eileen replied. 'You know that.'

'But it's been five days,' Peter complained.

'You can live with Auntie Ethel,' Eileen reminded him.

'I'd rather stay here,' Peter mumbled.

'It's Christmas soon,' Ian said. 'It's not fair that we're sleeping on the beach. We missed the Christmas Pageant.'

'Perhaps we can ask Father Christmas for a house,' Peter taunted.

'That's enough,' Eileen cautioned.

'I'm hungry,' Ian murmured.

'So am I,' Peter added, opening the newspaper wrap to expose two pieces of fish and a handful of chips. 'Is this all there is?'

'Leave some for Mum and me,' Eileen advised. 'And be grateful you have something to eat.'

Peter picked up a chip and held it towards Ian, asking sardonically, 'Which half do you want?'

'Mind if I come in?' a voice interrupted, and a familiar balding head protruded through the tent opening.

'Of course you can,' Eileen said, and added apologetically, 'There's hardly enough room.'

'There is enough,' Father Cavanaugh responded. He kneeled beside the boys, who shuffled to make room. 'There,' he said, settling and crossing his legs. 'Good afternoon, Clarice,' he added. 'Sorry for the intrusion.'

Clarice rolled over and sat up, adjusting her tousled hair. 'Oh, Father Cavanaugh,' she said. 'I am terribly sorry. I am in a such a state.'

'No need to apologise. I have been told the story of everything that has happened. You should have come to see me when things started going badly. I may have been able to help.'

'It's not seemly to beg,' Clarice said.

'Serving God's children in need is very seemly,' Father Cavanaugh replied. 'It is what I do, whether they ask or not.' He surveyed the tent. 'Where are the younger ones?'

'Wally and Josie are with Missus Nicholls,' Peter said. 'Judy is with Auntie Ethel.'

Father Cavanaugh nodded, before saying, 'Well, by the grace of our Lord, I have some good news. The Church has a house at Brighton you can rent.'

'We have no money,' Clarice said.

'Your husband will pay,' Father Cavanaugh told her.

'He hasn't done anything for us,' Clarice said. 'Why now?'

'God and I have spoken to him,' Father Cavanaugh replied, adding, 'So have the police,' and he winked. 'A man may choose to abandon his family, to suit his own selfish means, but there are laws that hold him to account, in Heaven and on earth. Your husband will be responsible, and he will pay the rent.'

Clarice caught her breath to say, 'Bless you, Father.'

'Bless you and your family,' Father Cavanaugh said. 'Mother Cassidy will send Sister Bernice to help you shift your belongings to the house this evening. The Church can organise places for the younger children because there are only three bedrooms, but you will not stay here any longer.'

'Josie and Wally will come with us,' Eileen said. 'We can make room for them.'

'As you wish,' Father Cavanaugh replied. He made the sign of the cross and exited the tent.

'We get a new house!' Peter said. 'Everything will be all right again.' Eileen appreciated her brother's joy, but she wasn't convinced everything was going to be all right ever again. Too much was broken.

1947

"You can be much more alone with other people than by yourself, even if it's people you love."
Lucy Muir

Eileen walked through the street shadows in the balmy night air, house roofs and patches of bitumen highlighted by weak moonlight, the sun's lingering breath rising from the road. For three long months, she arrived at work before nine at night, and returned home after breakfast when the city was commuting to work and the morning sun was bearing down. She knew she ought to be grateful. She was making earnings to help feed and house her family, but she hated the job, and she resented being responsible for everyone else. She was still angry that her father curtailed her employment at Ingerson's more than a year beforehand because he was determined his daughter would not be drawn into the hedonistic city world where everyone smoked and drank and wore lipstick and lived lascivious lives. Instead, she was kept within the confines of the Glenelg home, made to help her sick mother with house duties and care for the children, and expected to shop for groceries and goods using coupons and the pittance her father provided when he chose to drop by the family home. He kept telling Clarice money was hard to come by because he was struggling to re-establish his building trade in a post-war market where everyone was impoverished from the extended austerity. And then he stopped paying for anything, and they lost their house on The Broadway. Everything about him was double-standards and lies; he could cheat and leave his family, he could avoid paying support and leave them to be evicted, but she couldn't wear make-up.

Father Cavanaugh's intervention saved them from living on the beach in destitution and for that Eileen gave prayers to God in the church. Housed in a two-storey eccentric house they dubbed Hatters Mansion, the children manufactured spooky stories about the building's imagined unsavoury past. Eileen applied her memories of favourite radio horror shows and was pleased with the effect of her terrifying tales on her siblings. She shared one of two upstairs bedrooms with Judy and Josie, and the three boys crammed into the other room, but she was grateful to sleep in a comfortable and dry bed after sleeping on the beach, although the room was stiflingly uncomfortable in the summer heat. 'It is a temporary measure,' Sister Bernice explained when she helped Clarice carry her suitcases into the house. 'Quarters are cramped all over Adelaide. It's difficult to find a suitable place for so large a family.'

Clarice's spirits lifted when they moved in. Peter began an apprenticeship at John Martins in the city to help support the family and Ian sold newspapers outside The Broadway pub. There was food, although sustained rationing restricted what the family could purchase, leaving Eileen to wonder how long the war would continue to have an impact on Australian lives. Bruce was in Japan. Dudley returned to New Guinea and knew nothing of their plight. The war wasn't at all over; it morphed into a less tangible event that kept people struggling and in danger.

And then Donald arrived one afternoon to announce, 'I found you a job, Girlie. You start tomorrow night. I'll take you there now,' and he drove her in his white Bedford truck past the open fields along King George Drive and into the Minda Home grounds with its sturdy formal buildings where he introduced Eileen to Matron Adams.

'You work ten pm to eight am. Arrive fifteen minutes before your shift starts. Sister Watkins will be your supervisor. She is Head Nurse of Rogerson House, but she will also be your supervisor in the housing quarters. Listen closely to what she tells you and follow her instructions to the letter. Am I understood?' Eileen nodded mutely. 'Good,' said Matron Adams. 'I will take you on a short tour and introduce you to the staff with whom you will be working. Then we can return, and your father can sign the necessary papers while you organise your uniform. You begin tomorrow night.'

And it was done. She had no choice, no say. 'Whatever else might have happened,' Donald told her when he stopped outside her home, 'I am still your father. Never forget that, Girlie. I am still head of this family.'

As much as she wanted to dispute his claim, his authority, given all he had done and not done, she held her tongue, knowing she had no right to challenge him, or to be disrespectful, so she thanked him for finding her work again, and promised that she would give her wages directly to her mother to feed the family. And, with that promise made, she climbed out of his truck, and Donald drove away.

Eileen yawned at the entrance to Minda Home, weeks of long nights weighing on her. The walk to the administration buildings led to yet another night of monitoring the sometimes silent, sometimes cacophonic housing quarters, depending on whether the children were sleeping or traumatised by waking nightmares, and how many messed their beds. Eileen corrected her blue uniform and white apron before she entered the building to clock in for her shift, greeting Dorothy in the office.

'Busy night ahead, Bonney,' Dorothy said, shaking her head. 'Sarah threw a terrible wobbly an hour ago and made a mess of her room. The other kids are still awake in the next dorm, waiting to go back to bed.'

'Thank you, Dorothy,' Eileen said, appreciating the warning. The oldest girl in the first cottage, Sarah was notorious for her fits. Eileen did not understand why she continued to share a room with five other girls, all of them much younger, but the bosses knew what they were doing, and it wasn't her place to question what was done or why.

Eileen left the main building and headed for the first cottage at the edge of the sand dunes. She mounted the wooden walkway joining the cottages and entered to discover Sister Watkins and Nurse Maslen, both of whom finished at ten pm, ushering the girls into their room. Sarah was curled on her bed. 'Evening, Bonney,' Watkins said. 'You missed the excitement.'

'What can I do?' Eileen asked.

'Help Maslen get the girls into bed would be a good start,' Watkins said. 'Then she can go home, and you can start your rounds. Keep an eye on Pearce in the third cottage. She's being cagey tonight.'

Poopy Pearce, Eileen mused, as she moved to the first bed to help little

Vera Williams. *All I need is another night of cleaning poo.* 'There,' Eileen said, tucking the sheet firmly around Vera. 'Comfortable?'

'Thank you, Miss Bonney,' Vera haltingly replied, a smile lighting her cherubic face.

Eileen patted Vera's shoulder and moved to help Christine snuggle into her bed. 'Will Sarah be a good girl now?' Christine asked, as Eileen settled her into the white sheets.

'Sarah is sleeping,' Eileen said. 'You can too,' although she wondered how long the drugs Watkins used to calm Sarah would keep the girl sedated.

Goodnights given to Watkins and Maslen, Eileen crept into the second cottage and moved quietly from room to room, checking on the sleeping girls. The prevalent odours of vinegar, baking soda and naphthalene interspersed with whiffs of excrement and urine permeated the cottages, as Eileen methodically passed the cots, sniffing to determine who needed a change of linen and bedclothes. When she found each event, she gently woke the girl, helped her remove her wet clothes and changed the sheets. If the bedwetting or pooing was extreme, she guided the distressed child to the shower and bathed her. Most girls stood obediently or sat in sleepy compliance as Eileen cleaned their mess, but some, like Poopy Pearce, or Sarah, or little Audrey, grizzled or cried or wrestled with Eileen, and she collected her share of bruises from the hits the girls doled out as she tried to console them. Eventually, she accepted it was circumspect to walk past certain bedwetters who were aggressive in the middle of the night, and deal with the issue when they were woken in the morning at seven am.

'Honestly, Bonney, they don't even realise it,' Watkins advised a couple of weeks into the role, after she asked about a bruise below Eileen's right eye. 'I know it makes you feel bad to ignore someone peeing in their bed, but you'll learn some of these girls don't even know they've done it, and they forget about it even when you've helped them. Don't do dangerous things, Bonney. No one will thank you for it. The girls need management and care, but not your heart.'

First round of the cottages completed, Eileen returned to the initial building to check the medication roster on the wall, noting which girls required treatment during the night. She memorised the long-term patients, the ones permanently sick or on controlling drugs, but the girls were always contracting colds or getting infections, so the medication schedule changed weekly, depending on when the doctor came and who caught what. Watkins sorted the drugs, labelled clearly for each girl by name, cottage, room and bed so there would be no mistakes. All Eileen had to do was administer the medicine at the right time during the night; often at midnight and, for a couple of girls, again at four in the morning.

At midnight, she moved through the cottages quietly, gently waking the girls who needed attention, and checking again for those who soiled their bedding. When her round was completed, she settled into a chair in the first cottage and closed her eyes to nap.

Eileen jerked awake and looked around, before reading the wall clock. Six-fifteen. She rubbed her eyes and tried to recollect the last task she completed before she sat in the chair. Cottage Three. Medicine for Audrey. She hurried along the path to the cottage and gave Audrey her the belated medication. The girl didn't complain, for once. Then Eileen came to the front room of the first cottage and sat in the chair, exhausted. But she was afraid to close her eyes again. There was no more time to sleep. The next task was waking the girls for breakfast, after which she had to bathe Anthea Jones. Anthea required individual and specialised attention. 'She looks like a six-year-old,' Watkins told Eileen as she swapped shifts on the first day, 'but she's twelve. She's such a delicate little creature. Quiet. Polite. Always smiles. You will love her. We all do.'

After the wake-up round, Eileen wheeled Anthea to the main building and into the white-tiled cubicle where Anthea had to be showered in her chair. Eileen was ordered to wear a mask and rubber gloves, while bathing the girl, and use a special sudsy soap. Out of curiosity, the first morning, Eileen asked Watkins why the extra precautions were involved.

'Doctor's orders,' Watkins replied. 'He insists that whoever washes the girl wears the protective gear. I don't know any more than you do.'

Although Eileen accepted Watkins' answer, it puzzled her that the Head Nurse was no more informed than she was about the girl's condition, and she worried that she was washing a patient with an infectious disease, or with a contaminant that no one else was willing to be near, but she had no one with whom to raise the issue. Watkins was right. Anthea was sweet and polite, and Eileen felt obliged to help the girl whatever the reason behind her illness.

When she had Anthea dressed, she wheeled her to the cottage and sat her among the other girls to eat breakfast. She left the troop under Lottie Walker's supervision while she undertook the laborious duty of changing and making beds before finishing her shift at a little after eight. Glad to be finished, Eileen clocked off and walked out of the main building. The morning sun was bright and angry, and that meant the walk home would be warm, but warmth made her happy because it would drive out the night shift chill. She yawned. Sleeping in her bed would be luxurious.

*

The water shimmered, flickering images and glittering waves rippling between the boundary of sea and sky, portent to the day's impending heat. A seagull drifted low over the water, mid-morning sun glowing on its white feathers. Closer to shore, beyond the white water, three black and white pelicans cruised majestically, orange bills poised, watchfully intent on fishing the silver streaks flashing through the shallows. The low tide exposed a long, curve of sand where a handful of people wandered in pairs and threes, or singularly, engulfed in worlds of their making. Others frolicked and swam in the water, but Eileen was alone, her feet barely skimming the bottom, languidly moving her arms to keep her balance in the gentle ripples. A red convertible cruised along the Esplanade, windows glinting, top down, and she fancied she saw a white scarf trailing languidly behind a young woman in the passenger seat. Houses nestled between the dunes, homes of an older generation, wealthy people from wealthier times, times before the Great Depression and the Second World War stripped middle class and poor people of dreams and hopes beyond what there was to eat the next day.

Eileen closed her eyes, dipped her head beneath the water, and swam a handful of strokes until she could stand, waves lapping softly against her back. She watched a young couple strolling hand-in-hand across the beach and up to the base of a dune where they paused, and the man leaned forward to kiss the woman on her cheek.

Her heart ached for Dudley. She dreamed of him when she wasn't too exhausted from her shifts at the Home. Her lips tingled, remembering how he patiently, tenderly taught her to kiss. She imagined his hand in the small of her back as they danced, recalled his scent, his dreamy brown eyes and soft-spoken tone, his whispers in the darkness when he pressed against her, arms entwined. She wished he would write, but he couldn't because he would have no idea where she was living after the eviction, and she had no way of letting him know. The disconnection amplified her pain.

The six months he said he would be away in New Guinea were almost passed, but she did not know how she would meet him when he returned from active duty. She figured she would sing at The Argosy and he would see her like the last time, and they would continue where they left off, but the location of the church refuge in Brighton, Bruce away and unable to chaperone, combined with the night-shift job she was taking that included working weekend nights, meant she could no longer sing with the band or even dance at The Argosy. She was confined to a life of servitude, a caged bird prevented from growing wings and flying. She was Cinderella after the ball, already kissed by the Prince who offered possibilities of a better future, but trapped again by her family's needs, with the Prince unable to rescue her.

She floated on her back in the gentle water, its velvet touch soothing her soul and helping her to imagine Dudley caressing her arms, her thighs. All the boys she stared at and dreamed about until Dudley entered her life never prepared her for what it really was like to be embraced and kissed. It was magical, scintillating, enthralling. She wanted more of it. She wanted Dudley.

Eileen rolled onto her stomach and swam towards the shore, wading in the shallows through schools of shimmering silver minnows. She guessed it was ten o'clock and figured she should be home before her mother panicked. She told Clarice she would stop by the beach for a swim, but her mother always feared the worst for her daughter's safety. Time to go home.

As she crossed the sand, heading for her towel, she noticed two young women sitting under a pastel blue and yellow umbrella, but she paid them little attention, until a voice called, 'Bonney!' Recognising the dark blond

Patty Ivers, a woman with whom she worked at Ingerson's, Eileen altered direction to the umbrella, studying Patty's pale pink and frilly two-piece bathing suit as she approached. 'Sit down,' Patty invited. 'This is Di. You remember her?'

Eileen sat on the edge of the blue plaid blanket, acknowledging the brunette, but said apologetically, 'I'm sorry. I don't.'

Di extended a hand. 'That's all right. I operate an overlocker. You worked with Mary and Susan in buttons, didn't you?'

'Yes,' Eileen replied.

'Didn't you like working with us?' Di asked.

'Oh, I did!' Eileen replied. 'I loved it.'

'So why did you leave?' Patty asked.

'Oh,' Eileen gasped. The memory of her father's anger flashed before her. 'I had to care for my mother,' she said. 'She's been very ill.'

'Oh, so sorry,' Patty said. 'I didn't mean to pry.'

'Yes, you did,' Di said, grinning. 'She's such a gossipmonger!'

'I am not!' Patty retorted indignantly, and the young women laughed, until Patty caught her breath to confess, 'Actually, I am,' and they broke into another gale of laughter. Eileen smiled at their self-indulgent amusement because it reminded her of the fun she had with Joyce at Primary School when they bantered about the teachers and other students and shared playground gossip.

'You really should get a better swimsuit,' Patty said, assessing Eileen.

Eileen drew up her knees and wrapped her arms around them to hide her skinny torso and her two-tone grey cotton bathing suit. 'Aren't you afraid of being arrested?' she asked, raising a querying eyebrow at Patty.

Di laughed and Patty replied, 'In this old thing? Hardly. I wish I could get one of those proper French bikinis everyone's wearing in Europe.'

'And get arrested like that girl on Bondi Beach in Sydney!' Di chorused. 'Did you read about that?'

'Yes!' Patty squealed. 'That would be something.'

'I wouldn't want everyone staring at me,' Eileen said.

'As if they can't see everything already in that outfit you're wearing,' Patty said, and the girls laughed again, leaving Eileen embarrassed. Seeing her discomfort, Patty touched Eileen's arm in a gesture of friendship, saying, 'Honey, it's all right. We're being silly. Look at Di's sorry little outfit.'

Di stared indignantly. 'And what's wrong with this?' she asked and stood, angling her black and white one-piece suit and body in accentuated modelling poses. 'Bet you are both screamingly jealous now,' and she bent forward, pushing up her ample breasts and sticking out her bum.

'Betty Boop!' Patty screamed.

'With bazookas!' Di cried, pressing her breasts together. 'The boys would kill for a picture of this on their lockers.'

'Knock it off,' Patty mocked petulantly. 'You're making a scene.'

Di resumed her place under the umbrella and winked at Eileen, saying, 'You've nothing to be afraid of. Let them stare.'

'I figure your boyfriend doesn't mind what he sees,' Patty said. 'You do have a boyfriend?'

Eileen blushed, and replied, 'I do.'

'Ooh,' said Patty. 'Is he meeting you down here?'

'He's still overseas,' Eileen replied.

'That's a shame,' said Di. 'So's my squeeze. He's in Japan. Where's your boy?'

'New Guinea.'

'Is he back soon?' Di asked.

'Yes,' Eileen said.

'What's his name?' Patty asked.

Eileen wondered whether Patty's question was fair, but she answered, 'Dudley.'

'Dud the spud,' Di teased. 'Bet he's very cute. Is he?'

'He is,' Eileen replied, smiling.

'Describe him so we can imagine him,' Patty said. 'Look. We'll even close our eyes.' She winked at Di who immediately closed her eyes.

'I don't know,' Eileen said.

'You don't know what he looks like?' Patty asked. Di opened her eyes.

'No. I mean, I don't know if I should describe him.'

'Go on!' Patty urged. 'Be a sport.' She closed her eyes and Di followed suit.

Eileen hesitated and began, 'Well, he's my height.'

'Not tall,' Diane said.

'Sh,' Patty ordered. 'Go on.'

'He has dreamy brown eyes.'

'Ooh,' Di said. 'Getting better.'

'Sh,' Patty urged again.

'He has a soft mouth and a sweet smile,' Eileen continued. 'He holds himself confidently and he knows how to dance.'

'I bet he does,' Di said, and the girls sniggered.

'What's his last name?' Patty asked.

'Why?' asked Eileen.

'It's a game,' Di explained. 'You see if his name is going to fit with your name. See what its sounds like. You don't want to marry a man with a weird last name. You could end up as Eileen Schnozzlewotz or something.' Di laughed, and added, 'Or a rude one that everyone makes fun of for the rest of your life.'

'Like Smallcock,' Patty said, and the girls burst into laughter again.

'Or Numbottom,' Di stammered, and the laughter gained momentum.

'It's Wright,' Eileen said.

Patty and Di gathered their composure, and Patty said, 'Eileen Wright. That sounds all right.'

'His name is Dudley Wright?' Di asked.

'Yes,' Eileen replied. 'Why?'

Di glanced at Patty, but to Eileen she said, 'Oh, nothing really.'

'Do you know him?' Eileen asked.

Di laughed lightly, and answered, 'No. Not really. I think I must have heard the name before. It sounds familiar. That's all.'

'It's not an uncommon name,' Patty said, looking quizzically at Di, who shook her head. 'Where did you meet him?'

'At The Argosy,' Eileen replied.

'I love that place!' Patty said. 'We go there all the time, don't we, Di?'

'We do!' Di said. 'Perhaps we'll see you there.'

'I haven't been for a while,' Eileen said. 'I work Friday and Saturday nights.'

'Really?' Di asked. 'Where?'

'Minda Home.'

'Where they put the simple kids?' Di asked.

'Nightshifts?' Patty added. 'That must be spooky.'

'It's not that bad,' Eileen explained. 'Most of the girls are good.'

A horn echoed across the beach. Di stood and waved towards the Esplanade where a tall young man in a white shirt emerged from a dark blue sedan and waved in return. 'That's Bertie!' Di said. 'Time to go.'

'Sorry we can't stay, Eileen,' said Patty, rising and scooping up the blanket. 'It was so nice to bump into you like this. Perhaps we can catch up another time.'

'It was nice seeing you, too,' Eileen said as she stepped out of the way of the two young women who were frantically packing their wares into bags.

Eileen returned to where she left her towel and clothes and waved to Patty and Diane as they trudged across the sand and up to the road where their escort waited. The sun was beating down on the earth, the heat rising, and she was late heading home. Exhaustion oozed through her muscles, the ocean's massage forgotten, and it was time to sleep, if her mother let her. Clothes in hand, she headed for the nearest change hut.

*

'Girlie!' Clarice called from the hall. 'There's someone here to see you.'

Eileen put down the cutting knife and the potato she was dicing, wiped her hands on her flowered apron and took it off. Exhausted from another long night at work, all she wanted was to sleep. 'Who is it?' she asked, as she traipsed towards the front door.

Resplendent in his army uniform, framed in the doorway against the morning sunlight, his light brown hair combed neatly to the left and his face clean-shaven, his brown eyes dark and alluring, Dudley smiled, and said, 'I wasn't sure if this was the right house. I was told you moved when I went to your old house.'

'I presume this is the young man you met at the Botanic Gardens last year?' Clarice asked.

'Yes, Mum,' Eileen replied, trying to recover from her shock. 'This is -'

'That's all right,' Clarice interrupted. 'Mister Wright already politely introduced himself. He seems to have a notion to introduce you to his parents.'

Eileen's eyes widened at the news, and she looked at Dudley for an explanation. 'I asked your mother if she minded that I took you to meet my family for lunch today. They're all at home and, as I'm going back to New Guinea tomorrow, I thought it would be appropriate you all met one another.'

'I-' Eileen stammered, looking at her mother, before saying, 'Yes. I'd like to do that.'

'I thought we could also go to a movie and then dancing,' Dudley added.

'Before you get too ahead of yourself, Mister Wright,' Clarice warned, 'I remind you that it is Sunday, and there will be no dancing, and you will be home by ten o'clock. Is that understood?'

'Yes, Missus Bonney,' Dudley agreed.

'Of course, Mum,' Eileen confirmed. 'Oh,' she said, as if suddenly realising what was happening. 'When are we leaving?'

'As soon as possible,' Dudley prompted. 'We have to catch the train to Goodwood and swap to the train to Mitcham to make lunch in time.'

'I need to change,' Eileen said, becoming flustered. 'I'll be quick.'

'Mister Wright and I will have a quiet chat in the parlour while you get ready,' Clarice said, and she invited Dudley to follow her into the house.

Eileen hurried to the bathroom where she washed her face and underarms quickly, applied baby powder, and checked that her hair was tidy, brushing and puffing it out for greater body. She pinched her cheeks for colour to mask her exhaustion. She pushed past Ian in the bathroom doorway, who asked, 'What's the rush?' but Eileen ignored him. She rushed upstairs to her bedroom, avoiding stepping on Josie's doll, chose the best dress she owned, a dark green A-line with white buttons, put on her white socks and brown shoes, and checked her hair again in the mirror.

As she turned to leave the room, Judy appeared in the doorway, and asked, 'Where are you going?'

'Out,' Eileen replied. 'You have to look after Mum.'

'Are you going out with that man downstairs in the parlour?'

'Yes.'

'He's too old,' Judy said.

'Mind your own business,' Eileen warned. 'Go finish the potatoes in the kitchen for Mum.' She trotted down the stairs and took a deep breath, before she strolled calmly into the parlour.

'You'll need this,' Clarice said, holding up Eileen's dark grey trench coat.

'Can I talk to you?' Eileen asked, looking at Clarice. 'Privately?'

Clarice followed Eileen into the kitchen, where Eileen whispered, 'Please can I wear some lipstick, Mum?'

'You most certainly cannot,' Clarice replied brusquely. 'I don't even like the idea of you going anywhere with this man. Does he know how old you are?'

'Of course he does. He's really nice,' Eileen argued.

'Yes, I can see that, and he is very polite, and he has served his country,' Clarice replied. 'But he is a man, and you, Girlie, are still a child. Your father would not allow this.'

'I don't care what Father would or wouldn't allow,' Eileen retorted. 'He doesn't live here.'

'That is enough!' Clarice ordered. 'I have a good mind to say no right now.'

'I'm sorry, Mum,' Eileen apologised desperately. 'Please let me go. He's leaving on Monday, and I might never see him again. He's been so nice to me. Please?'

Clarice hesitated, meeting Eileen's pleading gaze, tilted her head as if she was going to shake it, but said, 'Home by ten o'clock. Make sure you go exactly where he says you are going. No shenanigans. No lies. Am I clear? By rights, you should not be seeing someone like that at all.'

'Yes, Mum,' Eileen agreed. 'Thank you, Mum,' she said, and she hugged her mother until Clarice pushed her back, to say, 'And do not let him lead you on. Hear me? Men are the ruin of us.'

Walking to the train station, and travelling to reach Goodwood, gave Eileen time to talk with Dudley, hold his hand, feel close and learn about him. 'Before the war, I was keen to go into my father's wholesale furniture business, but I joined up at the Wayville recruiting centre and was posted to Darwin,' Dudley told her.

'My Auntie was in Darwin,' Eileen said, rocking to the train's clackety rhythm. 'She was on the toilet when the bombs started dropping.'

Dudley grinned. 'I was at Winnellie the day of the first raid. Glad I wasn't on the toilet, but I could have used one.'

Eileen laughed and hugged Dudley's arm, but her tone was filled with concern as she said, 'It must have been horrible.'

'It was a dog's breakfast,' Dudley replied. 'The Japanese came back quite a few times, but mostly to mess up the airfield. After that, I was posted to New Guinea.'

'What is New Guinea like?'

Dudley shook his head. 'Hot. Wet. Pretty awful in the main. I don't like to talk about it.'

Eileen leaned in, filled with an urgent need to kiss Dudley, but he pulled away, leaving her stupefied. 'Sorry,' he apologised awkwardly. 'It's not seemly to be kissing in public.' Eileen blushed and looked down at her shoes. 'Hey,' Dudley said, gently lifting her face towards him. 'There's nothing more I'd like to do than kiss that beautiful mouth of yours, but you know what people are like. Don't fret. We'll have plenty of time at the movies.' He grinned mischievously and winked.

Amused by his affability, Eileen laughed, but she glanced around the cabin, conscious of people staring, and decided Dudley was right not to be overly affectionate on the train. 'How long have you been back?' she asked.

'Two weeks,' Dudley replied. 'It's short leave. We're mopping up and sorting out the natives. Some blokes are still hunting Japanese in the forests, but lucky we're not there for that.'

'How come you've only caught up with me now?'

'Strewth,' Dudley gasped. 'You weren't exactly easy to find, you know. I went to your old house and there was someone else living in it. Lucky one of your neighbours knew where you'd gone, or I would never have found you.'

'Sorry,' Eileen said.

'Why the change of house?'

'It's a long story.'

Dudley laughed. 'We're on a train. I have time to listen.'

Waiting on the platform at Goodwood station to change trains, Dudley pulled a tobacco packet from his pocket, and a small paper, and deftly rolled a cigarette, sealing the rolled paper with a lick of his tongue and slide of his fingers. He held the cigarette towards Eileen, who shook her head. 'I don't smoke,' she said.

'Never?' Dudley asked.

'I tried one with Lorna at The Argosy,' Eileen explained. 'I wasn't very good at it.'

'It's like kissing,' Dudley said, and winked again. 'Just takes practice.' When Eileen shook her head again, he said, 'You should practise. It will make you look more sophisticated. That's why film stars smoke.' He popped the cigarette in his mouth and pulled out a box of matches, again expertly flicking a match into life, cupping it in his hands and lighting the end of his cigarette. He drew a deep breath and sighed as he breathed out smoke. 'Best friend in the army,' he said. 'If you're on smoko, it means you're not digging a trench in mud and rain, or on night duty staring into the jungle.'

Dudley ushered Eileen aboard when the train arrived and, after they alighted at Torrens Park, he steered her across Belair Road into a steeply inclined street with established solid houses and large properties. Eileen spied a lofty old building peeping between trees and houses, and asked, 'What is that place?'

'Scotch College,' Dudley replied. 'My Alma Mater.'

'Oh,' Eileen said. The Latin phrase meant nothing to her, but she knew of Scotch College, a posh school where only the very privileged attended.

'And this is my home,' Dudley said, stopping at a white picket gate. 'Or rather my parents' home.'

Eileen stared up the curved paved driveway at the two-storey Second Empire styled house nestled among gum trees and bushes and roses. A dark blue and black sedan sat on the driveway and parked behind it was a low-slung red sports car. 'Nice cars,' Eileen murmured.

'Do you like cars?' Dudley asked.

'Yes,' Eileen replied.'

'Can you drive?'

'No.'

'I'm sure you'll learn soon enough,' said Dudley, leading Eileen towards the house. 'Dad's old Bentley is nothing special, but my sister's little

Triumph Roadster is brand new, freshly imported.' He paused beside the sports car and opened the passenger door. 'Hop in,' he invited. 'If you're lucky, I'll take you for a spin in it later.'

'You will not,' a woman said frostily. She stood on the stone steps leading to the porch. Stockily built, wearing a green plaid cardigan and brown skirt, her hair was tied fiercely in a bun like a school mistress or an older woman.

'Ah, Jean,' Dudley said, closing the car door. 'Welcoming as always.'

'And who is this?' Jean asked, descending the steps.

'Eileen Bonney,' Dudley said. 'This is the young lady I told you about who sings at The Argosy Palais.'

'A singer,' Jean said, assessing Eileen as she approached. 'Why did you bring her here?'

'She's a good friend,' Dudley said. 'I thought it would be nice for her to meet Dad and Mum.'

Jean raised an eyebrow. 'Does Carol know?'

'Yes, she does,' Dudley said irritably, 'and stop being so nosey.'

'I am your older sister,' Jean replied. 'It's my responsibility to be nosey.'

'Come on,' Dudley urged, and he took Eileen's arm and guided her up the steps, past his sister and her disparaging expression. 'Let's find Dad and Mum. They are far more hospitable than my biddy of a sister.'

'It's just as well you are going back overseas,' Jean said from behind. 'You still have a considerable amount of growing up to do.'

'Who is Carol?' Eileen asked as they passed through the front door.

'An old friend,' Dudley replied.

'Why would she need to know about me?'

Dudley turned Eileen to face him. 'Carol is very good friends with my nosey older sister. They feel like they can both boss me around and so she wants to know everything I do.'

'That sounds terrible,' Eileen said.

'It's not so bad,' Dudley replied. 'But I am a soldier, and I can bloody well do whatever I like, and that fact annoys them.' He chuckled and grinned, adding, 'Come on. You have other people to meet.'

The house interior overwhelmed Eileen: high ornate ceilings, glittering chandeliers, tapestries, paintings and mirrors adorning the walls, wide double doors, and hand-crafted wooden furniture. Two of her mother's sisters were wealthy women – Auntie Fay, who fostered John, and Auntie Hirelle, who lived at North Adelaide in a grand old house – but Eileen had never been inside a house as opulent as the Wright's mansion, and it filled her with a sickening maelstrom of awe, envy and inferiority. Dating Dudley was a cruel mistake. He lived in a different class, a different world. She could not rise so high.

And another matter niggled her. She wanted to know more about Carol. But before she could ask another question, Dudley ushered her into the parlour, a room filled with high-backed armchairs and gilt-framed paintings, dominated by a large fireplace with a marble mantlepiece. A grizzly-whiskered man, wearing grey trousers, a white shirt, and a maroon vest, rose from an opulent armchair.

'Father,' Dudley announced, 'this is Eileen Bonney.'

'Miss Bonney,' Mister Wright said, with a vague nod, and Eileen noticed he cast a questioning glance at Dudley.

'The singer I told you about,' Dudley perfunctorily explained.

'Oh,' Mister Wright said, and he sat again. 'I believe lunch is ready.'

Dudley took Eileen's arm and steered her towards a glass door, saying, 'I'll show you the back garden. Then we can eat.'

Eileen was fascinated by the fare placed on the table. Though sparse in quantity, there were meats and condiments, butter and bread and cheese and sugar, nothing suggesting the family's lifestyle was affected by post-war rationing.

Dudley's parents were polite but aloof in their manner throughout lunch. Dudley tried to engage Eileen in conversation with his parents, but they turned every topic around to Dudley's tour of duty, and their family friends and businesses, and his plans after returning for good, showing minimal interest in talking to Eileen or asking questions about herself or her family.

Dudley's younger brother, Arthur, a bright-faced, fair-haired youth dressed in tennis gear, arrived as lunch was finished. Unlike Jean, he was sociable, and Eileen learned he was attending college and planning on going to university to study medicine, but Jean drew Arthur away from Eileen as soon as she was able, and, as soon as the meal was politely finished, Dudley's parents excused themselves and retired to other pursuits.

Dudley hurried Eileen back to the train station where they caught a train into the city, watched Bogart and Bacall in "The Big Sleep" at West's Cinema in Hindley Street, shared cigarettes, kisses, cuddling, and made a mad scramble to catch the train to Hove, all of which melted into a warm, embracing cloud of happiness for Eileen. She leaned against Dudley on the clacking, swaying train, wrapped in his presence, slipping into euphoria and exhaustion simultaneously. Only when the train stopped at the Hove station, and Eileen checked Dudley's watch to discover the time was close to eleven, did her drowsiness dissipate and panic storm in. 'We have to hurry!' she urged. 'Mum will be furious.'

'It's all right,' Dudley reassured her, wrapping his arm over her shoulders. 'I'll sort it out with your mother. I'll say the train was held up.'

'She won't believe that,' Eileen said.

The pair walked briskly along Brighton Road and down Hulbert Street, until Dudley stopping Eileen in the shadows, and pulled her close. 'This has been a wonderful day, Eileen,' he murmured. He leaned in and kissed her, slowly, softly, lingering in the sensuality of the contact. Her body tingled, whispered of deeper, darker promises, and she pulled away in trepidation. 'Are you all right?' Dudley asked.

Eileen fought to catch her breath, and whispered, 'Yes. Yes, I'm perfectly all right. It's, well, Mum might be waiting up.'

Dudley glanced at the house across the road, saw a light glowing and said, 'I'm sure she is.'

'We best go in,' Eileen insisted.

Holding hands, the couple crossed the road, but as they reached the steps the front door opened, revealing a familiar tall figure, dressed in his Military Police uniform. Gasping, 'Father!' Eileen released Dudley's hand.

'Inside the house now, Miss!' Donald barked.

'We didn't mean-' Eileen began.

'Inside!' Donald repeated.

Cowering, Eileen ran into the house, past her mother, and up the stairs to her bedroom, and she heard Donald close the front door. Desperate to know what was unfolding, she left the bedroom light off and crept to the window. 'What's going on?' Judy's sleepy voice asked from her bed.

'Sh!' Eileen ordered. She gingerly lifted the window sash and listened, frustrated because the roof hip and angle meant she couldn't see Dudley or her father below.

'I don't care who you think you are, mate,' Donald snarled, 'but no self-respecting soldier would be chasing up the skirt of a fifteen-year-old girl. You turn right around now, and leave, and I never want to see your face anywhere near my daughter again! Am I clear about that?'

'Listen, Sergeant Bonney, I wasn't-'

'See this uniform, soldier? Means I can do whatever I want to the likes of you. On your bloody bike, mate! Now!' Donald roared.

Eileen stood on her tiptoes to see if she could glimpse Dudley leaving, but the roof line and darkness conspired against her. Emotions roaring into her throat, she threw herself on her bed, sobbing hysterically, unable to stop when Judy shook her, and she was still wailing when her mother appeared and turned on the light. 'Time to calm down now, Girlie,' Clarice said, sitting on the edge of Eileen's bed. 'It's done with.'

'I want Dudley!' Eileen sobbed. 'I want him back!'

'That's not going to happen,' Clarice said firmly. 'And you should know why.'

Eileen rolled onto her side. 'Why is he here? He has no right to be here anymore!'

'I asked your father to come,' Clarice said.

'Why?' Eileen asked.

'He's still your father, and he knows what's best for you,' Clarice reminded her.

'Why was he wearing his uniform? He's not in the army anymore!'

'He wore it to make a point. I think Mister Wright understood.'

'It's not fair!' Eileen screamed and she buried her head in her hands again.

'Shush now, Girlie,' Clarice asked. 'You're not making it any better. You're upsetting Judy and Josie, and you need to get some sleep. This will look very different in the morning.'

'Go away!' Eileen bawled between sobs. 'Leave me alone!' She buried her head under her pillow, howling and blubbering. The world was cruel.

People were cruel. Her father was cruel. Dudley was the only brightness in her drab existence, the only hope she had to escape her prison. She hated her father more than ever for what he was doing.

*

Eileen ushered little Anthea to the breakfast table, glad the bathing session was over. She was keen to shower before doing the morning bed-making round. As she stepped back from Anthea's chair, Watkins called her to the door. 'Matron wants to see you, Bonney.'

'Where?' Eileen asked.

'In Rogerson.'

'Do you know why?'

'No,' Watkins replied, shaking her head. 'Best hurry.'

Disappointed not to be able to cleanse herself of the chemicals she was certain were in the soaps used on Anthea, Eileen adjusted her soiled white apron and blue uniform and walked through the dull morning light towards the red brick Rogerson building, yawning, her legs like leaden pedestals. Sleep pulled at her, willing her to lie down and close her eyes. 'Matron wants to see me,' she said tiredly, as she entered the front door.

'Down the right corridor in the first dormitory,' a nurse directed, a young black-haired woman Eileen hadn't previously met.

Matron Adams greeted her as she entered the dormitory. 'Good morning, Bonney.'

'Good morning, Matron,' Eileen replied. She liked the Matron. She dressed crisply, wore her blond hair tied back in a neat bun, and she spoke with an educated British accent, but, despite her taciturn appearance, Matron Adams was kindly, and she loved the children in her care. 'Watkins said you wanted to see me.'

'Indeed,' Adams said. 'We have a problem to solve. Seems Hughes and Smith have both come down with a nasty bug and can't come in today. I need you to do an extra shift. Would you mind?'

Flabbergasted by the request because she was expecting to leave and go home to sleep, Eileen gathered her thoughts, to reply, 'I haven't fully cleaned up after washing Anthea.'

'Of course,' Adams said. 'You can bathe in the nurse's bathroom and have a quick breakfast to freshen up. It's eight now, so if you could be ready at nine that would be an enormous help. Shall I see you here, then?'

'Yes,' Eileen replied. 'Thank you, Matron.'

Adams turned her attention to another nurse, so Eileen returned to the front reception where, stifling a yawn, she asked the black-haired woman, 'Where is the nurses' bathroom?'

'Along there, love,' the woman replied with a gracious smile.

Eileen headed through a door into a short corridor and into a bathroom with two showers and a bath. She studied the bath's inviting white enamel curves, decided that was her best option because she could keep her hair dry, and the bath water would remind her of the ocean. She put in the black plug and turned on the taps and yawned, before stripping away her clothes, the cool air prickling her skin, while she tested the water. When she was satisfied with the temperature and the level, she climbed in, slid down until the water lapped around her neck and her knees, and sighed. Dudley was in New Guinea, probably forgetting all about her, thanks to her father's meddling. She cried until she ran dry of tears for him. Her world was horrible. And she was so, so tired. She closed her eyes.

*

'You could have drowned,' the skinny nurse was saying. 'People drown in baths like that.'

'Hush, Jennifer,' the dark-haired reception nurse chided, as she patted Eileen's legs with the towel. 'Stop scaring her.'

Eileen snatched the towel, embarrassed to be towelled by someone else.

'Only trying to help,' said the dark-haired nurse.

'Matron's having a blue fit wondering what happened to you,' Jennifer said.

'What time is it?' Eileen asked.

'Nine-fifteen,' the dark-haired nurse told her.

'Oh,' Eileen gasped, hurrying with her drying. 'I can do the rest. Thank you.'

'Lucky we knew you were here,' said the dark-haired nurse. 'I'm Pam.'

'Thank you, Pam,' Eileen replied. 'And Jennifer.'

'We'll leave you to it,' Pam said. 'Tell Matron you had to go to the loo. We have to get back to our stations, love, Will you be all right?'

'Yes,' Eileen replied. 'Thank you.'

After the nurses left Eileen to finish dressing in the bathroom, she glanced at the bath. Understanding how close she came to death made her skin crawl. She hastily adjusted her uniform and apron, checked in the mirror that her hair was up, pulled on her cap and hurried to the dormitory.

The pervasive tang of disinfectant and urine greeted her as she entered. A nurse was bent over, talking to a girl sitting on a bed, but Matron Adams wasn't in the room. Unsure of what to do, Eileen approached the nurse, who looked up and asked, 'Bonney?'

'Yes,' Eileen replied. 'Sorry. I was – I was on the toilet.'

'It doesn't matter,' the nurse said, smiling. 'I'm Margaret – Sinclair in here – and this is Olive.' The girl on the bed in the ubiquitous Minda Home white smock grinned toothlessly.

'Hello, Olive,' Eileen said.

'Olive gets nervous when the other girls go out to play,' Margaret said. 'One of us normally stays in here to talk to her. She likes to talk about cooking, don't you, Olive.'

'Yes,' Olive said shyly.

'Would you like Bonney to stay with you while I make the beds?' Margaret asked.

Olive glanced at Eileen and looked down at her own socked feet, murmuring, 'Yes.'

Margaret patted Olive's hand and stood, saying to Eileen, 'I'll be here, making the beds. First, though, I'll fetch fresh linen. The other girls will be back in a little while. Matron will probably tell you what she needs next.' She smiled at Eileen and headed for the door.

Eileen's chat with Olive began awkwardly because Olive was reluctant to engage, but slowly the girl gathered courage, especially when Eileen broached the topic of soup. 'I like tomato soup best of all,' Olive confided.

'Chicken broth for me,' Eileen replied.

'How do you make chicken broth?' Olive asked, and the conversation gained momentum as Eileen explained how she made chicken broth for her family, while Sinclair methodically made her way along the beds, changing linen exactly as Eileen did in the cottages by the dunes.

Matron Adams returned, shepherding girls into different rooms in the dormitory and kitchen and laundry areas. She beckoned to Eileen and told her, 'You can help in the kitchen, please. The girls generally know what to do. You need to make sure they do the right thing.'

'Yes, Matron,' Eileen said. 'Sorry, I was late. I␠␠was-'

'On the toilet,' Matron Adams finished, her eyebrow raised mockingly. 'Yes. Most young women are when they run late. Off you go.'

Dismissed, Eileen entered the kitchen to find half a dozen girls donning aprons over their smocks, supervised by another nurse. 'Where's Hughes?' the nurse asked when Eileen approached.

'I think she's sick,' Eileen explained. 'Matron asked me to help. I'm Eileen Bonney. Just Bonney to everyone here.'

'Copley,' the nurse replied. 'All right then. You can keep an eye on Heather and Dawn over there. They're boiling water for the other girls. The larger one is Heather. She thinks she's the kitchen boss. Humour her.'

'Thank you,' Eileen said, and she moved to the stove area where two girls were watching water pans heat up.

'Who are you?' Heather challenged.

'Hello,' Eileen replied, smiling. 'I'm here to help today.'

'I don't know you,' Heather said, irritation rising, and she straightened, flexing her square, broad shoulders.

'I'm Bonney,' Eileen said, assessing the girl who looked much older than the other girls, as she tried to placate her. 'I guess you're Heather?'

'You don't know my name,' Heather said. 'You shouldn't be here.' She started flexing her pudgy hands, her anxiety rapidly increasing. 'You should go.'

Eileen recognised the warning signs, familiar in other girls when their emotions were escalating in the cottages where she worked, and she backed away. 'What's going on?' Copley asked.

'Her!' Heather said angrily, pointing at Eileen. 'She's not meant to be in here!'

'Bonney's taking Hughes' place today, Heather. Matron asked her to help.'

'I don't like her!' Heather replied angrily. 'Tell her to go away!'

Copley turned to Eileen and advised, 'Probably best if you help the girls with the plates and cutlery.'

Glad to move away from Heather's obdurate mood, Eileen crossed the kitchen to where three girls were sorting the crockery. She introduced herself and asked what they were doing. A short, dark-eyed girl with an obvious lisp said, 'We are counting everything, so everything is right.'

'Can I help?' Eileen asked.

'Yes,' the girl replied. 'You can count the bowls.'

'Bonney!'

Eileen turned at the warning shout from Copley to see Heather storming towards her, yelling, 'You don't belong here!' and carrying a full bowl of boiling water that she was clearly intent on dowsing Eileen with. Eileen bolted for the kitchen door to escape, but before she reached it the door swung open and Matron Adams entered. Eileen rushed past Adams into the corridor, but she slipped on the polished floor and landed unceremoniously on her back. As the door swung shut behind her, Matron Adams yelled, 'Heather!' Eileen rolled onto her stomach in the corridor, wrapped her head in her hands, and bawled.

*

'I am never going back to that place!' Eileen whimpered, and she broke into another burst of heaving sobs, clutching the grey woollen blanket between her hands, and burying her face into her pillow. 'Never!'

Clarice stroked her daughter's dishevelled brown hair. 'No one will make you go back,' she whispered.

'She tried to kill me!' Eileen cried. 'I hate that place! I hate it!'

'It's all right, Girlie. You're not there now, and I won't make you go back,' Clarice crooned. 'No one will make you go back.'

'Promise?' Eileen asked, between sobs.

'I promise.'

Eileen looked up. 'And you won't bring Father into this?'

Clarice hesitated, but she assented.

As Eileen eased up onto her elbows, wiping her nose and tears, she noticed her mother sat at an odd angle on the bedside. 'What are you doing?'

Clarice adopted a sincere expression and lifted a blue bucket, saying, 'I thought you might need this.' Eileen's puzzled face made Clarice smile. 'To catch your tears.'

Her mother's absurd gesture made Eileen snigger, and then laugh, and Clarice laughed with her. It was a comedic act, Eileen decided, as Clarice left her room, but she understood her mother's intention. She knew she should get up and go downstairs to help Clarice, but she was too physically and emotionally exhausted to do anything except collapse.

When she woke in the evening, and realised she was still on her bed, undisturbed, she sat in the dark and listened to muffled voices downstairs. She pulled back the curtain to discover the last pastel orange vestiges of sunset glazing the western horizon above the houses. She headed downstairs.

Light and voices spilled from the kitchen. Ian, Peter Judy, Josie and Wally were at the table, finishing a meal, and her mother was by the stove, wiping her hands with a pale blue dish cloth. 'You look like death warmed up,' Peter said, lowering his spoon.

'Don't talk with your mouth half full,' Clarice reminded him.

'No,' Ian said, lifting his spoon of custard. 'Fill it up!'

'And no need for you to be cheeky, Ian Charles, or straight to bed!' Clarice snapped.

'I think he should go straight to bed now,' Judy suggested.

'Nobody asked you,' Ian retorted.

'Hungry?' Clarice asked, looking at Eileen.

'No,' she mumbled. 'Not really.'

'Sit down. I'll make you a cup of tea.' Clarice turned to the children. 'The rest of you can wash and clean up. Then off to your rooms.'

'I want to listen to the radio,' said Ian.

'Not tonight,' Clarice replied. 'You can read in your rooms.'

While Peter, Ian and Judy tidied the kitchen table and washed the dishes, Clarice organised a cup of tea and asked again if Eileen wanted to eat. Eileen declined. After the cup was placed on the table, Clarice supervised the children, leaving Eileen to sip at the tea. 'Goodnight, Girlie,' Peter said as he left with Ian and Wally in tow. Judy repeated the goodnight as Josie and she followed the boys, and Clarice ushered the children upstairs, saying, 'I'll be up to check you're in bed in an hour.'

'I work now, Mum,' Peter called down.

'So do I!' Ian added.

'Then you both need your sleep,' Clarice advised. 'Early start in the morning.'

When the upstairs doors closed, Clarice made herself a cup of tea and sat on the end of the table. 'Feel better?'

'Thank you,' Eileen replied. 'I'm just so very tired, Mum.'

'You're a very brave young woman,' Clarice said. 'I'm proud of you.'

'But what are we going to do if I don't work?' Eileen asked. 'We have no income again.'

'We will get by. Sister Bernice has found a cleaning job I can do, part-time, for a local parishioner.' Clarice sipped her tea and cleared her throat. 'I also spoke to your father this afternoon. He might have found another job for you.'

Eileen looked up, angry tears flooding her eyes. 'You promised you wouldn't tell him!'

'He has a right to know.'

'He has no right!' Eileen cried. 'All he cares about is himself!'

'That will do!' Clarice said bluntly.

'It will not do!' Eileen yelled. 'He's why we're all in this horrible mess! Can't you see that, Mum? Why can't you see that? Why can't you accept it?'

'Because he is all I have,' Clarice answered. 'I can't keep taking money from Bruce, or from you, and Peter and Ian.'

'From Bruce?' Eileen asked, flabbergasted. 'Bruce is giving you money?'

Clarice lowered her head. 'He has been.'

'For how long?' Eileen asked. When Clarice stayed silent, Eileen pressed her. 'For how long, Mum?'

'Bruce was sending his pay from the Airforce,' Clarice explained. 'He was helping when your father stopped – stopped coming home.'

Eileen stared at Clarice, smashed her fist on the table, upsetting her half-empty cup, and walked out, slamming the front door in her wake. She strode along the street, heading for the ocean, her mind bristling with anger and disbelief. Headlights lit her face as a car turned into the street from the Esplanade, and someone wolf whistled as the car swept past. She crossed the Esplanade into the dunes, and onto the cold beach sand, and stood at the edge of the waves crashing onto the shore, letting the broken shells and ocean-rolled stones etch the soles of her bare feet as she stared into the dark void of the Gulf. *Why has it ended up like this*? she silently asked. *Why me, God*? *What did I do so wrong*? She sank onto the wet sand and a sob wrenched from her chest into her mouth, choking her. She rolled onto her side and cried – for herself, for her mother, for Dudley, for Bruce, for her broken family, for Clive who had to run away, for everything that had gone so terribly, terribly wrong.

*

Her fingers rested on the dial, shaking with uncertainty, as she read the number scribbled in Dudley's educated scrawl, the number he gave her the day she lunched with his family. 'If you need anything,' he told her, his gracious smile lighting his face, 'ring. If I'm not home, I'm sure Mother will be happy to chat.' With his voice whispering in her memory, Eileen dialled the numbers, one by one, listening to the burr as the dial retracted after each number. The phone rang at the other end, and she waited, hoping no one would answer, but it clicked, and a woman asked, 'Hello?' Eileen hesitated, afraid to answer, and the voice repeated, 'Hello?'

'Oh,' Eileen stammered. 'Is this Missus Wright?'

'If you mean my mother, Alice Wright, no,' the voice replied. 'This is her daughter, Jean. To whom am I speaking?'

Eileen paused, deciding whether to be prudent and hang up, but she chose to press on. 'Hello, Jean. This is Eileen Bonney. We met at your parents' house a few weeks back.'

'Yes, I remember you,' Jean said. 'You really made a mess of my brother, didn't you?'

'I'm sorry?' Eileen asked, perplexed by Jean's observation.

'He's madly in love with you, which is, of course, absurd,' Jean said. 'But I heard your father told him you weren't up for auction yet. At least someone showed good sense.' Baffled by Jean's comments, Eileen was unable to answer, but Jean broke the silence. 'My heroic brother's not here, you know. He's still in New Guinea. Seems they need him to win the peace now the war's over.'

'Oh,' Eileen said. 'Have you heard from him?'

'One letter,' Jean replied. 'You know they still censor half of what he writes. The war's over and they're still afraid the Japanese will get secret information. No idea what a defeated enemy could do with it.'

'Is he all right?' Eileen asked.

'Apart from pining for you?' Jean asked sarcastically, and chuckled. 'He's soddenly wonderful, as always. I suspect he actually likes being in New Guinea. He says he can't wait to get home, of course, but I think that's only because he can't find a beautiful girl to lead astray where he is. You know you're not the only one, don't you?'

'Sorry?' Eileen asked.

'Oh,' Jean replied. 'You didn't know, you poor thing. Didn't mean to break it to you quite so rudely, but then it is best you know these things.'

Eileen felt a rush of despair and wished she hadn't called. 'Sorry, I better go. I'm sorry for calling.'

'A pleasure,' Jean replied diffidently. 'I'm glad you have our number. So convenient for you, if a little awkward for us. Spud is always generous like that.' And the connection ended.

Eileen hung up, digesting what she learned from the conversation, comprehension dawning like cancerous tentacles around her heart. The girl at the beach – Di? – she knew something. *You're not the only one*. Jean's blunt reveal was enough. She stumbled upstairs and sank on her bed. She was alone, as she was almost every day after quitting Minda Home. Peter was working. The other children were at school. Her mother was cleaning houses. The world was dreary and cruel, and she was growing sick of its monotony punctuated by weather, light and dark, drudgery in the house, meaningless conversations with her siblings and her mother's endless depression. Her heart ached for Dudley and Jean drove a cruel stake through that same heart.

*

The knock was familiar. Eileen turned from drying the dishes, but Clarice said, 'I'll see who it is,' and left the kitchen. Eileen heard her mother open the door, the soft background August rain, and a man's voice. She put down the towel and waited until her mother led her father in.

'Good evening, Girlie,' said Donald cordially, as he placed a battered and rain-spattered brown cap on the kitchen sideboard. He was tanned and leaner, and the hair around the sides and back was longer and greyer than when he was Military Police Sergeant Bonney. His damp and dirty grey overalls and sweat-smudged grey shirt reminded her of the father she knew before the war, the man who could laugh and surprise everyone with puppies and songs, the generous but firm man who loved his children, but that man was lost to the war. He never came home.

'Are you going to say anything?' Clarice prompted.

'Good evening, Father,' Eileen said.

'I see I am too late for a meal,' Donald observed.

'I can put leftovers on a plate,' Eileen offered.

'That would be nice,' he replied.

'Cuppa?' Clarice asked.

'Thanks, Mother,' Donald said.

Clarice filled the kettle and put it on to boil, while Eileen scooped the remaining mashed potato, peas and half a sausage onto a plate and placed it and a fork in front of her father. 'I'll be glad when the meat rationing is finally over,' Donald said as he picked up the fork. 'Men working on building jobs need good tucker to see them through. Time the government realised we don't need to keep feeding the British and Americans at the expense of our own working men.'

'But you are working,' Eileen said. 'I heard work is hard to get.'

'It is,' Donald said between mouthfuls, 'but the Government is talking about big building projects in electricity and housing, especially up in the northern cities around Port Pirie, Port Augusta and Whyalla. A smart man will make money out of that.'

'And that will be you,' Clarice said.

Donald chewed, swallowed, and replied, 'That will be me.'

'So why are you here?' Eileen asked, anger simmering from her last encounter with him.

'It happens that,' said Donald, mouth half-full, 'the Government has an initiative that gives you a nursing job, Girlie, if you want it.'

'I am not going back to Minda Home,' Eileen said bluntly. 'That place is horrible.'

Donald chuckled and said, 'Much better than that.' He lowered his fork. 'They have finished refurbishing Military Hospital 105 on Daws Road, and they are turning it into a general repatriation hospital. They are taking in new staff.'

'How do you know this?' Eileen asked.

'I still work with the Military Police when I am needed.' Donald replied. 'That is how I know. It will be a trainee position and you will live in the new Nurses' Quarters.'

'Why are you doing this?' Eileen asked.

'You cannot stay at home, Girlie,' Donald said. 'It's unhealthy for a girl your age to have nothing but idle time.'

'It's so you can avoid paying for us,' Eileen accused.

'Eileen Bonney!' Clarice gasped.

'You know it's true, Mum. He's making all of us pay for what should be his responsibility.' Eileen's voice trailed off as her father glared at her.

'Best go to your room and think about what you said,' Donald ordered coldly, his face reddening around his cheeks and ears.

Eileen eased around the kitchen, keeping as far from her father's reach as she could, although to get to the door she had to pass close by. 'You owe your father an apology,' Clarice said. 'He goes out of his way to look after you.'

Eileen lowered her eyes and crept past, anticipating a hand grabbing her. As she stepped into the hall, Ian called from upstairs, 'Is Father here?'

'Yes,' Eileen replied.

'Father's here!' Ian yelled, and he came barrelling down the stairs, followed by Wally, Judy and Josie. Eileen pressed against the wall to let the children pass.

'Coming?' Peter asked.

'Maybe,' Eileen replied. 'I'm tired.' She watched Peter descend and heard the greetings and joy of the others at seeing their father, and wished she felt the same, but they didn't know what she knew. Instead, she retreated to her bedroom, switched off the light and sat at the window, staring into the rain.

That her mother didn't keep her confidentiality disappointed her and, given all he did to Clarice, all the pain and sorrow she endured, Eileen couldn't fathom why her mother remained steadfastly loyal to him. He found her work at Ingerson's and took it away to punish her. She was sure the job at Minda was punishment as well, his way of controlling her. She wanted to hate him for it all, but she couldn't entirely hate him. And that made it all the more difficult to understand.

'Mind if I come in?'

Clarice's question snapped Eileen from her thoughts. 'You can put the light on.'

'No,' Clarice replied, sitting on the bed. 'It is nicer here in the dark watching the rain on the window.'

'It's soothing,' Eileen said, and she was silent, before asking, 'Is he gone?'

'He is spending time with the children,' Clarice explained. 'They don't get to see him as much as they should.'

'That's not their fault,' Eileen argued.

'No,' Clarice replied. 'And it's not entirely his fault either. I only let him come here when I feel it's necessary, or he has something important to discuss with me.'

'Why do you let him come here at all?'

Clarice sighed. 'He is still my husband, Girlie. And he feels responsible to be a father to you. I need him to be a father to you.'

Eileen had no energy or desire to argue with her mother. The rain and dark room were peaceful and all she wanted was peace from her personal turbulence. When Clarice was silent, she waited to see what her mother would say or do next rather than break the silence herself.

'It's a great opportunity,' Clarice finally said.

'What is?'

'The work he found. At the hospital. Many young girls would like a job like that.'

'Is it really an opportunity?'

Clarice shifted on the bed and took her daughter's hands in hers. 'There's nothing here for you, Girlie. You cannot waste your life looking after me and your brothers and sisters, moping away your days. You should be out working and getting on with your life.'

'But you've been sick.'

'I am much better,' Clarice said, squeezing Eileen's hands. 'The cleaning jobs give me something different to do in the daytime, and the children are getting bigger. I have been talking to Father Cavanaugh. There might be a better place coming up, with more room. And Donald might also have somewhere for us. And if you live at the hospital, you will be better off than living here.'

'I don't want it to be like last time,' Eileen said. 'I hate that place.'

'Oh, Girlie!' Clarice gently scolded. 'It won't be. You will be working with brave young women and men who saved our country, people not much older than yourself, people like Bruce. You will be doing an important service. There is no better job than being useful to others.' She placed an arm over Eileen's shoulder. 'I think you should take this opportunity.'

*

Peter passed the telephone receiver to Eileen. She lifted it to her ear, and said, 'Hello?'

'Jean Wright, Miss Bonney. Bet you're surprised to hear my voice.'

Eileen drew a breath, before she replied, 'Yes. I am.'

'No more than I am to be calling you,' Jean said caustically. 'Seems I've become a tout. I really don't approve of this, but I'm doing this for my little brother. Anyway, to the point. My errant brother is home on leave this Thursday and is hoping you might meet him at the train station in the city when he arrives. What do you say to that?'

'Oh,' Eileen gasped, and her heart raced. 'Thursday,' she repeated. 'What time?'

'Ten forty-five. Sharp, I believe. The army's been good for Spud. Finally made him punctual.' Eileen wrestled with writhing, conflicting emotion, until Jean prompted with, 'Well? Can you?'

'No,' Eileen said, and repeated, 'No. I'm sorry. I can't.' She thought she heard a muffled chuckle at the other end.

'Well, I'll let him know. You have finally got some sense, it seems. Bravo for you. Poor Spud will be devastated, of course, but what can he expect, really? Anyway, that's done. I won't keep you,' Jean said, and she hung up.

Eileen clutched the receiver, wondering if she made a mistake, wondering why she chose to say no when her heart was thumping furiously at the mention of Dudley. He came to her in dreams with promises and teased her with lingering memories of caresses and kisses, even after she knew she was not the only one in his sphere. She waited for him to say he was coming home again, hoped he might call. Now that he was coming home, he suddenly seemed less important.

She hung up the phone and walked into the kitchen where Clarice was scrubbing a pot, and Peter was seated at the table finishing a game of Solitaire, laying out the cards and studying them with greater relish than he ever studied his schoolbooks. 'Who was it?' Clarice asked.

'A woman,' Peter interrupted, without raising his eyes from the cards. 'A rather posh one,' he added, exaggerating the educated tone of his voice.

'A friend,' Eileen said. 'She was asking if I wanted to go out on the weekend.'

'Where?' Clarice asked.

'It doesn't matter,' Eileen said. 'I said no.' She flipped a card on Peter's playing deck before he could stop her, turning up a Two of Spades.

'Did I ask you to do that?' Peter challenged.
Eileen ignored him and said to Clarice, 'Can you ring Father, please, and tell him I will take the job?'

1948

"And then to see her the way she was that day leaves you with something you can't ever forget.'
Ulysses Johnson

The light was on, dowsing everything with a yellow hue. Eileen rubbed her eyes and stretched in her narrow bed, feeling the mattress lumps shift beneath her back. Women around her shuffled and sighed and yawned. Someone – Violet Baxter she guessed – said, 'It's another beautiful morning, girls! Rise and shine!' and Eileen smiled ruefully at Baxter's boundless enthusiasm and sarcasm. Grabbing her towel and toiletries bag, Eileen headed for the showers, hoping to be there before too many others, but the line-up was as long as every morning, so she waited in the bathroom block, feet shuffling on the cool concrete floor, until a cubicle was free. She recognised the petite dark-haired girl preparing to leave the shower, and said, 'Good morning, Kolesche.'

'Morning, Bonney,' Betty Kolesche replied cheerfully. 'I think there's still enough hot water. You know how quickly it runs out.'

Eileen showered swiftly, and skipped washing her hair, conscious the water was losing its heat. Dried and in her underwear, she pulled on her thick brown stockings, donned her grey nurse's dress, slipped into her starched white apron, tucked her hair neatly as high as she could, put on her white cap and laced up her brown shoes. 'Hurry up, girls,' Sister Overton urged. 'Breakfast is on.'

Eileen hurried to the canteen where she collected a bowl of porridge, a cup of tea – 'white and one' – and ate breakfast, listening to the chatter. Just before seven am, morning sunlight angling through the windows, she signed into the ward under the watchful eye of Sister Edwards and set to the first task; emptying bed pans. That odoriferous chore completed, she worked methodically along the line of beds, checking sheets for wetness, stripping those that were damp, making beds for patients who were able to be up and about, adjusting the pillows for those who were bed-ridden. Every day, since starting her cadetship at the Repatriation Hospital, the routine was monotonously maintained, minor variations excepted for visiting doctors or patient issues. Military routine ran the hospital.

'Bonney,' Sister Edwards called from the nurse's station. 'You can help Newton with Bed Seven please.'

Eileen emptied the bed pan she was holding, washed her hands at the sink and crossed the ward floor. 'Change the sheets,' Newton recommended, as Eileen reached her. 'A new one's coming in.'

'Where's Claire?' Eileen asked, naming the brunette WAAF with the lingering stomach wound who occupied the bed.

'Died last night,' Newton replied. 'Septicaemia.'

'Oh,' Eileen sighed. She started stripping the sheets from the bed. 'I thought she was doing all right.'

'So did Sister,' Newton said. 'Shame. She was a nice one.'

'Fifteen minutes to smoko!' Baxter announced as she strode past with an armful of linen. 'See you outside, girls.'

'When you finish the sheets, you might want to check on Missus Redwood in Bed Fifteen,' Newton advised. 'She's been very dehydrated. Make sure she's drinking and there's enough water for the poor dear.'

Eileen snapped the sheets tight in the stiff fashion demanded in training and checked for wrinkles before she moved to Bed Fifteen. 'Hello, Missus Redwood,' she said, smiling. 'How are you feeling?'

'Not good,' the woman croaked through cracking lips.

'When did you last have a drink?' Eileen asked, as she assessed the water level in the jug on the bedside cabinet. She filled a glass and carefully lifted Missus Redwood's head to assist her. As she lowered her patient's head, Missus Redwood whispered, 'Thank you.'

Eileen adjusted the pillow and sheet and said, 'I'll drop by later to see how you're going,' before she patted Missus' Redwood's arm and headed for the station.

'You'll need to remove that stain,' said Edwards as Eileen entered the space, nodding at a soiled mark on Eileen's starched white apron. 'Can't be tacky on duty.'

'Only off duty,' another nurse, Cooper, riposted, winking at Eileen.

'That is enough, Cooper,' Edwards warned, although the trace of a smile graced her lips.

Eileen grinned, and asked, 'Is there anything else I need to do before I go on break, Sister?'

'You can take these files to administration,' Edwards said, handing Eileen a manila folder. 'Chandler will know what to do with them.'

Eileen walked along the corridor and across the garden towards the Administration building, enjoying the warm February sunshine bathing the garden and bitumen drive. She delivered the folder before she headed to the plot closest to the Nurses' Quarters where she expected to find Baxter and fellow nurses coming off morning duty.

As she joined the circle of seated and standing women, Cooper held out a small red packet, saying, 'Fag?' Eileen withdrew a cigarette and waited for Cooper to offer matches.

'Shame about that girl in Bed Seven,' a short, stocky nurse named Gwen Henderson said. 'She was nice.'

'That's three this week,' Lyla Mann, noted softly, shaking her head.

'They say it's worse in the men's quarters,' Baxter said. 'Some of those poor bloody souls have all kinds of long-term illnesses.'

'I feel saddest for the ones with messed-up heads,' said Henderson. 'There's no cure for that. They scream all the bloody time. They must have seen terrible things.'

Eileen drew in smoke and exhaled. 'Becoming a professional smoker, Bonney,' said Baxter. 'You weren't that keen when you started.'

Eileen laughed and replied, 'Didn't know how good they could be.'

'Learned something about our Bonney, I did,' said Baxter.

'What?' Mann asked.

Eileen cocked an eyebrow. 'Yes, Baxter? What did you learn?'

Baxter gestured for the group to gather conspiratorially around her. 'It seems, 'she said, slowly, 'someone told a big fib about their age.'

'Oooh,' Mann and Henderson chorused, with accusing stares at Eileen.

'No.'

Eileen blushed and straightened. 'Someone isn't yet seventeen,' Baxter concluded, and she looked at Eileen with innocent eyes.

'Who told you?' Eileen challenged, feeling the heat in her cheeks.

'I might have looked in some records,' Baxter replied.

'Are you allowed to do that?' Mann asked.

Baxter laughed, and said, 'Of course I'm not bloody allowed to do that. But I did. I happened to be helping in Administration and I chanced upon the drawer with all our records.' She turned to Cooper who was strolling from the ward to join the group and said, 'For instance, this woman has a dark and mysterious past.'

'And to whatever are you referring, darling?' Cooper asked in an exaggerated tone.

'Your secret engagement,' Baxter announced.

'There's no secret about that liaison,' Cooper replied, reaching for a cigarette. 'I simply choose not to advertise personal disasters.'

The girls laughed and Eileen was glad to have Cooper's separation from her duplicitous boyfriend obliterate the discussion around her father's subterfuge to ensure she was taken in as a nurse cadet. The memory of his lies plagued her conscience. Dressed in his military uniform, he brought Eileen to the hospital Administration block and judiciously supervised the completion of her application form and interview. In the process, he made sure her birth year was registered as 1930, so she would meet the minimum age for the cadetship. He even waited while she underwent the mandatory medical and measurement for her new uniform, so adamant was he that she was to take the job. Not that she was contemplating otherwise. She was glad to be leaving the chaotic circumstances of family life at Brighton to live in the Nurses' Quarters, even if, as she discovered, it meant working regimented hours and sharing a room with other nurses.

'When are you seventeen, Bonney?' Mann asked.

Surprised by the conversation circling back, Eileen swallowed and replied, 'Next month. Please don't tell anyone.'

'Date?' Cooper asked.

'Twenty-fourth,' Eileen said, looking around guiltily.

'That will be a Monday,' Mann said.

'Oh, then we will have a party that week on the Saturday night!' Baxter declared.

'I'm rostered on that Saturday,' Eileen told them. 'I already checked.'

'Then we'll have a party when you're not rostered on!' Baxter announced and the other women applauded. 'Leave that to me.'

'Time to be back on deck,' Mann reminded the group.

'I just got here,' Cooper complained.

'Then you'll be here all on your little lonesome,' Baxter teased, running a hand over Cooper's shoulder as she passed her.

'I can do plenty on my own,' Cooper retorted, smiling wickedly. 'I'll see you girls inside.'

Eileen followed the others until she veered into the ward under her care. She smoothed down her apron, conscious of the stain that Sister Edwards pointed out, straightened the edges of her uniform, and adjusted her cap, acknowledging Kay Lambert, a friendly patient who waved.

Sometimes, especially in the early weeks, she had flashbacks to her weeks in Minda Home, remembering the sweet girls who needed her help, their endearing smiles and laughter, watching them sleep. Sometimes Eileen remembered the darker moments when the girls pitched tantrums in piques of frustration or had meltdowns that led to anger and throwing objects. The patients in Daws Road Repatriation Hospital were still coming home from the war, some with terrible wounds that were refusing to heal, infections, many with recurring diseases like malaria and tuberculosis, some with cancer and the like diagnosed while they were serving their country, even illnesses the doctors whispered about but did not explain to nurses like Eileen. For whatever reasons, mostly money and space Eileen assumed from comments made by her friends, patients were treated and moved on from the beds quickly – too quickly in certain cases because they returned with complications from surgery, regressions, secondary infections. Most improved and eventually went home. Some slowly got worse. Some died in the hospital. Some died at home.

And some patients were in the Repat because the ravages of the war were locked in their heads and souls, plaguing them with terrible visions and black thoughts requiring constant sedation and observation. They couldn't escape the war.

'When you finish staring out the window, Bonney, how about taking that pile of sheets across to the laundry?'

Eileen shifted her attention to Sister Edwards who cocked her head towards the linen basket, and said, 'Yes, Sister.' She wheeled the basket along the corridors to the laundry, the clacking wheels reminding her of the trams, collected a fresh linen trolley, wheeled it back to the ward, and continued her round, taking time to chat to the patients who were looking for company.

At lunch, the other nurses were waiting for Eileen in the canteen. 'All organised,' Baxter announced.

'What is?' Eileen asked as she placed her lunch tray on the table.

'I've checked the rosters and made sure we are all off on the Saturday after your birthday. We're going to a movie, then on to a dance in the city, and that's how we'll celebrate your birthday!'

'Sh,' Eileen urged, looking around. 'You'll get me in trouble.'

'For turning eighteen?' Kolesche asked. She winked and laughed. 'Unlikely,' and the nurses laughed with her.

'A few of the orderlies are coming along as well,' Mann said.

'How did you have time to organise this so quickly?' Eileen asked.

'Not what you know but who you know,' Baxter replied enigmatically.

*

Beneath a clear blue March sky, Eileen pedalled along South Road, clattering over the bumps and ridges in the bitumen, enjoying the cool breeze in her face and the freedom of her day off. Bruce left a message at the Repat to meet him at Auntie Fay and Uncle Spot's house, so Eileen borrowed Lyla Mann's bicycle and headed for Kurralta Park, eager to see her brother. Next pay, she would keep a little aside from sending it to her Mum and buy her own bike, a blue one that an orderly named Clarence was selling. The mid-morning traffic meant she rode with the other cyclists. She was wary of cars, trucks, and buses, but she liked cycling since she took to it at the hospital as a means of getting around, and she was enjoying the chance to ride, working her legs and lungs. She negotiated the traffic at the Anzac Highway intersection, crossed over, and cycled into the suburban streets of Kurralta Park until she reached her relatives' Federation-style home with its manicured front garden and trees. She halted, dropping a foot onto the kerb, and saw Uncle Spot standing in the front garden with a hoe, his Walker hat tilted back on his head. He looked up, recognised Eileen, and greeted her.

'Hello Uncle Spot,' she replied. She lifted the green bike onto the footpath and leaned it against the cream picket fence. 'Mind if I leave this here?'

'Bring it to the porch,' Spot urged. 'Someone might think it's up for grabs if you leave it there.' He strode to the gate and opened it for Eileen to wheel her bike through. 'What brings you here?' he asked as Eileen parked the bike against the cream porch pillar.

'Bruce said he wanted to see me,' Eileen explained.

'Well, go inside. I'm sure Fay will be very pleased to see you,' Spot said, and he waited for Eileen to open the door before he returned to hoeing weeds in a rose bed.

Eileen entered the house, appreciating its dark and cool interior, smelling the blend of musty wood, soap and mothballs when she passed the lushly furnished front parlour and bedrooms on her way to the kitchen. Auntie Fay was stirring a brown mixture in a red cake bowl and fresh cooking fragrances filled the air. 'Eileen!' Fay cried cheerily. 'Bruce said you might be here today. Come in. Sit down. I'll make a cup of tea.'

Eileen thanked Fay before she asked, 'Where is Bruce?'

'Where else but down the back with the horses,' Fay replied. 'Did you come by tram?'

'I rode.'

'On a bike? All the way from Daws Road?' Fay asked, and when Eileen grinned and nodded, Fay added, 'You must be exhausted, you poor thing.'

'It's not far at all,' Eileen replied.

'Would you like a cool drink first?'

'Water would be nice.'

'I can add lemon cordial,' Fay offered, and she opened a cupboard to retrieve a Cottee's bottle.

As Fay prepared and delivered the lemon-flavoured drink, she inquired about Eileen's work. Eileen told her she was learning a lot, and that she was generally enjoying it, but she admitted, 'The saddest part is when patients die. Sometimes it's obvious they're not going to make it, and it's hard to pretend they will when you work with them. But, when they go, it's a little easier because you know it's coming. The hardest is when we lose people who look like they will make it through, and then they suddenly die, and no one expects it.'

'Surely the doctors know what's happening to them,' Fay said.

'Maybe they do,' Eileen replied, 'but if they do, they don't tell us, and we're the ones who find them, and we have to lay them out.'

'That must be terrible,' Fay commiserated. She looked up at the back door and said, 'Here comes your brother.'

Bruce stomped his feet on the outside mat and removed his cap respectfully before he entered. Spying his sister, his face creased into a broad grin. 'Girlie,' he said. 'It's good to see you.' He hugged her and asked Fay for a glass of water, after which he said, 'Come down the back. I've something to show you.'

'I'm making a cuppa,' Fay said.

'We won't be long,' Bruce promised, and he took Eileen's wrist to lead her out.

Eileen followed her brother along a white gravel path into the back garden with its trimmed lawn, multi-coloured roses, pink oleander, purple lavender bushes and a large cypress shading the corner. The rear wire fence opened into the adjacent vacant block where three horses – one chestnut, one bay and one black – were grazing. All three raised their heads when Bruce and Eileen reached the fence, and the chestnut trotted towards them. 'This is Bayside Boy,' Bruce said, stroking the horse's nose as the horse presented it. 'Just "Boy" to us.'

'He's beautiful,' Eileen said.

'Go on,' Bruce urged. 'Pat him. He's quite the charmer.'

Eileen reached for the horse's neck and stroked it. Boy turned to her, and she rubbed his soft silken nose, crooning, 'Hello, Boy.'

'Boy is quite the pacer,' Bruce said. 'Uncle Spot is training him, ready to race next year.'

Eileen asked, 'You're happy here?'

Bruce grinned. 'I am now. I wasn't sure for a while, you know, the war, always a bit restless after coming back. Thought about travelling north, like a few mates have done, but Uncle Spot made it clear I had to make up my mind about what I wanted to do. I like working with the horses, so I stayed. I get a place to live, Spot pays a wage, and Auntie Fay makes a nice cup of tea.'

'Where's John?' Eileen asked.

'Mister Hoity-toity is working in the city at Faulding's,' Bruce replied dismissively.

'Why do you call him Mister Hoity-toity?'

'Ah, you know what he's like. Too college-educated for the rest of us. Thinks we're all stupid,' Bruce explained. 'Prefers to spend time with his business college chums, going to the theatre and other fancy things.'

'But you live together. You must spend some time with him?'

'I hardly see him,' Bruce said. 'He comes home, has his dinner with us when he feels like it, and goes to his room to read or play his records, or he goes out and doesn't come home until late. Anyway, Uncle Spot and I work with the horses, and he's not interested in them, so we don't have much to talk about.'

'I haven't seen John in months, not since early last year,' Eileen confessed.

'You haven't missed much.' Bruce paused, and added in a conspiratorial tone with a wink, 'But I have seen the fugitive.'

'Clive?' Eileen gasped. 'Where?'

'He's around,' Bruce teased.

'Around where?' Eileen pleaded.

'Now I promised not to lag,' Bruce said, his tone becoming serious. 'He's working.'

'Doing what? Is he all right?'

'I'll organise for us to all meet at the trots,' Bruce promised. 'He's labouring, doing odd building jobs, making a few bob, here and there. Says he has a business prospect in the wind.'

'I really want to see him,' Eileen said. 'It's been far too long.'

'Blame the old man for that,' Bruce said. 'How's Mother?'

'Struggling,' Eileen said. 'I send most of my money home to help out, like you did when you were away.'

'I still do,' Bruce told her. 'You know he doesn't give her anything.'

'He's meant to-' Eileen started, but Bruce cut her off.

'That mean bastard wouldn't give anyone the sweat off his back in a heatwave. You know that, Girlie. He's a mean bastard. If I hadn't sent Mum my service pay, you would have been out of that house long before you were kicked out. I was so surprised when I came home and learned you'd been living in a tent down on the beach. No man with a spine does that to his wife and kids.'

'He found me jobs so I can help out.'

'He got you jobs so he didn't have to pay anything. He was doing that to me and Clive before he started on you. He was trying to get me to leave the Navy patrols on the Port River to join him in the Military Police so he could use me for his own ends. That's why I went and joined the Airforce – to get away from him.'

'Clive told me he knew things, but he wouldn't say what,' Eileen remembered.

'He made Clive join the Navy before the poor kid was old enough, but Clive went AWOL before they put him into training,' Bruce said. 'Cheeky bugger.'

'I didn't know anything about that. Is that why Father was chasing him?'

Bruce laughed, replying, 'And couldn't catch him. Cunning as a sewer rat and slippery as an eel.' He shook his head. 'It will catch up with the old man one day, mark my words.'

'Have you seen him lately?'

'The old man?' Bruce asked. 'I see him around. He's still in the Military Police. He can't seem to make anything out of building.'

Boy nudged Eileen with his nose. 'Yes, I'll pat you,' Eileen said, stroking the horse.

'Do you want to help me feed these lads?' Bruce asked.

'Yes please,' Eileen replied.

Riding home in the late afternoon, the low sun over her shoulder throwing long shadows ahead, Eileen mused over the fun with the horses and Bruce. Bruce was lucky he had Uncle Spot to mentor him, fortunate to find a place and purpose. Since working in the Repat, she learned how so many young men returned from the war to unemployment, broken families, lost dreams, and hopelessness. Like Bruce mentioned, some drifted deeper into the country, some headed interstate in the hope of finding work and new lives, and some sank into the depths of bottles. And the afternoon's happiness helped her to push down the bubbling anger she felt rising against her errant and irresponsible father who left scars across everyone. She wanted to be happy. Happiness was the best feeling, like the wind on her face and through her hair when she rode fast. She was definitely buying Clarence's bicycle.

*

Doctor Longridge sat on his stool before Eileen, repositioned his rimless glasses, and said, 'For your own health, Bonney, having those rotten teeth removed will be a fillip, and will save you and your family a lot of money in dental care. You are very lucky you're working here in the hospital because we can do all this for free.'

'Completely free?' Eileen asked.

'That, young lady, is one of the benefits for serving your nation. Free dental and medical treatment.'

'Do I have to have all my teeth out?'

'All teeth rot, sooner or later. It's a natural thing. Some people seem to be lucky and escape it, but most people don't. Unfortunately, you have chalky teeth, and they are more susceptible to decay than normal teeth. You don't want this type of pain coming back into your life every six months for the next twenty years, do you?'

Eileen shook her head. The thought of recurring toothache for years terrified her. 'So, I'll have dentures?' she asked.

'The dentures we will make for you will be bright, like a Hollywood starlet's smile, and the latest vulcanite and ceramic moulds will fit you perfectly and look totally natural. They are easy to care for, too, because you only clean them overnight to start fresh the next day. If the truth was known, it's better than having your own teeth.'

'How long does all this take?'

Longridge adjusted his glasses on his nose. 'We'll take impressions and a mould today to get the best possible natural fit organised. We'll send that to the lab, and they will make your dentures. Then you pop back in here, we remove the rotten teeth, and fit the new ones.'

'Straight away?'

'Generally, yes,' Longridge replied. 'Sometimes we may have to allow the gums to heal, but we will avoid that if we can.'

Eileen listened as Longridge explained how long it was going to take her to adjust to the new set of teeth and what she should expect, and she asked her final questions before Longridge ended the consultation. Freed from the dental chair, Eileen walked through the feeble sunlight to the Nurses' Quarters where she lay on her bed, wondering if she was making the right decision. She winced when a nerve jangled beneath her decaying molar.

'Penny for your thoughts?' Baxter asked when she strolled in.

'Have you had all your teeth out?' Eileen asked.

Baxter sat on Eileen's bed as she answered. 'Not yet. I know Ellison has, and O'Docherty. Why?'

'Doctor Longridge said I should,' Eileen explained. 'He says my teeth are chalky and won't last.'

'He is a dentist,' Baxter said. 'He should know what's good for you.'

'It's scary,' Eileen murmured.

'Perish the thought,' Baxter said, 'but, if Longridge told me what he obviously told you, I'd get it done.'

'What's going on?'

The young women turned to Mann, who stood at the door. 'Bonney's been advised to get her teeth out,' Baxter explained.

Mann approached, grinned, and said, 'You should do it. You'll have all new shiny white teeth and no toothache ever again.'

'It scares me,' Eileen replied.

Mann sat beside Baxter. 'Do you know that, in Scotland, parents buy a set of new teeth for their daughters when they're engaged to be married? It's a personal gift to ensure the newlyweds aren't saddled with expensive dental costs in the time of their life when they least need expensive bills.'

'Surely that's not true, is it?' Eileen asked.

'Claire McGinty's parents did it for her last year,' Mann said.

'Who's Claire McGinty?' Eileen asked.

'You haven't met her. She left after she got married,' Mann replied.

'Was she happy?'

'About getting married, or getting new teeth?'

'Her teeth,' Eileen pressed.

'Her teeth looked amazing!' Mann said. 'She said she couldn't have made a better choice.'

'There's your answer,' Baxter said.

'I'll think about,' Eileen decided.

'In the meantime, we have a big party to organise,' Mann said. 'And you, young lady, get to be another year older.'

*

Sister Edwards held up the receiver in the nurses' station, saying, 'There's a phone call for you, Bonney.' Eileen smoothed down the sheet she was changing, shrugged at Kolesche, who was staring quizzically, and crossed the ward to the station, glancing at the clock. Seven-fifteen pm. 'Personal calls are not allowed on duty,' Edwards reminded her, as she handed the receiver to Eileen. 'Your brother better have a very good reason for ringing.'

Eileen took the receiver and said, 'Hello?'

There was a pause on the other end, before a familiar voice said, 'Eileen, I have to see you.'

She drew a sharp breath and glanced at Sister Edwards who was busy shuffling a pile of files on the bench. 'You shouldn't ring me here.'

'I told the Sister I was your brother and there is an urgent family matter I needed to speak to you about,' Dudley said. 'And I do need to see you urgently.'

'You know why I can't see you.'

'That's all over, Eileen. It's in the past.'

'How can I believe you?' Eileen challenged. 'You lied before.'

'I owe you the biggest apology,' Dudley said. 'And I want to make that apology in person. Please. I'm back for good now. Let me take you to the movies on Saturday. We can talk. I can explain.'

Eileen saw Edwards' glowering gaze. 'I have to go.'

'Meet me at West's city cinema, two in the afternoon,' Dudley pleaded. 'Please.'

Eileen hesitated, before agreeing. 'All right. Saturday. Goodbye.' She didn't wait to hear his reply. She hung up the receiver and apologised to Sister Edwards for the interruption.

'See that it doesn't happen again, Bonney,' Edwards said. 'I should report this incident, but I will overlook it this once.'

'Thank you, Sister,' Eileen said, and she withdrew from the station.

'Is everything all right?' Kolesche asked when Eileen returned to continue changing the sheets.

Eileen tried to smile, but her emotions betrayed her. 'Something's come up,' she said.

'What?' Kolesche asked.

'I can't really say,' Eileen replied, 'but I can't go Saturday. You have to explain it to everyone for me.'

'Oh,' Kolesche said, disappointed. 'That is a shame. We were all so looking forward to dancing and playing up a little.'

'You should all still go. It's just I can't go – because – well, because of what's happened.'

'You can tell me,' Kolesche coaxed. 'I won't gossip, not like the others.'

'I know,' Eileen said. 'You're a good friend, Kolesche, but this is a very private thing. I can't tell anyone.'

'What do I tell the girls?'

Eileen stopped turning down a sheet. 'Say I've got to be home for my Mum. Say it's something to do with her being very unwell.'

'I will,' Kolesche promised. 'But remember, I am here if you need to talk to someone about this.'

Evening shift over, the ward glowing with low night lights, Eileen walked into the grounds between the buildings and sat on a step in the shadows. She fished in her pocket for a cigarette she half-smoked earlier in the evening shift break, lit it, drew a draught, and exhaled with a long sigh. Common sense warned her not to meet Dudley, like when she decided not to meet him at the train last October. He was meant to be the past. Time should have healed her pain. But it didn't. Instead, Dudley came to her in dreams, lingered at the edges of daytime musing, haunted her when her guard was down. Hearing his voice again, hearing him beg to see her, ignited the past and sent shock waves through her heart, reminding her of his disarming smile, the light in his soft brown eyes, the passion he brought to life in her, tingling lips, the spark in his touch. Logic warned her, but her heart dared her, begged her with the same desperation as Dudley begged.

She dropped her cigarette and stamped on the butt, outraged sparks flaring and vanishing. Meeting Dudley was sure to be a mistake, but, if he had ended the other relationship, would she miss an opportunity to pursue her heart's desires if she didn't go this time? She replayed his phone call over in her mind. The timbre of his voice was different, altered, softer. Something was changed. *I will go*, she decided. *I need to know.*

*

She pedalled harder when the railway bridge and road underpass appeared on Goodwood Road and lifted her feet, crying 'Wheeee!' as the blue bike sped to the bottom. At the base, she pedalled furiously to make it to the top, bike chain straining, pedals groaning, and Eileen puffing and grinning with pride at her success. She checked for traffic, let a black Ford sedan cruise by and three cyclists, and crossed the road to the Millswood railway station. She originally planned to ride into the city, but halfway along Goodwood Road she changed her mind. She also wondered why Dudley chose not to meet her at the Torrens Park station near his family home, but perhaps he was planning to be in the city during the day. Not that it mattered. She enjoyed the opportunity to ride. Ticket bought, bike stowed, train arrived, she boarded and settled into the leather seat to watch houses roll by.

Yesterday, when her friends learned she wasn't going out with them, Baxter and the other nurses pressed her for an explanation. 'We organised this for you,' Baxter complained. 'Can't your mother wait one day?'

'Oh, Baxter,' Kolesche intervened. 'That's not fair.'

Baxter shook her head. 'Yes, I know,' she agreed, 'but we're so bloody disappointed.'

'Another time,' Eileen vowed. 'It hasn't worked out this weekend, that's all.'

'Bet there's a boy,' Cooper teased.

The accusation made Eileen blush, which only worsened the attention of the others. 'There bloody is!' Baxter said. 'Look at her go red!'

'Who is it?' Cooper pressed. 'What's his name?'

'There is no boy!' Eileen retorted. 'You girls are terrible!'

'A girl's face tells no lies,' Mann stated. 'That's what my Mum always says when I try to pull a porky over her.'

'If it is a boy,' Cooper said, 'we can only forgive you if you tell us his name.'

'There is no boy!' Eileen insisted.

'We believe you,' Baxter said, winking at the others. 'Please look after your poor old mum, and make sure she is very comfortable.' The young women giggled provocatively, and Eileen warned them to be respectful.

The train pulled into Adelaide railway station and Eileen alighted on the platform, the air tainted with the piquant railway odours of steam and grease and oil. People hurried from the carriages, singles, couples, groups and families heading into the city to shop, to be entertained, or to simply kill time. She noted there were fewer military uniforms and people were wearing less austere styles and seemed happier. The immediate world was assuming a sense of order, although radio reports and the newspapers portrayed a world seething with turmoils, some created directly from the war's aftermath, many re-emerging from the pre-war past. An Indian man named Gandhi was assassinated in January, and some of Eileen's nursing friends said it was a shame he was killed, especially with India establishing autonomy from England, although Eileen couldn't see why so much fuss was being made over one man's death in a foreign land. She thought the bigger issues were that the British Empire was crumbling all over the world, Communism was spreading through Europe and Asia, threatening democratic freedoms, and people in the Middle East were wrestling over whether Israel should exist. Baxter told everyone she thought it was only right the Jewish people were allowed to have their homeland given back, after everything that happened to them in the war and, while everyone agreed in principle, Cooper said she wasn't so sure it was fair to the Arabic people who'd been living around Jerusalem for a very long time. Eileen shrugged. In the end, even these issues were far away in foreign lands, and less important than what was happening to her right now.

The clock showed one forty-five when she passed through the main hall and ascended the stairs onto North Terrace. She crossed the road and headed along Victoria Street towards West's cinema in Hindley Street where Dudley was waiting. She couldn't see him among the people milling to enter the solid white Art Deco façade. The billboards advertised "Arch of Triumph", a movie Eileen hadn't heard of, but Ingrid Bergman was in it, so she expected the movie to be serious and interesting.

Eileen entered the foyer, marvelling at the swanky interior with its plush carpet and colourful murals, but her eyes were drawn, as they were the first time she came to the cinema with Dudley, to the sweeping curved staircases, and for a moment she imagined herself as a princess in a European palace, waiting for her lover, the music building towards a climax as her eyes roved the room for him.

She spied Dudley on a maroon couch, dressed in a brown cable knit sweater and tan trousers, with polished brown shoes, his brown hair parted and combed neatly back. He held two tickets. He rose as she approached, and he looked unnaturally thin. 'Eileen,' he said, reaching for her hand. 'I'm so glad you came. I've missed you terribly.' His hand was warm and sweat beaded on his forehead.

'Are you all right?' Eileen asked.

Dudley squeezed her hand, replying, 'I am so much better now that you are here. I've bought the tickets. Do you want an ice-cream?'

'No, thank you,' she said. Although the idea of an ice-cream appealed to her, the mention of it caused her aching molar to twinge.

'Let's go in, then,' he urged.

She wanted to ask the important question, the matter that determined whether she should even be with him, but he led her up the grand staircase and into the cinema before she could do more than tell him she was pleased to see he had returned from New Guinea. 'It must have been terrible,' she said, as they took their seats.

'Not as bad as people think,' he replied dismissively. 'I forgot to ask. You haven't seen this movie, have you?'

'No,' Eileen answered, conscious that he abruptly changed the topic.

'Good,' he said. 'Let's enjoy this time together.'

The lights dimmed and the shorts began. The curtains shifted, the music swelled as the main feature commenced, revealing the famous Parisian structure, the actors and the reference to Erich Maria Remarque's 1945 novel. Dudley held Eileen's hand and patted it with his other hand, but she was sensitive to the heat and clamminess in his contact, and he was shaking. 'Dudley,' she whispered, 'you're ill.'

'It's nothing,' he replied. 'A cold.'

'This isn't a cold. You need to see a doctor.'

'After the movie,' Dudley replied. 'Please. Let me have this moment.'

Eileen acquiesced despite her fear that he was suffering from something far more sinister than a cold. Patients in the Repatriation Hospital who presented with symptoms like Dudley had malaria. She'd seen it enough times. So many returning personnel came home with malaria from the South-East Asian jungles.

Halfway through the movie, as Charles Boyer and Ingrid Berman sped along a highway, Dudley's shaking worsened. 'That's enough,' Eileen said. 'You're very sick. I'll take you to the hospital.' She stood and led him along the row, to the chagrin of other patrons, and down the stairs into the foyer. Sweating profusely, trembling, pale, Dudley fumbled in his pocket and fished out a metal container. He opened it and swallowed a tablet. 'I'll fetch water,' Eileen said.

Dudley was seated on a sofa when she returned with water from the confectionary bar. He drank and sat forward, elbows on his knees. 'I am so dreadfully sorry,' he apologised.

'It's malaria, isn't it?'

Dudley nodded. 'Afraid so. Bloody Port Moresby mosquitoes.'

'I'll get you to the hospital,' Eileen offered.

'No,' he replied. 'Won't do. They'll just prescribe what I already know. Ask someone here if you can ring my father. He'll come and get me. Or my sister.' He grabbed Eileen's hand. 'I'm so sorry, Eileen. I wanted tonight to be something special.'

'I'll ring your father,' Eileen promised. 'Wait here. I'll be right back.'

*

Baxter and Cooper danced into the canteen, twirling as though they were still on the Saturday night dance floor, and they swept onto seats beside Eileen who was stirring her mushy Weetbix. 'You missed a fabulous evening,' Cooper said, fluttering her eyelashes.

'The music, the dancing, oh, and the boys,' Baxter said, feigning a swoon.

'The boys indeed,' Cooper agreed, and the women laughed.

'We all absolutely missed you, Bonney,' Baxter said. 'How is your mother?'

'My mother is fine,' Eileen replied, and she scooped a spoonful of cereal and milk. 'I did the right thing by going.'

'Well, that's nice to hear,' Baxter said, and added, 'Besides, the boys didn't miss you at all,' and she winked conspiratorially at Cooper.

'The boys certainly were enraptured with Baxter,' Cooper said raunchily, and she dodged a lazy slap attempt from Baxter, laughing as she straightened.

'Girls!' Kolesche remonstrated as she approached from the servery with her breakfast tray. 'Far too much frivolity! Best behaviour please!'

'Yes, Miss Kolesche,' Cooper and Baxter chorused, and they sat obediently, hands crossed on their laps, imitating chastened and angelic schoolgirls.

'Much better,' Kolesche said. She sat beside Eileen. 'How was Saturday?'

'Fine,' Eileen replied. 'Not as good as yours, it seems.'

The women laughed, and Kolesche said, 'Dancing is always fun, and finally, after all these years, there are men to dance with. You must come next time, Bonney.'

'I will,' Eileen promised. 'I will.'

Breakfast eaten, teas swallowed, the nurses headed for the wards, hurrying across the open spaces as grey clouds dumped a steady drumming rainfall on the metal roofs. Eileen clocked in with Sister Edwards and worked in tandem with Kolesche to attend each patient's needs, administer medicines, check and change beds, chat where asked, and sort through arriving breakfasts. By morning break, she was exhausted. She headed outside, under the shelter of a veranda, fished a cigarette from her pocket and leaned against the wall, watching the rain pool in puddles on the pavement as she smoked.

Her thoughts wandered to images of Dudley on Saturday night, his saddened and exhausted brown eyes, his shaking hands and sweaty face, his voice cracking as he persisted in apologising for his illness. And then Jean Wright strode into the foyer in loose grey trousers and a brown vest, her blond hair tied in a ponytail, accompanied by a tall and broad-shouldered stranger. 'Really, Spud! You simply never listen to reason, do you?' Jean scolded, as her male companion hoisted Dudley to his feet and steered him towards the doors. She glared at Eileen. 'I'm surprised to see you here,' she remarked. 'My brother really isn't very clever, you know.' And she strode out, leaving Eileen standing alone with the cinema attendants staring at her.

Seeing Kolesche emerge from the ward, Eileen wiped away her tears and offered her friend a cigarette. 'You've certainly taken to smoking with a vengeance,' Kolesche observed. She accepted the offer and waited for Eileen to use her lit cigarette to light Kolesche's.

'Something to do,' Eileen replied, 'and it's relaxing.'

'The woman in bed twenty-one isn't looking good this morning,' Kolesche noted. 'Sister doesn't think she'll see the night.'

'Poor thing,' Eileen murmured.

'Guess we'll get the laying out job again.'

'Someone has to treat them right,' Eileen said. 'Her husband will take it bad.'

'Sister is ringing him.' Kolesche paused, after she drew a breath of smoke, before she inquired, 'Are you all right?'

'Why?' Eileen asked, wondering what Kolesche saw.

'You look like you've been crying.'

'Oh,' Eileen said, leaning forward and wiping her cheek again. 'It's nothing.'

'Your mother isn't well?'

Eileen shook her head. 'No. Mum is fine. I was remembering something – from my past.'

'Do you want to talk about it?'

'No,' Eileen replied. 'There's not much to talk about.' She sat against the wall, drew in a lungful of smoke, and exhaled, hoping Kolesche would let the topic drop. She did, and Eileen was grateful.

*

'Missus Wright?' Eileen queried hopefully.
　'Speaking,' said the woman on the other end of the line. 'Who is this?'
　'Eileen.'
　'Eileen who?' Missus Wright asked.
　'Eileen Bonney.'
　'Have we met?'
　Eileen hesitated. 'Yes. I had lunch at your house.'
　'Oh. Are you a friend of Jean's?'
　'No,' Eileen replied. 'Dudley brought me to meet you last year.'
　'Yes, dear. What do you want?'
　'I was hoping I could speak to Dudley.'
　'Dudley is out,' Missus Wright replied. 'Would you like to leave a message for him?'
　'I was wanting to know how he is. You, know – his malaria.'
　'Oh, he has good days and bad days. These poor boys have given a lot for their country, dear. Coming home so sick isn't supposed to be part of it, is it?'
　'Please tell him I called.'
　'I will, dear. What was your name again?'
　'Eileen Bonney,' Eileen replied.
　'I will let Dudley know you called,' Missus Wright said. 'Goodbye.'
　'Goodbye,' said Eileen. She waited until she heard Missus Wright hang up before she lowered her receiver, her hand trembling.
　'Finished?' asked the duty orderly at the office desk.
　'Thank you,' Eileen said.
　Walking between the Administration office and the Nurses' Quarters, Eileen felt emptiness gnaw at her gut, stringing her nerves tight. Missus Wright' indifference made her feel estranged and uncomfortable, as if the woman never acknowledged Eileen's place in Dudley's life; as if Dudley

never mentioned her in his home. She remembered Missus Wright as neatly attired with glasses perched on her nose like a school mistress. She seemed polite, clever. The day Eileen visited, Missus Wright listened rather than talked, and she didn't ask Eileen more than a couple of generic questions. Where did she live? What school did she go to? What was her father's occupation? Did she mind peas without gravy? The conversation was inane, the conversation a person sustained when they had no interest in the other person. It wasn't that Missus Wright was rude, but now Eileen realised that she treated Eileen's presence as a momentary aberration.

Baxter was leaning against the Nurses' Quarters entrance when Eileen arrived, surreptitiously finishing a cigarette, since they were not meant to smoke around the dormitories. 'Evening, Nurse Bonney,' she said, pretending to be a person of authority. 'Shouldn't you be in bed?'

'Shouldn't you?' Eileen retorted.

'Enough of your sass, young lady,' Baxter warned. 'Now, off to bed!'

Eileen sashayed into the Nurses' Quarters, but Dudley and his mother's disaffected phone conversation lingered in anticipation of her dreams. It seemed Missus Wright, like Dudley's sister, thought Eileen wasn't good enough for Dudley. *Well, that isn't true*, Eileen decided. Dudley sure thought otherwise, and Eileen wasn't ready to let a pair of snobby women tell her who she could or could not love.

*

The lights flickered. Eileen paused, pan in hand, listening to the wind whistling across the metal roof and rattling the windows. Ward Sister Ambrose opened the fuse cabinet and checked the issue wasn't with the electrical wiring. Eileen glanced at the clock. Four pm. The patient she was assisting, Colin Lyons, said, 'Never seen a storm like this in April.' The lights flickered again and went out. Ambrose closed the cabinet in the Nurses Station and picked up the phone.

Pan emptied and sanitised, Eileen returned to the ward as the lights blinked back on. 'Electricity wires are down somewhere,' Ambrose said. 'Generators will keep us going. This is a wild old Sunday.'

'There might be something more to hear on the radio,' said Rodney

Ellis, in the nearest bed. 'Can we listen, Sister?'

Radio reports confirmed the gale was wreaking havoc across Adelaide, especially along the shoreline. The Glenelg jetty was dramatically torn apart by ferocious waves, and a man named Archie Pudney was stranded at the kiosk on the end of the jetty, despite valiant efforts by lifesavers to rescue him. HMAS Barcoo, a wartime frigate and survey vessel, was beached between Glenelg and West Beach, several crew still aboard. City centre businesses were damaged. Beams from the roof of the old Ozone theatre in Prospect smashed through houses and the local police station, narrowly missing a woman. The Thebarton police barracks and a factory on Port Road lost roofs.

The news unsettled Eileen. Even though her family were several streets from the beachfront at Brighton, the suburb was in the teeth of the gale, and she feared for her mother's safety. She asked Sister Ambrose if she could call, but when she tried the telephone lines were dead.

'It's a terrible situation,' Ambrose agreed. 'But I'm sure your mother will be all right.'

'I really have to go to Brighton at the end of this shift,' Eileen said.

'And how would you do that in this weather, Bonney?' Ambrose asked. 'I wouldn't allow it.'

'But what if my family are in danger?'

Ambrose took her hand. 'We all have family out in that storm, Bonney. My husband works for the Fire Department, so I know he will be right in the middle of all this mess, and I can't do anything about it. All I can do is pray the Lord will look after him. And that's all you can do, too. Say a quiet prayer. God will look after your family. Go on. Say a prayer. And then see to our patients, please.'

Shift finished, Eileen retreated to the Nurses Quarters where she listened with her friends to the reports coming in about the state-wide damage, heard the squally wind and driving rain tormenting the Repat buildings and trees, and wondered if her family were safe from the brutal tempest tearing through Adelaide.

*

'We're moving to Port Neill,' Judy announced.

Eileen was dumbfounded by her sister's revelation. She rode to Brighton when it was safe to do so to check how her family weathered the freak autumn storm only to discover they were leaving Hatter's Mansion. 'Why?' she asked.

'Dad has a building contract,' Judy explained.

'You're going with Father?'

'Why wouldn't we?' Judy asked.

Eileen had a raft of reasons why the family shouldn't go anywhere with their father, but she felt obligated not to tell tales. 'Where is Port Neill?'

'On Eyre Peninsula.'

'But that's hundreds of miles away,' Eileen gasped. 'How will you get there?'

'Dad is driving us. We're going in his truck. It will be an adventure.'

'Everyone?'

Judy laughed. 'No, Girlie. Peter is staying in Adelaide because he has a job. Ian's going as Dad's apprentice to learn the building trade. So that's Mother, me, Josie and Wally. I'm hoping I can get a job there, too.'

'Doing what?' Eileen asked.

'I don't know. Working in a shop? I've finished school.'

Eileen studied her little sister who wasn't little any longer. 'Where is everyone?'

'Josie and Wally are at school. Peter and Ian are working. And Mum's out cleaning. So, there's only me.'

'Is there a bike?' Eileen asked. 'We could go for a ride and look at what's left of the jetty.'

'Dad's old bike is out the back. I'll go get it,' Judy said.

As she rode with Judy along sections of the Brighton to Glenelg foreshore in the late afternoon sun, Eileen marvelled at the detritus of broken planks, tree boughs, half-buried boats and smashed bathing huts littering the sand, and the gouges scooped from the seawalls that were meant to protect the esplanade and houses. The sisters stared at the pitiful remnants of the Glenelg pier. The walkway planks were gone. The solitary aquarium stood stranded at what had been the midway point along the jetty and further out the marooned pavilion leaned precariously on the surviving L-shaped pier.

'Did you hear about the warship?' Judy asked pointing north towards West Beach. 'I heard they are going to try to re-float her today or tomorrow. It's all very exciting, isn't it?'

'It is,' Eileen agreed, although she wondered who was going to pay for repairing everything and who was going to do it. The jetty looked irreparable. 'We best get back,' she said. 'I'll talk to Mum when she gets home.'

'She doesn't get home until late,' Judy said.

'That's all right,' Eileen replied as she turned her bicycle and mounted the seat. 'I'm not on shift until tomorrow morning. I can wait. I need to know what's happening.'

Cool night wind in her face, streetlights throwing silver patches across Daws Road, Eileen pedalled towards the hospital, her mind whirling with the changes her mother explained as they shared an evening meal. Everything Judy told her was corroborated by Clarice. With the children at the table, Eileen could do little more than listen and ask plain questions – When? How long? Where were they going to live? She had no opportunity to ask her mother the bigger questions – Why? Why was she going to live with Donald again? What was going to happen after his work at Port Neill finished? She couldn't understand why Clarice was willing to give her father another chance after the way he treated her. Port Neill was so far away.

Headlights enfolded her as a solitary bus came from behind and rattled past, hot exhaust air engulfing her, before she pedalled into the Repat driveway and stopped at the gate to identify herself to the guard. 'Evening, Bonney,' the soldier said as he lifted the boom. 'Late night.'

'Family,' she replied, walking her bike into the grounds. *Family*, she thought as she headed for the Nurses Quarters. *Complicated, mixed-up family*.

*

Eileen straddled the BSA's black leather pillion, tucking her dark green dress up and in to maintain dignity, wrapping her arms around Bob's waist, her bony knees angled away from his thighs. The bike bumped and vibrated and chattered as it growled in acceleration. An orderly on Ward Six, Bob asked her to be his partner at dances several times in the preceding weeks, but Eileen politely declined each time, using work or being tired as her excuses. This time, however, she relented. The occasion was a special event in the city at the Embassy Ballroom designed to raise money for her bid to be crowned Queen of the Repat. Everyone from the hospital was going, except those rostered to work, like Baxter, who was frustrated she couldn't be there. 'I run around and get all these people to raise money and get behind you, and then Sister rosters me on tonight. Where's the bloody justice in that?' she asked. 'It will be so much fun, and I miss out!'

'We'll dance for you,' Kolesche promised. 'I won't steal all the good-looking men.'

'That's because none of them will dance with you,' Baxter teased, and the group laughed. 'And how is everyone going to get there?' Baxter asked.

'Well,' said Henderson, pausing for effect, 'most of us are catching the bus. Mann is getting her brother to take her in. And the Queen-in-waiting,' she said, bowing affectedly to Eileen, 'is going on the back of a certain bloke's motorbike.'

The girls teased Eileen. Bob, a broad-shouldered, bespectacled and handsome orderly, made it very clear to everyone he was keen on Nurse Bonney. 'There'll be one very happy man at the dance,' Baxter concluded. 'Treat him nicely, Bonney. He has a fragile heart. It won't take well to a shock.'

'Whatever do you mean by that?' Eileen protested, and everyone laughed again.

The BSA engine thumped and Eileen held tight to Bob's waist as he sped along Goodwood Road. The city was settling into evening, the final vestiges of sunset fading in the west, travelling vehicles turning on their headlights, streetlights winking on. Eileen thrilled to the motorbike's speed and power as Bob accelerated and weaved along the road. 'Lean with me through the corners!' he yelled, as they approached Greenhill Road, and Eileen obediently leaned with him as they turned right. 'Very good!' he yelled, 'You're a natural,' and he opened the throttle briefly, before slowing, turning left onto Brown Street towards Gouger Street.

She was reluctant at the outset when her friends nominated her to participate in the charity event as an entrant. Baxter, Mann, Kolesche and Henderson gathered around her in the canteen. 'Come on, Bonney,' Baxter urged. 'You have to do this. We all want you to do it.'

'You're the prettiest girl on the ward,' Kolesche told her. 'What with your new teeth and amazing smile, you're a movie star!'

She smiled at Kolesche's remark. The weeks of pain after having her dentures fitted were worth it. Apart from initial discomfort, and the unexpected and awkward experiences of learning to eat and speak again, the dentures fitted flawlessly and when she smiled in the mirror the young woman smiling back had that Hollywood lustre of perfect teeth. The processes of removing her teeth to clean them and placing them in a glass of vinegar and water overnight were strange, but she adapted to the routine and the sensation of sleeping toothless. When her friends asked her to take part in the Charity event, she was confident that at least she would have a dazzling smile. 'All the orderlies and nurses I talk to say they'll raise money for you,' Henderson added. 'You have to do this.'

'Queen of the Repat!' said Mann, grinning. 'And we can be your princesses!'

'Princess Violet,' Baxter said, pretending to be dreamy. 'I do like the sound of that.'

'You don't need a title to be a princess, Baxter,' Kolesche taunted.

'You are definitely our entry,' Baxter said. 'I'll let the organisers know.' She turned to the canteen and announced loudly, 'Listen up! Bonney is our entry in the Queen of the Repat competition. Start shelling out your donations, people!' Her declaration received a ragged cheer and several more nurses gathered around the group.

'I'll do your hair,' Kolesche offered, and she began to undo Eileen's cap.

'Stop that,' Eileen protested, pushing Kolesche's hands away. 'I have to do evening roster.'

She was conscious of the build-up of traffic as they reached the intersection of Gouger Street and King William Street, but Bob's relaxed riding skill boosted her confidence, and she trusted him to deliver her safely to the Grenfell Street ballroom venue. It was fun on the back of Bob's motorbike. Although her older brothers owned motorbikes, she never rode one by herself, although she longed to do so. Motorbikes were popular because cars were too expensive to buy and run on rationed petrol, and pushbikes were too slow. The pillion experience was exciting, wind brushing her face and streaming through her hair. It gave her a sense of freedom, like floating in the ocean, only more exciting. She leaned with Bob as he turned into Victoria Square, concentrating on her centre of balance to help him, so she didn't see the approaching car, only felt a solid thump that sent her spinning.

*

The white walls and curtain perplexed her. She was meant to be standing, looking down at a patient, not be the patient in the bed. 'I will come back shortly,' the brunette nurse with a dark mole on her left cheek said. 'You have visitors.' She held the curtain aside, allowing Kolesche and Mann to enter.

'You're lucky to be alive,' Kolesche said, as she stood beside the bed and touched Eileen's arm. 'We were so shocked when we heard. We came straight here. Everyone wants to know how you are.'

'What about the ball?' Eileen asked, remembering where she had been going.

'Oh, sod the ball!' Kolesche said. She looked at the scrapes and bruises on Eileen's face and her bandaged right arm and leg. 'You look terrible.'

'Where's Bob?' Eileen asked.

Kolesche glanced at Mann, before she replied, 'We're not sure. The nurse said he's in Intensive Care.'

'Oh,' Eileen gasped. 'Poor Bob.'

'It's not really serious,' Mann quickly explained. 'It's his leg. Apparently, it was pretty badly smashed up because it got caught between the car and the bike, but he's all right otherwise.'

'They told us you were thrown clear,' Kolesche said, shifting the topic. 'You still copped some nasty bangs and scrapes.'

'Sit down,' Eileen invited.

'Do you want a drink?' Kolesche asked, reaching for the water jug on the cabinet.

'Thank you,' Eileen said. She waited for Kolesche to pour a glass of water and pass it to her, lifted it, and sipped, realising the right side of her lip was swollen.

As she lowered the glass and Kolesche returned it to the cabinet, a man asked, 'Mind if I come in?' and Bruce appeared at the grey curtain.

'Bruce,' Eileen said. 'How did you -?'

'The hospital rang Mum, and she rang me because she can't come in quickly,' Bruce explained, as he moved into a space beside the bed. 'Uncle Spot drove me in. He's going back to fetch Mum.' He acknowledged Eileen's friends with a respectful nod, saying, 'Evening. I'm Girlie's brother, Bruce Bonney.'

'Lyla,' said Mann.

'Betty,' Kolesche replied.

'Nice to meet both of you,' Bruce said.

Eileen saw her brother's eyes linger on Kolesche. 'Get a chair,' she urged.

'I'll organise that,' Bruce said, breaking his gaze, and he fetched two more chairs so all three visitors could sit by the bed. He took his seat, after Kolesche and Mann sat, and said, 'I presume there's story to tell, Girlie.'

*

Eileen was grateful her injuries were superficial – bruises, abrasions. Her friends came and went, keeping her informed about hospital and work gossip, teasing her for finding a very silly way to get time off the roster, bringing her a clipping from the paper that reported the motorcycle accident, and telling her how much fun the charity ball was. They let her know when Bob Andrews was out of the Intensive Care Unit, although they told her he was unlikely to leave the hospital for some time, at least until his shattered leg healed. She had time to reflect. Bob was kind, and she prayed that he was healing, but she was not attracted to him, and she felt guilty for letting him take her to the ball because if she hadn't acquiesced the accident may not have happened. She wondered how her family were faring on Eyre Peninsula and what life was like in a small country town so far from anywhere. Memories of Dudley haunted and teased her, and she hoped he was healing from his malaria. As much as he hurt her with his cheating and lies, she couldn't push him away from her thoughts, no matter how hard she tried. She hid her tears from the nurses who came to her bed, and she wished he wasn't what he was.

Her brother John visited with Uncle Spot and Auntie Fay the second day after the accident. 'The things a girl will do to get attention and her name in that paper,' John said when he entered the room in his dark blue pinstriped suit, his curly hair flamboyantly brushed to one side. He kissed Eileen on the forehead before ensuring Auntie Fay sat on the chair by Eileen's bed. 'So, my dear, tell us the full story,' John invited. 'It must be a doozy.'

Eileen abbreviated the events for the sake of her relatives before she asked if they had news about her family at Port Neill. 'I spoke to Clarice on the phone,' Auntie Fay told her. 'Donald is busy with a building project, and Ian is learning the trade. Judy is working in the local pub. I told your mother I did not approve of a young girl working in a pub, but my advice, it seems, is not sought. Nevertheless, Clarice is well, and the little ones are at school.'

'And Faulding's?' Eileen asked, looking at John.

'Divine,' he replied. 'Making a living out of drugs seems to be quite fashionable.' He winked and smiled wickedly. 'I like it.'

Bruce returned on the third day, curious about Eileen's friend with the dark hair. 'Betty Kolesche,' Eileen explained, and she understood why Bruce was inquiring. 'You're keen on her, aren't you?' Bruce blushed, making Eileen laugh. 'Brucie has a crush,' she teased.

'I wanted to – I mean, I really like how she looks,' Bruce clumsily explained.

'I'll organise for us all to go dancing when I'm up and about,' Eileen offered.

'I'd like that,' Bruce said.

'I bet you will,' Eileen teased.

Bruce's confession of interest in Kolesche kept Eileen smiling long after her brother left the ward. Kolesche was one of her best friends and Bruce her favourite brother, and in her eyes they would make a perfect match, if she could engineer getting them together.

On the fourth morning, a doctor stopped by Eileen's bed to say, 'Miss Bonney, I believe you can go home today.' Excited to be released, she dressed after breakfast, thanked the ward nurses for taking care of her, and made her way down to the front desk to complete her discharge.

As Eileen explained who she was to the discharge nurse, a cheerful older woman with a harelip, the nurse interrupted to say, 'I forgot to tell you. There's a gentleman waiting to see you,' and she nodded to indicate where Eileen should look. In the foyer was a familiar figure in brown slacks, a grey shirt and brown cardigan holding a bright bouquet of flowers.

Eileen smiled at Dudley to mask her surprise, turned back to the discharge nurse, signed the paper, and said, 'Thank you,' before walking towards the waiting room.

Dudley greeted her warmly and held the flowers for her to accept, saying, 'I rang, and the ward nurse said you were leaving this morning, so I came to give you a lift back to the Repat. I'm so very sorry I didn't visit earlier. I didn't hear what happened until yesterday.'

'They are beautiful,' Eileen said, accepting the flowers. 'You shouldn't have come. I was going to ring my brother.'

'I wanted to come,' Dudley said. 'I've missed you.'

'Are you feeling better?' she asked.

'The malaria? Better than I was. Good doctor and drugs. Seeing you now makes me feel even better.'

'You shouldn't be here,' Eileen said, fighting her rising emotion. 'I know there's someone else.'

Dudley took her arm and said, 'I have a car. Let's go down to Glenelg, have a bite to eat and see a movie. We can talk in the car.'

'Is there someone else?' Eileen asked, refusing to be guided forward.

Dudley hesitated, sighed, released Eileen's arm, and said, 'All right. Yes. There was someone else. But that's in the past, Eileen. It's over. It wasn't ever serious, really. You have to believe me. It's you I want to be with. Only you.'

As much as Eileen's head warned her not to go with him, her heart urged her otherwise, like it always did. She felt connection with Dudley, an inexplicable need to be with him. From the first time he danced with her at The Argosy, the first kiss in the Botanic Gardens, the fondling and cuddling in the cinema back rows, he made her feel special and alive in a way no one else made her feel. She wanted him. She needed him. 'I'll come,' she said. He grinned and swept her into his arms, crushing the flowers that spilled around them in a rainbow shower.

*

Eileen crossed the footpath and ascended the steps into the Administration building, wondering why Matron summoned her between shifts. She told the duty woman at the desk why she was there and made her way to the Matron's office, knocking politely on the part-open door. 'Come in, Bonney,' Matron Archibald called. Eileen corrected her cap and apron and entered. Archibald, a stout, imposing figure, her hair tied back hard in the military style, rose from her chair to say, 'You're wondering why I sent for you.'

'Yes, Matron,' Eileen replied.

'I will tell you. But, first, how are you recovering?'

'Very well, thank you, Matron,' Eileen replied.

'Motorbikes,' Archibald said with disdain. 'Nasty machines. Men like them because they are loud and dangerous.' She approached Eileen. 'Do you know how Andrews is faring?'

'I heard he's still in hospital,' Eileen said.

'He is, indeed,' Archibald confirmed. 'Leg broken in three places, and a crushed ankle. He is very lucky the doctors decided not to amputate.'

'Oh, poor Bob!' Eileen gasped. 'I didn't know it was so bad.'

'Stay away from motorbikes, Bonney,' Archibald warned. 'Like men, they look like fun, and they sound enticing, but they are dangerous to your health.' Archibald's face creased into a broad smile. 'Now, to the matter I asked you here for. While it was a shame you never won the Queen of the Repat competition, I wanted to congratulate you for individually raising more than seven hundred pounds. That is quite an accomplishment.'

Eileen drew a sharp breath. 'I didn't realise,' she began, but left her sentence unfinished.

'It seems your sojourn in the Royal Adelaide Hospital earned you more donations than you might have got by attending the ball,' Archibald remarked and chuckled. 'A very effective sympathy vote. Anyway, well done, Bonney. I wanted to thank you personally, on behalf of all the staff. You should be very proud of your effort, as should your friends. They worked very hard for you.'

Eileen left the Administration building and skipped towards the canteen, keen to share her news. She spotted Kolesche leaning against a wall and ran to her, beaming. 'You'll never guess?' she said as she reached Kolesche.

'You're getting married.'

'Don't be absurd!' Eileen chastised. 'We raised more than seven hundred pounds for the charity!'

'Ooh!' Kolesche cooed and straightened. 'That's wonderful!'

Eileen clasped Kolesche's hands, and the two nurses danced gleefully. 'Where's Cooper?' Eileen asked when they stopped to catch their breath.

Kolesche winked and replied, 'Checking out the shelter with Alan and Pat.'

Eileen's face shifted to shock. 'Both of them?' she blurted. 'Together?'

'Cooper likes challenges,' Kolesche replied.

'That's disgusting!' Eileen declared, and they sniggered and then laughed, only controlling their mirth when they saw an orderly striding towards them.

'Nurse Bonney?' the orderly asked.

'Nice looking young man,' Kolesche noted with a wink.

'Stop it,' Eileen said. 'Yes?' she replied to the orderly.

'There's a telephone call for you,' he informed her.

Eileen looked at Kolesche who raised an eyebrow. 'Better hurry,' Kolesche urged.

Eileen followed the orderly and accepted the receiver when it was handed to her. 'Hello?' she said.

'Eileen Bonney?' a woman's voice queried.

'Speaking,' Eileen replied. 'Who is this?'

'Carol. Dudley Wright's fiancée,' the woman announced. 'Does that mean anything to you?'

Eileen's heart raced.

'I didn't think you would have much to say,' Carol said curtly. 'I'll keep this brief. Stay away from my fiancé. Do you understand?'

'I haven't seen him,' Eileen said. 'Honestly.'

'I don't want to hear excuses and don't lie to me. Keep your evil paws off my Dudley or, I promise you, you will be very sorry you ever met him.' The phone disconnected.

Eileen began shaking. She was bewildered and upset and felt brutally sick. She hung up the receiver clumsily, looked at the orderly who was watching politely, and burst into tears, before she ran outside, slumped against a wall, and sank to the ground, sobbing.

Later that night, celebrations and congratulations echoing in her ears, Eileen tried to sleep, but sleep eluded her, replaced with Carol's recrimination and Dudley's smile. Why was he being so cruel? Why couldn't he let her go, leave her alone, get on with his life? Or why didn't he tell Carol the truth and leave her? Why? Questions, fears, hopes, frustrations bubbled and swirled through her head, infected her dreams, kept her tossing and turning throughout the night, until the grey light of dawn crept through the window to announce another day was ready to begin. And she was exhausted.

*

'Are you sure this is what you want to do?' Matron Archibald asked.

'Absolutely sure,' Eileen replied, edging the transfer application form across the desk towards the Matron.

'This will take a few weeks to be fully approved,' Archibald explained, perusing the details on the form. 'And the Heidelberg team will have to approve your application in the first place.' She looked up. 'Have you been to Melbourne?'

'Never,' Eileen replied. 'It's a good reason to go.'

'A curious spirit,' Archibald murmured. 'Well, yes, I guess some of us have that. But beware. It can lead you into trouble, Bonney.'

'I will be careful,' Eileen promised.

'We will miss you.'

'And I'll miss everyone here,' Eileen replied.

'Does your mother know you're leaving?'

'I'm talking to her tonight.'

The conversation with Matron Archibald flowed through Eileen's memory as she dialled the number and waited for the Port Neill exchange to connect lines. The whir of the ringing phone stopped with a click and a voice asked, 'Hello?'

'Mum!' Eileen said hopefully. 'It's Girlie!'

'Girlie!' Clarice yelled. 'Where are you?'

'At the Repat, Mum,' Eileen replied. 'How are you?'

The line crackled and part of Clarice's reply was muffled as she replied, 'I am fine. Tired, Girlie. But I am always tired. I go to work and come home, and the children need things done and the housework must be done.'

'How are the children?'

'They are fine, Girlie. Everyone is fine.'

'And Father?'

'Your father is working all the time, very busy. So is Ian. They are nearly finished the houses.'

'What happens then?'

'I think we are coming back to Adelaide,' Clarice said.

'When?'

'Maybe next month. Could be sooner.'

'Has Father got another job?'

'He will continue working for the Military Police. He says they have work for him.'

'What about building?'

'He is looking for more building projects.'

'Do you have enough money?'

'Of course,' Clarice said. 'Donald and Ian are bringing in enough. And Judy is working too. Your sister is really growing up. She misses you.'

Eileen swallowed before saying, 'Mum, I have some news. I've been offered a position at the Heidelberg Repat.'

'Where?' Clarice asked across the crackle.

'Heidelberg Repatriation Hospital.'

'Where is that?'

'Melbourne,' Eileen replied guiltily.

'But isn't that in Melbourne?' Clarice asked, as if she had not heard Eileen.

'Yes.'

'But -' Clarice started, and asked, 'Why are you going to Melbourne?'

'They need more nurses there, Mum. Lots of returned men and women are being sent to Heidelberg because it is so big.'

'We need lots of nurses here, too,' Clarice argued.

'I've already signed the papers and been accepted,' Eileen told her. 'I can't back out now.'

'But who can I call on if things don't go well?'

'Judy's old enough to help, especially now that she's working. So is Ian. And Bruce and Peter and John will keep an eye out for you.'

'But you will be in Melbourne,' Clarice argued.

'I promise I'll write every week, Mum. I'll write twice a week, to you, and to everyone.'

'When do you go?'

'Next Friday.'

'We won't see you,' Clarice protested. 'Can't you wait? We are coming back to Adelaide very soon.'

'They expect me to be there to start next week. Mum, I need to do this. I can't stay in Adelaide forever. You travelled when you played piano for the silent movie company. It's my turn to do something like that. I need to leave, Mum. I'm sorry.'

When the conversation ended, Eileen lowered the receiver and walked into the evening air. She lit a cigarette, drew a long draught, and stared up at the starlit sky. 'I'm sorry, Mum,' she whispered, 'but I can't stay here anymore.'

1949

"If you wish for things you can get, you're gonna be happy. If you wish for real big things, all you're gonna get is real big disappointments."
Connie Ennis

'Three, two, one...Happy New Year!'

Caught in the euphoria, Eileen was swept into the arms of a brash young man who kissed her firmly on the mouth. 'Happy New Year!' he shouted, as he released her and turned to kiss another young woman. Another young man leaned in and kissed Eileen on the cheek, whispering, 'Happy New Year.'

Voices took up "Auld Lang Syne" and people linked arms and sang with gusto. Eileen took a swig from a beer bottle when it was passed to her and joined in the singing, and she was overwhelmed with happiness.

Later, in her bed, the night's revelry swirling through her intoxicated mind, she tried recalling the ghosts of New Years past, favourite memories of the family gathered around the piano in the Black Forest home before the war, her father, her mother playing, and everyone's joyful faces as they sang. There were images from celebrations in The Broadway house, sombre because Clive, Bruce, John and their father were absent, even though the piano echoed with music and the children sang "Auld Lang Syne" like adults. She missed her family. Despite the staff in the Heidelberg Nurses' Quarters, she felt alone. And yet she was also as far from her Adelaide pain as she could be.

Mid-morning New Years' Day, she went to the canteen with a pad, a fountain pen and ink bottle and set herself the task of writing to her mother. "Dear Mum," she wrote, her nib scratching across the beige paper, her lettering diligently imitating the Copperplate style enforced in her schooling, although she regularly lapsed into capitals. "Happy New Year! I hope everyone is well, and settled back in Adelaide, and the new year brings everyone good things.

The trip on The Overland was exciting, and I loved the sounds and smell of the steam engine. Because it was an overnight journey, I managed to sleep across a seat after travelling through Tailem Bend. An orderly from the Heidelberg Repat met me at the station in Melbourne and we travelled by bus to the hospital. He is nice young man. His name is Kenneth, although everyone calls him Ken, and we have become good friends. Matron Wilkes welcomed me and showed me where I sleep, and the bed is comfortable, a lot like my old bed at Daw Park. I do like it here."

Eileen paused to organise her thoughts and remembered her promise to write regularly. It was six weeks since she arrived in Melbourne and she hadn't written, and she felt guilty. She bent forward on the table and continued.

"I received your letter. Thank you, especially for letting me know your new address. I know I promised to write twice a week, but it has been very busy settling in and getting used to the new place.

The morning after I arrived, the doctors gave me the compulsory medical. All clear of course. Then I was fitted for my uniform. Here the dress is military khaki, with a white apron and white cap. I was assigned to a ward and started work. It is the same work as I was doing at Daw Park; stripping, cleaning and making beds, emptying pans, helping the patients with their medicine and taking them to the toilet, bathing those who cannot help themselves. It is sad seeing so many people still recovering from the war after all this time. One patient in the ward has been here for seven years, on and off, suffering from relapses in malaria and an infection that keeps gnawing at her flesh. The doctors do not understand it. They keep cutting bits out and amputating parts, and it is altogether awful for her. She is such a brave and positive girl, but everyone knows she is not getting better.

I heard there was a body found on Somerton Beach not long after I left last year. Have you heard any more about it? I read in the paper that no one knows who he is. That is so mysterious. I hope the police work out what happened to him. Please tell me what you know about it.

Anyway, must finish and get the letter ready to send. I hope you are all well and happy. Give my love to everyone."

She signed with "Yours truly, Girlie" and waited for the ink to dry before she folded the paper in three, slid it into an envelope and scribed the address.

*

'This one is the six-twenty Brownie C,' the chemist assistant explained, putting the black camera box on the counter for Eileen to consider. 'Kodak introduced this model in 1946 and they're very popular for budget photographers. Takes six-twenty film rolls. It's very easy to use.' Eileen watched the assistant open the camera, slot in a film roll, close the box and turn the side knob to ready the film for the first photograph. 'And when you're done with the roll, it shows up in this little rear portal and you can wind off the roll, open it, address it and send it for processing.' He slid a small yellow booklet forward. 'All the instructions are in your brochure. That's why this one's so popular.'

'How much?' Eileen asked.

'For you, young lady, I can do it for two pounds and six shillings.'

Transaction completed, two additional film rolls bought, Eileen strolled out of the chemist shop and headed for the Bourke Street Myer building, intent on buying a floral blue dress she saw a week earlier.

Buying the camera excited her. Her friends at the Heidelberg Repat had cameras and photographing each other was fun. Now she could take her own photos to record the memories. Away from home, the ability to capture her adventure meant she could share what she saw and the people she met with her family in Adelaide.

Events in Adelaide still troubled her conscience. In her most recent letter, her mother intimated the family was shifting for the third time since returning from Port Neill. They had already moved from Semaphore to Hindley Street, where they were living in a cellar and behind a pool room. Her father seemed incapable of holding down a permanent job or providing a steady income. She felt guilty living away, but she wanted to escape the responsibility that belonged to her father and mother, and in Melbourne she could keep the family woes at a distance, live her life, be the person she chose to be. But it didn't stop her thinking about her mother, her brothers and her sisters. She would return home, she knew it, but not yet. Not now. Adelaide still harboured agonising memories.

The floral blue dress beckoned through the display window. She smiled, balanced the weight of her new camera in her bag, and headed into the store.

*

'Have you ridden a horse before?' Ken asked as they strolled towards the white wooden enclosure.

'I've patted and fed some,' Eileen replied, remembering times she spent with Bruce and the pacers. 'Does that count?'

Ken laughed. 'I take that as you haven't. That's fine. I can teach you.'

'Where did you learn to ride?' she asked.

'My father owns racehorses,' he replied. 'He's part-owner of a stud farm on Mornington Peninsula.'

'My brother works for my uncle, and he trains horses in Adelaide. We can't ride them. Bruce says they're too valuable.'

'Racehorses are,' Ken explained as they passed through the gate. 'They can make you rich, and they can break you.' He stopped a few paces from the horses. 'Which one is best for a novice?' he asked the wiry youth who was wearing a brown Akubra, a tan shirt and dark brown trousers, and holding the reins of both horses.

'Who's the novice?' the handler asked.

'The young lady.'

'Then she'd be best on Starlight here,' the handler replied, pulling on the bay roan horse's reins. 'He's a gelding with a few years under his hide. Very gentle and forgiving codger.'

'Go meet Starlight,' Ken said to Eileen. 'What's the black one called?' he asked, but before the handler could reply Ken said, 'No. Wait. I sense a theme here. He would have to be Midnight. Right?'

The handler laughed and replied, 'Good guess, Mister,' and held the reins towards Ken.

Eileen stroked Starlight's velvet nose and crooned to him in the way Bruce taught her to coax horses. 'The best way to mount your horse is to put your left foot in the left stirrup,' said Ken moving beside Eileen. 'I'll help you up, but don't pull on the saddle very hard if you can avoid it. Push up with your left leg.'

Eileen fitted her shoe into the stirrup, and, with Ken's lifting assistance, she swung onto the saddle. 'Stroke his mane and talk to him,' Ken advised, 'but keep a firm grip on your reins. Don't let them dangle loose near his face or he'll think he's free to wander away.'

'Starlight won't wander away,' the handler said. 'He's too old and lazy to do much more than what he's told.'

Ken mounted Midnight and reined in beside Eileen. 'How's it feel?'

'High,' she replied. The earthy odours of horse, dust and faeces surrounded her.

Half an hour after walking through basic riding lessons, Eileen's back and legs and wrists were aching. Ken reined in beside her, grinned and asked, 'Ready for a trail ride?'

'Of course,' Eileen replied, eager to enjoy the experience.

'Follow me,' Ken said, and he led her onto a riding track.

They wound along a creek bank, ducking under boughs and skirting bushes, watching birds flit through the branches and skim across the babbling water. Light glittered on the stream. 'This place is beautiful,' Eileen said, as she concentrated on keeping her back straight and reins even.

'Merri Creek,' Ken replied. 'Means very rocky in the Wurundjeri language, although they would say "merri merri" for very rocky.'

Eileen laughed and repeated, 'Merri merri. How do you know this?'

'My mother,' he explained. 'She's an historian, of sorts. Works at the State Library. She likes to collect all kinds of information about the people who lived here before white settlement.' He reined in and waited for Eileen to draw alongside. 'The creek starts up north, near Wallan, and runs down to join the Yarra. It's famous for being the only place where white people made a treaty with the local blacks. Apparently, John Batman met with the local Wurundjeri elders somewhere around here and made an agreement on sharing the land. Only none of the higher authorities wanted a treaty with the local people, so it was over-ruled by Bourke, the New South Wales Governor, to protect the English notion of the country being terra nullius.'

'What's terra nullius?'

'Latin. It means empty or unowned land. That's what the Europeans called it when they arrived. It really means the white settlers didn't have to negotiate with the Aboriginals. They could take whatever land they wanted.'

Eileen listened to Ken's history lesson, but she was studying his face, his straight nose, his firm chin, his lips. Since he met her at the station when she arrived, she was interested in his friendly personality, and he invited her to nurse and orderly outings, but for the first time she assessed him more deeply and liked what she saw.

'Should I call you Bonney or Eileen?' Ken asked. 'I mean, it's always Bonney at work, and you call me Evans, but I'd prefer if you call me Ken when we're out and about.'

Eileen blinked, considering the question, and replied, 'I'd like you to call me Eileen rather than Bonney.'

'Eileen it is,' he said. 'Do you want to ride on further, Eileen?'

'I'd like that, Ken,' she replied.

*

'Why are you walking so slowly?' Shirley Turner asked, her face screwed up, as she paused with an armful of sheets to wait for Eileen to catch up in the corridor. A third nurse, Dot Parker, stopped beside Turner.

'Ken, I mean Evans, took me for a long ride on the weekend,' Eileen replied.

'Too much information!' Parker declared, and Turner snorted as they laughed.

'Don't be so crude!' Eileen complained. 'It was horse riding at Merri Creek.'

'Ooh,' Parker said mockingly. 'Don't need to apologise to us for what you do on the weekend, Bonney,' and she winked at Turner.

'Don't be mean, either. He's a gentleman.'

'They're all gentlemen, until they can get their hands inside your blouse,' Parker warned. 'Or elsewhere,' she added and winked again.

'And you would know all about that,' Turner teased. Parker pulled a face and the women laughed. 'So, are you going out with him again?'

'To the races in a fortnight,' Eileen replied.

'A fortnight?' Parker said. 'Your boy's a bit slow on the uptake.'

'Too much of a gentleman for my liking,' Turner added, and they giggled.

'He works in surgery,' Eileen said. 'They have long shifts.'

Turner nodded. 'I'm only teasing, Bonney. I know Ken Evans. He's a nice young man. You could do a lot worse around this place.'

'You should see if he's free for the pictures when you're off next,' Parker suggested. 'Can get pretty close and dark in the back row.'

'You really do have a one-track mind, don't you Parker?' Eileen accused.

'I like a fast-track mind,' Parker said, and she blew Eileen a kiss.

'Do you have anything better to do than stand in a corridor giggling like loons?' a voice challenged from a doorway. The nurses turned to discover a stocky, blond ward Sister glaring at them, her arms crossed fiercely across her ample bosom.

'Sorry, Sister Oxenham,' Turner said. 'Come on, girls,' she urged. 'Work to do,' and she led her companions along and out of the corridor.

*

His fingers searched for her hand, and she willingly let his warm hand enfold hers in the flickering silver light and shadowy cinema patina. His touch sparked along her arm and into her body and she was glad he took the initiative. She pressed her arm against his, basking in the thrilling sensations, but memories of another cinema and a man's touch crystallised. Angry and sad, simultaneously, that those memories dared disrupt the present moment, she forced the past down and focused on the shimmering screen, laughing at Lou Costello's antics in the forest with the Wolfman.

Later, in the corner of a corridor, Ken pulled her close and she let him kiss her, remembering what she learned from another lover, annoyed with herself for wishing it was that lover.

Later still, lying in her dormitory bed, she dreamed she stood at the end of The Broadway in Glenelg South, watching the sunset paint tendrils of amber, purple, gold and pink across a deepening blue sky, listening to the whispering waves, with her arm linked in a man's arm, someone who was Ken and Dudley, and yet neither. She felt safe, warm in her heart despite the cooling evening breeze, and the world was at peace and beautiful beyond words. This is what she wanted; someone who made her world perfect, someone who made her feel safe and loved. More than anything, that was what she craved.

*

"Dear Mum," Eileen began. "I hope everyone is well and that Josie's cold is better." She paused to remember what she knew from her mother's most recent letter, but only Josie's cold came to mind. "I have met the most interesting young man here in Melbourne. I may have mentioned him before as the orderly who met me at the station when I first arrived. His name is Ken Evans. He assists doctors in surgery theatre, so he is very clever, and one day he hopes to be a doctor too.

Ken has been taking me to interesting places. We went to the Melbourne Zoo last weekend. I have never seen such beautiful and strange animals in one place. We saw Commandant Charco's dogs, the ones he was meant to take on expedition to Antarctica, and Peggy the elephant. There's been a lot in the papers about the zoo not caring enough for the animals, but what I saw did not show anything bad happening, although it is cruel seeing animals locked up that should be running free.

Tell Bruce I have been to the races and that Ken's father owns a stud for breeding racehorses, and that later this year we are going to the Melbourne Cup. I love the grey horses best of all, and if I see one, when we are at the races, I have to bet on it.

Ken lives in Carlton. It is a nice suburb, a little way out of the city, but there is a lot of sadness there because people live in very poor conditions.

The girls at work told me Carlton is full of slums, and I did see some very run-down places when I went walking with Ken. We ate at an Italian restaurant in Lygon Street and the food was lovely, especially the pasta, although I could not get the noodles onto my fork properly. It seems funny being served food by people Father used to guard in Loveday, but Ken said a lot of Italians were immigrating to Australia now the war is over.

Will write again soon. Sorry it has not been as often as I promised, but we are very busy at the hospital, and we do not have a lot of free time after hours. Love to everyone."

Eileen stared through the window at the rain bathing the concrete and grass, glass and stone. It rained often in Melbourne, at least that's how it seemed to her in the three months since she arrived. Adelaide already felt like a lifetime away, someone else's life. In the paper, yesterday, she spotted an advertisement for student nurses to begin training as general nurses at the Repatriation Hospital. The entry minimum age was eighteen. That made her smile. Her eighteenth birthday was coming in two days, but she was nineteen officially in the hospital records. She was nineteen and no one knew otherwise in Melbourne. No one called her Girlie. She wasn't running after her siblings or trying to make ends meet day by day. Her father's shadow no longer loomed over her life. Her dentures were finally comfortable, and she could smile confidently. And a man wasn't cheating on her or tormenting her heart. She was someone else entirely.

*

'We're rostered to work in the TB ward this coming week,' Turner said, turning from the lists on the brown pin board.

'Do we have to work on the TB ward?' Eileen asked.

'Everyone gets their turn in the ward,' said Petersen, who was walking past.

'I heard we get extra pay for part of the shift,' Williams said, leaning in to check her roster. 'Besides, it's raining all next week. Better to be inside, dry, warm and busy.'

'Probably get a bonus cup of tea and a biscuit,' Turner remarked, and snorted. 'Come on, Bonney. We have two days off to enjoy. Can't keep

Mister Evans waiting.'

'Bonney!' a voice called, and Eileen saw Pat Fryar beckoning her to peruse another pin board. She crossed the hall to learn what Fryar wanted, Turner following. 'Are you going to do this?' Fryar asked, pointing at a flyer.

"Repat Amateur Hour Open Mike Singing Competition," Eileen read. 'Why me?'

'We know you can sing,' said Fryar. 'We've heard you in the quarters.'

'You should enter,' Turner urged.

'I don't know,' Eileen replied. 'I haven't sung in front of anyone for a while.'

'So, you have sung before?' Fryar noted gleefully. 'That's wonderful! Let's sign you up.'

'No sign up,' Turner said, pointing at the smaller print. 'We arrive in the hall and whoever grabs the mic sings. Come on, Bonney. Be a sport. It will be fun. Do it for us.'

'But I will have only come off duty next Friday night,' Eileen said, noting the date and time.

'Perfect!' Fryar declared. 'You're in! We will cheer for you!'

*

Eileen slid off her protective grey rubber gloves and bent to lather her hands over the basin, scrubbing furiously, keen to ensure she carried no infection from her patients. The week spent on the ward caring for bed-ridden men in the hardest stages of the disease was difficult and sad. The care she had to take in the Tuberculosis Ward reminded her of the bathing she did for little Anthea in Minda, and it set her wondering again exactly what was wrong with the little girl. Poor Lenny Owens was the worst. He coughed and moaned, and he needed constant care with drinking and changing his sheets. Ward Sister Franklin was strict concerning nurse contact with the patients, insisting all procedures were followed precisely and she urged Eileen to be vigilant when she worked with seriously infected patients, like Lenny. 'I won't have nurses on my watch coming down with anything,' she told Eileen and Turner when they started their rostered week. 'If you feel even a tickle of a cold, I want to know, and I will take you off duty. Tight masks, gloves on, scrub down regularly.'

Turner quickly learned how to mock the Sister's manner. 'Bonney!' she would snap under her breath. 'Tight mask!' or she would say, 'Scrub yourself, girl!'

Eileen tried in vain not to giggle, complaining, 'You are a terror!' and she looked up guiltily in case Sister Franklin was watching.

Scrubbed, disposable wear removed and binned, Eileen headed for the showers to bathe and change. Half an hour later, she hurried to the hospital hall. 'We thought you forgot!' Fryar declared as Eileen entered.

'I came as fast as I could,' Eileen replied, catching her breath.

'Where's Turner?'

'Coming,' Eileen told her. 'Sister made her stay back an extra ten minutes to finish tidying up in the station.'

'Ranklin' Franklin,' Fryar said. 'Tough old biddy that one.'

'Needs to be,' said Williams. 'Wouldn't want her responsibility for twice the pay.'

'Twice our pay is still two times not much of half of anything else,' Fryar replied.

'Master of ceremonies is up!' Williams announced, pointing to the makeshift hall stage where a reed thin man in a tuxedo appeared from a side curtain. 'Band is ready.'

'What do I do?' Eileen asked.

'Nothing except wait your turn,' Fryar advised. 'We put your name and song choice on the list.'

'Song choice?' Eileen gasped.

'"It's Magic!"' Fryar replied. 'We heard you singing it in the showers.'

'That was in the showers, not in public,' Eileen argued.

'Best place to find talent,' Williams remarked. 'Which is why Fryar isn't going up.' The women laughed and Fryar poked out her tongue.

Eileen stood with her friends at the back of the small crowd in the hospital hall and made room for Turner to join when she arrived. 'Sister was especially picky this afternoon,' Turner said. 'You got off lightly.'

'I'm glad I did,' Eileen replied. 'It's nerve-wracking enough doing this.' She noted the band had a piano, a bass, a trombone and a trumpet, a saxophone, drums, and a guitar, an impressive ensemble for a hospital event, and her nerves jangled. She reminded herself of The Argosy, and that singing was her love, but the reminiscence did not placate her nerves.

'Welcome!' the master of ceremonies began. 'Let's kick off tonight's singing and dancing with that favourite, "Manana"! Hit it, boys!'

'That's Doctor Richards,' Fryar said, as the drummer began a Spanish rhythm and Doctor Richards took up the castanets.

'Now that's a talented doctor,' Williams remarked, raising an eyebrow. 'He can check my pulse with his stethoscope!'

'Evelyn Williams!' Eileen chided.

'Let's dance!' Parker said, grabbing Eileen's arm, and the nurses surged onto the dance floor.

At the end of the opening instrumental, Doctor Richards announced, 'First on the microphone tonight is croonin' Eddie Nunan and his rendition of Crosby's "Swinging on a Star!" Come on, Eddie! Come on up and join the band!'

A thin, dark-haired man, presumably an orderly, strode onto the stage, stood at the microphone, and said, 'Good evening, everyone. This is one of my personal favourites. I hope you like it too!'

'Sing it and we might!' a man shouted from the dance floor, and everyone laughed. Eddie nodded to the band who swung into action.

'Love this song!' Fryar said as she joined Parker and Eileen, towing an orderly for her partner. 'This is Graham.'

Eileen swung to the rhythm, letting Parker take lead, and the day's work in the ward melted away in the melody. Everyone applauded as Eddie finished. 'He is good,' Eileen said.

Doctor Richards returned to the microphone and announced, 'Next up, ladies and gentlemen, are Adams, McCarthy and Sheffield, straight from the pharmaceutical department, and wowing us with the Andrews Sisters' hit, "Boogie Woogie Bugle Boy"!' Everyone cheered and clapped as the three nurses joined the stage and shook out their hair in unison as they gathered at the microphone. They pointed to the band, the trumpet player swung into the song's opening riff, and everyone prepared to swing again on the dance floor. 'Oh my goodness!' Eileen gasped. 'I can't sing like these people! They're professionals.'

'Don't be silly,' Parker chided. 'They're nurses like you. Of course you can sing as good as them.'

Two more performances and dances came and went before Doctor Richards announced, 'And now, our girl from Adelaide, Eileen Bonney, is leading us in a romantic waltz with that gorgeous Doris Day hit from last year, "It's Magic"! Find that partner you want to hold close and join the soiree of love!'

'You're up!' Turner said, extending her arm towards the stage and bowing.

Eileen smiled at people she recognised as she crossed the floor, stepped onto the stage and stood at the microphone. Dread threatened to overwhelm her, but she drew a deep breath, shook her arms and hands, and glanced at the piano player, who grinned, raised his hands theatrically, and began the opening bars played by strings in the original song. Pushing down her nerves, Eileen hit the high opening note on 'You sigh,' and moved effortlessly into the song, feeling the music sweep through her as she sang and watched the small crowd shuffle their waltzes, some for the fun of dancing, some closer, more intimately in love. She held the note on the final 'you', letting the band finish as her voice faded, beamed when the applause and shouts of encouragement flowed towards her, and headed to join her friends as Doctor Richards called up the next singer.

*

Eileen leaned against her bedhead and angled her mother's letter in the dull light. "Bruce is engaged," she read. "He is going to marry Betty, that lovely young girl you worked with at the Repat. She is such a dear, and your brother is love-struck, which is very nice to see. He said to tell you that you found him an absolute treasure. He sends his love."

Eileen lowered the letter and stared at the shadows on the opposite wall. Her big brother was going to marry her good friend. There was a moment, not so long ago, when she imagined she would be the first to marry, that Dudley and she would break the news to everyone, and her life would move onto a different trajectory, away from chaos and poverty. But Dudley ruined that dream. She sighed. She was delighted for Bruce and Betty. She would see what she could do to be in Adelaide for the wedding.

Marriage was inevitable, she decided. So many nurses she worked with were married, or engaged, or about to be engaged, racing into a life of keeping homes, raising children, caring for husbands. Sometimes, she imagined married life as a romantic idyll – not working, quiet days cleaning and shopping and cooking, sharing time with friends, playing with children, reading magazines – but sharp experience would jog her memory with her mother's cruel marriage. Clarice's fate was less than idyllic: abandoning an artistic career, perpetually pregnant, impoverished, jilted by an unfaithful man, working low-paid menial jobs to make ends-meet, bitterness and sadness, and the truth left Eileen confused and wary. As much as she tried to rationalise her mother's fate – marrying late, victim of a poor choice of husband, too many kids, wartime – she couldn't reconcile the social fantasy with the reality her mother endured. What if she married the wrong man? What if she couldn't say no to a large family? What if her marriage wasn't what she hoped it would be? What then? Marriage wasn't simply a means to an end. Whoever she married would have to be someone she could love and trust, someone who loved her equally. She wasn't rushing blindly into marriage. Dudley taught her not to hang her hopes on a fantasy. She intended to be sure before she married anyone.

*

The weather was predicted to reach 62 degrees Fahrenheit by the middle of the day with swirling, brisk northerly and westerly winds, and showers. Eileen huddled in her coat, collar up against the strong wind, arm linked with Ken's arm, sheltering under his umbrella from a light drizzle on their walk to Victoria Park. Instead of the races, Ken insisted they go to the football. 'I follow Carlton, obviously, because I live in Carlton,' he said, when he asked Eileen to go with him the Thursday before, 'and we're playing for top spot. Collingwood are on top, but if we knock them off today we could move to the top.' He grinned and asked, 'Do you follow the footy?'

'A little, when I was in Adelaide,' she replied.

'Which team?' Ken asked.

'Glenelg,' she replied. 'The Tigers. We lived around the corner from the football club. I went to Glenelg Primary School.'

'Did you go to games?' Ken asked.

Eileen laughed and said, 'No. I was always working or looking after the kids.'

'Well, on Saturday I'll take you to see some real football,' Ken said proudly. 'The Navy Blues are one of the oldest clubs, and we were premiers in '45 and '47, and we're on track to win again this year.'

'Did you play football?' Eileen asked.

Ken laughed. 'I did as a kid, but I wasn't good enough to get into the big league. Took up medicine instead.'

Eileen heard the crowd long before they reached the Victoria Park gates, the noise and milling mob reminding her of the races. She stood with Ken in the queue, among the supporters draped in club scarfs, Carlton faithful with navy blue and white, Collingwood followers with black and white paraphernalia, most people in austere brown and grey winter clothing. Ken bought tickets, and the pock-faced ticket seller said, 'They reckon we'll see thirty thousand today.'

'Better not be a debacle like that game between Carlton and Richmond back in June,' said a bullish man behind Eileen.

'Nah, cobber,' the ticket seller replied. 'We wouldn't be that stupid here on our home turf.'

'What was that all about?' Eileen asked as she walked into the ground with Ken.

'They let too many people into Punt Road,' Ken explained. 'Ground only takes slightly over forty thousand people, but nearly fifty thousand squeezed in and broke fences and gates. A handful were taken to hospital. Papers made it sound worse than it was.' He laughed. 'Besides, we won. That's all that matters.' He led Eileen through the bustling crowd, pushing towards the fence, although it was obvious they would never reach the front. 'We can watch from here,' Ken said. 'I'll keep the umbrella handy,' he said, glancing up at the threatening grey sky. 'The main game starts in half an hour.'

While they waited for the Reserves game to finish, Ken explained finer aspects of the rules, especially a new rule where teams could use two substitute players during the game.

'Still a bloody stupid idea,' a thickset, pot-bellied man beside Ken intervened. 'Takes the toughness out of the game.'

Eileen sensed the growing expectation as the bell sounded the conclusion of the Reserves match and the crowd continued to swell. Chatter rose, people pressed closer on the low mound where they stood, and the anticipation climaxed as the teams ran onto the ground to a chaotic crescendo of cheers and boos. Carlton wore their navy jumpers and white shorts as visitors to the Collingwood home ground, and Collingwood their black and white jumpers and black shorts. To Eileen, the men on the field looked larger than life, physically impressive, fit, strong warriors surging into battle. The captains tossed a coin to choose which end to attack, the players took their positions, the umpire bounced the ball, and the spectacle began, as the wind whipped across the ground and light rain started falling.

The crowd yelled and hooted, and gave the players directions, cajoling and berating them and the umpire who seemed to be loosely in control, cheering when a goal was scored. A ball over the boundary line was signalled with a white handkerchief before the umpires retrieved the ball, sometimes tossed out of the crowd, and they hurled the ball high into the milling pack of players to continue the game. Eileen found herself caught in the spectators' enthusiasm, with Ken waving his fist and yelling, 'Go, you Blues! Go!' and she imitated the people around her, urging on the Carlton players.

A bell jangled to signal the end of the first quarter. The umpire collected the ball and walked to the middle, while the players trudged across the field, swapping ends. Then the ball was bounced, and the game swung into action again. 'Who's winning?' Eileen asked.

Ken pointed to the scoreboard. 'We're down thirteen points. They killed us that quarter. Terrible conditions to play football, but the wind favours us this quarter.'

By the time the bell concluded the second quarter, and coaches and players huddled to talk tactics, Carlton had taken the lead by eleven points, and Ken's spirits were buoyed. 'How was that, Eileen?' he asked rhetorically. 'That was a great comeback. See? The wind made a difference. Now we have to hold them this quarter and come home with it in the final.'

As rain tumbled from the overcast sky and more umbrellas opened around Victoria Park, the bell and the bounced ball set the third quarter in motion. The players crashed and slid in the muddier parts of the oval, and the slippery ball eluded desperate hands in the wind and the rain. Carlton defied the conditions and added two more goals to Collingwood's one, although to Eileen's eyes Collingwood seemed to have much greater possession of the ball and were only behind because they were scoring points instead of goals.

When the third quarter ended, the tired, muddy and wet players changed places. The rain eased enough for Ken to lower the umbrella. 'Last quarter,' he said. 'We have the wind and we're three points up. The boys should bring this one home.' He grinned, hugged Eileen, and asked, 'So what do you think? Is this fun?'

'It's great fun,' Eileen replied, and she leaned against Ken's chest, glad to be loved.

*

Introduction written, Eileen dipped her nib in the dark blue ink and returned to the letter. "Ken took me to see Carlton play Collingwood last Saturday at Victoria Park. It was not the nicest of days because of the wind and rain, but I did enjoy it. There were so many people cheering and barracking for their teams, and the men were fierce on the field. I think I will go again if Ken asks, although he was devastated that his team, Carlton, lost by three points.

The work here is hard. I have been doing shifts on the TB ward, because we all have to take our turn, which I can see is fair to everyone. I am very careful to wash thoroughly after I work with patients and Sister is very strict to make sure we are systematic and careful. Hospital life is generally good, though. There are movie nights and dance nights and I have been singing with a band the orderlies and doctors put together."

Eileen paused to compose what to write next. The canteen light flickered, and she looked up. This late in the evening, the canteen was empty, but Turner was walking towards her. 'Why are you up?' Eileen asked.

Turner slumped onto a chair opposite Eileen and leaned on her elbows on the table. 'Can't sleep.' She saw the pen and ink and paper. 'Who are you writing to?'

'My family,' Eileen replied. 'I promised to write twice a week, but mostly I manage once a fortnight.'

'I promised my sister the same,' Turner said. 'I said I'd write every week, and she said she would do the same.' She chuckled. 'Of course, we haven't, but I miss her.'

'What's her name?'

'Sandra. We all call her Sandy.'

'Older or younger sister?'

'Older by three years,' Turner replied. 'She's twenty-two.' She sighed and brushed back her auburn hair. 'You know, I might go home soon, to see Sandy. I've been thinking about it for a while. I miss home.'

'Where's home?' Eileen asked.

'Ulverston,' Turner replied. 'It's in Tasmania, middle of the northern coast, west of Davenport. Do you know it?'

'Not at all,' Eileen said. 'I've never been anywhere, except Adelaide and here.'

'You should come with me,' Turner proposed. 'We could run away together.'

'Sounds like fun.'

'It would be so much fun! We could visit Sandy, and she would let us stay with her and Bob. Bob Maxwell is her husband and he's a sweet man. You and I could travel around Tasmania on bikes and find jobs.'

'Doing what?' Eileen asked.

'Picking fruit. Picking hops for the beer factories. Boxing fish. We could roam around, and meet boys whenever we wanted, and be as free as the birds.' Light glittered in Turner's eyes. 'You would love it.'

'I would,' Eileen agreed. She leaned towards Turner to say, 'If you miss your sister so much, you should definitely go.'

'I think I will,' Turner said, rising from the chair. 'Let me know if you'd like to come too.'

As Turner walked out of the canteen, Eileen glanced at a couple of orderlies who entered and sat at a table. One produced a deck of cards. The wall clock told her it was getting late, and she was on duty at seven in the morning, so she put her pen in its case, screwed the lid onto the ink bottle, folded her letter and headed for the dormitory.

*

'You like pasta, Signora?'

Eileen looked up at the young man in his white shirt and black trousers, his handsome teenage face darkened with the shadow of an emerging moustache and beard. 'I do,' she replied.

'Okay,' the youth said. 'I bring pasta for you, Signora. And aqua and pane della casa, si?'

Eileen was perplexed by the waiter's hybrid language, but Ken intervened to say, 'Water and bread would be fine.' The waiter nodded and weaved between the small cluster of tables towards the kitchen, and Ken turned to Eileen. 'He called you Missus - Signora. They're still learning English, at least that young lad is. He's new to Australia, but the owners have had this café since the 1920s.'

'I didn't realise so many Italians lived here,' Eileen said, looking around at the patrons.

'Well, we'll see a lot more soon enough,' Ken explained. 'I read the government is encouraging European immigrants to come to Australia, starting either this year or next. Something about building new capital works. Now that we're all officially Australians instead of British citizens, Calwell wants the immigrants to be called New Australians.'

'We've always been Australians.'

Ken shook his head. 'We were British citizens until the start of this year. We became Australians in January.'

'But George the Sixth is our king,' Eileen said.

'He is indeed, and we are still British as well.' Ken looked up as the waiter arrived with bread, water and a bottle wrapped in a green cloth, and said, 'Grazie, buon lavoro!'

'Grazie, Signore Evans. Mi scusi,' the youth replied, bowing and smiling. 'I bring your meal now.' He hurried back through the café.

'I didn't know you spoke Italian,' Eileen said.

'I can't,' Ken replied. 'I know enough to say thank you and hello, how are you. Not exactly fluent.'

'I don't know any other language.'

'You don't need to,' he reassured her. 'English is the only language we need in Australia. New people coming here have to learn it.'

'It must be very hard, coming to a new country and not be able to speak the language.'

'Probably,' Ken agreed, 'but these people managed when they came from Italy before the war. It comes down to how hard you're willing to work and learn. And we certainly don't want lazy people coming here.' He grinned, winked, and added, 'We have enough of them already.'

The waiter returned with two steaming bowls of pasta and placed them on the table. 'Buon appetito!' he invited and turned to another table.

'Looks good,' Eileen said, studying the curled noodles, 'but I'm afraid I won't be any better at this than last time. They're so slippery.'

'I'll show you the technique using a fork and spoon that Mario taught me a few weeks ago,' Ken offered, but as Eileen reached for her fork he took her hand and said, 'Before we eat, I have something to ask.'

Eileen met his steady gaze. 'Whatever is it?'

With an earnest expression that astonished her, he said, 'Eileen Bonney, will you marry me?'

*

'Ken asked me to marry him,' Eileen announced to her friends as they shared a smoko outside the wards.

She heard gasps, and Fryar exclaimed, 'And?'

Eileen extended her left hand to display a diamond ring on her finger. 'Let me look at that,' Williams said, and she grabbed Eileen's hand, turning it to study the diamond and the thin gold band.

'And?' Fryar repeated.

'I think it's real!' Williams declared, and the women laughed. 'He's no cheapskate either,' Williams added. 'That's a bloody sizeable rock.'

'Size of the rock tells you something about the size of the man,' Fryar asserted.

'I beg your pardon!' Eileen retorted.

'When did this happen?' Fryar asked.

'At the Italian café, on Lygon Street.'

'You like Italian food?' Fryar asked, crinkling her nose.

'It's awkward, but tasty,' Eileen replied.

'Give me fish and chips, or a lamb chop and mashed potatoes!' Fryar declared. 'I feel sorry for the immigrants who want to open eating places. Most Australians won't eat their food.'

'When's the big day?' asked Williams.

'We haven't chosen one, yet,' Eileen replied.

'Why ever not?' Fryar asked, raising an eyebrow. 'Get married and get out of here. He's going to be a doctor eventually. You won't have to work for a living. You can live a posh life with a big house.'

'Have lots of kids,' Fryar urged. 'You'll be too busy at home to have to work.'

'Now you're being silly,' Eileen said.

'Have you, you know, been back to his place yet?' Fryar asked, grinning.

'I'm not that kind of girl!' Eileen protested.

'No one starts out as that kind of girl,' Williams said, and winked at Fryar, who smirked. 'You must have done something right to get him to propose,' and the women sniggered.

'We can be your bridesmaids,' said Fryar.

'Sister can be your Matron of Honour,' Williams suggested.

'Speaking of Sister,' Fryar said, coughing, dropping her cigarette, and stepping on the butt. Eileen and Williams dropped their cigarettes and snuffed them out with their shoes.

'I suspect you young ladies are up to no good again? I believe you all have work to do,' Franklin said. 'Williams, you can come with me. I need a hand.'

'Yes, Sister,' Williams replied, and she turned to follow as Franklin strode past, swivelling to Fryar and Eileen to pull a face before falling into step with the Sister.

'You must be excited,' Fryar said.

'I am,' Eileen answered quietly, hoping Fryar didn't notice her hesitation. 'We better go inside.'

Moving to the ward beds, checking reports, adjusting pillows and refilling water, between conversations with patients and responding to bells, Eileen fingered and twisted the new ring on her finger, contemplating what it meant. She imagined marrying a different man in Adelaide, before he proved to be like her father. Instead, she ran to Melbourne and decided she wouldn't rush into marriage. And now she accepted a proposal from another man, a different kind of man, one a little less handsome, less passionate. Not that Ken was any less a man. He was kind, a gentleman, a man with prospects, generous. He was keen for racehorses, football, Italian food. They kissed and canoodled at his flat and in the shadows of the evenings, and he was a good kisser, but there wasn't the same spark she felt when she kissed Dudley, as if something was missing, something wasn't quite right, and she didn't know what it was, or why she felt that way. She accepted his offer of marriage as an obligation for his kindness and attentiveness, but she wasn't deeply in love with him, and that confused her.

*

Soft rain pattered against the dormitory windows beneath the dull October sky. 'I don't know what to do,' Eileen said, flopping onto her bed.

'There's no point marrying a man you don't love,' Turner advised. 'Too many women do that, and they live miserable lives.'

'I know,' Eileen replied. 'My mother did exactly that. Threw away a career for a man who turned her into a baby machine and, when he was done, he left her for another woman.'

'Oh, that's horrible!' Turner exclaimed. 'Your poor mother.'

'I don't want to be like her,' Eileen stressed.

'Is Ken your first boyfriend?'

'No.'

'That's lucky, then,' Turner said. 'First loves are the hardest to forget. Mine was a boy named Lincoln Braithwaite. I was sixteen. He was an apprentice carpenter who lived in our street, and I was madly in love with him. Blue eyes. Dark hair. His smile went straight through me, like a warm knife. I melted when he touched me.'

'What happened to him?' Eileen asked.

'Killed in Borneo, right at the end of the war when it was all but over. His plane was shot down, but no one found it. So unfair.'

'Oh, Turner, I'm so sorry,' Eileen commiserated.

'I was heart-broken. I locked myself in my room and cried for days.'

Eileen reached for Turner's hand, searching for something to say in consolation. 'I know what you mean about being heart-broken. I did the same when I broke up with my first boyfriend. It's why I came here,' Eileen explained. 'I couldn't cope with knowing I might run into him walking down the street. It was easier to run away from it all.'

'You did the right thing,' Turner said. She squeezed Eileen's hand and looked her in the eyes. 'You need to do the same now,' she said. 'If you don't love Ken – and you know the answer to that question in your heart – you need to tell him. You need to tell him before it gets too late.'

'I don't know how,' Eileen said, looking down.

Turner squeezed Eileen's hand excitedly. 'Come with me to Tasmania!' she urged. 'It will give you a good reason to break it off with Ken. You can tell him you have to go away for a while.'

'But what about work?' Eileen asked, sitting up. 'And where will we live?'

'We can stay at my sister's, at least until we settle in. And there's plenty of work in Tasmania, like I told you before.' Turner squeezed Eileen's hand harder. 'Come on, Eileen! It's a perfect idea. You and me. We can make a fresh start to everything, and we'll have so much fun. Tasmania is beautiful and green and cool. It's like being in England. We can run away from all the drudgery and promises and pointlessness of all this. We can start afresh. Please.'

*

The milling spectators studied the form as trainers paraded horses in the square enclosure before leading them onto the track. The overcast sky kept the air cool and the rain-washed grass moist under foot. Patches of brief sunlight appeared and vanished across the grandstand. Eileen followed Ken through the crowd, and she stood on tiptoes to peer at the horses in the enclosure. 'Which one do you fancy?' Ken asked.

'I don't know,' Eileen replied. 'Which one are you choosing?'

'Delta's the favourite,' Ken replied. 'Won the Victorian Derby. Odds are six-to-one.'

'Which one's Delta?' Eileen asked.

'The jockey is wearing the brown and blue stripes.'

'Are you betting on Delta?'

'Favourites never win the Cup. At least that's what people say, although some have,' Ken said. 'I like the look of Foxzami, the bay horse coming into the pen. Number five. The jockey's wearing the red helmet and purple top.'

'Why that one?' Eileen asked, as she jostled with a woman who tried to push in front.

'His sire sired Hiraji, the horse that won two years ago,' Ken explained. 'Maybe this horse has the goods too.'

'I think I like that one,' Eileen said, pointing to a bay horse parading in the enclosure, the jockey in red sleeves and blue diamonds on white.

'Comic Court,' Ken said. 'Is that the one for you?'

'He looks proud, and I like the colours. Do you know anything about him?' Eileen asked.

'Trained in Adelaide, I believe. Rumours are he's got potential.'

'I'll have Comic Court,' Eileen decided. 'He's from Adelaide, so he must be good.'

'Go up to the stand and I'll find you,' Ken said. 'I'll place our bets.'

As Eileen watched Ken's broad back weave through the crowd, heading for the bookies, she felt a deep ache, not of impending loss, but sadness for Ken. She would tell him her decision today. She sighed deeply and returned to watching the horses leave the enclosure and move onto the field. She attended enough events to understand a little of the conditions and how they affected race outcomes. Morning rain made the track heavy, and horses struggled with the wet grass and muddy soil in the earlier races, but the sun bursting through since midday, pushing aside the rain-sodden clouds, meant the track was drying, if slowly. Even so, it would still take a strong horse to run the two miles and win.

She headed for the grandstand, weaving between people as she climbed the steps, and she chose a place from where she could see the track and the finish line. *I'll tell Ken about my plans after the end of the races*, she mused, as she watched the horses walking and trotting towards the starting barrier. *That will be the right time.* Another pang of sorrow wounded her as she realised this day was most likely the last day they would spend together, and she twisted the engagement ring on her finger. *No*, she thought. She slid the ring from her finger into her pocket. *This is the right thing to do*, she decided, but when she saw Ken climbing through the crowd towards her she retrieved the ring and slid it guiltily onto her finger.

'Bets are placed,' Ken announced as he sidled across the row to stand beside Eileen. 'I put a pound each-way on Comic Court for you, and ten pounds to win on Foxzami.'

'That's too much money!' Eileen protested.

'Only if my horse doesn't win,' Ken said, grinning. 'That's what we do in the racing game, my love. We bet big. If Foxzami wins at sixteen-to-one, I'll make a pretty packet.' He leaned across and kissed Eileen's cheek, before straightening as the crowd hubbub erupted in a roar. 'And we're away!' Ken cried.

Eileen watched the horses thunder past on their first lap, admiring the animals' speed and strength as they carried their riders, and she cheered for Comic Court who was among the front runners. 'Who's in front?' she yelled.

'Looks like Bruin,' Ken replied. 'It's too early yet.'

The horses steamed around the far side of the track and the pack behind the leaders jostled and pushed for position. Two horses were checked and dropped out of contention, but Comic Court valiantly stayed with the front runners. Bruin, though, was leading and looking strong, and as they turned into the final straight towards the finish, it seemed the race was coming down to four or five horses. Eileen's heart sank as her choice faded into the trailing pack, but Ken became agitated, yelling, 'Now! Take the run now!' The bay, Foxzami, having stayed with the leaders for the race, began to pull away, along with two more horses, and halfway down the straight it was a desperate sprint between Benvolo and Hoyle, with Foxzami streaming past on the outside. Swept up in Ken's wild yelling and gesticulating, Eileen stood on her tiptoes screaming, 'Go, Foxzami! Go!' over and over, her throat straining as the crowd became one passionate orgy of urging betters. Hoyle tried to stem Foxzami's inexorable run, but the bay number five flashed past the winner's post a solid length and a half ahead, and Ken jumped and yelled ferociously, before he swept Eileen into his arms and kissed her passionately.

*

"Dear Mum," she wrote. "This letter is only for you, not for my brothers or sisters. I will write them a separate letter." She paused, dipped her nib into the ink, and continued. "I know this will come as a surprise, but I am leaving the hospital here in Melbourne and travelling with my very good friend, Shirley Turner, to visit her sister in Ulverston, Tasmania. We have already bought our tickets to travel on the SS Taroona and I am excited to be going, but also a little nervous because this will be the first time I have ever travelled on a ship. We are planning to stay in Ulverston for several months, but I will write every week." She paused to replenish her ink, and to compose her next lines.

"I never told you, but Ken Evans, the nice young man I mentioned in our letters, proposed to me, just before the football Grand Final. I accepted, of course, but I do not think it was a very wise thing to do, and so one of the reasons I am leaving Melbourne is to end our engagement. I have not found a way to tell him yet. I was going to tell him last Tuesday at the Melbourne Cup races, but I could not because he was so happy, having backed the winner, and I did not want to ruin his happiness. I know it is wrong to run away like this, but I do not want to go through everything that will happen if I keep pretending that I love him when I do not, and I do not want to break his heart. He is a nice man who deserves better. If I go away, I hope he can forget me and find someone who will love him as much as he deserves to be loved." She re-read her words before she dipped her pen and continued.

"I will not be home this Christmas. I will miss singing carols together and seeing everyone. I will miss Bruce's wedding. I feel terrible for this, but I do not know what else to do. Please tell everyone that I miss them and love them all very much."

Eileen sat back and stared at the letter. She wanted to tell her mother she understood her, that she learned not to make the same mistakes, that she wanted to become a different person when she came to Melbourne, but that hadn't really happened at all, so she was going to start afresh in Tasmania instead. She didn't have the words and phrases to say what she wanted to say. She wanted to be a grown-up, sensible, wise, and free, but she didn't understand how to be those things. The year in Melbourne was full of new experiences, new places, new people, new food, a new lover, and yet she still felt like the child she was in Adelaide whose life was determined by the decisions of others. She wanted to break the invisible emotional yoke that tormented her and escape the social burdens threatening to hold her down. That's what she wanted to tell her mother. Written words weren't doing what she wanted them to do. She scrunched the letter in her right hand and crushed it into a tight ball.

*

Eileen bent over the bucket, convulsing as she tried to vomit nothing again. Her stomach, neck and arm muscles tightened, and she moaned as she heaved a sliver of green bile and was left with a thread of saliva hanging from her lip. She wiped the saliva aside, slumped onto her haunches and leaned against the side of the bed, sweating and clammy, feeling the ship yaw and roll beneath her. 'I should have made you stay,' Shirley said from her bunk. 'Do you want my help?'

'I'm fine,' Eileen muttered clumsily. 'I only need to die, and I'll be okay.'

'If I catch it from you, I will kill you,' Shirley swore.

'You can't catch seasickness,' Eileen said.

'You know what's wrong,' Shirley said. 'Lots of people were infected at the Repat. Your skin was yellow when you were in the bath. You should have listened to us and stayed to recuperate.'

'If I stayed, we wouldn't be here,' Eileen agued.

'And I wouldn't be stuck in a cabin with someone retching in a bucket,' Shirley complained.

'I need water,' Eileen said.

'You'll throw up again,' Shirley reminded her.

'What time is it?' Eileen asked.

'After midnight,' Shirley said. 'You need to sleep.' She climbed out of her bunk and took Eileen's arm to help her up from the floor. 'My goodness, you positively reek, girl,' she said, as Eileen sank onto her bunk. 'You need a wash.'

'In the morning,' Eileen muttered, rolling onto her side.

'The bucket is by the bed, if you need,' Shirley told her, and she returned to her bunk. 'I'd empty it, but it's dark and rough out there.'

'You don't want to fall off,' Eileen warned.

'Not like the poor man who fell overboard in September,' Shirley said.

'Poor man,' Eileen murmured. 'Why would someone do that?'

'We never know what people are thinking,' Shirley said. 'They said in the paper that there was nothing suspicious. You know, no murder. He was probably bankrupt, or something didn't work out in his life the way he wanted, and he had enough.'

'I still don't understand why anyone would do that,' Eileen said. 'There's always something to live for.'

'Like sausages and eggs for breakfast,' Shirley said. 'That's what we can have to calm your stomach.' She switched off the light.

'Ew,' Eileen groaned. 'Shirley Turner, you are so mean.'

'Go to sleep,' Shirley ordered. 'I've put your teeth in the glass by your bed. At least you won't throw them up again.'

Eileen lay on her side, sweating, feeling the waves thud against the steel ship and the world yaw and pitch like her stomach. The nausea was less intense, though it came and went throughout the evening. She had nothing left in her stomach, nothing to throw up, so she prayed there would be an end to vomiting. She knew Shirley was right. She should have stayed in the Heidelberg hospital and recuperated from her illness, but she had to leave before Ken had an opportunity to draw her deeper into his plans; before she capitulated and accepted what he planned for them both. She knew she should have told him the truth – she planned to – but circumstances interfered. *It's better like this*, she decided, as the first wave of sleep rolled over her. *He will know, now, and I won't have to deal with the fallout or pleading. Dudley tried that on me, twice. It was enough. Not again. Not ever again.*

1950

"I was born when she kissed me. I died when she left me. I lived a few weeks while she loved me."
Dixon Steele

Cloth gloves protecting her from the rough wood fibre, Eileen hoisted the stack of wooden packing crates and carted them to the concrete block where the canvas fire hose hung on the water tap. She wrenched the stack apart, sitting the individual crates on the concrete, and hosed off the fetid fish remainders before she took up a hard-bristled wooden brush and scrubbed the interior of each crate, working methodically to remove traces of fish from the sodden wood. When she was satisfied the crates were clean, she shifted them to the drying rack and collected another stack to recommence the cleaning process. As she put down her newest load, she paused to wipe her brow and watched two gulls circling over the factory's iron roof, the white and grey birds expertly riding the air currents as they searched the world beneath them for food. The air reverberated with the ocean's distant murmur, the chugging of fishing boats and cranes and engines, infrequent voices, horns and gull cries, cannery machinery, and a low whispering morning breeze carried a salty seaweed tang. The sun glittered on corrugated iron and patches of water, promising a clear, cool February Friday to finish the working week.

Like every morning since starting work at the International Canners factory in December, time passed quickly. After smoko break, Eileen moved into the factory to scale fish from the fishermen's morning catch until lunch. After lunch, she joined the production line where she packed ice boxes with fish for transport and that task went through to afternoon smoko. She mended packing boxes until knock-off time. The routine was constant and easy, the work varied if malodorous.

She least enjoyed scaling the big fish, constantly wary of the keen knives and their capacity to nick fingers through the work gloves or take a finger completely off as happened to poor Anna Minchin a week earlier. Eileen heard her scream and saw the blood pooled on the floor after the men carted her out back and drove her to the doctor, and she knew what the nurses faced who would be consoling and attending to Anna. She fancied working in the cannery section, which seemed cleaner and more organised, but a job was a job, and it paid enough to eat and go out on the weekends. At least she escaped the Melbourne trap. She drew a deep breath and bent to cleaning the crates.

'Let's go!' Shirley called from the pallets, wiping her hands on a rag. 'Smoko!'

Eileen turned off the tap and lowered the hose, conscious of the light breeze cooling her arms. Sleeves rolled up on her blue shirt, dark grey trousers damp from overspray and her knees sodden from kneeling to scrub the wet boxes, Eileen trudged in her Wellington boots to the side of the shed where the gathered workers lit cigarettes and drank from their water containers. She accepted a hand-rolled cigarette from Shirley and waited for the matches to be passed before she lit and inhaled the first lungful of smoke.

'Who's going to the dance tonight?' inquired Wendy Dowd, the thickset brunette who weighed fish.

'What dance?' Richard Tanner, asked in return. He flicked his blond cowlick away from his eyes with his left hand that had only four fingers, one lost a year ago in the factory.

'There's one at the football club,' said Wendy.

'What about the pictures?' Matthew Bond asked. 'I'm going to the town hall.'

'What's on?' Shirley asked.

'Twelve o'clock High,' Matthew replied. 'Has Gregory Peck in it.'

Eileen leaned against the shed as she smoked and listened to the conversation, the same conversation the workers had every Friday, sometimes at morning smoko, sometimes at lunch, almost always in afternoon smoko. Who was going where? Who with? What was the best option? In the weeks since arriving and living with Shirley's sister and her husband, Eileen and Shirley explored Ulverston and the countryside, cycling west along Penguin Road and east out to Turners Beach when the weather was fine, dancing and going to the movies on weekends, picnicking along the banks of the Leven River. On the ocean rocks, they stripped to their bras and panties and photographed each other posing like movie starlets, laughing, and relishing the freedom of being alone in a world of sea spray and sunshine. For Eileen, the experience was exhilarating and liberating, partly because Shirley was a positive soul, a happy, carefree person who loved being back in Tasmania because she had a strong connection with her sister, Sandy, a relationship Eileen envied. But Eileen's feeling of freedom also came from being uncontrolled by Ken and Dudley, from being a complete individual and not a girl hoping for a good-looking prince to sweep her off her feet and make her life complete.

'Eileen,' Shirley called. 'Foreman's up and about.'

Eileen stubbed her cigarette butt with her boot heel and followed the others towards the factory. She spotted Mister Herring at the office door, watching the workers finishing smoko, and she smiled inwardly at the stocky and balding man's appropriate if amusing surname for a fish factory foreman. She never saw him berate a worker. He simply stared with the expression of a strict school master that warned everyone tomfoolery would not be tolerated. She knew his stern manner was bluff, a man playing a role, but everyone obeyed him without complaint.

When the afternoon bell rang to end the day shift, Eileen stacked her last box and pushed her hair back from her forehead to wipe away a film of sweat. She grabbed a white cotton rag to clean her hands, and her left cheek where she smeared dirt and sweat earlier, threw the rag onto the boxes, and headed for the door.

Shirley was waiting. 'Thank God that's another week over,' she remarked. Fellow workers wheeled their bikes away from the fence, saying, 'Have a good weekend,' and 'See you Monday.' Eileen turned her handlebars towards the road, mounting as Shirley joined her, and they pedalled into the town centre, chatting and laughing.

The sun lay low in the west, the day was rapidly losing its heat, and seagulls and terns circled and dipped over the ocean, their white wings glowing when the golden rays caught them. The Australian mainland and Melbourne were invisible, almost three hundred miles to the north, a distant place where an old life was left behind.

*

'Are you sure you don't want to come?' Shirley asked, leaning out the window of Bob's shiny dark grey 1948 Holden. 'There'll be lots of people at the dance. You might meet Mister Right.'

'I'll be fine,' Eileen replied. 'I'm tired. I'd be no fun tonight.'

'But Neil and Brian and the others, they'll be expecting you,' Sandy said from the front passenger's window.

'The boys will find someone else to dance with,' Eileen replied, grinning. 'They can't have too much of me.'

Shirley laughed and said, 'I'll dance with as many of them for you as I can.'

'You'll dance with Luke,' Eileen corrected. 'You know you will.'

'He's so dreamy,' Shirley crooned, swivelling coquettishly.

'Stop it, Shirley. You're drooling on your dress,' Eileen teased.

'There's fresh apple cake on the kitchen bench,' Sandy told Eileen. 'Help yourself.'

'Thank you,' Eileen replied.

'All right, we're off!' Sandy called, waving.

'Bye!' Shirley yelled.

Eileen leaned against the wooden porch balustrade, watching the red taillight recede and the brake light flare as the car reached the end of the street to turn towards the town centre. The last vestiges of sunset coloured the western horizon, silhouetting the birds drifting effortlessly towards roosts against the apricot glow. She reached into her pocket for a half-smoked rollie and her matches, lit the cigarette, drew back, and enjoyed the warmth spreading through her body. *Going to the dance would have been fun*, she mused, but she really was tired from the work, and she wanted a break from people and fussing and bustling, so she chose to stay home when Sandy and Bob announced they were attending the dance. Eileen was content. The house was hers for the night. Besides, Shirley's interest in Luke was more than a passing fancy and Eileen knew she would end up a third wheel, whatever the night's outcome.

She heard a light meow and Sandy's black and white cat, Thomas, stared up with soulful eyes. 'Come on, Thomas,' Eileen cooed, and she bent and hoisted the hefty cat into her arms, and Thomas smooched her cheek as she cuddled him. 'At least someone loves me,' Eileen murmured. Thomas purred.

Pushbike tyres crunched on gritty gravel. Thomas shuffled insistently to be released, flowed to the ground, and scurried around the side of the house. A man cycled into the neighbouring driveway, calling 'Evening,' as he leaned the bike against the side of the house.

'Good evening,' Eileen acknowledged, and she self-consciously dropped her cigarette butt.

The man sidled to the dividing picket fence and said, 'My name's Mervyn Jones. I live here with my parents.'

'Eileen Bonney,' Eileen reciprocated. 'I live here with -'

'Bob and Sandy Maxwell,' Mervyn interrupted, 'Yes. I know. You're friends with Sandy's sister. I've seen you a few times.'

'I don't remember meeting you,' she said, assessing the man in the darkening light.

'No,' he said. 'We haven't met, but it's a small town and everyone knows what's going on in everybody else's life. Not going to the dance?'

'Not tonight. I thought I'd spend the night in.'

'Sounds a splendid plan,' Mervyn replied.

'Did you just get home from work?'

'Oh, no,' he said. 'I was at a friend's house, having a few quiet Friday drinks to celebrate the end of the week. That's most Friday nights really.'

'Where do you work?' Eileen asked, her interest rising.

'You ask a lot of questions,' Mervyn replied.

'If I don't ask, I won't know. My Auntie Fay used to say that to us.'

'Mind if I join you for a smoke?' Mervyn asked. 'That's if I'm not intruding?'

'I'm not going anywhere.'

Mervyn strolled to the driveway entrance and into the yard to stand beside Eileen on the porch. *He's tall, but not too tall*, she decided, and she liked the look of his face, even in the evening light; square jaw, straight nose, face framed by loose, combed brown hair. He pulled a red and white cigarette packet from his top shirt pocket and opened it, offering Eileen a fresh cigarette.

'What kind are these?' Eileen asked, accepting a cigarette.

'The best kind,' Mervyn said. 'Craven A.' He took one for himself, drew a lighter from his trouser pocket and leaned forward to light Eileen's cigarette, an act of manners she duly noted. 'I see you smoke roll-your-owns.'

Eileen glanced down at the glowing butt by her foot and stubbed it out. 'Filtered cigarettes are too expensive,' she said.

'They're healthier for you,' Mervyn asserted. 'That's what the doctors say.' He lit his cigarette and rested against the porch balustrade. 'It's a beautiful night,' he said, gazing up at the array of glittering stars.

'You didn't tell me where you work,' she reminded him.

'At the cannery,' he said. 'I supervise unloading of the trucks.'

'I work there too!'

'Oh? Which section?'

'Nothing special,' Eileen replied. 'In the crate and fish section.'

'You're not a local though,' Mervyn noted.

'I'm from Adelaide.'

'What did you do there?'

Eileen smoked between questions and answers, enjoying Mervyn's relaxed companionship, learning how he was born in Ulverstone, was an apprentice plumber with his father but chose to take a job as a supervisor at International Canners when the new factory opened, how he played football for Ulverstone until he injured his knee the previous year. She didn't ask, but it became apparent he wasn't married, and she wondered why a man so well-spoken and handsome didn't have someone.

'If you're not doing anything tomorrow, I was wondering if you'd like to go for a drive to Delaney's Falls,' Mervyn said. 'I assume you haven't been?'

'I haven't,' Eileen replied. 'How far is it?'

'Half hour drive and a short walk.'

'I can come after church.'

'I'll be waiting,' Mervyn said as he straightened to leave. 'Goodnight, Eileen.'

Eileen watched Mervyn's slim silhouette walk to the road and up the adjacent driveway. He stopped to wave before he disappeared through the front door. She drew on her cigarette and stared up at the stars. Ulverstone was not going to be so lonely after all.

*

Mervyn was waiting as he promised, resting suavely against the mudguard of his dark blue Nash sedan in grey trousers and a white shirt, sleeves rolled up, brown hair combed loosely to the left. He greeted everyone with a charming smile, and nodded to Bob and Sandy, and Shirley gave Eileen an inquisitive look, saying, 'Who's been sneaking around the back of the chook house?'

'You don't have to know everything, Shirley Turner,' Eileen said, blowing her a kiss.

'Where is he taking you?' Shirley asked.

'Delaney's Falls.'

'Very romantic,' said Shirley. 'And a beautiful day for it too.'

'I have to go,' Eileen said as she walked towards Mervyn. 'I'll be home before tea.'

'Make sure you are, or there will be hell to pay,' Bob growled in his mock fatherly voice, before he laughed and gave Mervyn a thumbs up.

Mervyn held the passenger door open for Eileen to climb in, and when he settled in the driver's seat, Eileen said, 'Nice car.'

'Bought it last year,' he said. 'Nearly bought one of those new Holdens, but I like the drive of this one and its slipstream design.' He slid the car into gear and, as they moved away, he added, 'Big solid six-cylinder motor too.'

The conversation swung back and forth, Eileen telling part of her tale around her family and nursing, Mervyn unfolding his family and how his older sister and brother were killed in the war. 'Len was in Singapore when it fell. He was marched north to work on the railway. We never heard from him after that. Maggie was on the *Centaur* hospital ship, a nurse, like you. The Japanese sunk the *Centaur* in 1943, off the Queensland coast. Maggie didn't make it.'

'Oh, that's terrible,' Eileen commiserated.

'Never understood why the Japanese attacked a hospital ship,' Mervyn said. 'The war might be over now, but I know Mum and Dad will never forgive the Japanese for that. I'm not sure I can either.' They drove in silence, Eileen imagining what it must have been like for the poor souls trapped aboard a sinking ship, until Mervyn announced, 'We turn off here. Up the track is a place from where we can walk to the falls. The weather is holding so we should get a good view.'

Parked, Mervyn ushered Eileen out of the passenger door before he opened the boot to produce a cane picnic basket with a blue and white check towel folded on top. 'Thought we could grab a bite after the viewing,' he said. 'Hope you don't mind.'

Eileen was impressed that Mervyn brought the basket, and it fixed him in her mind as a thoughtful man, someone who wasn't focused on self-interest. She fell into step behind him, and he led her through shafts and pools of sunlight along a rough dirt path between the blackwood trees and blackberry bushes. The rising thunder of cascading water surrounded them as the path descended into a gully, but Mervyn turned from the main path, stepping over clumps of grass and weaving between mossy rocks and ferns and, when the ground underfoot became moist and slippery, he turned to help Eileen negotiate the steep slope. 'I thought we could see the falls from a different vantage than most people,' he explained as they crossed a rivulet. 'Locals know this side track. Tourists don't. They cross Preston Creek to get to the usual view.' He led Eileen a few more yards before he halted and announced, 'There it is.'

Eileen silently revelled in the wonder, fascinated by the narrow, glittering torrent plunging over the gorge lip and landing on a cluster of sharp, glistening rocks before foaming and spilling along the creek's course. She was enfolded in the rich, humid tang of rotting vegetation, soil and water, and the rumble of the falls, until Mervyn asked, 'What do you think?'

'It's beautiful,' she murmured. 'Truly beautiful.'

'There are other falls along the creek. This one is mixed up sometimes as Preston Falls, but the land around here belonged to a bloke named William Delaney.' Mervyn waited, before saying, 'Shall we find a place to set up the picnic?'

'Can we stay here a moment more?' Eileen asked.

'We can stay as long as you like,' he said.

As Eileen watched light glitter and shatter into rainbow shards in the plunging water, she sensed Mervyn's presence beside her, and she expected him to reach for her hand, and knew she wouldn't mind if he did, but he kept his hand to himself, like a gentleman, and she was content with that choice as well. The moment was perfect, and she was at peace and happy.

*

Sandy picked up a cooking pot and her green tea towel at the basin, as Eileen and Shirley emerged from the bathroom, giggling and adjusting their hair. 'Where are you two off to now?' she asked.

'Devonport!' Shirley replied.

'There's a special dance tonight at the Town Hall,' Eileen added.

'Hindu dancers!' Shirley interrupted. 'Shivaram and Tenaki.'

'Janaki,' Eileen corrected.

'It's something really exotic,' Shirley said.

'And I presume you're being escorted by Luke and Mervyn,' said Sandy, wiping the pot.

'You would be presuming correctly,' Shirley replied, and the young women giggled again.

'So, which one of you is going to be first married?' Bob asked as he entered.

'Bob Maxwell!' Sandy growled tersely. 'You know I don't appreciate smoking in the kitchen.'

Bob glanced guiltily at the cigarette between his index and middle fingers, before replying, 'I was simply curious as to who was laughing so much.'

'Parlour,' Sandy ordered. Bob grinned sheepishly and slunk out of the kitchen into the hall.

A car horn honked at the front of the house. 'That will be the boys!' Shirley declared. 'We'll be home late.'

'Don't do anything I wouldn't do,' Sandy said, her face comically serious.

'I'm not that type of girl,' Shirley replied coquettishly. Linking her arm in Eileen's arm, she said, 'Come on, Miss Bonney. Our chariot has arrived. We must be gone.'

'Come home late and I'll have a shotgun ready!' Bob called from the parlour as Shirley and Eileen reached the front door.

'Like Dad had for you!' Shirley retorted, and she pulled Eileen into the front yard before Bob could reply.

The Nash sat idling at the kerb, Mervyn at the wheel. Luke leapt out of the passenger's seat and opened the rear door, ushering Eileen in with a gentlemanly sweep of his arm, and stealing a kiss from Shirley before she climbed in. Doors closed, Mervyn pulled away from the kerb, tooting the horn and waving to Bob who emerged to stand on the porch.

Between short bouts of conversation, on the drive to Devonport, Eileen smoked and reminisced about the passing weeks in Ulverstone. Factory labour was much better than working the hospital wards. The only pernicious odour was from fresh fish brought in for processing, not the persistent stench of hospital antiseptic mingling with sweat and urine and fear of dying. Shirley and Sandy and Bob were fun to live with. There was no burden of siblings, no pressure to keep a family together, and they all had enough money to get by and have fun. Sharing a room with Shirley was freer than the drudgery of maintaining a bed under the watchful eyes of dormitory Sisters in the Nurses' Quarters. Evenings spent cycling the countryside, swimming and bush walking opened a world of natural beauty along the northern coast and into the hinterland, and Eileen captured all she could on her Brownie camera. Tasmania was idyllic.

And now there was Mervyn. Gentle, smart, polite, fine to look at, not possessive and pressing like her former beaus, he showed her his world and he was interested in her world. He danced and sang, and played football and tennis, worked hard and relaxed when he wasn't working. He was the icing on her Ulverston cake, sweet and completing her taste of a new life. She thought Melbourne and Ken were the changes she needed to escape the stifling pressures of Adelaide, and Dudley, and her family, but they melded into the same stifling experience. Ulverston and Mervyn were refreshing, revitalising, the fresh start she was seeking.

'Penny for your thoughts?' Shirley asked as the lights of Devonport filled the windscreen.

'Thinking how lucky we are,' Eileen said. 'How glad I am that I came with you.'

'Aw,' Shirley cooed and hugged Eileen. 'I'm glad you came too.'

Mervyn drove through Devonport's outskirts, turning left before the bridge over the Mersey River and heading onto Rooke Street towards the Town Hall. 'Plenty of people here tonight,' Luke observed.

Car safely parked, the foursome walked briskly along the street, and they joined the throng milling outside the Town Hall. Inside, Eileen admired the colourful flower arrays and lights set up for the performance. 'What is the production called?' she asked.

'I believe it's called "Indra Vijayam",' Mervyn explained. 'An Australian woman, Miss Lightfoot, is credited with organising it.'

'Fascinating,' Shirley remarked, as they took their auditorium seats. 'I wonder what possessed her to go looking for Indian performers?'

The prelude swelled, the Hindu dancers emerged, and Eileen was drawn to the lithe, athletic movements of the principal dancer, Shivaram, his dark bushy hair and golden jewellery glittering against his brown skin, his white teeth shining in the stage lights. When the performance ended, the crowd stood and applauded to show their appreciation, before Eileen and her friends flowed into the night air, carried by the exodus.

'So, what did you think?' Mervyn asked, when they reached the corner and could stop to talk.

'I thought it was wonderful,' Eileen replied. 'The dancers are so talented.'

'I think I'd rather smoke a cigarette,' Luke said, fishing in his coat pocket for his packet. He pulled it out, flipped the lid and offered everyone a cigarette.

'You didn't like it?' Eileen asked, taking Luke's offering.

'I guess it takes some skill to do that sort of thing, but the music was odd, and I didn't understand the story,' Luke replied. He returned the packet to his coat and produced a lighter, the tiny flame creating flickering shadows on his face.

'It was about an Indian god named Indra,' Shirley said, 'but I didn't understand the rest of it.'

'It was beautiful to watch,' Eileen said. 'I enjoyed it.'

'Would you like to walk for a few minutes?' Mervyn asked, raising his left arm towards Eileen.

'We'll meet you at the car,' Luke said, offering his arm to Shirley.

Eileen and Mervyn crossed the road and strolled in the moonlight along the footpath beside the river, chatting about the performance and the night, until Mervyn asked, 'How long do you think you'll stay in Tasmania?'

'I don't know,' Eileen replied. 'Perhaps forever.'

He stopped her and said, 'Would you consider staying in Ulverstone?'

She laughed. 'I honestly don't know.'

'Why don't you know?'

Eileen shrugged. 'Sometimes I feel guilty about abandoning my mother. Sometimes I miss my brothers and sisters. Sometimes I miss Adelaide.'

'I'd like you to stay.'

'Maybe I will,' Eileen said. 'It's too early to know for certain.'

Mervyn took her hand in his, and said, 'I'm growing very fond of you, Eileen.'

She squeezed his hand, replying, 'And I of you, Mervyn Jones.' She looked up at the moon scudding between wisps of dark cloud. 'Work in the morning. We best be heading home.'

They walked, hand-in-hand, back to the car, Mervyn coughing in exaggerated fashion to break up a passionate kiss between Shirley and Luke. 'You're such a spoil sport!' Shirley complained as she parted from Luke.

'We're in the back seat on the way home,' Luke announced, winking at Mervyn.

'And I'll keep an eye on both of you in the rear-view mirror,' Mervyn warned.

'You will do no such thing, Mister Jones!' Shirley snapped, and everyone laughed.

*

'Luke proposed to me!' Shirley announced elatedly as Eileen entered the bedroom.

'No,' Eileen replied. 'When?'

'Tonight. Before we returned to the car. Are you excited for me?'

'I wondered why you two were being so fresh in the back seat,' Eileen said, grinning.

'Stop it!' Shirley retorted. 'Are you happy for me?'

'Oh, of course I am!' Eileen replied and she embraced Shirley emphatically. 'You are so lucky. Luke is a lovely, lovely man.'

'I'm so thrilled!' Shirley said.

'Is there a ring?'

'Not yet. We're going to choose it together in Launceston on Saturday. You and Mervyn can come with us.'

As Eileen stripped off her dress and bra and put on her nightie, she said, 'I know this is a terrible question to ask, but are you really sure about Luke? I mean, he's lovely, but is he the one you want to spend the rest of your life with?'

Shirley flopped onto her bed, hands beneath her chin. 'Oh, yes! He is. He really, really is. He's so, so perfect, so kind, so gentle, and soooo sexy!' Both women laughed at Shirley's exaggerated emphasis.

'Have you told Sandy and Bob?' Eileen asked.

'Tomorrow morning,' Shirley replied. 'I'll tell them at breakfast.'

'How about I get up and make breakfast?' Eileen suggested as she sat on the edge of her bed.

'We both will,' Shirley said. 'Let's surprise them. It will be fun.' She stared at Eileen with a soulful gaze.

'I'm really so very happy for you,' Eileen said.

'Has Mervyn said anything?' Shirley asked. 'He's dead keen on you.'

'No,' Eileen said, 'at least, not a proposal.'

'But, if he did, you'd say yes, wouldn't you?' Shirley urged, and bubbled over with excitement, adding, 'We could have a double wedding!'

'You are a dreamer, Shirley Turner,' Eileen retorted. She eased under her bed covers. 'I'm tired, and we have to be up early to make breakfast and get to work on time. Go to sleep.'

'I can't,' Shirley said. 'I'm too excited!'

'Then go have a warm milk and calm down,' Eileen suggested.

'Yes, Miss Bonney,' Shirley replied with mock obedience. She crossed the room and jumped onto Eileen's bed, shaking Eileen, and saying, 'I'm getting married!'

Eileen fought Shirley's grip and broke into a giggling fit, gasping to catch her breath. 'Get off!' she cried.

Shirley relented, and rose from Eileen's dishevelled bed to calmly announce, 'I think I will go have a warm glass of milk.' She sashayed to the door and flicked off the bedroom lights as she exited, saying, 'Sweet dreams!'

Eileen sat up to adjust her bedclothes and settle her emotions in preparation for sleep. Faint noise came from the kitchen where Shirley was warming milk on the wood stove and Eileen smiled at her friend's eager energy, but when she snuggled into her pillow and rolled onto her side she could not sleep. Her mind rallied every memory she had of lovers, from the skinny red-haired boy she spied on from her backyard in The Broadway, to Dudley and his charming smile and sensual lips, to Ken's educated voice and kind eyes, to Mervyn's solid shoulders and big hands, and she reflected on each one and speculated what if possibilities. What if she had called out to Tim one afternoon? What if Dudley wasn't already engaged? What if she kept going out with Dudley even if he was engaged? What if she stayed in Melbourne with Ken? What if she accepted Mervyn's inevitable proposal? What if she said no to all of them?

She was awake when Shirley crept into the bedroom and she heard Shirley whisper, 'Are you awake?' but Eileen kept silent and listened as her friend climbed into bed, rolled over and nestled into sleep. She knew Mervyn was positioning himself, steeling himself to propose to her, because their intimacy of late was familiar and tender, and he was asking her what she saw for her future. *The truth is*, she thought, *I don't know my future, and now that Shirley is marrying my future is even less certain.*

Before they left Melbourne, Shirley and she made plans to travel as much of Tasmania as they could together but, so far, they only stayed in Ulverstone, held by Shirley's infatuation with Luke. The engagement spelled the end of the original plans because Shirley would embrace married life, leaving Eileen stranded. As much as Mervyn was a nice man, possibly even a good prospect for marriage, he reminded her of Ken, and she was not yet ready to settle and bear children. *I am nineteen*, she thought. *I haven't seen enough of the world.* As much as she felt sad for her mother's life, her mother at least lived an interesting single life until she was twenty-nine. Clarice Stephens, young woman and musician, lived before she became Clarice Bonney, wife and mother, drudge, forsaken woman.

When sleep did finally envelop her, she dreamed a man walked with her through a forest, the trees and bushes more essence than corporeal, and the man held her hand and his touch tingled teasingly through her body. And he turned her gently towards him, tilting her chin softly with his hand and kissing her with a lingering caress and, when she opened her eyes to gaze into his face, expecting to see Mervyn, it was Dudley Wright.

*

'I think it's good the government banned all Communists from holding government jobs,' said the busty red-haired woman in the bus seat beside Eileen. 'We can't trust those people. Look what's happened in China and Korea. The same as what happened in Russia.'

Eileen nodded agreeably. Since the start of the year, the new Prime Minister, Robert Menzies, led a style of government focussed on internal growth and external mistrust. She knew, with inner pride, that Dame Enid Lyons was in the Federal Cabinet, one of two women first elected to parliament before the war, but otherwise she had little interest in political matters, although the news that people were talking of more wars breaking out, so soon after the last one ended, saddened her and made her uncertain of the future.

'They say the Chinese are spreading their Communism all through Asia, like the Russians have been doing in Europe, and the Red Peril is the new

Nazi threat to us all,' the woman continued.

Eileen wished she was sitting in the window seat so she could turn away and watch the Tasmanian countryside whiz by, and ignore the woman, but she was trapped in the aisle seat. Away to the west, through the rain that dogged the bus since leaving Launceston, she glimpsed the mist enshrouded silhouette of Cradle Mountain and made a promise to visit it.

'My son is talking about going to fight the Communists in Korea,' the woman said. 'He fought in Borneo against the Japanese.'

Why would you want your son to go to another war, so soon after he's returned from one? Eileen wondered. *I wouldn't want Bruce to go again. Ever.* She hoped that, by keeping silent, the woman would grow tired of a one-sided conversation, but the woman seemed determined to persist, as if she preferred the sound of her voice to dialogue.

'At least they finally stopped rationing petrol,' the woman said. 'I hear they might stop butter rationing soon. Not that it matters to me. My brother Jack has a dairy farm, so we always have plenty of butter, even in the tough times. Silly, isn't it? That they stopped rationing petrol, but they're still rationing butter?'

Eileen opened the novel on her lap.

'What are you reading?'

'*The Heart is a Lonely Hunter*,' Eileen replied.

'Is it good?' the woman asked.

'It's strange,' Eileen replied. 'I think I'd like to keep reading now.'

'I like books like *Gone With The Wind*,' the woman continued. 'I saw the movie, of course, but it wasn't a patch on the book. That Vivien Leigh did a good job, though, and Clark Gable was as debonair as always, but they missed so much of the book in the film. That's what made it disappointing.'

Eileen focussed inward, remembering how her favourite character in McCuller's novel could escape to her inner private world. She could relate to Mick Kelly, even having never seen snow. *But maybe I will see snow on Mount Wellington*, Eileen reminded herself, and anticipation rippled through her veins.

Leaving Ulverstone was not easy. Mervyn was devastated. 'You will come back?' he asked pensively in the porch light, after she told him her plans.

'Of course I will,' Eileen reassured him. 'Only I need to see what I came to see. Surely you understand that? I want to explore more of Tasmania than Ulverstone and Devonport.'

'I do understand,' Mervyn replied. 'It's, well, I hoped we might be like Luke and Shirley. They're very happy.'

'We can talk about it when I come back from Hobart,' Eileen said. 'It won't be for too long. I promise.'

'It will seem like forever to me,' Mervyn said.

She didn't miss his reference to Shirley and Luke's wedding. Engaged less than four weeks, they married in the Ulverstone Holy Trinity church, with Eileen and two of Shirley's workmates as bridesmaids, along with Mervyn and Bob and Jeff as groomsmen, and Sandy as Matron of Honour. The couple spent a week on honeymoon in Devonport before moving into a small timber-framed house at the edge of town, leaving Eileen alone at Sandy and Bob's house.

'They love having you with them,' Shirley told Eileen after Shirley informed her Luke bought a house. 'Sandy said you can stay as long as you like.' She giggled and added provocatively, 'You could stay with Luke and I, but it might be too noisy.' When Eileen told Shirley she was heading for Hobart, Shirley was disappointed. 'I hoped we would spend lots of time together still,' Shirley said. 'This isn't because I got married, is it?'

'Of course not,' Eileen refuted. 'But you have a man to take care of now, and I have spare time on my hands, so I thought it would be a perfect opportunity to head south.'

'What about Mervyn?' Shirley asked.

'He said he'll wait for me,' Eileen told her, although at that point in time she hadn't yet told Mervyn her plans, because she knew Shirley would use him as a lever to keep her from going away.

'Where will you stay?' Shirley asked. 'Have you got a job?'

'I think so,' Eileen replied. 'There's a maid's position at the Custom's House Hotel. I wrote a letter to the manager and hopefully I will make it in time for an interview.'

Sandy gave her the McCullers novel after Eileen found it on the parlour sideboard. 'I was reading it,' Sandy explained, 'but I lost interest. I read, or heard somewhere, it's the writer's first novel. You can read it if you want. Take it on the bus with you. It might fill the time.' Eileen politely refused, but Sandy insisted the novel really wasn't worth keeping and she was going to give it to the bookstore to re-sell, so Eileen accepted the gift and began reading on the first leg of her bus trip from Ulverstone to Launceston.

She turned the novel's page. Mick had a job at Woolworth's to support her family. Eileen understood what that meant, how that felt, why Mick believed it was a mistake.

The woman beside Eileen finally gave up on her one-way conversation and opened her copy of *Women's Weekly*, the cover displaying a cherry-cheeked child in a blue cardigan struggling with knitting needles and balls of yarn. Released from the woman's unsolicited intrusion, Eileen read while the rainstorm darkened the countryside and the bus driver turned on the interior lights.

*

'My name's Ruby, Ruby Ballard,' the young woman said. She folded a white cotton sheet and laid it neatly on the pile on the dolly cart.

'Eileen Bonney,' Eileen replied.

'You're new, aren't you?' Ruby asked. Her smile revealed her perfect teeth.

'Yes,' Eileen confirmed. 'I started on Friday.'

'I've been here three months,' Ruby said. 'Live local?'

'No,' Eileen replied. She pushed the rattly dolly cart to the first doorway. 'Can you open the door, please?'

'Where are you from?' Ruby asked. She unlocked the door and swung it open, announcing, 'Maid!'

'Around,' Eileen replied. 'Adelaide originally.' She lifted a set of sheets from the cart and Ruby grabbed the white towels and soap.

'Muswellbrook, myself,' Ruby told her. 'You've probably never heard of it, right?'

'No, I haven't, Eileen admitted. She headed for the bed and put the fresh sheets on the brown armchair.

'It's in New South Wales, north of Sydney!' Ruby yelled from the bathroom. 'Coal and cows, and not much else! That's why I left; that and an abusive father who drank too much! Why did you leave Adelaide?'

'Lots of reasons,' Eileen said. 'I needed to see more.' She stripped the sheets from the bed and threw them on the floor.

'No boyfriend?'

'Too many,' Eileen replied.

Ruby emerged from the bathroom, laughing. 'Well, it might be we have the same problem,' she said, catching her breath and winking. She put down a towel she was folding. 'Can you stand still a moment?' Eileen arched an eyebrow, but she stopped fitting the sheet and straightened. Ruby approached and inspected her. 'You see it, don't you?'

'Twins,' Eileen replied.

'Yes!' Ruby exclaimed. 'It's true. Same brown hair, same blue eyes, same height. Oh my gosh!'

'Same uniform,' Eileen said, and they laughed.

'It's uncanny. It's like looking in a mirror.'

'Your nose is straighter.'

'Your eyebrow arches more.'

'I think that's why I like you already,' Eileen said, grinning.

'Oh, Hobart is in big trouble if there's two of us on the prowl. Where are you staying?'

'In the hotel, until I find somewhere,' Eileen explained.

'Then you better move in with me,' Ruby suggested. 'My flatmate moved out last week and I need someone else to use the second bedroom. It will be cheaper than staying where you are now. And you'll have me for company.'

'I'll come and look,' Eileen agreed.

'After today's shift,' said Ruby. 'I'll take you there, and we can eat together.'

*

Ruby opened her refrigerator and produced a long neck bottle of Cascade beer, holding it up for Eileen to view. 'Thirsty?'

'Where did you get that?' Eileen asked.

'Bought it,' Ruby replied.

'How old are you?' Eileen asked.

'Twenty-two,' Ruby replied. 'How old did you think I was?'

'I assumed -' Eileen paused and added, 'I'm nineteen. That's all.'

'I won't tell anyone,' Ruby said, grinning. 'I repeat my question: thirsty?'

'Yes,' Eileen said. 'Yes, I am.'

Ruby expertly poured the beer into two long glasses, generating a frothy head on the golden liquid. 'Tonight's menu consists of local pork sausage, mashed potato and carrots, accompanied by a large dollop of fresh-out-of-the-packet gravy, and garnished with a sprig of parsley I stole from the neighbour's garden.' She took up one glass, pointed it towards Eileen and said, 'Cheers!'

'Cheers!' Eileen echoed and drank.

'And after we've eaten, we're going dancing at the Belvedere,' Ruby announced.

'But I'm in these dowdy old work clothes,' Eileen complained. 'I can't go out. My hair is a mess.'

'You can wear one of my dresses,' Ruby told her. 'I'm sure it will fit. And I can fix your hair, and you can fix mine. We'll have a great time. You like dancing, don't you?'

'I love dancing,' Eileen replied.

'Then let's eat and get ready!' Ruby declared.

Meal completed, Ruby led Eileen into her bedroom, opened the wardrobe and threw four dresses onto her bed, saying, 'Choose one. Although I think the best one for you is the green check with the white trim. I love that one.'

'Then you should wear it,' said Eileen.

'Oh, I can't,' Ruby said. 'I wore it last time at the Belvedere.' She pouted, altering her voice to imitate a movie star, saying, 'Darling, seriously, I can't be seen in the same outfit twice.' Eileen lifted the green dress and held it against herself. 'Perfect!' Ruby declared. 'Have a quick wash in the bathroom, use a splash of my vanilla essence perfume, and get that dress on, girl. Then we'll do our hair and make-up and set Hobart alight!'

Wrapped in trench coats, hair curled and set, lipstick and mascara applied, tipsy from beer and a shared glass of gin, Eileen and Ruby headed for Argyle Street along the lamplit streets in a brooding winter night, walking briskly and chatting, singing snatches of popular tunes, until they arrived outside the art deco Belvedere building. 'This is a car shop,' Eileen said, staring at the ground floor showroom windows with the shadows of cars lurking within.

Ruby pointed to the lit windows on the first floor. 'That, girl, is where all the action is. Upstairs we go.'

Swing music enshrouded them as they entered the stairwell, and it reached a crescendo when they burst through the door at the top. Couples whirled and stepped to the rhythm of "The Hucklebuck", a song Eileen knew well, and she smiled as Ruby grabbed her hand and said, 'No standing around, girl, Let's dance!' Eileen flowed into the dance, letting Ruby take the lead, pleased by Ruby's fluency and confidence, and laughing as the first song ended and the eight-piece band swung straight into the next song, fronted by a female vocalist.

When the band leader announced the end of the set, Ruby asked if Eileen wanted to share a cigarette and the young women headed for the toilets to smoke. The toilets were busy with women coming and going, adjusting makeup and hair, peeing, smoking. 'Where did you learn to dance, girl?' Ruby asked.

'My brother Bruce used to take me to the Aubrey Hall Dance Studio and The Argosy Palais. You?' Eileen asked between puffs on the cigarette.

'Boyfriends,' Ruby replied. 'The best was an American. He was on leave in Sydney, and we had some swell nights, dancing. All kinds of dancing.'

'Goodness me, Ruby Ballard, you shameless thing,' Eileen gasped, feigning shock.

In the background, the band started playing, and an exodus of women from the toilet pushed through the smoke and perfume haze. 'Let's go, girl!' Ruby exclaimed, and she took Eileen's hand again and led her back into the ballroom. The band was playing the "Twelfth Street Rag" and the women leapt into the rhythm, kicking their feet and jiving on the parquetry floor as the clarinet player riffed through his solos. The jive continued into the next song and then the band leader announced, 'Ladies and gentlemen, the next piece is for a Foxtrot. Take your partners please.'

'I need a breather,' Eileen said. 'A glass of water would be good.'

Ruby led Eileen to the edge of the dance floor where soft drinks were being served and they each took a water. Eileen studied the dancers, the women in formal ball gowns, and said, 'I think we're under-dressed.'

Ruby laughed, replying, 'Yes, we are. We should be at the Royale. We'll go there next time.'

Eileen was about to respond when a tall, hawk-nosed man in a black suit stepped between the women and asked, 'Would you lovely ladies like a couple of dashing gentlemen to dance with?' He indicated his friend, a dark-haired man with a thick moustache and steel blue eyes.

'Thanks, but we're fine,' Ruby said before Eileen could respond. She took Eileen's glass, put it on the bench and led Eileen back to the dance floor. 'Can you Foxtrot?'

'Of course,' Eileen replied, and as Ruby took the lead role Eileen asked, 'Why aren't we dancing with the men?'

'You want all the complication that goes with dancing with men?' Ruby queried. 'Seriously? I thought you ran away from that.'

'I did.'

'Then I saved you from more complication, girl,' Ruby said, and she steered Eileen between the other couples, laughing and spinning elegantly through increasingly complicated variations of the dance steps.

And then another suited man with a grave expression on his blotchy, moustached visage intervened mid-dance, stepping between Eileen and Ruby as he indicated the door with his arm. 'I think you both better leave,' he said gruffly.

'On what grounds?' Ruby challenged.

'You are not appropriately attired, either of you,' the man said. 'The Belvedere has a sound reputation for excellent dress and good manners, and you will not blemish that reputation.'

'We're only dancing,' Ruby argued.

'Please do not make a scene,' the man warned bluntly. He nodded over Ruby's head to another man with sharply combed slick hair, a burly character in his formal suit, who moved towards them.

'Let's go,' Ruby said, taking Eileen's arm. 'Some people think they're way better than others.' Ruby sniffed disparagingly at the man before she led Eileen onto the stairs into the wintry night.

Lightning flashed over the city, rain gushed along the gutters, and Eileen pulled her coat over her head, feeling the cold rain splash against her legs. 'Well, here's another fine mess you've gotten me into!' Ruby declared in a poor imitation of Oliver Hardy.

'How do we get home in this?' Eileen asked.

'Like any other poor soul without a car or a bus ride,' Ruby said. 'We walk.'

Collars up, arm in arm, the two women launched into the downpour, flinching at every burst of lightning and chasing thunderclap as they hurried along Argyle Street towards Ruby's apartment block. Car headlights swung alongside, and a man called, 'You girls want a lift?' but Ruby waved him on.

'We could have taken the lift,' Eileen complained.

'And save ourselves from what?' Ruby asked. 'Getting wet? We're already soaked!' she declared, and laughed, and Eileen laughed with her.

They clambered up the slippery front steps from the pavement into the apartment building and climbed two flights to the landing and Ruby's door. Ruby fumbled with her key before she swung the door open. She flicked on the single light globe, threw her keys onto the couch, sighed, and announced, 'Home sweet home. Let's get out of these sodden garments and get dry.' Eileen stripped off her coat and the borrowed dress and stood shivering in the centre of the room, until Ruby handed her a dressing gown. 'This was Janine's, but she forgot it. Now you can use it, girl.'

Eileen laughed.

'What's so funny?' Ruby asked.

'You keep calling me girl.'

'It's a habit from my Dad,' Ruby said. 'He used to say it to every woman.'

'My family all call me Girlie back home,' Eileen explained.

Ruby grinned as she slid out of her bra, and said, 'Girlie it is, then.' She towelled herself quickly, put on a sweater, and asked, 'Hungry, Girlie?' as she headed for the kitchenette.

'Not really.'

'Cup of tea, then,' Ruby said. 'A hot cup of tea will dry us out.'

'I will, thank you, but then I better get going,' Eileen said.

'In this weather, Girlie? I won't allow that. There's a spare room and you can sleep there tonight. You've got your work clothes. You can rinse your bra and knickers and air your uniform overnight. And tomorrow night you'll bring your goods and chattels over here and settle in. I insist. Agreed?'

'You're too kind,' Eileen said.

Ruby approached and hugged Eileen. 'We're sisters.'

In fresh sheets, the rain humming against the window and wall, Eileen remembered she had a letter to write to tell her mother where she was and what she was doing. The last exchange was more than a week ago, when she said she was heading for Hobart. She promised she would write when she had an address to receive letters. Ruby had given her one. She snuggled against her pillow. *Ruby is fascinating*, she mused, *and it's strange how we look so much alike, like we are almost twins*. She smiled. The thought of having a doppelganger appealed. Hobart wasn't going to be so bad a place to stay, after all.

*

Eileen admired the steep, rifted hills descending through thick verdant forests onto the undulating landscape as she cycled along the winding narrow road, and she breathed in the fresh, crisp air. 'The valley is so beautiful!' she exclaimed, when she stopped her bicycle beside Ruby. 'Everywhere is endlessly green.'

'England is like this,' Ruby said, catching her breath.

'You've been to England?'

'No,' Ruby replied. 'My brother Clarrie wrote me letters, before he was lost over Europe. He told me about places he visited when he was on leave. He had a brilliant way of describing things with words.'

'You miss him,' Eileen said softly.

'I do,' Ruby replied. 'I wanted to be like him.'

'I guess he was very handsome.'

Ruby grinned. 'He was very handsome, and smart, and nothing scared him,' she said. 'I idolised him. I wish he came home.' She stared across the valley, and the quiet moment of unspoken pain flitted by like the clouds scudding across the hilltops. 'Do you have brothers or sisters?' she asked.

'Eight,' Eileen answered. 'Six brothers. Two sisters.'

'Wow!' Ruby gasped. 'Nine of you. How did your mother cope?'

'She didn't,' Eileen said quietly.

'Oh,' Ruby said. 'Sorry.'

'I'd love to live out here,' Eileen remarked, changing the topic. 'I feel free.'

Ruby laughed, shook out her hair as she remounted her bike, and urged, 'Catch me if you can,' and she pedalled swiftly away. Caught off guard, Eileen pushed her bicycle forward and chased Ruby, grinning as she closed the distance on a low climb. An orange apple-laden lorry suddenly rose over the crest, forcing the young women to cycle in single file on the edge of the road as it swept past, the driver hanging out the window to wolf whistle. 'Well, that made his day,' Ruby said sarcastically. 'I hate it when men do that.'

'Whistle?' Eileen asked.

'Ogle and make stupid bloody noises,' Ruby said. 'I'm not a lump of flesh for their pleasure.'

'But they all do it.'

'Good men don't,' Ruby argued, and she sped up again, forcing Eileen to pedal harder to catch her. They rode up and down three more hummocks before Ruby slowed and slewed her bike to a stop beside a hand-painted roadside sign. 'Here we go!' she announced, gesturing for Eileen to look at the sign with painted blue lettering, *Pickers Wanted: Experience Not Needed: Food and Board Provided*. 'We can live here for free and earn money. Fresh air, quiet, beautiful views. Just what you wanted.'

Eileen looked over the fence at the farm spreading across the hill slope, the white and green painted wooden house surrounded by trees and bushes and large wooden sheds, paddocks with rows of apple trees, a Border Collie loping across a track ahead of two figures, and immediately compared the view with her memories of Hobart and Melbourne and Adelaide streets with their trams and cars and trains and crowds. 'It would be very different,' she murmured.

'I'm up for it, Girlie!' Ruby declared. 'You?'

'What about our jobs?' Eileen asked.

'We quit!' Ruby replied.

'And the apartment?'

'We leave. It's too expensive anyway. We can save money out here. Are you in?'

Eileen nodded to her smiling friend, laughed, and said, 'I am.'

*

'Mick Warner's the name,' the fair-haired foreman announced, holding his hand out to shake. He led Eileen and Ruby towards five wooden huts at the perimeter of the apple orchard, where he continued his introduction. 'You'll hear some of the regulars call me Two-Up. That's 'cos I like a game of Two-Up after work on Fridays, and I'm not bad at it either. You sheilas play Two-Up?'

'I've played a few games,' Ruby said.

'Save up your money, then, cos I'm betting it'll be mine soon enough,' Mick warned. He opened the door to the first hut, revealing two long trestle tables with benches. 'Mess hut,' he said. 'You get fed here, morning and night. You take something along with you for lunch. Cook's name is Jenny. She makes a good stew, and an apple pie better than anyone.' He closed the door and led them to a smaller hut. Eileen wrinkled her nose at the familiar stench of excrement. 'Dunnies are inside. Hope you're not prudish, cos you could be sitting next to someone else when you're busy. Sheilas on the left door. Blokes on the right. Newspaper stacked inside the door.'

Two young men emerged from the right door, buttoning their trousers, and looking sheepish when they spotted Mick with the young women. 'Say g'day to young Arnie Tiller and Paddy Moran,' Mick said, waving to the young men. They grinned and returned the greeting, before heading for the orchard. 'Lads are passing through on their way to set up a farm further down on the Huon. Making a few shillings before they move on.' He led the young women to a larger wooden hut where a tan Kelpie rose from her curled sleep and wagged her tail slowly. 'This here's the women's quarters,' he said. 'Over there,' he said, gesturing to another hut several yards away, 'That's where the blokes sleep.' He approached the dog and patted its ears. 'And this is Maybelle. She keeps an eye on the blokes and makes sure none of them stray across the compound at night-time. Does a good job, she does,' he said, chuckling as he patted the dog. 'None of the blokes mess with Maybelle. You're sharing with four other sheilas. They're out in the orchard right now. Two of 'em are leaving end of this week cos the work's getting lean. Any questions?'

'What time do we start?' Eileen asked.

'MacAvoy's rooster is pretty good, but I do the wake-up round at five, breakfast is ready at six, in the orchard by seven-thirty,' Mick explained. 'Lunch at midday. Smokos mid-morning and mid-afternoon. Knock off at five-thirty. Tea at six. Five days a week, until harvest is finished. Paid weekly on Fridays. Do what you like on a weekend. Any other questions?' Mick raised an eyebrow. 'No? Good,' he decided. 'You done this work before?'

'No,' Eileen replied.

'Thought not,' said Mick. 'Soft hands. Neat hair. Maids or nurses or something, eh?'

'Close enough,' Ruby said. 'Show us what we need to know.'

'I'll take you through the ropes today,' Mick said. 'You don't get paid for that. Tomorrow morning, you get up and start like everyone else. Then you earn your money. I will tell you one thing. You chose the wrong time to come, you know. Best time for picking apples is the first half of the year. Season's right at the end now. But then no one is around either, being the start of winter, so maybe you'll get a couple of weeks of work. Follow me.'

*

Eileen hefted her basket to the lip of the wooden bin, tilted it to empty the apples, then hung the basket in her left hand while she wiped sweat from her forehead with her right. The temperature was low beneath the grey early winter sky, but the work was hard.

Mick looked up from the grading table, glanced towards where Ruby was approaching with her basket on her shoulder, and shrugged. 'I warned you the season was done,' he said in his laconic manner. 'I reckon by tomorrow there won't even be second-grade fruit left on the insides of the trees. The lads left this morning. You sheilas probably ought to move on as well.'

'Is there any other work we can do?' Eileen asked.

Mick slid off his leather cap and scratched his thick bush of brown hair. 'The Everston's prune their vines hereon in. It's only been a month, but I can put in a good word for you because you've worked hard and honestly. Their vineyard's next paddock over.'

'Could you?' Eileen asked, as Ruby arrived to empty her basket.

'Could he what?' Ruby asked.

'Talk to the neighbours so we can get more work.'

'I thought this was the last of it,' Ruby said. She emptied her basket and leaned against the wooden bin.

'Vine pruning,' Eileen explained.

'Well, that's a good choice of an easier job,' Ruby said, shaking her head.

'You won't find vine pruning easier,' Mick warned, wiping his hands on a black rag as he approached. 'You ever done it?' Before they replied, he chuckled and said, 'No, you two sheilas wouldn't have done it.' He pretended he had a grape vine before him and he started explaining what the job involved, imitating the actions of finding the main framework and cutting the shoots back to twin buds. 'The foreman will be watching like a hawk,' Mick said. 'Forewoman, actually. Missus Everston. She's tough on workers who don't understand how important their job is. Good pruning leads to good harvests. You been paid by the weight in apples you pick here. Everston's will pay by the number of vines you successfully prune. Still interested?'

Eileen looked at Ruby who was listening keenly to Mick's explanation. 'I'm in for it,' Ruby announced, and she looked at Eileen, who nodded.

'I'm not promising a job,' Mick said, 'but, after work today, I'll go visit the Everstons and see if they'll take you.'

'So, we're finishing up?' Ruby asked.

'There's nothing but scraps for the birds on that orchard now,' Mick said. 'I'll get Mister MacAvoy to sort out your pay packets, and then you've got the weekend to yourselves.'

'I guess we'll need to find somewhere else to stay,' Eileen said to Ruby.

Mick snorted, and said, 'If Everstons take you on, I reckon I can talk Mister MacAvoy into letting you sheilas stay in the hut, at least for a while. No one else is using it.'

*

The rain pelted the road and melted the forest into grey. Eileen followed Ruby onto the shoulder, dismounted and ushered her bike under the canopy of two large eucalypts where the rain gushed through the branches and leaves, but without the ferocity of the August storm. Saturated, the two women stared out at the hazy world. The shadowy outline of a timber truck appeared through the rain and swooshed past, disappearing around the bend they negotiated only a moment earlier. 'No drinks in Huonville for us,' Ruby said disconsolately. 'We might not even get back to the hut in this debacle.'

'We can't exactly sleep under a tree out here,' Eileen argued.

'We could,' Ruby replied. 'Sometimes it's not much warmer or drier in that bloody hut on MacAvoy's.'

'It's free accommodation. My family slept on Brighton beach one Christmas.'

'Why would you do that?'

'We lost our home. We had nowhere else to go,' Eileen explained.

'How did you lose your home?'

'It's a long story.'

Ruby chuckled, shrugged and said, 'So, tell it. I'm not exactly going anywhere right now.' Interrupted twice by cars sweeping past that Ruby tried to flag down, Eileen told Ruby all she needed to know about the eviction and beach living. When she was finished, Ruby said, 'My father nearly strangled my mother.'

Eileen gasped. 'Really?'

'We were in our beds, my brother and me. I think I was maybe six. It's hazy now,' Ruby said, gazing into the rain. 'I remember waking up hearing shouting, and screaming, and something shattered in the parlour. I got up and found Clarrie crouching in the hall peering into the parlour. I might have said something to him, I don't really remember, but I do remember looking into the parlour, and there was my father with his hands around our mother's throat, and she was red in the face, and her eyes were bulging.' Ruby stopped.

Seeing her friend shaking, Eileen enfolded her in her arms, and the two women stayed protected from the outer world in the embrace, Ruby sobbing softly, Eileen feeling her friend's pain shivering in her soul.

A horn broke their embrace. Eileen peered out to the road to see a red Bedford truck parked on the shoulder and a man's blue-capped head sticking out of the window. 'Are you girls all right?' he yelled. 'Do you want a ride?' He opened the door and jumped down, slipping awkwardly in the mud as he approached. 'Where were you girls going?'

'Into Huonville,' Eileen replied.

'I'm headed there,' the driver said. 'I can take you in.'

'Thank you,' Eileen said. She helped Ruby to her feet, and they wheeled their bikes towards the truck, crossing rivulets running along the edge of the road as they kept balance in the muddy slush.

'Hop up in the cabin,' the driver instructed. 'I'll put your bikes on the back.'

Eileen and Ruby and climbed into the truck. 'You are sodden wet, girl,' Ruby chided with a grin as they settled on the seat, and Eileen was glad to see her friend's spirit lift.

The truck rocked as the driver climbed onto the running board and into the cabin. He slammed the door. 'It's a bloody monsoon out there!' he declared, and reached behind Eileen, extracting a striped, orange towel. 'All I got, ladies,' he said, handing the towel to Eileen. 'Ain't the cleanest rag, but it might help you get a bit of that water off you.' He fossicked in his pocket, his elbow digging into Eileen's side, pulled out a large handkerchief and wiped the rain from his face. 'Name's Richard Porter,' he said, and he extended a big, dirty hand towards Eileen.

Ruby reached in and shook Richard's hand, saying, 'Ruby.'

'Eileen,' Eileen said, shaking Richard's hand after Ruby.

'All right then,' Richard said, pressing the starter and putting the Bedford into gear, 'we better get you ladies somewhere dry.'

*

The morning light filtering through the curtain threw a long blade of light across the floor. Eileen watched dust motes, before she rolled over and pressed against Ruby's warm arm. 'Are you awake?' she asked.

'I am now,' Ruby replied.

'It's not raining.'

'I know.'

'We better get going while we can,' Eileen suggested.

'Not until I've had a good breakfast,' Ruby asserted.

'What time did you come to bed?'

'You were already snoring.'

'I don't snore,' Eileen replied indignantly.

'And the Pope isn't Catholic,' Ruby retorted.

Eileen sat up on an elbow, looking at Ruby. 'Do I really snore?'

'You drank enough last night to snore for two weeks,' Ruby replied.

'No,' Eileen refuted. 'I didn't get drunk. You know I don't get drunk.'

'How did you get into this bed?'

'What do you mean?' Eileen asked in return.

'If it wasn't for Richard and his two friends, you'd still be sleeping down in the shed,' Ruby said. 'They carried you up here, very quietly.'

Eileen sat up, taking in the room, the fogged window, the chintzy furnishing, clothes hanging over every opportunity to dry. 'We're in the Grand Hotel?'

'I got a room,' Ruby told her. 'We needed somewhere. Don't worry. The publican looked after us. He didn't think it was good that two women would have to sleep outside on a wintry night, or sleep in a shed with strangers, and he was happy to take my money.'

Eileen lifted aside the white sheets and sat on the edge of the soft bed, feeling dizzy. 'My head is thumping,' she complained.

'I'm not surprised,' Ruby said. 'You drank more beer and wine last night than I've seen you drink anywhere.'

'I think I remember now,' Eileen murmured. She stood and carefully stretched, and turned to Ruby who was also rising from the bed. 'Did I do anything I shouldn't want to remember?'

'If I tell you, you'll remember,' Ruby said, grinning salaciously.

'Oh, I didn't kiss that wall-eyed man with the beard, did I?' Eileen asked, and answered herself with, 'Ugh. I think I did. What was I thinking?'

'Jack is lovely, a kind man,' Ruby said. 'He doesn't get on with his wife.'

'He's married?'

'I'm teasing!' Ruby said, laughing. 'He's not married.'

'You are so mean, Ruby Ballard!' Eileen accused, and she hefted a pillow at her friend who knocked it aside.

'Put your teeth in, wash up and get dressed,' Ruby urged. 'I'm hungry.'

*

The return ride to MacAvoy's orchard along the winding road under leaden skies was arduous, but the fresh, cool air slowly eased Eileen's aching head. Three vehicles trundled past, coughing fumes. One driver tooted his horn and waved enthusiastically, and Ruby muttered obscenities in return. The women chatted on the easier sections, laboured up the winding hills, and freewheeled down the slopes, laughing, relishing the breeze billowing their hair and stimulating their faces. *How many miles have I ridden?* Eileen pondered as her legs pushed hard against another gradient. *I could ride everywhere.* She recalled reading in the newspaper about a nurse who rode her bike all over New Zealand and was doing the same in Australia, starting from Brisbane. *Maybe I could do that*, she considered – ride around Australia. *Maybe I will*, she decided.

When the pair dismounted at MacAvoy's, and wheeled their bikes towards their hut, the orchard was quiet. Maybelle appeared from beneath the rainwater tank, with her ears lowered and tail wagging, pleased to greet familiar people, but as Eileen stooped to pat the dog she sensed another presence and saw Mick Warner.

'I have a letter that arrived Friday,' Mick announced, holding out the envelope. 'Missus MacAvoy forgot to give it to you Friday with your pay.'

'Thank you,' Eileen said. When she saw the postage mark was from Ulverstone, she unsealed the envelope and read.

'Everything all right?' Ruby asked.

Eileen looked up to see Mick was walking back to the main house. 'I was meant to go back to Ulverstone, to see Mervyn. He asked a question I promised to answer.'

'He proposed?' Ruby asked.

'In his way, yes,' Eileen explained.

'Don't do it,' Ruby advised. 'Why would you burden yourself with a man?'

'I can't stop thinking about him,' Eileen said. 'He would be a good husband.'

Ruby put both hands on Eileen's shoulders and squared her up to stare into her eyes. 'You don't need a man to make your life right, Girlie. You know that. If you search deep enough, you know a man doesn't make you *you*.'

'I feel obliged,' Eileen argued.

'Obliged?' Ruby queried. 'Can you hear yourself? Obliged isn't enough, surely?'

'It's more than that. If I can't stop thinking about him, it must mean something.'

'I can't stop thinking about chocolate,' Ruby countered, as she fossicked in her trouser pocket for her cigarettes, before flipping open the pack and offering one to Eileen. 'Or having a drag.'

Eileen accepted the offer. She waited for Ruby to produce matches, lit her cigarette, drew back, and savoured the smoke.

'See?' Ruby said. 'There are lots of things we desire, things we think we want, things we think we can't live without, but they're not all good for us, Girlie, and we can't have everything.'

Eileen wanted to argue, wanted to tell Ruby that the way she felt for Mervyn was nothing like wanting a cigarette or a chocolate, but she knew Ruby would rebuke her. Instead, she asked, 'Are you going to get married some time?'

Ruby blew a smoke ring and chuckled, before replying, 'I'll get married when I've seen enough and done enough, and if I am still in the mood to get married.'

'What's that meant to mean?'

'It means I'm finding out who Ruby Anne Ballard is before I let someone come along and make me into someone else,' Ruby explained. 'Once a man makes his surname mine, I cease being who I am.'

'That's not true,' Eileen countered. 'You'll still be you.'

'Think so?' Ruby asked. 'You told me about your Mum, and the things your father did to her. I bet she was much happier before she married. My Mum was never happy with my drunken, abusive old man. In fact, I don't know any woman who's happy in marriage. They get by. They put up with men's disgusting behaviours. They work like servants. And fake everything.'

'That's a very sad way of looking at marriage.'

'It's a very sad way to have to live,' Ruby countered. 'I'll marry when, and if, I find a man who sees me as his friend, and partner, and equal. Until then, I'll have fun, and treat the ones I find interesting as part of the fun.'

'What about children?' Eileen asked. 'Surely you want children of your own?'

Ruby shrugged. 'I like the idea. But that's another reason why I have to find them a good father, not just a bloke who gets me pregnant and stays out with his mates all night because he doesn't want to be home with me and the kids.'

'I better pack,' Eileen said. 'I have to ride into Hobart first thing tomorrow morning and make a phone call before I catch the bus.'

'So, you're running to this man?' Ruby asked.

'I have to answer his question,' Eileen replied. 'I can't live with myself if I don't do the right thing.'

'Then you better go. I'll let you get sorted,' Ruby offered. 'I'll see you shortly. I have something to discuss with Mick.'

*

Leaving Ruby at the bus station in Hobart was as hard as it was to leave Mervyn in Ulverstone in May, and the longer the bus journey ran through the pouring rain the more regret ate at Eileen. Ruby talked Mick into driving the young women into Hobart on the Sunday night, and Ruby wrangled a room at the Customs House hotel. 'Mister Lowell owed me a favour,' Ruby explained when Eileen asked how she could get a room so easily. They spent the night in Hobart, in the hotel room, Ruby organising drinks and a maid bringing a meal to their room. 'This is how the well-to-do live it up,' Ruby remarked when they were set up. 'No need to go out. Only you and me tonight. Even our own maid.'

'How can you afford all this?' Eileen asked.

'We made good money picking fruit.'

'It was hardly good money,' Eileen said, remembering the long, cold and wet days of hard labour for little pay.

'Well, there wasn't much to spend it on,' Ruby said, and she poured a fresh beer for Eileen and passed her a cigarette.

Staring through the rain-streaked bus window into the grey evening world leading into Ulverstone, Eileen reflected that Ruby was easily the best friend she ever had, a twin sister, a confidante, and she felt as if she was betraying her better self to leave, but she promised Mervyn she would come back, and she missed him more than she expected. The dreary weather meant she skipped between waking and sleeping for the hours aboard buses from Hobart to Devonport and from Devonport to Ulverston. She tried reading a book Ruby gave her as she left, a new novel called *A Town Like Alice*, but she couldn't concentrate because of the conflict between her turbulent emotion and exhaustion, so she laid the book aside as a task for when life settled into gentler routine, and she leaned her head against the rattling glass. *I never even got to see the snow on Mount Wellington*, she mused. *One day, I'll come back for the snow.*

Mervyn was waiting in the electric light at the Ulverstone bus station in his black hat and overcoat, umbrella ready to shelter Eileen, broad smile creasing his cheeks. His embrace was the welcoming she imagined throughout the weeks apart, and she let the first kiss linger, reminding her why she returned. 'I'm so glad to see you,' he said as he picked up her case. He led her to his car, opening the door to shepherd her in, and stowed the suitcase in the boot. After he settled in the driver's seat, he paused to stare at Eileen.

'What's wrong?' she asked.

'I'd forgotten how beautiful you are,' he replied. He leaned in and they kissed again and, when their embrace ended, he started the car and drove until he parked outside his home. 'I've asked Mum and Dad to let you have my room, for now, until we find somewhere more appropriate,' he explained.

'Where will you sleep?' Eileen asked.

'I've set up a bed on the back porch.'

'You'll freeze.'

Mervyn laughed. 'Dad and I put up a partition to keep the weather out. It's actually very comfortable. Come on,' he urged, opening his door. 'Mum has a hot meal waiting.'

Mervyn's parents graciously greeted Eileen, and his mother, Rita, laid a meal of lamb chops, mashed potato and vegetables before Eileen at the kitchen table, along with a freshly brewed pot of tea. 'I hope you like it,' Rita said.

'You shouldn't have gone to so much trouble,' Eileen replied, but she was keen to eat after the long bus journey and the aromas were teasing her.

Part way into the meal, there was a knock at the front door, and Mervyn's father led in Sandy, who was wearing a green dress and yellow sunflower apron. 'We heard you were coming back,' Sandy said, hugging Eileen. 'Shirley will be so excited to see you. It's good to have you back.' She stepped away, appraising Eileen, and said, 'You're so fit and strong. What on earth have you been doing?' Eileen briefly described the apple picking and vine pruning work. 'My goodness,' Sandy said. 'You have been on an adventure.' She reached into her apron pocket and retrieved three letters. 'These came for you while you were away. We didn't know where to forward them, but Mervyn said he hoped you would be back before Christmas.'

Eileen looked at Mervyn. 'Thank you,' she said, accepting the letters.

'I'll let you finish eating,' Sandy said. 'Pop by tomorrow morning for tea and scones. I'm making a fresh batch right now. You can tell me all about your adventure.'

The evening passed in sharing stories, and after Mervyn kissed her goodnight, Eileen closed her bedroom door, careful not to make noise, and she listened to Mervyn's footsteps on the wooden floorboards and the backdoor open and close. Her lips tingled from his kiss, and she could smell the lingering scent of his aftershave. She surveyed the room, noting Mervyn's football photos, photos of his parents, one of him in his army uniform, and one with him standing proudly by his new car. She studied each, examining his smiling face, observing how handsome he looked in his military outfit, how confident he carried himself in the football photos, how proud he was of his car. She picked up the letters Sandy delivered, and shuffled through the envelopes, studying the postmark dates. All three were from Adelaide. The first two were recognisably her mother's handwriting, but the third and most recent was addressed by someone else. She unsealed the envelope, curious because of its elegant cursive, and unfolded the letter.

"Dear Girlie," it began. "I trust this letter finds you well. I know you will be surprised to hear from me, but I am writing to let you know our mother has fallen extremely ill, perhaps gravely so. She is currently quarantined in the Royal Adelaide Hospital and the doctors say she has Typhus. Unfortunately, Ian and Wally are in the Kent Town Home for Boys, and Josie is in the Fullarton Girls' Home, because no one is able to look after them. I am sending this letter to the last address you sent to Mum, so I hope you receive it."

Eileen read the closing lines and the flourish of her brother John's educated signature. She lowered the letter. Her mother was dying. She checked the franking date on the envelope. July. It was almost September. Her hand started shaking. What if her mother was already – she didn't want to think or say the word. She couldn't stay in Ulverstone. She had to go home. The younger ones – Ian, Josie and Wally – couldn't be left in Homes. Where was her father in all this? She left the bedroom and headed for the rear porch.

'What's wrong?' Mervyn asked when Eileen appeared at the end of his bed in the flickering kerosene lamplight.

'My mother,' Eileen said, haltingly. 'She's, she - she might be dying.'

Mervyn's eyes widened. 'That's terrible.'

'I have to go home.'

'When?' Mervyn asked, sitting up.

'Tomorrow. As soon as I can,' Eileen said.

'But –,' Mervyn began, hesitated, and said, 'I was hoping – well, I wanted to ask you to marry me.'

Eileen sighed. 'I know,' she said. 'I know that's what you wanted.' She sat on the edge of the bed. 'Mervyn, it's what I think I wanted too. That's why I came back. But I didn't know this was happening. I can't ignore my family. They need me. I have to go home.'

Mervyn took Eileen's hand in his, and said, 'Then I'll get you home. Quickest way is to fly out of Burnie to Melbourne.'

'I can't afford a plane flight.'

'I'll organise the plane, Eileen.' He pulled her close and hugged her, and whispered, 'It will turn out all right, you'll see.'

*

Pressed against the shuddering hull, engines clamouring, Eileen gazed out of the ANA DC3's window at the white clouds and metal grey ocean. Ahead lay Melbourne and the train to Adelaide. Behind was Burnie airport and Mervyn waving from the terminal gate. Her world was running at speed, buckling and tilting towards a life that stifled and threatened to smother her two years earlier. For two years, she tried to find balance, reason, freedom, purpose, but those things kept eluding her.

At the root of her problems were men. Dudley made false promises and lied to her. Ken wanted her, but not as much as he wanted himself. Shirley, who was meant to be a good friend, was caught up in Luke's web and married him. Mervyn – poor Mervyn – he wanted her too, and perhaps he might have been a good husband, but now the world tilted away from him.

And Ruby.

Ruby was the one shining light, the one person in two years with whom Eileen truly felt free to be herself. And she abandoned Ruby for Mervyn's promise.

She glanced guiltily to her left at the man reading his newspaper and smoking, before she turned to the window to wipe creeping tears from her eyes as the world raced below.

1951

"It's no use going back to yesterday, because I was a different person then."
Alice

Eileen smoothed her mother's hair on the crumpled pillow, saddened to see her brown hair greying so rapidly. 'Comfortable?' she asked. Clarice smiled and Eileen was pleased there was sparkle in her mother's blue eyes. When she arrived in Adelaide, in September last year, her mother was a shadow of herself, thin and grey and so very sick the doctors would only allow Eileen to speak to her wearing a mask and gloves. Death crouched over her. Now, January, the shadows of illness receding, her mother was alive and growing stronger by the day. 'I'll fetch a lemon and honey tea,' Eileen offered.

In the kitchen, Auntie Ethel asked, 'How's Clarice this morning?'

'She's much better,' Eileen replied. 'I can't thank you enough for taking her in.'

'Family look after each other,' Ethel said. 'She was too ill to be by herself.' She opened the upper kitchen cupboard. 'Tea, Girlie?'

'I'll make it. Do you want one?''

'Yes, I do,' Ethel replied, as she put the kettle on the stove. 'I'll see if Len wants one too. I'm sure he will.' Ethel headed for the back garden and the shed where Len was always pottering and making things and keeping to himself in the privacy of his corrugated iron and wood-framed castle.

Eileen listened to the grandfather clock ticking in the hallway before she opened the Bushell's can and scooped black tea leaves into the pot. Through the kitchen window, the garden with its spreading tree and expanse of lawn held a surreal aura, reflecting a life and a place Eileen envied, an ordered, peaceful suburban home like the one they all lived in before the war tore their world and family apart. She learned that so many unfair and cruel things happened to her family in the two years after she left for Melbourne. With her mother's failing health, and her father's itinerant work between the military and building, and no home after their father took them to Port Neill, the younger children were shifted from sleeping on tables in a billiard hall in Regent Arcade, to the Coffee Palace in Hindley Street, the Grosvenor Hotel, St Morris theatre and the cellar of a house in Semaphore, until Wally and Ian ended up in the Kent Town Boys Home and Josie was sent to the Fullarton Girls Home. Family intervened to rescue the children. She felt guilty she was absent and unaware of the circumstances. If she hadn't left, perhaps things might have been different.

The boiling kettle broke her reverie. She poured the steaming water into the teapot, the warm aroma pleasing her senses. She searched for honey in Ethel's pantry and squeezed a lemon that came from Ethel's tree into an enamel mug painted with petunias against a white background. She poured in the tea and stirred the mixture, testing the balance of sweet and sour.

'Hello, Girlie,' Len said, as he followed Ethel through the back door. Eileen returned his greeting. She poured three more cups, and asked, 'Black or white?'

'White with four,' Len replied, washing his hands over the kitchen sink.

'White with two,' Ethel said. 'Anzac biscuits anyone?'

'Thank you, yes,' Eileen replied. 'I'll take this to Mum,' she continued, organising the lemon and honey tea on a small tray.

'Put a slice of the carrot cake on the tray, Girlie,' Ethel suggested. 'I'll take it to Clarice. You have a seat, love.'

Eileen protested mildly, but she let Ethel take the refreshments to her mother while she sat at the kitchen table with Len. 'So, they took you back at the Repat?' Len asked, after sipping his tea.

'They were very kind,' Eileen replied. 'The Head Matron treated my time away as leave. It's as if nothing happened, although the people have changed. I am back in the Nurses' Quarters. With Mum not in a place of her own, I wasn't sure where I was going to live when I was coming home.'

'We would have let you stay with us,' Len said. 'You're always welcome here.'

Ethel returned from the bedroom and sat to drink her tea, and Eileen enjoyed the chat. When the morning tea was finished, she excused herself and sat with her mother again. 'When you're better,' Eileen said, 'I'll take you to Waterfall Gully. It's so pretty. The fresh air will be good for you.'

'You will go see Josie and Ian and Wally?' Clarice asked.

'Of course, Mum,' Eileen replied. 'I'm also visiting John today. Uncle Spot and Auntie Fay invited me to lunch, so I'll leave soon. Peter is dropping by the Repat later this week.'

'You be careful on that bike,' Clarice urged.

'I know how to ride, Mum,' Eileen replied.

'But there are more cars about,' Clarice said. 'Everyone is starting to buy one. The roads are busy. I have seen it.'

'I'll be careful, Mum,' Eileen reassured her.

Later, crossing Anzac Highway on her bike on her way to lunch, Eileen was conscious there were many more cars and trucks and buses on the roads than when she left for Melbourne, although the traffic paled in comparison to Melbourne streets, but when she rode back to Daw Park in the warm January evening, her head buzzing with John's gossip about who was where and doing what with whom, she felt less confident riding on the road, her mother's warning teasing her sense of security.

In the Nurses' Quarters, she changed and showered, chatted with three friends in the canteen as they shared a late evening tea and biscuits, and commandeered a chair to read a few pages of *A Town Like Alice*. She was surprisingly fatigued from the day's exertions, so she made a mental note to maintain her riding regime, having made cycling a daily occurrence in Tasmania.

Thinking of Tasmania sent her thoughts racing in separate paths, one chasing disappointment at having left Mervyn heart-broken at the airport, promising to return when her mother was better, the other kindling sharp moments with Ruby, laughing at the antics of other people, dancing in the ballroom, standing in the rain drenched to the bone, sleeping together to keep warm. As much as she tried, the novel persistently dropped out of focus, and she felt a pressing need to climb into her bed and pull the blankets close and be alone. She rose from the chair, shivering despite the warmth in the air, and retreated to her room.

*

'You have a very nasty fever, Miss Bonney,' Doctor Ketteridge said through his white mask while he pressed his palm against her forehead. 'Somehow, you have caught a good dose of influenza, but because it is out of season, with what is current, we are keen to run a few more tests.'

Eileen listened to the doctor's assessment and his discussion with the Sister and two orderlies who were also masked and heard the word x-ray. 'Excuse me,' she interrupted, 'but why an x-ray?'

'Your cough,' Ketteridge said. 'It's especially rattly and persistent. We want to make sure you haven't developed pneumonia.' He returned his attention to the Sister and issued more instructions.

'How long before I can go back to work?' Eileen asked.

Doctor Ketteridge raised a bushy eyebrow and said, 'I suspect a little more rest in bed is required. I'll come back on Thursday morning.' He motioned to a masked nurse, a colleague Eileen knew as Janet Addison, who produced a hypodermic.

'Now what?' Eileen asked.

'We are doing a Mantoux test,' Ketteridge explained. 'You know what that is, don't you?'

'I worked in the TB ward in Heidelberg,' Eileen replied.

'Yes. That is what the records show,' Ketteridge said.

'But I didn't get sick.'

'Just a precaution,' Ketteridge answered. He nodded to Addison, who began the intradermal procedure.

'You think I have TB?' Eileen asked.

'We are being cautious, Miss Bonney,' Ketteridge said. 'You should know that is standard practice in a hospital.'

Eileen waited for Addison to swab the point where her arm was injected with tuberculin serum. She watched the doctor speak to the Sister and orderlies at the end of her bed, before he placed the records in the holder and led the Sister and orderlies from her room.

'Are you drinking?' Addison asked.

'Yes,' Eileen replied. 'Do they think I have TB?' she whispered.

'I don't know,' Addison replied. 'Let's check the notes.' She retrieved the records from the end of the bed and scanned the information. 'It doesn't say,' she told Eileen. She replaced the records, came closer, and said, 'But you are in Daw House so they must be suspecting something.'

'We do put flu patients in here,' Eileen remembered.

'Sometimes,' Addison agreed. A knock at the door interrupted. Addison turned and said, 'You have visitors.'

Bruce entered with Betty, both wearing surgical masks. 'Brucie!' Eileen cooed, blowing her brother a kiss.

'They told us we should be wearing masks to visit,' Bruce said. 'I told them my sister already knew I was ugly.'

Eileen laughed. 'I may be infectious. You should wear the mask.'

'I should have asked for one for this bloke then,' Bruce said. He clicked his finger and a craggily handsome man, with combed and slick black hair, stuck his head around the corner of the doorway.

'Clive!' Eileen cried and held out her arms.

'It is I,' Clive said theatrically with a flourish of his arm, as he crossed to embrace his sister.

'Oh, Clive, I've missed you!' Eileen declared. 'Where have you been?'

'A lot of places, Girlie. A lot of places.' Clive sat on the edge of the bed. 'Some of them you wouldn't believe.'

'I didn't know I was allowed visitors.'

'Some of us know who to talk to and where to go,' Betty said, grinning and winking. 'This place is my second home.'

'You'll get in trouble,' Eileen warned.

'For you, Girlie Bonney, it'd be worth it,' Bruce said. 'We have a lot of news to catch up on.'

*

Yesterday there was blood in her sputum. Behind their masks, she recognised Doctor Albury and Doctor Perkins from the Heidelberg

Repatriation Hospital at the end of her bed, and she was surprised they travelled from Melbourne, until she understood why they might be there. She was isolated in Daw House. The pieces fell into place. Doctor Ketteridge cleared his throat and tapped the clipboard. 'I think you might be guessing at what we are about to say,' he began. 'The Mantoux test is positive.'

'I know,' Eileen replied quietly.

'Yes,' Ketteridge said, glancing at his colleagues. 'We thought you might. The x-rays show a dark patch on the lower lobe of your right lung.' He paused to acknowledge his companions. 'I think you know Doctors Albury and Perkins.'

'Yes,' Eileen said. 'I saw them when I was working on the TB ward.'

'We have discussed your case very closely, Miss Bonney. There are rapid advances being made in the treatment of tuberculosis. New drugs are being developed to contain and eradicate the infection. At the moment, however, as we see it, you have two choices. We send most patients at your stage of development to the Birralee Sanatorium to recuperate. It is a laborious regime, and involves performing a lung collapse, but with care and a good environment you might hope to recover in two years. Of course, there is a chance the tuberculosis will recur after you leave the sanatorium. We would, of course, treat that eventuality as and when – or if it happened.'

'And the second choice?'

'We think you are a good candidate for a partial lobectomy,' Ketteridge said. 'The x-rays show the infection is concentrated and localised in the lower lobe of your right lung, and it has not at all affected your left lung.'

'And what happens after the surgery?' Eileen asked.

'Resection is very effective. You will need at least six months to recover, but you could be back on your feet before the year's end,' Ketteridge explained. 'It is much quicker and more effective than the recuperative process, and you would be highly unlikely to have a relapse.'

'But because it's surgery, there are risks involved,' Eileen said, recalling words she heard many times from doctors to patients in her care.

'Yes,' Ketteridge agreed. 'There are risks. There is always risk with surgery, as you know full well. And the first month or two will be difficult, because we have to drain fluid from your chest cavity and keep the antibiotics up to prevent secondary infections. But we believe the benefits far outweigh the risks in your case.' He took a breath and continued. 'Of course, in the end, the choice is yours, Miss Bonney, and you still have a short window of time to make your decision before there is no choice. We will give you time to consider.'

'I'll have the operation.'

'You don't have to rush into this,' Ketteridge reminded her.

'My mind is made up,' Eileen replied. 'I'll have the surgery.'

Doctor Ketteridge nodded. He spoke to the other doctors before making notes on the records. 'Very well,' he said, turning to Eileen. 'We will start the preparation. First, we will monitor you for a week or two to make sure you are ready. You are a very fit young woman, which will speed your recovery, but we must ensure everything is in order before we operate. There are more tests to do, and more x-rays to be taken. I will speak with you again, at the end of the week, to confirm you are comfortable with your decision. Good afternoon, Miss Bonney.' Ketteridge excused himself and led his entourage out of the ward.

Alone, Eileen closed her eyes. 'Well, this is another fine mess I've gotten myself into,' she murmured, remembering how Ruby parodied Laurel and Hardy. *What would you say now, Ruby Ballard*? Eileen pondered. *I have TB. And now I'm going to lose half my lung. That's hardly fair. Why me*? Tears welled in her eyes and trickled down her cheeks. She sniffed and suddenly coughed, a wracking cough that strained her throat. She grabbed the handkerchief from her bedside cabinet and coughed into it, feeling her lungs spasm, and she spat into the handkerchief. When the coughing eased, she opened the cloth, knowing what she would see, the tell-tale smear of blood, and another tear coursed down her face.

*

Tedium. Every day the routine kicked in. Wake and wash. Meds. Breakfast. Tests. More meds. Lunch. And on. More x-rays. More tests. Doctor Ketteridge came and went, each time reassuring her everything was taking good shape, each time leaving her with no new information. Days passed.

A week. A month. She felt her body wasting with inactivity.

Family came and went. Her mother arrived. 'Oh, Mum,' Eileen said, seeing Clarice enter her room with John. 'You're better.'

'My poor child,' Clarice said. She sat on the edge of the bed to take Eileen's hand. 'The doctor told me how sick you are and I had to come.'

'I'll be fine, Mum,' Eileen assured her. 'The doctors and nurses here are the best.'

'But surgery?' Clarice said. 'Why surgery?'

'I'll get better quicker,' Eileen said, and she explained what the doctors told her. 'But how are you?'

'Much better,' Clarice said. 'The doctor said I can go back to work next month.'

'You can't keep doing cleaning jobs,' Eileen protested. 'That's how you got sick in the first place.'

'I need to pay to live somewhere,' Clarice replied.

'Aren't you staying with Auntie Ethel?'

'It's time to find my own place,' Clarice replied. 'It's not fair on my sister to do what she's been doing.'

'It will be all right,' John said. 'I'll see what I can find for her.'

'And the children?'

'They won't be going back into any Homes,' John said.

'And how have you been?' Eileen asked, turning to her brother.

'Wonderful,' John replied. 'Life couldn't be better.'

'John was promoted,' Clarice said proudly.

'Yes,' John confirmed. 'I'm moving up in the company. Who knows, Girlie? Manager one day perhaps.'

The afternoon visit passed quickly, and after John and Clarice left the evening routine began. Medication numbed the pain, but nights seemed to last longer than they should, and then it was morning again and the routine repeated. She felt so helpless, a failure. She came home to make things better, returned to help her family, and now she couldn't help herself. When the lights went out each night, she prayed she would heal, prayed there was an error, a poor diagnosis, that she would be up and about very soon. *It's not fair, God*, she thought over and over. *My family need me. Why this? Why now?*

And then, a Thursday morning, three days before her birthday, Doctor Ketteridge arrived with two trainee doctors in tow to announce, 'We will be operating on you tomorrow, Miss Bonney.'

Eileen murmured, 'Oh,' and waited.

'Do you have any questions?' Ketteridge asked, peering over his spectacles.

'What time tomorrow?'

'I have scheduled you for nine am. You should be out of surgery a little after midday. Any more questions?'

'No,' Eileen replied. 'Thank you, Doctor.'

'We are extremely confident it will be a success, Miss Bonney. I will see you in the theatre in the morning.'

Nurses and orderlies came and went, the routine continued as it did every day, and Eileen tried to read a copy of Grahame Greene's *The Heart of the Matter* between the medication and note-taking and tests, but she gave up and snoozed.

At times, her mind swarmed with possibilities the operation might present and buzzed with what she saw and remembered from the TB ward in Heidelberg, the complications, the disappointment, infections, death, but she pushed aside the negatives, knowing she also saw relief, happiness, and health in patients. She had no reason to doubt Doctor Ketteridge's belief that all would go well. Still, the night was restless, and her dreams vacillated between sadness for Mervyn and Ruby and Ken and Dudley and her family, and fascination of a journey she could not describe, only take, that led her down through a beautiful forest to a waterfall thundering into darkness.

She was pleased to see a nursing colleague, Janet Oxley, accompanying the orderlies who came for her in the morning. The orderlies helped her onto the barouche and wheeled her to the theatre in Ward Two, passing her to the operating team. She fancied she recognised the anaesthetist – perhaps it was David Sinclair behind the mask – but relaxants clouded her mind. She knew there would be chrome implements lined up on the table beside the doctor, and the bottles and tubes and hoses with a mask beside the anaesthetist, but she couldn't quite see much more than the overhead lights hanging below the shadow of the ceiling and figures moving around her in surgical gowns and masks. Doctor Ketteridge appeared above her, and asked through his mask, 'Are you ready, Miss Bonney?'

Eileen murmured, 'Yes, Doctor.'

'Good,' he said. 'I will see you on the other side.'

*

She opened her eyes. Her mother's face appeared. 'I'm glad you're awake,' said Clarice. She placed her hand on Eileen's left hand and squeezed gently. 'How do you feel?'

'Like a truck ran over me,' Eileen whispered, mindful of plastic tubes running from her side and her hand.

'They have to drain fluid from your chest,' Clarice said. 'I don't know much else.'

'I'm glad you are here,' Eileen rasped, struggling to draw in air to speak.

'I brought Mum,' a male voice said to her right.

Eileen turned her head to Peter. 'Thank you,' she mouthed.

'We were told we can only stay a few minutes,' Peter said. 'You need lots of rest.'

'The operation went for four hours,' Clarice told her.

'How do you know that?' Eileen wanted to ask, but her lips moved silently.

'I waited,' Clarice said.

'Mum made me bring her here after she rang the hospital this morning, and they told her what time you were going into theatre,' Peter explained.

'I couldn't let you go through this alone,' Clarice said. 'Not my Girlie. You came all the way from Tasmania to look in on me. The least I can do is come down the road to look in on you.'

A thin, ruddy-faced nurse entered and skirted Clarice. 'Nice to see you're awake,' she said as she checked the drip. 'I'm going to ask your guests to leave, though. Sister said they could have a few minutes, but you need your rest.'

Clarice squeezed Eileen's hand again, and rose, saying, 'I'll come in to see you when I can. Everyone says to wish you a happy birthday for tomorrow.'

'Get better,' Eileen whispered.

'I'll let Lyla know you're doing all right,' said Peter. 'She's working tomorrow.'

'Say hello-,' Eileen started to reply, and coughed, shooting a sharp pain through her chest and back.

'Easy,' the nurse said. 'Doctor says you're not to talk, or cough, or move around.'

Clarice and Peter waved, and Eileen waggled her fingers in response. 'What's your name?' she mouthed to the nurse when her brother and mother were gone.

'Alice Wilson,' the nurse replied. 'And no more talking.' She produced a thermometer and asked Eileen to open her mouth. 'You've probably got lots of questions, but you'll have to save them for when Doctor Ketteridge comes to visit. You've done a very brave thing, but now you need to get your strength back and let your body heal.'

Eileen watched Wilson fuss about, doing the same jobs Eileen did for her patients, knowing why she was checking how much fluid was in the drip bag against the measure on the record, why she checked the reservoir where fluid was draining from Eileen's chest, why she checked the bed and the bandaging. Eileen had questions, many questions, but a great weariness was enfolding her. She had to sleep. Sleep was the greatest healer.

*

Doctor Ketteridge came to see her three days after surgery, clipboard in hand, glasses perched on the end of his nose. 'How are you feeling, Miss Bonney?' he inquired.

'Very tired,' Eileen whispered.

'You have been through a tough fight and come out the other side,' Ketteridge said. 'You have certainly earned a long rest.'

'Did it go well?' Eileen whispered, gasping for breath.

'No more talking, please,' Ketteridge advised. 'And to answer your question, Miss Bonney, precisely as planned. Not using clamps or sutures on the lung surface seems to be very effective.' He glanced at his clipboard. 'I see you are receiving Streptomycin. That will speed your recovery.' He looked up and studied the tubes running from Eileen's chest and checked her pulse. 'Rest,' he said. 'No talking. And no visitors for some time, I am afraid. We cannot risk infection. I did speak with your mother and explained that you need to be given as much rest as possible for the time being. Your mother is a very gracious lady. The hospital will let her know when she can visit again.' He released Eileen's wrist and moved to the end of the bed. 'I will drop by in a few days to check on your progress. You are in very good hands.' And he was gone.

Nurses and orderlies came and went in the Intensive Care Unit under strict instructions not to talk to Eileen, so her communication was limited to nods and smiles and hand gestures. Tubes running from the right side of her back restricted her movement, keeping her on one side, making her left side ache. Despite relievers, the pain remained dully incessant throughout her chest, back and neck and the pillow gradually felt as comfortable as stone. A catheter siphoned her urine. Constipation curtailed her need to defecate, until a nurse appeared with the dreaded enema kit and the matter was resolved. The evening nurses bathed her and massaged her gently where her left side was most uncomfortable. Sometimes the nurses brushed her hair. Mornings. Days. Afternoons. Nights. Drip. Drainage. Checks. Bathing. Awake. Sleep. No talking. She tried reading a book. She tried reading magazines. Staying awake, staying aware, was a step too far. A week. Two. More. And then the tubes were taken out and she could lay on her back, gingerly. She feared coughing.

Doctor Ketteridge strolled in on a Tuesday morning with an entourage of doctors and orderlies, greeted Eileen, and said, 'Well, you are definitely on the mend. I think it is time you moved back to Ward Two and began the next phase of healing.' He tapped his clipboard. 'These are very pleasing results.' He talked to the group, pointing at the clipboard as he explained procedures, before he turned to Eileen and said, 'The next phase will involve rebuilding your strength, and teaching you how to utilise air in your lungs. Still a lot of time ahead in bed, I am afraid, but we don't want to undo all the good work, do we? You have come along very well, young lady.'

'Thank you,' Eileen rasped, smiling.

'I will come by again when you are in Ward Two,' Ketteridge told her, and he moved on.

Eileen settled into her pillow, wrapped in the news she was escaping the Intensive Care Unit. She was getting better. The signs were good. When Alice Wilson came to check on her, Eileen whispered, 'What's the date?'

'April twenty-fourth,' Wilson replied. 'Is it a special day?'

'Yes,' Eileen whispered, and she smiled. One month after her birthday and she was alive and healing. It was a special day.

*

The picture of Elaine Brodie on the *Woman's Weekly* cover entranced Eileen because, as the short article on page eighteen revealed, the young woman was feeding ice-cream to her pet cocker spaniel, Bonny, and the image of the dog and the dog's variant of her family name resonated, sending Eileen drifting through memories of days playing with the red setter her father used as a breeding dog for additional income in the early years.

She flicked through the magazine, stopping to read the page-length stories to break her monotony. Since returning to Ward Two, she was allowed to talk – in fact the orderly, Alan Clifford, came every day to ensure she carried out deep breathing exercises to adjust her lungs to their new state – and she could have visitors for short periods, but she still had a catheter because she was not allowed out of bed. Nurses came to move her periodically to prevent bed sores, and help with the bed pan, and bathe her. Nurse Baxter, her friend from her first years at the Repat, took her dirty linen and spent time every morning washing and brushing Eileen's hair. 'Can't have a pretty girl like you not looking her best,' Baxter told her as she groomed her hair. Eileen luxuriated in Baxter's attention, glad to have a familiar face for company, laughing as Baxter reminisced past stories and shared the latest staff gossip.

Every day she waited expectantly for someone to visit. Her mother and her brothers and sisters came and went, but their stays were brief; long enough to find out who was doing what and not much else. Wally was living with Bruce and Betty in Whyalla and going to school again. Peter and Ian had apprenticeships. Judy and Josie were working. Apart from nursing friends, no one else came. She understood why. People were afraid they might contract tuberculosis if they spent time in the hospital among tuberculosis patients, even after treatment. She didn't blame them. After all, she was sure she caught the disease in a very similar way. She heard, when she was working at the Heidelberg Repat, there was a national authority being formed to control and reduce the spread of tuberculosis in Australian and that a woman in Adelaide, Doctor Nancy Atkinson, was developing a vaccine to reduce the spread and impact of tuberculosis, but even so many people were still afraid of the disease. It wasn't so long ago that TB was the major killer of Australian men and women. She shuddered. She was very lucky.

One afternoon, a tall figure in a long grey overcoat, cap in hand, walked towards her bed and stopped at the end. 'Hello, Girlie,' he said in his taciturn voice, his face stern. 'I thought I should come to see how my favourite girl was doing.'

Eileen hesitated, before taking in a strained breath to reply, 'You can sit, if you want.'

'I will,' Donald said, and he settled on the visitor's chair by the bed. 'I hear you've been pioneering medicine.'

Eileen smiled at his laconic humour. 'It's not what I wanted to do.'

'Hmm,' he breathed and was silent. After a short time, he said, 'I wanted to tell you, Girlie, if there's anything you need – well, let me know.'

'Thank you,' Eileen said. What she really wanted to say was 'You could take care of Mum and the family. That would be a big help.' But she didn't. That would demand more strength than she knew she could muster. Instead, she said, 'I will be happy when I am up and about.'

'How long does the doctor expect you to be here, like this?'

'Until September. That's what my friends tell me.'

'You're lucky I got you that job back in Forty-six,' Donald said, a faint grin creasing his cheeks. 'You'll get the best care here, having been a nurse.'

Her father didn't stay long. There wasn't a great deal either could talk about. He said he was getting plenty of work from the new government housing initiative, but he didn't speak about much else. He didn't mention Clarice. He said he saw her older brothers occasionally, but he didn't elaborate.

After Donald left, Eileen lay in her bed wondering what drove a man to do what he did – to marry a woman, have nine children with her and leave. Of course, he justified himself by keeping a fatherly interest in the children, especially the older ones like herself, but she knew he was only trying to expiate his guilt. She should have told him to never come again, but she couldn't. His eyes told her he did deeply regret leaving, that he was still attached to her as his daughter, and that was also why she couldn't say the hateful words, the accusations, the disappointment. Deep inside, she still loved him as her father. He still was her father. Nothing changed that simple fact.

*

'But I look terrible,' Eileen complained. 'My hair, my face -'

'Oh, stop it,' Baxter said. 'We'll fix all that, Bonney. Matron has given us permission to wash and set your hair, and help you do your make-up. You will be the most beautiful patient on the ward.' The other two nurses began fussing around Eileen, adjusting her nightie, and tousling her hair.

'Stop it!' Eileen pouted, joining in the laughter.

'I suggest you all hurry up,' a severe voice ordered from the doorway and Matron Morphett waggled her finger at the group. 'The photographer will be here in a little under an hour.'

'Let's hurry, girls!' Baxter urged. 'First, we wash and dry that hair and get the curls all in place. We're waiting on a magazine star! Snap to it!'
Eileen let the nurses laugh and cajole each other and wash and dry her hair and put on peach rouge and red lipstick and soft blue eye shadow as they eagerly prepared her for the photo shoot. 'You're such a celebrity,' Baxter remarked as she worked the curls into Eileen's brunette hair. 'Lobectomies and new drugs. The doctors are all so excited. You're the pin-up girl of the future of medicine!'

'Stop being such a drama queen!' Eileen replied.

'Keep still,' Baxter warned. 'I'd hate the photo to show a bang out of place. Think of the embarrassment!'

The nurses wheeled Eileen's bed to the corner of the ward and set up Eileen with multiple pillows five minutes before Matron Morphett led Doctor Ketteridge, a group of physicians, a mature woman dressed immaculately in black from the Red Cross, a photographer and a thin, young journalist into the ward. 'Here's the young lady we have been telling you all about,' Doctor Ketteridge said to the gathering as the people milled around the end of the bed. 'Miss Bonney was diagnosed with tuberculosis affecting the lower lobe of her right lung in March.'

Eileen half-listened to Ketteridge explaining his diagnosis, and procedures leading to the lobectomy, and on to the subsequent period of recovery, while she watched the suited journalist fiercely jot notes and the older, greying photographer survey the setting for best light and angles.

When Ketteridge was finished, he fielded questions from the group, while the photographer organised the Matron and the Red Cross woman. 'I think if we get you beside the bed here,' he said to Matron Morphett, 'and you stand here to present the Red Cross package, Lady Norrie,' he said to the Red Cross woman. The photographer straightened curtains behind the bed and checked the light on the vignette he was creating before he shuffled to the other side of the bed and pitched his camera on the stand. 'All right,' he said. 'Doctors stand back a little please.' He peered through his lens again, popped up, and said, 'We will take three shots. The first a test, the second should be the good one, and the third as a precaution. Are we ready? Look natural. Big smiles.' He ducked behind his camera and said, 'Three, two, one.'

Eileen smiled, but the flash startled her. 'Excellent,' the photographer said. 'This time, Miss Bonney, make sure you are meeting Lady Norrie's gaze. You're receiving a special gift. It's a special day.' He ducked again and counted. Ready for the second flash, Eileen gave her broadest smile and stared into Lady Norrie's eyes. 'And last one,' the photographer said, counted, and the shoot was over. 'I'll make sure I have everyone's details correct,' the journalist said, and he asked for names and checked spelling.

As quickly as they arrived, the entourage peeled out of the ward, and the nurses returned to wheel Eileen's bed back into position. 'Who's famous now?' Baxter teased, grinning mischievously as she packed

Eileen's pillows. 'Your picture will be in all the papers.'

'I think that young reporter liked you,' Nurse Smith teased. 'He couldn't stop staring.'

'You girls are terrible,' Eileen retorted.

'We're not the one in the spotlight,' Baxter said, and the banter continued while the ward resumed its daily activity.

*

The recovery routine continued unabated into August: waking, medicine, breakfast, checks, washing, breathing exercises, lunch, medicine, physiotherapy, dinner, medicine, sleep. Baxter brought Eileen the article created from the luminary visit, and they laughed about the artificial pose, although Eileen was quietly pleased with her appearance and momentary if minor fame. She was concentrating more easily on reading, but she was becoming increasingly frustrated by her bed confinement. The world continued through its cycles; sun, rain, wild wintry weather. The war in Korea threatened to suck Australians into its vortex and the Middle East was a violent cauldron. Turmoil. Chaos. Uncertainty. One world war was exchanged for multiple wars, as if humanity was determined to tear itself apart.

Baxter sat with Eileen whenever she was on duty. 'What I wouldn't do to be out of this bed,' Eileen said one morning, after the usual check-up was added to her record sheet. 'A short stroll, or even a wheelchair would be nice.'

'I'll see what I can do,' Baxter replied. She returned half an hour later with a wheelchair. 'Ward Sister says, so long as we stay inside, I can take you for a tour.'

Sitting in the wheelchair, rolling along the ward, stopping to chat with other patients, seeing the world through different windows raised Eileen's spirits in the ensuing days as she felt her strength returning, life surging through her.

*

Late in August, on a Saturday morning, Sister Norwich wheeled the chair to Eileen's bed and said, 'You have a visitor.'

'Who is it?' Eileen asked.

'A gentleman,' Norwich replied. 'I'll have Williams take you to the cafeteria.'

'Why not here?'

'He said he wanted to speak to you privately. I did tell him the hospital was not a place for secret liaisons,' she said, winking, 'but he insisted on seeing you alone.'

'Did he give a name?' Eileen asked, as she manoeuvred into the wheelchair.

'Mister Wright,' Norwich replied. 'Posh speaking. Very nicely dressed, too. Where do you know him from?'

'Oh,' Eileen stammered, befuddled by a sickening ripple in her gut and ice in her veins. 'He's – ah – a family friend. He knew my older brother.'

'Wait here. I'll send Williams to fetch you,' Norwich instructed, and she headed for the ward station.

Pat Williams wheeled Eileen to the cafeteria and, when they entered, Eileen saw Dudley standing near the wall. He wore a light blue shirt under his dark blue pin-striped suit, a dark blue tie and he carried a matching dark blue Fedora. His black shoes were highly polished, apart from a muddy scuff on the left heel. He smiled as Williams wheeled Eileen towards him, and he said, 'I can take it from here.'

'She's not allowed outside,' Williams told him. 'In here, and along the corridor only, if you want to wheel her around at all.'

'I'll bring her back to the ward, shall I?' Dudley asked.

'Ward Two,' Williams said. She patted Eileen's hand, winked slyly, and walked away, leaving Eileen with Dudley.

Dudley squatted before Eileen and reached for her hand, and she let him take it, although her heart was racing, and she had a strong desire to pull away. 'I am so sorry,' he confessed, his face forlorn, his usually sparkling brown eyes saddened, the hint of tears dulling them. 'I didn't know. I should have stopped you from leaving.'

His remorse caught her off guard and she asked, 'Leaving?' even as she understood his meaning.

'I should have begged you not to go to Melbourne,' he said. 'If I'd asked you to stay, this might never have happened.'

'I never told you I was leaving.'

'I heard,' Dudley confessed. 'Your nursing friends told me.'

'But you didn't come to speak to me,' Eileen accused, and she withdrew her hand.

'It was too late. I tried. I stood outside this place, trying to get the courage to come inside. I simply couldn't find it.'

'Because you were already engaged,' Eileen said. She watched his face change and darken, the blood sharpening his cheeks. 'She rang me, you know. She told me to keep away from you.'

'Carol had no right to do that.'

'She had every right,' Eileen countered. 'You had no right to cheat on her. Or on me.'

'You don't understand,' he pleaded. 'I thought I loved her, but when I met you I realised I wanted you more.'

'When it pleased you, Dudley. Only when it pleased you,' Eileen said. 'Are you still engaged?'

Dudley lowered his eyes, before meeting her questioning gaze and replying, 'We're married.'

'When?' Eileen asked, struggling to check her rising anger.

'Last year,' Dudley replied quietly, fingering his hat. 'June.'

'Over a year, already,' Eileen remarked, forcing a smile. 'Planning children?'

'Not yet,' Dudley replied. 'I'm not ready for children.'

'But she is.'

'Carol would like a family, yes.'

'Then why are you here?'

'Because,' Dudley said, and faltered, before saying, 'Because I can't stop thinking about you, Eileen. I dream about you. In the middle of a conversation, I hear your voice. When I hold Carol, sometimes I wish I was holding you.'

'Stop it!' Eileen snapped. 'That's terrible! It's cruel and it's unfair. You can't think these things. Carol is your wife.'

'But I want you to be my wife.'

'No. You don't,' Eileen said slowly. 'You want me to be your plaything, your amusement, your distraction from your responsibilities. And I won't be that.'

'It's not like that at all,' Dudley argued.

'Take me back to the ward,' Eileen said firmly.

'Eileen,' Dudley pleaded.

'Please take me back to the ward,' Eileen repeated. 'Now.'

Crestfallen, Dudley rose to his feet and stood behind the wheelchair. 'Your hair is beautiful,' he whispered.

'Shall I call Matron?' Eileen asked without turning.

'I'll take you back,' Dudley said.

'And you won't come again,' Eileen added. 'Not unless you come with your wife.'

Dudley didn't answer. He wheeled Eileen silently along the corridor and into Ward Two where Williams came to meet them. 'Thank you for visiting, Mister Wright,' Eileen said, as Williams took control of the wheelchair and turned it so Eileen could look at Dudley. 'Please give my love to your wife.'

Dudley flushed with embarrassment, coughed to clear his throat, and replied, 'I will.' He glanced at Williams, put on his hat, and walked away, the echo of his footsteps receding along the walkway.

'Everything all right?' Williams asked as she steered Eileen towards her bed.

'No,' Eileen whispered hoarsely, and she broke into tears.

*

'The good news is,' Doctor Ketteridge said, adjusting his glasses as he spoke to Eileen, 'you are ready to move to Saint Margaret's.'

'Where is Saint Margaret's?' Clarice asked.

Ketteridge turned to Clarice, who was seated beside the bed, John standing beside her, and said, 'Saint Margaret's is in Semaphore. We use it as a convalescence home. Your daughter is making very pleasing progress, and the next step is to get her ready for going home.' He returned his attention to Eileen. 'The tests show the surgical area is healing as it should, and there are no indications of the tuberculosis remaining in any part of your lungs. I am confident you are cured. You have been a model patient, Miss Bonney, and it has been a pleasure to work with you. I will have Matron make all the necessary preparation, and we should see you at Saint Margaret's by Wednesday.' He signed the report and handed the clipboard to Baxter, before saying, 'You will be in good hands hereon. Goodbye, Miss Bonney.'

'Thank you, doctor,' Eileen replied. Ketteridge nodded and moved to another patient in the ward.

'That's wonderful news, Girlie!' John declared. 'You must be very happy to hear that.'

'Relieved,' Eileen replied.

'My brave girl,' Clarice said, and she reached for Eileen's hand.

'We have exciting news, too,' John said. 'I have found Mum a place to live.'

'Oh, that is exciting!' Eileen said, smiling. 'Where?'

'A unit in Glenelg. Part of a set of units in an old bungalow in Augusta Street,' John explained. 'Very comfortable, and a short walk to Jetty Road.'

The conversation led into news about family, and what Eileen needed her brother to bring to her before she moved to Semaphore, and then it was time for her visitors to go.

After John and Clarice left, Baxter arrived and told Eileen she was so happy for her and excited she was leaving.

'I'll miss you,' Eileen told her.

'And I'll miss you, Bonney,' Baxter replied, stroking Eileen's hair. 'You've been very brave.'

'I'll visit when I'm able,' Eileen promised.

'I'll come see you when I knock off my shift,' Baxter promised. She adjusted Eileen's pillow, grinned, and returned to her duties.

Eileen settled into her pillow and looked around the ward at the beds and patients, people battling individual illnesses, minds and bodies wracked with struggles. Edith, in the bed opposite, was fighting a nasty secondary infection from a leg operation. The new drugs were helping, but her battle was so much harder because she learned last week her husband died in a train accident at Outer Harbour. Across from her was Colleen, who only arrived after two months in the ICU ward. Like Eileen, Colleen was a post-lobectomy tuberculosis survivor, but she was in the very early stage of recovery, and she reminded Eileen what she must have looked like when she first came to the ward. Colleen had an eight-month-old baby named Cyril, but she hadn't seen Cyril for almost three months. Life was cruel to so many people. Eileen was grateful that her journey was moving away from death. She couldn't wait to transfer to Semaphore, where she would be allowed to walk, bathe herself, and regain independence, and be among people who, like herself, were recuperating to get on with their lives. Life was precious. It had to be lived.

Mid-morning the following day, Sister Carter led two orderlies to Eileen's bed, one with a wheelchair, the other carrying a bag containing Eileen's personal possessions. 'Time to leave, Bonney,' Carter announced. An hour later, Eileen was being wheeled through the entrance of Saint Margaret's from Military Road, the hospital's iconic conical tower reminding her of the witches' hats from *The Wizard of Oz*. 'Built in 1874,' said the nurse who greeted Eileen as she took charge of her wheelchair. 'We'll look after you, Miss Bonney. You'll be right as rain soon enough.'

Her room was airy, with high ornate ceilings, a tall window that let in cool daylight, three other patients, and a bed more comfortable than the one she vacated in the Repat. A white vase of pink hydrangeas sat on the bedside cupboard. 'Your brother dropped this in from your family,' the nurse told Eileen as she placed Eileen's suitcase by her bed. 'I'm Jessie Mills; Nurse Mills, of course.' She indicated the patients and beds in the room with her arm, saying, 'That's Ann, Lynne, and Vera's out for a walk in the garden.'

Ann and Lynne waved. Ann, a robust woman with curtly curled brown hair cut in a bob, sat up in her bed with a magazine open. Lynne, a thinner, younger woman, was in a chair beside her bed, knitting, her grey dressing gown draped over her shoulders.

'I'll help you unpack and settle in,' Mills offered.

'Thank you,' Eileen replied. She leaned towards the card beside the flowers and read the "Get Well Soon" caption above a bright pink rose on the cover before she opened it. The printed script was "We pray each day that you will grow in strength and that God will speed your recovery to brighter and happier times," and in her mother's handwriting beneath the script she read, "Love from us all, Girlie, my brave, brave daughter. Mum, Bruce, John, Clive, Peter, Ian, Judy, Josie and Wally xxxxxxxxxx."

Tears welled and she sniffed, prompting Mills to put a hand on Eileen's shoulder, and ask, 'Is everything all right?'

'Sorry,' Eileen blubbered, but she couldn't explain why she was crying, her emotion choking her words.

*

'The nurse said we're not to rush you,' Peter said, 'and you know I don't argue with nurses.' He winked at Lyla who was sitting beside Eileen on the garden bench.

'Wise men who want to live long lives don't argue with their wives either,' Lyla quipped, and Eileen chuckled at her brother and sister-in-law's banter.

'So, what do you do all day?' Peter asked. 'I mean, you're stuck in this place. You can't go out or anything.'

Eileen glanced at Lyla, whom she knew would know the daily routine in the convalescent home, before she explained. 'Early breakfast, of course. Then a wash and dressed. In the beginning, they wheeled me down to the breathing and speech pathologist, but now I walk there every morning, and we exercise my lungs to build my strength and endurance. Then it's time to read, or do tapestry, before lunch.' She pointed to a half-completed maroon flower tapestry on an easel by her bed. 'That's my first project.'

'Very pretty,' Lyla commended.

'In the afternoon, the physiotherapist makes me exercise to rebuild my strength,' Eileen continued, 'and lately, I go for a short walk, if someone's around. Dinner. Reading. Sometimes cards. Plenty of chats with the other patients.'

'That's a busy day,' Peter said, nodding.

'It's better than it was before,' Eileen said. 'I hated being stuck in the hospital bed, not being allowed to move. Any news from Mum?'

'She's settled in her new unit,' Peter said. 'She's still doing cleaning jobs, but she's being fussier about the ones she takes. No cheap or dirty conditions anymore. I think she's cleaning at the cinema on Jetty Road, up the lane from where she's living.'

'She should find work as a musician. Radio stations must still be hiring people.'

'The stations don't use live bands as much now, not with the new records around. And I don't think she's gotten over the old bastard selling her piano,' said Peter. 'I haven't heard her play in ages.'

'When I'm better, I'm going to save up and buy her a piano,' Eileen said. 'It was her life.' She paused to watch a seagull coast across the grey sky and vanish above the roofs.

'Maybe we can all chip in to pay for it,' Peter suggested.

'Betty and Bruce send their love,' Lyla said. 'We saw them two weeks ago when they came down for the weekend from Whyalla.'

'I would really like to see them,' Eileen said, disappointed.

'Ah,' said Peter. 'You will.'

'When?' Eileen asked.

'Betty wants to know if you'd like to spend a while in Whyalla to recuperate?' Lyla explained.

'I'm not sure I'd be allowed,' Eileen replied.

'Apparently, you can,' Lyla said. 'Betty rang the Matron and asked if it was possible.'

'How did she know who to ring?'

Lyla laughed. 'Betty worked with her for a short while on wards at the Repat, before she left. They were friends.' She winked. 'Pays to have friends in high places.'

'I'd love to stay with them,' Eileen said. 'What's Whyalla like?'

'On its way to becoming an important industrial city,' Peter replied. 'Population's growing and a lot of the new migrants are being encouraged to go there for work in the shipyards and the refinery.'

'I'll ring Betty and let her know you're keen,' Lyla promised. 'We might even come for a drive while you're there. It'll be like old times.'

'We had fun, didn't we?' Eileen asked.

'We had lots of fun,' Lyla replied, holding Eileen's hand. 'If it wasn't for you, Betty and I might not have met your brothers.'

'I'm not so sure,' Peter suggested, with a broad and cheeky grin. 'I think

I would have found you.'

'That's very sweet,' Eileen said, smiling at her brother.

'He is such a liar,' Lyla accused. She rose from the garden bench, took Peter's arm in hers and extended her other arm to Eileen. 'Come on, Girlie. Let's go for a walk before it gets too cold.'

*

The late November Sunday was warm, but the breeze through the open car window took the edge off the heat. The drive from Adelaide to Whyalla took longer than Eileen expected, even though Bruce warned her they would spend at least five hours on the road. Between Port Wakefield and Port Pirie, she stared out the window at the long low line of eucalyptus blue and grey hills stretching north and south parallel to the highway beneath a cloudless deep blue sky. Scattered farms dotted the flat land between the road and the hills, marked by yellowing crops, tractors pulling harvesters and grain trucks raising dust. Town names swept past on white signs before the car ambled through them: Lochiel with its expanse of salt lakes, Snowtown, Redhill, Crystal Brook. 'Next stop, Warnertown,' Bruce announced from the driver's seat, and minutes later they were parked beside a humming petrol bowser, the black Holden sedan sucking in gallons of petrol, Eileen winding up her window to stop the fumes stinging her nostrils.

Outside Port Augusta, the sun at its zenith, the sky pocked with white lumps of cloud, the highway turned south-west and south, running between low, flat hills across scrubby saltbush red earth plains, and Betty passed a water flask and a biscuit to Eileen, saying, 'Almost home.'

'It's very dry out here,' Eileen said.

'We're on the edge of the desert,' Betty explained. 'Out west,' she continued, gesturing past Bruce's shoulder, 'there's nothing but dead land and dry salt lakes for hundreds of miles, all the way to Western Australia. It hardly rains out here, and there are no lakes or rivers.'

'Where do people get their water? Eileen asked.

'They built a pipeline all the way from Morgan to Whyalla, finished it in 1944,' Betty explained. 'That's it running beside the road.' Eileen gazed at the pale grey pipeline mounted on its concrete struts, trying to imagine how long the pipeline had to be to reach from the town on the River Murray to the industrial city on Eyre Peninsula, and pondered how people worked in the dry heat to build it.

The iron dust-red structures of the Broken Hill Proprietary's blast furnace and shipyards and the conical rise of Hummock Hill loomed above the dry red landscape over the Holden's bonnet. Away to the right, another hill rose sharply from the land like a breaching whale. 'Mount Laura,' Betty said as she described what lay ahead. 'It's a vibrant city growing out of the desert. Families from Europe are settling here, and the blast furnace and shipyard are getting bigger and better. That's why Dad and Mum came from Poland – to start a better life. And they have.'

Past the blast furnace and shipyards, Bruce turned left into McBryde Terrace, wove through Forsyth and onto Patterson Street, and gave Eileen a tour of the town shopping and business strip, stopping at the base of Hummock Hill. 'When you're up to it, we'll walk around the hill. You can see over the ocean from the slopes.' Bruce drove up a steep road and at the crest the fledgling city opened to the west, creeping in the wake of the Iron Knob railway. 'Those houses out that way,' Bruce explained, 'are the ones we're building for all the new workers. Cheap, Government-funded, good houses.'

'Everything is red,' Eileen remarked. 'Even the paint on the buildings is tinged with red. It's eerie.'

'Iron ore dust,' Bruce explained. 'Gets into everything. While you're working here, you don't notice it after a while, and then you drive in from out of town after a few days away and you see it. Red. Everything.'

Five minutes later they pulled into a driveway, Betty announcing, 'Welcome to our home!'

The weeks in Whyalla leading up to Christmas were full of mild mornings, hot days and warm evenings, and sporadic heavy rainfalls. The first days Eileen spent sitting on the back porch, chatting with Betty about the good times together at the Repat, sharing family tales, baking in the kitchen, tending the vegetable garden Betty and Bruce doggedly forced to grow in the unforgiving earth, reading the "Whyalla News" and a short Western novel titled *Shane*, and working on her flower tapestry.

Betty and Eileen walked in the mornings. In the evenings, after Bruce returned from work and they ate, they sat on the porch and talked.

Eileen walked around Hummock Hill as Bruce promised, but she went with Betty. She saw the gun emplacements set up during the war to defend the ship building site, and Betty told her the hill was the site of the first European settlement of the area. 'The first settlement was called Hummock Hill. They changed the name to Whyalla in 1914, or thereabouts.'

'Why Whyalla?' Eileen asked.

Betty shook her head. 'I don't know. Maybe it's an Aboriginal word.'

Eileen stopped to gaze at the deep blue water in Spencer Gulf. She missed the ocean, swimming, walking with the sand between her toes. It seemed a long time since she frolicked with Shirley on the Ulverstone beaches, and an eternity since she ran with her brothers and sisters into the waves at Brighton and floated in the calming water where her cares were washed away.

With strength returning to her legs, Eileen doggedly climbed Mount Laura and she was sweating heavily and her legs shaking by the time she reached the summit. She covered her brow against the morning sun to survey the shimmering grey and red iron ore countryside stretching into the western desert, and for the first time experienced the vastness of the Australian landscape, the sharp blue sky and earthy emptiness of bush legends. This was an alien place; dry, barren, hostile. She marvelled that the Aboriginal people could have lived successfully for so long in country like this. It wasn't a fit land for Europeans who piped water all the way from the Murray River to survive.

And she started smoking again. While she was recuperating in the Repat and at Semaphore, the craving stayed at bay, but with her returning strength her body began remembering past habits and the aroma when Bruce or Betty lit a cigarette pulled her into the need. 'I'll have one,' she said casually to Betty one morning as they conversed on the porch.

'I don't think you're allowed,' Betty said, 'not after your operation.'

'I read somewhere that cigarettes are good for your breathing,' Eileen argued. 'Isn't it Camels that have the doctor saying it's safe? They say it opens the airways and soothes the throat.'

'They say a lot of things about why we should smoke,' Betty replied, 'but I'm not sure they are telling us the truth. I heard scientists have linked smoking with lung cancer.'

'You're still smoking.'

Betty smiled. 'Yes, I am.' She paused, staring at Eileen, before she laughed, and held out her cigarette packet. 'One,' she warned.

Eileen drew a cigarette from the pack and rolled it in her fingers before adopting an exaggerated pose. 'Stylish,' she said, raising an eyebrow coquettishly. 'Light me?' Betty leaned forward to light Eileen's cigarette with her own and returned the cigarette. Eileen took a deep breath, held the smoke to savour it and exhaled, saying, 'I have certainly missed that.' Then she coughed sharply.

'I think that tells you something,' Betty said.

Eileen controlled her cough to answer, 'It tells me I'm out of practice.'

The week before Christmas, Bruce organised a crabbing expedition to Eight Mile Creek. The sun sparkled in the crisp blue sky and the rising heat late in the morning shimmered across the purple saltbush as they drove to the shoreline. They spent the Saturday afternoon with Bruce's workmates and wives and families dabbing for crabs, the men and older children catching the scurrying creatures as the Spencer Gulf tide raced in, while the women prepared a picnic lunch on the beach. 'The tide comes in so fast,' Eileen said as she folded a red-and-white checked napkin.

'Bruce says people have lost their cars out here,' Betty said. 'They park on the beach, go out to the waterline on low tide, and can't beat it back in before it gets to their cars.'

'That would be horrible,' Eileen noted.

'It's still a lovely place,' Betty said, and added, 'Here comes trouble.' Bruce strolled towards the women with his metal bucket full of squirming crabs. 'That's enough for us,' he said, putting the bucket on the sand. 'Good meal in this lot.'

'You'll miss this,' Betty said.

'Plenty of crabs to catch back in Adelaide, if you know where to catch them,' Bruce replied. 'Does a man have to die of thirst out here?'

Betty raised an eyebrow. 'Might have to if he doesn't learn to ask politely.'

'Get me a beer, woman,' Bruce growled playfully.

'You're leaving Whyalla?' Eileen asked, as Betty retrieved a beer for her husband.

Bruce sat on the ground and covered his eyes against the low afternoon sun. 'Yep. Time to pack up. We'll be finished what I came here for by mid-year.'

'But I thought you said there's work here for a long time.'

'There is, for the right kind of people,' Bruce replied. 'This place is growing fast. Some bloke named Gloede is wanting to start a taxi service, and another lot want to build more shops west of McEwin Street. Those are good signs the place is getting bigger. But I've got other things I want to do. We've made good money, Betty and I, so it's time to go back to Adelaide, buy a house and raise kids. The government is building a new city north of Adelaide. I might get in on that.' Betty handed Bruce a beer bottle.

'When are you leaving?' Eileen asked.

'No idea yet. Maybe middle of the year when the current projects are finished,' Bruce replied. 'For now, we can relax and enjoy.' He tilted the bottle towards Eileen. 'Cheers, Girlie.'

As the sun set, the men built a roaring fire around a forty-four-gallon drum of water and, when the water was boiling heartily, they tossed in their catch of crabs. Eileen listened to the air squeaking from the shells of the cooking crabs sounding like the creatures were crying with pain as they boiled. Eating fresh crab meat between slices of home-baked bread smeared with butter, drinking cold beers and smoking, the group told tall stories about their exploits and the outrageous acts of other identities across the region, laughed at smutty jokes, and discussed local and world events in the glow of the coals. The Korean War was running full throttle in northern Asia, Egypt was a cauldron in the Middle East, Menzies' government was finding its feet, and the Australian cricket team were all out for eighty-two runs against the West Indies in Adelaide. Eileen sat on the sand, bound in the warm evening, smiling, laughing and listening to the others chat and argue and speculate, glad to be alive.

1952

"All I do is dream of you the whole night through."
Kathy Seldon

'The poor Princess,' said the nurse leaning on the reception desk, shaking her head. 'She had to get all the way back from Kenya. That's where she was when they told her the King was dead.'

'They say it was a blood clot that killed him,' her companion added.

'Old before his time, I heard,' the first nurse said. 'The war wore him out.'

'He had lung cancer, I heard,' said the second nurse. 'Too much smoking.'

'Well, we have a Queen now. I wonder when they'll hold the coronation and all that? That'll be a do and a half.'

'You know she's only twenty-five,' said the second nurse. 'Can you imagine being Queen of an Empire at that age?'

'That's all I am now,' said the first nurse. 'Twenty-five, I mean, not Queen.' The nurses laughed.

Eileen sat in the reception, listening to the nurses' chatter while she waited for Matron Ogilvy to call for her. Everything was familiar in the Administration block – the light, the floor, the photos on the walls, the smell of disinfectant. Barely over a year earlier, she was lying in a bed in Daw House, seriously ill, possibly dying if her luck turned sour, and now she was waiting to resume work. She knew the place and yet she was nervous, like the first time her father brought her to begin a placement and lied about her age.

'Eileen Bonney?' a voice called. Eileen saw Matron Ogilvy beckoning, so she rose and followed the Matron's petite back into an office. 'Please, sit,' Ogilvy invited, gesturing to a chair before a large desk. Eileen sat, clasping her hands nervously on her lap. She was sure she'd seen Ogilvy before, perhaps on a ward as a nurse or Ward Sister. Her dark hair framed an oval face set with dark eyes and a button nose, making Ogilvy appear younger than she probably was. Ogilvy stood behind the desk, perusing a manila folder dossier, flicking over the pages with her small, thin fingers. Eileen glimpsed a gold wedding ring. 'Welcome back,' Ogilvy said, looking up and smiling. 'You've been through a remarkably tough time, according to all this, Bonney. How are you feeling?'

'Rested,' Eileen said, unsure of exactly what to say.

'And you told the doctor you're wanting to come back to work,' Ogilvy said.

'Yes,' Eileen replied.

'Are you sure you want to return?'

'The doctor thinks I'm ready. I think I'm ready. I like working here.'

Ogilvy nodded. 'Then back to work it shall be,' she said, and she smiled as she lowered the dossier onto her desk. 'It will be good to have you up and about.' She lifted a page from the file, glanced across the text, and said, 'The recommendation is that you begin on light duties. To accommodate that, we'll place you in Daw House, where you will help to look after the young ladies. There's to be no lifting, of course, not even to assist patients to adjust themselves in bed. That's strictly forbidden. You'll sort medicines for patients and there will be substantial clerical work involved. You can return to the Nurses' Quarters immediately, but you will have a strict curfew and there is to be absolutely no gallivanting around at night or on the weekends. The doctor says in these notes that your constitution will take quite some time to repair, and you are not to do anything that might jeopardise that.' Ogilvy paused before adding, 'I see you turned twenty-one two weeks ago.'

Eileen blushed and was about to correct Ogilvy that she was twenty-two, if the paperwork was correct, but realised matters may have been revised during her illness and convalescence. She hesitated, nodded, and said, 'Yes.'

'Were there celebrations?'

'I spent the day with my mother and brothers and sisters.'

'Well, now you can vote, you have the key to the house, and you can legally drink, although the first is probably of little interest to you and the last two don't apply because this is your home and there will be no drinking alcohol while you are rehabilitating,' said Ogilvy. She smiled wryly and added, 'Congratulations.'

'Thank you,' Eileen replied.

'Well, no dilly-dallying,' Ogilvy said, returning the page to the record. 'You know where to go to organise your uniform. The Sister in charge of the Nurses' Quarters will allocate a bed. Back on duty tomorrow.'

'Thank you, Eileen repeated.

'Nice to have you back,' Ogilvy said.

*

'Bonney!' Two familiar people walked towards her along the Nurses' Quarters hallway. 'We heard you were back,' Baxter said. 'It's wonderful to see you.'

'You've almost faded away,' Cooper remarked, appraising Eileen as she released her from a hug.

'There wasn't a lot of her before,' Baxter remarked. 'She's always been skinny.'

'Not this skinny,' Cooper said. 'Skin and bones skinny.'

'Give the girl a break,' Baxter urged. 'She's been on hospital food for a year,' and Baxter and Cooper laughed, bringing a broad grin to Eileen's face.

'That's more like it,' Cooper said. 'I can see the cheeky girl is still lurking behind the woman's façade.'

'Facade?' Baxter teased. 'Fancy word for you.'

'Some of us don't stop learning, do we?' Cooper retorted.

'When's your break?' Baxter asked.

'In half an hour,' Eileen replied, glancing at the wall clock to confirm the time.

'Perfect!' Cooper declared. 'We'll meet you outside the canteen.'

'It really is good to have you back,' said Baxter as she turned to leave with Cooper. 'I missed you.'

Eileen watched her friends walk away. So much remained unchanged in the Repatriation Hospital, and yet so much was different. Friends like Betty, and former colleagues, like Matron Archibald, moved on to other jobs, places and new lives. So many patients had come and gone. The wards were filling, now, with long-term patients, people whose illnesses and injuries were not improving after the war, or who had infections and wounds that had stabilised but not enough for them to return home. A few were victims of recurrent sicknesses that flared again after leaving the hospital. The women in Daw House, where she was on light duties, were all ex-army personnel still fighting long-term illnesses and mental exhaustion. The Repat atmosphere was different than when she started in 1947, less militaristic, and more like a place of organised, relaxed care.

She finished tidying the workstation, excused herself to go on break, and left Daw House, heading for where she knew her friends were waiting. As she approached, Cooper held out a cigarette pack.

'This is Eileen Bonney,' Baxter said to the nurses – Schubert and Brown – and orderlies – Reid and Norman – and introduced them to Eileen. 'She worked here before she had a lobectomy last year.'

'Should you be smoking?' Reid asked.

'The doctor said it will help strengthen my breathing,' Eileen replied. 'He said if I enjoy it, I should keep doing it. He said it had nothing to do with my TB infection.'

'Might need a different doctor,' Schubert mused. 'Latest research is showing a strong link between cigarettes and lung disease.'

'When did you get your degree?' Baxter challenged. Schubert shook her head. Baxter released Eileen's hand and said, 'They're making better cigarettes now, with filters and ingredients that soothe the throat and calm the nerves. I feel so much better after smoko out here.'

'I guess it's all new since you left for Melbourne,' Cooper said. 'Different people, changes in the buildings.'

'Yes and no,' Eileen replied. 'In some ways it feels like I haven't been away at all. I was back for a little while, before I got sick, and then I was in Daw House and Ward Two for a long time.'

The chatter shifted to gossip about staff and patients before Cooper turned to Eileen. 'We should celebrate you being back in the land of the living. How about coming out to a dance this Saturday?'

Eileen shook her head. 'I can't. I'm on strict rules not to engage in vigorous activity of any kind.'

'That will disappoint a few of the boys,' Cooper quipped.

Baxter took Eileen's hand. 'Not even dancing?'

'I want to,' Eileen said. 'I want to hop on a bike and ride madly through the streets and feel the wind in my hair, but I can't. I'm only allowed to walk a short distance and be here to do light work. That's all.'

'Oh, you poor thing,' Cooper said. 'That must be so hard.'

'I couldn't do that,' Baxter admitted. 'I don't have the discipline.'

'It is discipline,' Eileen confirmed. 'I don't like it at all, but it's what I have to do if I want to live a normal life later.'

'Speaking of discipline, we better go back in,' said Cooper, stubbing out her cigarette.

Baxter took Eileen's hand again, and repeated, 'It's good to have you back.'

*

Eileen alighted in grey and purple twilight from the tram at Wayville where Bruce waved to her from the platform stairs. She lifted the collar of her dark green raincoat and eased through the crowd to join her brother and she smiled when she recognised her mother sheltering under a broad umbrella beside him. 'Glad you could make it,' said Bruce.

'I told Sister I was visiting my mother,' Eileen replied. 'I'm not meant to do anything strenuous.'

'Well, it's not a lie, Girlie. You are visiting me,' Clarice said.

'Where's Betty?' Eileen asked, searching for her sister-in-law.

'She's not well,' said Bruce. 'Bad headaches.'

'Oh,' Eileen murmured. 'I hope she gets better soon.'

'She's annoyed she couldn't come tonight,' Bruce replied. 'Tonight's the last night of the trots season. Should be some good races. Shame about the weather, but track will still be good, maybe a little heavy.' Bruce's assessment of the conditions and the horses reminded Eileen of

Ken, and she was lost in her Melbourne memories until Bruce pulled her arm, and said, 'Come on, Girlie. Follow me. Clive's meeting us at the track.'

The crowd pooled at the metal turnstiles into the trotting arena at the Wayville Showground before flowing into the grounds, separating for favoured places in the stands and on the mounds. Rivers of umbrellas and hats bobbed and swirled under the yellow lights through the steady downpour and as the rain became heavier transparent glowing drops, visible in the arena spotlights, generated halos around the poles. Eileen huddled with Clarice under Bruce's umbrella and chatted about family and work while Bruce sought out bookies. The loudspeakers echoed with a welcome to the final night of the season, seven races and packed fields, a reminder that Wanda's Son was a scratching and a promise the rain would clear. Eileen heard and felt the crowd's excitement rising, and her anticipation rose with it.

Bruce reappeared, waving tickets in his fist. 'Several sure bets tonight,' he announced, grinning. 'Wet track, longer odds, should be a good night. Found a reprobate in the crowd.'

Clive appeared behind Bruce, grinning. 'Evening, Girlie,' he said, and his right arm encircled a woman shrouded in a beige greatcoat. 'Allow me to introduce Yvonne.'

Yvonne held out her hand to Eileen, who took it, saying, 'Pleased to meet you.'

'And you,' Yvonne replied. 'I've heard so much about you.'

'Most of it lies,' Clive interjected.

'Have you been to the trots before?' Yvonne asked.

'First time,' Eileen replied above the hubbub. 'So many people.'

'Some nights nearly forty thousand are here,' Bruce said. 'Probably twenty thousand tonight because of the rain. Wayville's a tiny track compared to most, only five hundred and fifty yards, but the crowd gets close, and you can see the whole race. It used to be a speedway track before the war.'

The crowd's liveliness and Clive's enthusiasm caused Eileen to recall people cheering and booing and yelling at the Carlton football games in Melbourne. The Wayville noise was different, more compact, immediate, but the energy was palpable, and the noise rose when the first horses and sulkies entered the track to parade. The announcer introduced each horse and driver as they prepared for the start of the Wakefield Handicap, and Eileen asked, 'Who will win?'

'My money's on Foidale Scott,' Bruce said. 'The bay gelding.'

'Why?' Eileen asked.

'Tips and talk,' Bruce replied. 'The horse has been in good form after last year's injury.'

'Injury?' Eileen asked.

'Horses get injured, sometimes training, sometimes in the races,' Bruce explained. 'This was more than a year ago.'

The announcer's voice echoed across the ground as the horses lined up at intervals. 'Why aren't they lined up together?' Eileen asked.

'It's a handicap race,' Bruce explained. 'Depending on their reputation and age, each horse starts at a different spot.'

'That's odd,' Eileen remarked.

'It's meant to even the chances for every horse,' Bruce explained. 'It makes it harder for the best horses to win and makes every race more exciting.'

'Race is about to start,' Clive said, and the crowd surged towards the fence, pressing around Eileen and Clarice.

The horses and sulkies flashed by as they headed into the second corner, two abreast, harnesses shining, wheels churning mud, hooves thundering on the earth, the announcer's voice struggling to call the race over the roaring crowd. Four laps later, the winner flashed past the post and Bruce pumped his fist in the air. 'Now that's a good start!' he yelled as the crowd noise quietened. 'I'll be back after collecting our winnings,' and he melted into the crowd, followed by Clive. Eileen and Yvonne huddled around Clarice.

When the last race finished, the announcer thanked everyone for coming and reminded them the new season was only weeks away. Eileen, Bruce, Clive, Yvonne and Clarice flowed with the throng to the tram station platform, where Eileen embraced Bruce and thanked him for inviting her.

'I hope you'll come again,' Bruce said. 'Betty will be here next time.'

'Give her my love and tell her I hope she gets better soon,' Eileen said.

'You look after yourself, Girlie,' Clarice urged, as she hugged her daughter. 'Make sure you visit.'

'I will,' Eileen promised. She turned to Yvonne. 'It is so nice to meet you.'

Then Clive hugged Eileen and said, 'Nice to see you out and about, Girlie.'

'You look after that woman,' Eileen whispered.

As Clive released Eileen, loud enough for Yvonne to hear, he replied, 'She doesn't know how lucky she is.'

On the tram, watching people talk and alight at their respective stops, rain spattering against the windows, Eileen was warm with happiness. She left the tram at Daw Park and strolled into the hospital grounds under the lights, exhausted by the night's expedition and the excitement of the trots, and extremely satisfied. She was lucky on so many levels – to be alive, to have a loving family, to have a place to live. She was delighted to see her itinerant brother, Clive, finding happiness. If anyone deserved a fresh start, he did. She snuggled into bed and slept soundly.

*

In the flickering silver light, Eileen reflected on the conversation that led her to the Curzon theatre's plush seats and screening of the noir film *Clash by Night*. 'I thought you couldn't go out,' Baxter said, handing Eileen a cigarette outside the ward.

'I can't go dancing or anything,' Eileen replied. 'I can only go to quiet places.'

'Wayville trots isn't exactly a quiet night out,' Cooper argued.

'How about the movies?' Baxter asked. 'We're going to the old Ozone tomorrow night. You should join us.'

'Baxter knows Paul, the manager,' Cooper said. 'And it's called the Curzon now.'

Catching the tram down Goodwood Road was easy, and Eileen was pleased to be out and about with friends. The movie was confronting, an adult story with Barbara Stanwyck in the main role, an actress Eileen admired. The film also included a girl Eileen recently saw on the front of a *Time* magazine, Marilyn Monroe, playing a ditsy blonde in a minor role.

Apart from her attractive looks, Eileen couldn't understand why the magazines were making so much fuss about her. She wasn't much of an actress, and Eileen knew there was more controversy around the young woman's risqué photos filling the magazines than there was about her acting ability. What did draw Eileen into the movie was how the central character was caught in a bitter love triangle. She couldn't imagine loving two men at once. That would be odd, uncomfortable, unworkable. Dudley wanted to have such an arrangement with his wife and Eileen. She knew no one would be happy in the end.

After the movie, Cooper led the group into the foyer to meet the manager, Paul Thomas, who offered everyone coffee and cake, compliments of the house, and the group sat and chatted while the crowd dispersed. As the women started to leave to catch the tram, Paul called Eileen aside and said, 'It was nice to meet you. I didn't realise Cooper had so many lovely friends.'

'I didn't know her male acquaintances hit on her girlfriends,' Eileen replied.

'Oh, I apologise. I didn't mean it like that.'

Seeing Paul flush with embarrassment, Eileen smiled and said, 'I'll take the compliment for what it is.'

'I was actually going to say that if you want to see some more movies here let me know and I can arrange tickets. Cooper told me you've been very ill.'

Eileen glanced at Cooper and Baxter who raised their eyebrows knowingly. 'Cooper perhaps should be more discrete,' Eileen told Paul. 'Thank you for offering. I might take you up on that.'

'What was that about?' Cooper asked when Eileen joined them to wait for the tram.

'Free tickets,' Eileen replied.

'Careful,' Baxter warned. 'Nothing is ever free.'

'What do you know about him?'

'Not a lot,' Cooper said. 'He's friendly whenever we've been to the cinema, a gentleman really. He said he keeps an eye out for us Repat nurses because we do important work.'

'Wish they paid us what important work is worth,' Baxter complained.

The ride home was filled with analysis of the movie and Marilyn Monroe's future, everyone agreeing she was a Hollywood stunt, a flash-in-the-pan peroxide blond who would never match the beauty on screen or stardom of Lana Turner, Ava Gardner or Rita Hayworth.

Back in her bed, lights out, Eileen's thoughts drifted through the movie and onto Paul. He was nice enough, companionable, and it was a while since she spent time with a man. Going to the movies was a safe adventure. She would accept his offer of the free tickets. She did ask Cooper if he was taken, but Cooper said she didn't know. Eileen decided she would find out.

*

'I'm glad you came tonight,' Paul said, pushing the white coffee cup towards Eileen. 'I wondered if I was too forward last week.'

'You were,' Eileen replied, 'but I've come anyway. I'm curious.'

'About what?' Paul asked, lifting his cup to sip.

'You. Who you really are. Why you chose to talk to me.'

'There's not a lot to tell,' Paul replied. 'I live in Colonel Light Gardens. I work as the manager of this cinema, and sometimes for the New Star next door.'

'Why are the two cinemas so close together?' Eileen asked.

'Business, I presume. They're owned by the same company. Cliffords wanted to build a modern cinema, so that's why the New Star is there. This one was built in 1911 as the Wondergraph. Then it was renamed the Ozone, the Star Theatre, and now the Curzon. I reckon the owners think the old girl is getting a bit long in the tooth.'

'They'll sell it?'

'One day,' Paul said. 'Or pull it down. You should drink your coffee.'

'How long have you been manager?'

'Two years.'

'And you like it?' Eileen asked.

Paul grinned. 'How many jobs are there where you can see all the latest movies for free? Yes, I do like it. Wouldn't you?'

Eileen sipped at her coffee before she answered. 'I think I would. But

I'm a nurse.'

'It's never too late to start a new job,' Paul urged. 'I was managing a goods factory before this, and before that I was a Sergeant in the Army.'

'My father was a Sergeant in the Military Police, and my oldest brother was in the Navy and RAAF,' Eileen said. 'Did you go overseas?'

'I enlisted in 1940,' Paul replied. 'We were sent to North Africa, Libya in fact, and then they brought us back home in 1942 because of the Japanese. I ended up wounded in New Guinea and repatriated. So here I am.'

'Were you in the Repat?' Eileen asked.

'A year when it was the military hospital,' Paul replied solemnly. '1943. That's why I go out of my way to serve you girls when you come to this cinema. I know what you do, and I'm thankful for it.' He glanced at his wristwatch. 'Now, what about you? How did you end up working at the Repat?'

Eileen gave him an abbreviated version of her Repat experience before the bell called her into the cinema. She meant to ask if he had a girlfriend and chided herself for forgetting, but she was certain he didn't because of his attentiveness, and, in all honesty, she felt it would be rude to ask him a blunt question.

After the movie, Eileen found Paul waiting in the foyer. 'It's pouring outside. Let me drive you back to the hospital,' he offered.

'It's out of your way,' Eileen said.

'Not at all,' Paul replied. 'You know where I live. It's a simple drive-by for me.'

Eileen acquiesced for the convenience of the ride to stay out of the heavy rain, and for Paul's company, and she chatted with him about the cinema business on the drive home. 'My mother used to travel to country towns with a movie man in the early 1920s, playing piano for silent movies,' Eileen told him.

'Was she married to the movie man?'

'No.'

'She was a brave woman,' said Paul. 'Travelling the countryside for women isn't safe anywhere. It certainly wouldn't have been safe back then. What does she do now?'

'She's a cleaner.'

'But she was obviously a talented musician to play for the silent movies.'

'She was,' Eileen replied, and told him about the family evenings spent in the parlour singing while Clarice played. 'That all changed in the war,' she concluded.

'The war changed a lot of things,' Paul said. He turned into the Repatriation driveway and stopped at the gate. 'Don't get too wet,' he advised. 'See you next Saturday?'

'If I'm not on shift,' Eileen replied, as she climbed out of the car. 'Thank you.'

*

The weeks dragged to the end of June and Eileen rugged up against a cold wintry evening to catch the tram to Goodwood. Paul was waiting for her in the theatre café as he had for almost a month. 'We meet again,' he said, smiling. 'Nice coincidence.'

'Life is full of coincidences,' Eileen remarked as she sat.

'Coffee?'

'Coffee is so American,' Eileen replied in her mockingly affected posh voice, changed tone, and added cheerily, 'Yes, please.'

She studied Paul while he spoke to the woman behind the café counter. He was slim, dressed smartly in his manager's grey striped suit, his light brown hair combed neatly to the left, average height. She preferred men close to her own height at five foot seven inches. Tall men intimidated her. Paul was a good height. He carried himself confidently, self-assurance gained from responsibility and leadership, she assumed. He spoke with an educated voice, and she liked that as well. He was simply being friendly, she accepted that, but she wondered if more might develop in the relationship. He seemed a good man, one with whom she could see herself sharing life. Paul returned, carrying two coffees, and placed one carefully before Eileen. 'How much?' she asked.

He laughed and said, 'Same price as last time. On the house.'

'Perks of management?' Eileen teased.

'Perks of having my wife serving behind the counter,' Paul replied.

Eileen suppressed her shock as she glanced at the brunette woman at the confectionary bar, her mind and emotions processing Paul's revelation. 'Wife?'

'Yes,' Paul replied. 'Aggie Thomas.'

'Oh,' Eileen murmured, crestfallen.

'Is everything all right?'

'Oh, yes,' Eileen said, trying to compose her disappointment and shame at being naive. 'I mean, I didn't realise...' but she left the sentence unfinished.

'You didn't realise I was married?' Paul asked. He sat back, shook his head, and sighed. 'Oh dear,' he said slowly. 'I am very sorry.'

'It's not your fault,' Eileen said.

'Oh, I think it might be,' he replied. 'Very poor form. I should have said I was married from the start.'

'I shouldn't assume. I feel so silly.'

'Don't be,' Paul said, smiling again. 'I'm flattered a beautiful woman would find me attractive.' He laughed, and leaned forward to say, 'Of course, we won't mention this to Aggie, will we? She might not see the funny side.'

Eileen smiled at Paul's candid warning, but inside she was embarrassed and wanted to leave and go home and cry at her stupid self for making ludicrous assumptions. She glanced at Aggie behind the confectionary bar. She was short, plain enough in her looks, but she had a cheerful face, a dimple in one cheek, and she was comfortable with the customers. She complemented Paul.

'Movie's about to start. I'll meet you afterward and I can give you a lift home again,' Paul offered.

'Oh, no, that won't be necessary,' Eileen replied hastily, meeting his gaze. 'I've made arrangements to be picked up.'

'You didn't need to do that,' he said. 'I could have dropped you at the Repat.'

'What about your wife?'

'Aggie?' Paul queried. 'She finishes up when the movie starts and goes home early. She leaves Lena and Wilma to do the late shift. She's not a silly woman.'

'I better hurry in,' Eileen said hastily. 'Thank you for the coffee, Paul.' She rose and headed for the auditorium.

The screen shimmered, and music and voices ebbed and flowed, but Eileen's heart raced as she played out her reactions to Paul's confession. *No*, she chided herself. *He wasn't confessing. He was telling the truth. But why did he take me home the other times and not say anything? Did he have to say anything?* she challenged herself. *He's just a nice man being nice to me. I didn't ask if he was married or not. I assumed. I shouldn't assume.* She tried to focus on Katherine Hepburn's struggle with Spencer Tracey, the message of the film aimed at women, a message she knew she needed to hear, but it was too hard. Everything was too hard. She crept out of the cinema before the movie ended, checked Paul wasn't in the lobby and headed onto Goodwood Road to wait for a tram.

On the ride home, and in her bed, the faces came and went – Dudley, Ken, Mervyn, now Paul – men she wanted and yet didn't want; men who played with her heart. Each one was different. Each one could have been the man for her life. But none of them were. None of them could ever be that man. It seemed that man did not exist, not for her. Ruby was right. Maybe she was better off not trying to find a man to fulfil her life. Maybe she could do that herself.

*

'I think you'll enjoy working in Ward Seven, Nurse Bonney,' said Sister Williams. 'The young men there are lovely. Most have long-term illnesses stemming from the war. I think the one who has been here the longest is Allan Rowe in Bed Eleven. He received shocking burns and wounds from an aircraft crash. No one thought he would live, but he has. He's a brave soul, but it's too hard for him to go home. That's why he stays with us. Some of the others came here from other hospitals, repatriated to their home states. And a few come and go, illnesses flaring up from time to time. You'll get to know each one. Part of being on light duties is to make sure the patients are comfortable. Talk to them. Play cards and board games. Take them for strolls around the grounds when you can. They will appreciate it.'

Eileen surveyed the ward and the beds laid out before her. Four months in the women's ward in Daw House passed quickly, and she made good friends among the patients, but she was looking forward to a different environment. Caring for men would be an interesting change. She collected the ward clipboard and walked along the ward aisle, introducing herself as she asked how each patient was feeling. A young man in the third bed grinned, and said in an American accent, 'Today's Independence Day, nurse. Did you know that? Back home, my folks will be celebrating.'

'It ain't Independence Day for a few hours yet, mate,' the man in the bed beside him remarked. 'You Yanks have always been behind us.'

'You Aussies don't ever accept that we saved your necks in the war now, do you?' the American retorted. 'Pay him no mind, Miss,' he advised Eileen. 'He came back a little messed up in his head.'

Eileen looked at her clipboard, and replied, 'I won't, Mister McAllister.'

'Plain old Davie, Miss,' Davie told her. 'And this degenerate's name is Michael Docherty,' he added, using his thumb to indicate the man in the next bed. 'Call him Micky. He don't know himself otherwise.'

'Thank you for the advice,' Eileen said, and she nodded at Micky who was grinning at her.

In the seventh bed, an auburn-haired young man was sitting up, reading a motor sports magazine, and as Eileen approached the patient in the adjacent bed told her, 'It's Bill's birthday today! And what a lovely present he's getting!'

The men laughed and the young man looked up from his magazine with a soft, crooked smile. 'Is that true?' Eileen asked, glancing down at the clipboard. 'Mister Shillitoe. Did I say that right?'

'You did,' the young man replied. 'And it's Bill please.'

Eileen cocked her head as she replied, 'Bill it is, then. I'm Nurse Bonney. Happy twenty-sixth birthday.'

A chorused 'Whoa' rose from the patients, and the man who announced that it was Bill's birthday called out, 'Maybe Nurse Bonney can give a bloke a kiss for his birthday,' which drew another chorus.

Eileen blushed and she noticed Bill also blushed. 'I'm sorry about my friends' behaviour,' Bill said, looking uncomfortable.

Eileen laughed. 'I have six brothers, Bill. I'm sure we will get along fine.' She moved along the aisle, chatting with the other men, learning a little about each of them, noting why each was in the hospital. Every man had a particular story, an individual reason for being in the hospital, but they all seemed polite and lively. She decided she would enjoy working in the ward.

Back in the nurses' station, curiosity piqued about the auburn-haired patient named Bill whose birthday it was, she searched the records, found his manila dossier, opened it and read why he was admitted.

*

'I joined up in July 1944, immediately after I turned eighteen,' Bill said, as he walked beside Eileen along the corridor. 'I was a mechanical engineer trainee in the RAAF Fourth Technical Training Unit. I love engines. I have motorcycles back home, and I fix tractors and trucks for the local farmers. They sent me to Darwin and out to Fenton airfield, servicing Liberator bombers.'

'But you got Scarlet Fever and Rheumatic Fever at the same time,' Eileen said.

'I did,' Bill confirmed. 'How did you know?' he asked, looking at Eileen for an explanation.

'I read the records,' she admitted. 'Do you mind?'

Bill grinned. 'Not at all. I don't remember a lot about it. I had a sore throat one morning, and then a fever and a rash, so they diagnosed Scarlet Fever and sent me to 129 AGH, the Darwin hospital.' He chuckled and continued, 'The rash was like bad sunburn.'

'Your skin peels away too, I think,' Eileen said, as she opened the door to let Bill outside.

'It does,' Bill confirmed. 'Everyone was telling me the Darwin heat was cooking me because I was blood nut, you know, red hair.'

'That's cruel.'

'Just blokes having fun. No one meant anything by it.'

'But you got sicker.'

Bill shrugged. 'The sore throat got worse, and I ached all over. That's when they decided I also had Rheumatic Fever. The base staff sent my father a telegram to tell him I was on the critically ill list. Dad was concerned, as you can imagine. But then they sent him a telegram a few weeks later saying I was no longer on the critically ill list and Dad was pretty happy to hear that. Only the clerical staff got it wrong. I wasn't better. I was sicker than ever. So they sent him another telegram, a week after the second one, apologising, because they had actually moved me from the critically ill list to dangerously ill.'

Eileen grabbed Bill's arm. 'That's horrible. Your father must have been sick with worry.'

Bill chuckled, and Eileen liked the cheekiness in his lop-sided grin. 'He thought I was dying. I probably was.' He shook his head, and said, 'I don't know how we won the war. Communications were pretty ordinary.'

'You haven't been in hospital all this time, have you?' Eileen asked.

'They discharged me for medical reasons in July 1945, because the fever messed up my heart valves, and they shipped me back here to Adelaide. I've been in and out of the Repat since then.'

'According to your notes, you've been here nearly three months this time.'

'Four,' he corrected. 'I came back in March. They're still treating me for the damage.'

'Rheumatic carditis,' Eileen confirmed. 'Basically, you have a leaky valve, although the treatment seems to have finally solved the long-term recurrence of the fever.'

'Is there anything else I should know?' he asked.

She smiled and said, 'I'm not allowed to discuss a patient's notes with them.'

Bill laughed. 'Of course. Confidentiality. We never had this chat. But is there anything else I need to know?'

'No,' she said. 'It seems you're on the mend. But you will always have a heart condition.'

'The doctors keep telling me that,' he said, looking ahead as if he was trying to see through the mists of a future time. 'They say I might not live as long as I should.'

'The doctors tell you what they know, but they are not always right,' Eileen said. 'You have to do the best you can to manage it.'

Bill nodded. 'Makes life a challenge. That's what Doctor Beaton said.' He turned to Eileen. 'But somehow it seems better coming from you.'

'We all have challenges,' Eileen said, her mind flitting to her own recovery and Doctor Ketteridge's prognosis during his last visit to her.

'You have done remarkably well, Miss Bonney,' Ketteridge said in his formal expression, nodding wisely. 'You will make a pleasing recovery. Of course, I do have to tell you that some things may not be the same as they would have been had you not had to go through this. You will probably never be an athlete.' Eileen laughed. 'It will be a long time before you can lift heavy things or do hard physical work. Your tendons and muscles all have to heal completely. And it is possible you are unlikely to be able to have children.'

His final statement shocked her. 'Why ever not?' she asked.

'Your body underwent major trauma, Miss Bonney. Sometimes that is enough to disrupt the natural bodily processes, especially in young women. I am not saying you will not ever have babies. I am simply advising you that you should be aware that may be an unfortunate consequence of what you have been through.'

'Are you all right?' Bill asked.

Eileen pushed the raw memory aside, to ask, 'Would you like to walk through the garden?'

'Very much so,' Bill said, and he offered Eileen his arm.

*

Clarice lowered *The Advertiser* onto the table, saying, 'Marjorie Jackson. Now there is a woman who chased her dreams.'

'I heard she set a new World Record,' Eileen noted, lowering her teacup.

'For the two hundred metres,' Clarice confirmed. 'She won by five yards. But that wasn't the World Record. She set that in the heats. She set a new Olympic Record in the final, and on a muddy track.'

'Two gold medals and two World Records,' Eileen said. 'Who would have thought?'

'It's something for you to remember, Girlie,' Clarice said. 'You can be anything, if you want to be.'

'I imagine she trained very hard,' Eileen said.

'Yes, she would have,' Clarice agreed. 'But if you want to achieve something big, the training becomes who you are. The hours and hours I put into music when I was your age,' she said wistfully, shaking her head.

'So why did you stop playing piano and violin?'

Clarice huffed and replied, 'I married your father.'

'You played for the radio shows during the war.'

'He let me play for the radio,' Clarice said. '"All part of the war effort," he said, "We all have to do our bit." But I don't think he liked me doing it.'

'Why ever not?'

'Your father is a jealous man.' Clarice shook her head. 'Ironic, isn't it?'

'He loved singing when you played. We all did.'

'He loved singing,' Clarice said. 'I was only a vehicle for his pleasure. That's what all men are like. We are only useful if we serve their purposes. He did not hesitate to sell my piano when it suited him to sell it.'

'We needed the money,' Eileen said, feeling obliged to defend her father's action, even though she, too, was angry and disappointed with what he did. 'It was a hard time, for everyone.'

'He needed the money for himself,' said Clarice. 'He used our money to impress his other woman.'

Eileen sighed, tears rising. 'Why was he so mean to you?'

Clarice lowered her teacup. 'Men are nice to get what they want, Girlie – someone to cook for them, clean up after them, keep their home tidy, give them children, look after their children. Some men are happy with that because they can go about their manly pursuits knowing they have a home to return to when they feel the need. They show their wives a little tenderness, even respect and appreciation, sometimes, so long as they don't have to look after themselves. Wives become the mothers they had before they married.' She caught her breath. 'Then there are others, like your father, who are plain greedy. They want a woman to keep their home and children in place, while they go out, drinking and gambling with their mates, and spending time with other women for a bit of extra dancing they don't get at home, because their wives are tired, and do not want any more children.'

'But most men are happy with their family,' Eileen said.

'Oh, Girlie, I was naïve like that when I was your age. My parents raised me to be like Marjorie Jackson – chase my dreams, believe anything was possible. So, I did. I learned and played music wherever I could. I believed music was what I was born to make, and I was not interested in getting married, or having a family, not in the way my friends, even my sisters, were. They all wanted to find the right man. I travelled and played music, and I was happy, while my friends found men, fell in love, settled down and started families. I was not rich like them. I certainly was not secure in my means. But I was happy. It was a new time, a new era after the Great War, the future was full of promise, and I certainly did not need a man to keep me happy or give me purpose. All I needed was music.'

'Then why did you get married?'

Clarice sighed heavily. 'I listened to what the others were saying,' she said. 'I heard the whispers, the gossip. Even my mother started to worry that I was becoming a doddering old maid living alone with my piano, relying on my family to look after me. And then I met Donald. And fell in love. Just like that.' She shook her head. 'And that was the end of it.'

'But, if he was so bad, why did you fall in love with him?' Eileen asked.

Clarice chuckled and leaned back in her chair, before asking, 'Can you remember how much you were in love with that soldier when you were a child, Girlie? Remember? Why did you fall in love with him?'

Caught unawares by the reverse question, Eileen blushed and hesitated, until she realised her mother was expecting an answer. 'He was kind,' she answered. 'He had nice eyes. He was a good dancer.'

'And he treated you like you were someone very special.'

'Yes,' Eileen agreed. 'He did.'

'And you could not stop thinking about him, could you?'

'No. I couldn't.'

'So, now you know why I fell in love with Donald,' Clarice concluded. 'For exactly the same reasons. He was tall, with cheeky eyes, and his smile was happy and broad. He was a hard worker, he owned his business, and he treated me as someone very, very special. And I was twenty-nine and starting to think everyone else was right; that life is not complete until you marry. So, I did. And here we are.'

Eileen saw her mother's wan smile and the tears gathering in the corners of her eyes. 'I'm sorry I asked,' she apologised.

'I am sorry we haven't had this talk sooner,' Clarice replied.

'Do you still see Father?' Eileen asked.

Clarice lowered her eyes. 'Sometimes.' She looked up. 'He tried to make it up to me, you know. He felt an enormous responsibility towards all of us, but I think that was more about guilt and pressure from others for him to do the right thing. That's why he took us to Port Neill, and into the city, and why he found jobs for you older kids, why he brought Freddo Frogs home to the little ones. But he was not cut out to be a father, or a husband, Girlie. He wanted more.' She stifled a sob. 'I try to accept that he has done what he has done, and I should be rid of him. But it's so hard. And it gets terribly lonely, alone, in this flat.'

'Maybe there will be someone else, Mum,' Eileen suggested hopefully.

Clarice laughed, sniffed, and said, 'Good grief, no, Girlie. I might be alone, but I have no interest in another man making my life miserable. Please do not wish that on me.' She lifted her cup. 'Or on yourself. You should be glad to be rid of men.'

'Well, that's not so easy,' Eileen replied, grinning. 'They've given me a whole ward of them at the Repat. All young and handsome, too,' and she outlined her new role in Ward Seven.

'Oh, my goodness!' Clarice cried, feigning horror. 'What have they done to you? They've put my poor little chicken in the fox house,' and she laughed, and Eileen laughed with her. 'Well, my advice is that you give them their medicine to fix their illness and do not get involved with any of them, dear girl.'

'Matron said the same thing.'

'You know they will all tell you that you are the sweetest angel they have ever seen,' Clarice said. 'They tell every girl that.'

'I know,' said Eileen. 'They already say things like that.' She chuckled. 'They're such sweet men.'

'Oh, goodness, Girlie! Listen to yourself.'

'I'm only teasing, Mum,' Eileen replied, grinning. 'More tea?' She lifted the white pot and refreshed her mother's cup and her own. As she lowered the pot, she said, 'But there is one young man I've grown quite fond of.'

'Girlie Bonney!' Clarice gasped.

'He's very shy,' Eileen continued, smiling at her mother's feigned disgust. 'He's from the country, near Meningie. You know where that is?'

'I travelled the South-East with the movie company,' Clarice reminded her. 'I know where Meningie is.' She lifted an eyebrow. 'And what is this young man's name?'

'William,' Eileen replied, 'but he prefers being called Bill.'

'And why is he in the Repat?'

Eileen summarised what she knew from Bill's records, and said, 'He's been very sick for a long time, but it looks like that's all sorted.'

'If he's been sick for so long, why would you want to take home a lame dog?' Clarice asked. 'Does he have a job?'

'He was training to be a mechanical engineer in the RAAF.'

'But does he have a job now?' Clarice asked. 'It's hard enough for ex-servicemen to get work as it is, let alone one who's been injured or has an ongoing problem. Don't go getting involved with a man who doesn't have a job, Girlie. There's no good in that. You've seen what happened with your father.'

'He's been working for local farmers where he lives,' Eileen explained. 'He hasn't said a lot about it.'

'If he doesn't have a job, Girlie, stay away from him,' Clarice warned. 'No matter how nice he might seem, if you must find a man, you need someone who has an income and a future. If he can't provide for you, you'll end up miserable and on the streets.'

'I only like him,' Eileen said to appease her mother. 'I'm not thinking at all about anything like marrying him.'

Clarice's eyes narrowed and she said, 'Be careful.'

*

'Nurse Bonney,' Matron Morphett said. 'A quiet word, please?'

Eileen lowered the files she was sorting at the nurses' station and said,

'Yes, of course.'

'We might go outside, if you don't mind?' Matron Morphett said. She led Eileen out of the ward, where the morning rain kept them confined to the small veranda. 'I will keep this brief, Bonney. It is a tad unpleasant out here,' Matron said. 'Are you enjoying your work on this ward?'

'Yes, thank you, Matron, I am,' Eileen replied.

'I'm pleased,' Morphett acknowledged. 'And the men are respectful?'

Eileen grinned. 'Some of them are cheeky, but, yes, they are very respectful.'

'Hmm,' Morphett mused. 'I'm not sure how to put this tactfully, Bonney – it is rather sensitive – but there are rumours you've been visiting one of the men after hours. Is that correct?'

Eileen shuffled uncomfortably and blushed. Summoning her courage, she replied, 'I have.'

'Mister Shillitoe. Correct?'

'Yes, Matron,' Eileen said.

'And do we have a policy on that sort of thing in the hospital?'

' There's nothing untoward going on,' Eileen blurted. 'He's a complete gentleman.'

'Whether or not he is a gentleman is not the issue here, is it?'

'No, Matron,' Eileen meekly replied.

'A nurse does not strike up relationships beyond professional care, do they?'

'No, Matron.'

'No,' Morphett confirmed. 'Which leaves me with a dilemma. We cannot have this kind of fraternisation taking place. It sets a poor precedent for your colleagues, and a rather unnecessary expectation among the patients,' she said, raising an eyebrow pointedly. 'I should discipline you by moving you to a different ward, one without men it seems, although the other patients on the ward don't seem to attract visits from you after hours, which is just as well.'

'Matron, I-' Eileen went to interject.

'I have not finished yet, Bonney,' Matron Morphett warned. 'Don't add impertinence to my concerns.'

'I apologise, Matron.'

'As you should,' Morphett agreed. The pair stepped aside to allow an orderly to enter the ward. 'As it turns out,' Morphett continued, after the door closed, 'your would-be beau is being discharged in two days. He's leaving.' She watched Eileen's reaction to the news before she continued. 'If I can be assured this will not happen again, I might be able to forget this happened at all. What do you think, Bonney? Will an indiscretion like this occur again?'

'No, Matron. Absolutely not,' Eileen confirmed quickly. 'I promise.'

'You made that promise when you signed the form to join us,' Matron Morphett said. 'I guess your only excuse is that your father lied about your age back then.' When she saw Eileen's eyes widen, she said, 'Yes, Bonney, I joined the dots when I read through your records.' She smiled. 'Luckily, that's in the past, and no one else needs to know. You aren't the first girl to lie about your age, although most try to tell everyone they are younger than they are, for vanity's sake.' She drew her breath. 'Now, we have an agreement, and I expect you to learn from this mishap and become a much more professional nurse. There will be no more favourites, and no inappropriate behaviours with the men. Correct?'

'Yes, Matron,' Eileen responded gratefully. 'Thank you.'

'Don't thank me, Bonney,' Matron Morphett replied, opening the door into the ward. 'Do the right thing, as you should already be doing.'

*

Eileen shook her head. 'I'm not in the mood to go out,' she said, flopping onto her bed in her slip and underwear.

'Oh, come on, Bonney,' Cooper urged, standing at the side of the bed. 'You need to come with us. You're forgetting how to be sociable. Besides, Betty and Lyla and your brothers are coming along. It's to celebrate Baxter's birthday. You must come.'

'I can't go dancing,' Eileen argued.

'Oh, that's tosh!' Cooper retorted. 'You've been working on Ward Seven for more than a month.'

'Light duties,' Eileen reminded her.

'When did the doctor last say you couldn't go dancing?' Cooper asked.

'A few weeks ago,' Eileen said.

'Months ago!' Cooper said emphatically. 'You have to start dancing again, sooner or later. Make it sooner. Look at you. You're strong enough. It's not about breathing any more. You're smoking and walking and getting around everywhere on the trams. You don't have an excuse, Bonney. You're coming with us tonight, and that's that!'

'I'm not sure,' Eileen said despondently.

'Look,' Cooper said, leaning towards Eileen. 'The man you're mooning over has gone back to his farm, and you'll probably never see him again. You can't lie around moping about every man you meet on the wards. If we all did that, can you imagine what this place would be like? There'd be no one left to look after the patients, that's what. Get up, smile, and put on something nice. Baxter and Fitzgerald and I will be waiting at the tram stop. And don't be late!'

Alone, Eileen looked in her wardrobe. She had her uniforms and two dresses. The last time she wore the green dress it was to meet Paul who turned out to be married. The blue one then. It was fancier anyway, more suited to ballroom dancing. It was cool outside, so she could wear her overcoat, the dark blue one she bought in Melbourne more than three years ago. Because she had little need for clothes in the past eighteen months, she didn't shop for new ones, making do with what she had. Cooper was right. She needed to get out and live again. That was what attracted her to Paul, a chance to start living again. And that was what Bill ignited in her. She wished he hadn't gone home.

She grabbed the Johnson's baby powder and sprinkled it under her arms and into her knickers, slipped the blue dress over her shoulders, straightened it over her hips and brushed off traces of powder. She carefully sprayed her *L'Aiment Coty* on her fingers and dabbed it behind her ears and on her neck and wrists, making sure it was subtle and she was not childishly over-scented. She brushed her hair. The final touches were red lipstick and a string of fake pearls around her neck. She slipped into her shoes, grabbed her navy carry bag with her cigarettes, perfume and her purse, and hurried into the corridor and downstairs.

The girls cheered when Eileen appeared at the tram stop. 'Now we are the three musketeers and D'Artagnan!' Baxter said.

'Quick fag,' Cooper said, handing Eileen a cigarette and producing a lighter.

'It'll need to be quick,' said Fitzgerald. 'Tram's here.'

'Save it for Ron,' Cooper said, and Eileen slid the cigarette into her bag.

*

Lying on her back in her bed in the middle of the night, Eileen could feel her heart racing from the night of fun and laughter and dancing. She had almost forgotten what it felt like to be alive, full of music and energy and joy. Her brothers took turns sweeping her onto the dance floor, choosing the slower songs so she could ease into dancing again – Two-Steps, Three-Steps, Waltzes. Though she was asked to dance by other men, she refused, choosing to wait for either Bruce or Peter or John to dance, mainly John, who seemed less interested in dancing with other women than with her. 'Really, Girlie,' he said, as he steered her gently in a slow Fox Trot, 'I don't see what all the fuss is about. The best part is getting all glammed up and dancing, not swooning over the prettiest girls.'

'Have you ever had a girlfriend?' Eileen asked.

'Hardly,' John replied. 'I don't need the competition, darling. And, tonight, I don't need one because I'm already dancing with the most beautiful girl in the room.'

Eileen smiled, remembering John's compliment. Despite his haughty, aloof nature, he was generous with how he looked after their mother, and he was the only one who seemed to be rising above their family situation in his business world. He was the one who appreciated the arts and music in the way the Chaplin and Stephens families on their mother's side appreciated them.

Baxter's birthday celebrations were fun. Late in the evening, dancing coming to a close, Eileen joined a group who trooped out of the Palais and down to the riverbank, the Torrens glittering under the September moon. The men produced hip flasks which were passed around before a raucous rendition of 'Happy Birthday' was sung to Baxter. The men lined up for a birthday kiss and chased second kisses from their spouses and girlfriends amid rebukes and laughter. Eileen was exhausted from the dancing, although she wished she had the strength and energy and breath to swing dance like she did with Dudley and Mervyn. Ken was less of an energetic dancer, she recalled. He would have been at home with ballroom dancing at the Palais Royale where the level of sophistication and dress code and dance styles better suited his refined attitude.

Eileen rolled onto her left side, and her thoughts shifted to the auburn-headed ex-RAAF man to whom she became attached in Ward Seven. With her eyes closed, she could picture his face, his green eyes, his freckles, his lop-sided grin. She could hear his quietly spoken voice and feel the rough texture of his hand in hers when they secretly held hands in the back pew of the Repatriation chapel at Sunday prayer. She would love to dance with him tonight, but he was on a farm in the Upper Southeast, a hundred or more miles away. She sighed and pressed the side of her head into the pillow. Cooper was right. She had no excuses not to get out and enjoy life.

*

Cooper dropped an envelope on the table in front of Eileen in the canteen. 'I picked this up for you from the post office,' she said. 'Interesting postmark,' she added, raising an eyebrow.

Eileen studied the spidery handwriting, the Queen Elizabeth stamp, and the name "Ashville" on the postmark, before she opened the envelope and unfolded the letter.

'Well?' Cooper asked. 'It's from him, isn't it?'

'Yes,' Eileen said, without looking up from reading.

'And?' Cooper prompted.

'He wants to ring me.'

'When?'

Eileen turned over the page. 'Friday evening.'

'That's tomorrow night.'

'I better book in at the exchange,' Eileen said, and she stood.

'Did he say anything else?'

'He asked how I was.' Eileen headed for the door with Cooper in pursuit.

'And anything else?' Cooper persisted.

Eileen stopped and met Cooper's smiling gaze. 'No, Cooper, he didn't say anything else, whatever that's meant to mean.'

'No kisses at the bottom?'

'Oh, Cooper, seriously! He's a gentleman,' Eileen retorted, and she marched out of the canteen.

The rest of the day on duty was filled with swirling thoughts of Bill and her anticipation of his phone call, and Eileen took a long time to settle to sleep that evening, imagining his face and voice and recalling details he shared on their walks. Bill told her he lived with his father on a small farm, and that his father was a boundary rider for the Bowman family. Bill's mother had been a teacher, but she passed away when Bill was thirteen. His younger brother, Colin, was a horse trainer in the Adelaide Hills. Bill loved motorcycles and everything mechanical with engines. His grandmother lived in Meningie. Try as she did to suppress her anticipation to talk with Bill on the phone, she could not sleep.

Friday became an anxious flurry for the day's duties to end. She hurried from the ward, shared a cigarette with Cooper and Baxter, and all three waited at the Repatriation telephone exchange for the promised phone call. When it came, Eileen's nerves danced as the operator handed her the headset. 'Hello?' Eileen asked tentatively.

'Is this Eileen?' a tinny voice inquired.

'Yes,' she answered. 'Speaking.'

'It's Bill here, Eileen. How are you?'

Eileen waved at her friends to move away, before she replied, 'I'm fine, thank you, Bill. And you?'

The conversation was brief, over before Eileen wanted it to end. She thanked the operator as she handed back the headset and walked into the cool evening, ignoring her friends' immediate inquisition, until Cooper grabbed her arm and said, 'Eileen Bonney! We're talking to you. What did he say?'

Eileen beamed and replied, 'He asked me to go to a ball.'

'Where?' Cooper asked.

'Ashville.'

'Where in blue blazes is Ashville?' Baxter asked.

'I'm not sure,' Eileen replied, 'but I think it's near Meningie.'

'Meningie?' Baxter asked.

'It's a town on the lakes on the way to the Coorong,' Cooper explained. 'That's right, isn't it Eileen?'

'Yes,' Eileen confirmed.

'How on earth are you going to get to a dance in that bloody place?' Baxter asked. 'It's out woop-woop.'

'There's a bus,' Eileen said. 'Bill is going to buy me a ticket and send the information in a letter.'

'And where will you stay?' Cooper asked.

Eileen shrugged, replying, 'I'm not sure, but Bill said he was organising that.'

'It's a trap!' Baxter warned. 'He's luring you into a dark, out-of-the-way place and you'll never be seen again.'

'I like the sound of that,' Cooper said. 'Mysterious man. He might tie you up and keep you prisoner and use you as he sees fit.'

'That's terrible!' Eileen declared, and she started giggling.

'I think she likes that idea,' Baxter teased, and all three women broke into raucous laughter.

*

'Gentlemen, please take your partners for the Military Two-Step!' the master of ceremonies announced. The huddle of men in suits at the Ashville school hall entrance separated and fanned out as they headed to choose partners from the women seated around the hall perimeter.

Bill walked towards Eileen in his dark grey suit, smiling shyly, his auburn hair parted on the side and slicked down with pomade that made his hair appear darker, and her heart quickened when he bowed and held out his hand. She took his warm hand and rose, and they joined the circle of dancers on the freshly sawdusted floor, waiting for the piano, accordion, and drums to begin. Following Bill's lead, Eileen flowed into the two-step rhythm, back and forth, facing Bill and finishing with a twirl as he placed his right hand in the small of her back and spun her gently into the pattern. Her smile widened with Bill's grin as they danced, and she contemplated how the adventure brought her to this magical moment.

The journey began early afternoon at the Franklin Street bus depot, after catching the tram from Daw Park into the city. Dressed casually in a floral green full pleated skirt and dark green cardigan, her hair pinned, she carried a small brown suitcase containing her change of clothes for the evening, her new sky-blue dress carefully folded with a long white shawl, stockings and gold-flowered shoes. She bought the dress especially for the ball, her sister Judy taking in the seams to make it fit snugly, the shawl borrowed from Cooper. As he promised, Bill sent the bus ticket, so she boarded Bob Mitchell's bus and settled into the hard seat to watch the scenery pass on the two-hour trip as the bus climbed and descended the steep and winding highway through the Adelaide Hills before heading across the lake plains through Strathalbyn, onto Langhorne Creek and over the Wellington ferry at the Murray River. Everything was new, fresh, exciting, and she experienced the same exhilaration as she remembered from discovering new places and vistas in Tasmania.

The shimmering grey expanse of Lake Albert came into view as the bus neared Meningie. Pelicans camped on the shoreline and white gulls soared over the rippling water. The bus whisked by the first houses and a church on the town's outskirts and then houses and shops lined the left side of the road in the town's centre. At an intersection, the bus wheeled into a petrol station on the right side proclaiming itself as Kruse's Garage.

Bill was waiting to greet her when she climbed down from the bus. He apologised for wearing his dirty brown work trousers and a sweat-stained khaki shirt, but he was going home later to dress for the ball. He took her case and led her across the road to the two-storey Meningie Hotel where he checked her in with the hotel owner before taking her case to the allotted upstairs room. 'I thought it would be appropriate for you to stay here,' he said, lowering the case. 'It's a small community. People are friendly, but they talk. I'll come back at seven to take you to the ball. It's a few miles out of town at Ashville.'

Eileen thanked him for being thoughtful. After he left, she prepared for the ball, taking care to unpick and lengthen her hair with the brush and apply make-up without smudging. She opened her case and unfolded her blue dress, admiring its pastel colour, checking there were no creases, and draped the white shawl over it, satisfied the lighter colours would accentuate her brunette hair.

Dressed, she stared out the upper storey window at the fading light and setting sun glittering over Lake Albert while she waited for Bill. The pale blue sky was streaked with cirrus clouds painted apricot by the sinking sun. Bird silhouettes flew purposely towards hidden roosts. The view was serene and beautiful, but she was nervous. She was standing in the room of a hotel after a bus trip to a country town she never before visited, waiting for a man who was still a stranger to her.

Bill arrived after sunset on an AJS motorcycle, headlight glowing in the evening light, and the single bore engine thumped in hefty rhythm as he slowed and stopped at the hotel. He wore a grey suit, a white shirt with a thin black tie, and his black shoes were sharply polished. The vision of his shoes caused a flashback for Eileen to her father's boots, a memory that evoked sadness, although she pushed the emotion aside when Bill presented her with a small corsage of white sweetheart roses. 'I wasn't sure what colour you would wear tonight,' he said shyly, 'so I chose white.' 'It's perfect,' Eileen said. 'Would you pin it on please?'

Bill nervously pinned the corsage to Eileen's blue dress, his timidity in doing so not lost on Eileen who smiled at his coyness, and she wondered if his shyness was because he had never been with other women. 'How's that?' he asked, stepping back to check his handiwork.'

'Exactly as it should be,' Eileen said. 'Thank you.'

'Then we best go to the hall,' he said. 'Have you ridden on a motorbike before?'

'I have,' she replied confidently, although uneasiness stirred in her stomach as she remembered the accident with Bob Andrews.

Bill led Eileen to the motorbike, straddled the leather seat and waited for her to take position on the pillion behind him. As she shimmied up her gown to take her seat, Eileen was self-conscious of the amount of leg she had to expose to sit comfortably, and she was grateful the street was empty. 'It's only a few miles,' Bill reminded her. 'Not far, but hold on. I'll take it slowly, of course. I don't want to mess up your hair or dress.' She slid her arms around his waist, keenly aware of the intimacy, the smell of his aftershave, the strength of his waist and back. Bill repeated, 'Hang on,' slipped the bike into gear, accelerated gently, and puttered along the highway heading into the dark countryside.

The road outside Meningie was flat and generally straight for the first couple of miles and Eileen settled into the sensations of the bike's vibrations, the rattling engine and the wind in her face. Slow curves meant she leaned gently with Bill, and as they climbed into the hills closer to Ashville and the turns became frequent and sharper, she relaxed and enjoyed the ride. In a short time, they were turning into the grounds of the Ashville school where cars, trucks and carts were lined up outside the solitary lit stone building. Curious as to why the dances were held in such an isolated venue, as she climbed from the pillion seat, she asked, 'Why is the school the only building out here?'

'It's a farming community,' Bill replied, offering his arm to her. 'There's a post office further down the road, but mostly it's all farms around here. The school was built way back last century, but this hall was opened in 1918. It serves as the community centre.'

Bill presented Eileen to Pamela Lloyd when they entered, a young woman who introduced Eileen to the other young women at the ball, and they welcomed her into their circle. She met different people throughout the night, especially during the Progressive Barn dance where the women moved after short intervals to the next man in the circle. The dances moved through fast and slow cycles, and she appreciated Bill's dancing ability when they circled the floor in a waltz. She warmed to the people she met because they were open and friendly, and they were curious to know her. She felt as if she was already invited into their community. The dancing was over too soon, Eileen decided, when the band finished the final song and the master of ceremonies wished everyone a good night and safe travels home.

After a generous serving of supper, an offering of cakes and biscuits and scones and hot sausage rolls cooked by the local women, and more conversations, Bill led Eileen outside and onto his motorbike. 'It might be a bit cool,' he said as Eileen climbed aboard behind him. 'Sorry.'

'I will be fine,' she replied cheerily, wrapping her shawl tight.

The return journey to Meningie through the moonlight, the motorbike following the shuddering path of its headlight along the rough road, didn't seem to take as long as the outward trip earlier in the evening, but she appreciated the warmth and the security generated from her embrace of Bill's waist.

They dismounted outside the hotel, and Bill escorted Eileen to the hotel entrance, where he said, 'I hope you enjoyed the evening.'

'It was so much fun,' she replied. 'Everyone is so nice. Thank you for asking me to come.'

'Thank you for coming,' he said. He hesitated, before adding, 'You look beautiful this evening, and you dance much better than I do.'

Eileen blushed, hoping the colour in her cheeks was hidden in the shadows under the streetlight. 'I didn't know this was such a pretty town,' she said.

'Would you come again?'

'Of course!' she replied eagerly, adding, 'If you ask.'

'I will definitely be asking,' he confirmed. He paused again, and then said, 'I'm sorry I can't see you off in the morning. The bus to Adelaide leaves early and Dad's place is twenty miles north, past the Ashville school. I start work at Lloyd's at sunrise. But the hotelier will wake you in time.'

'I'll be fine,' she assured him. 'Thank you for everything, especially organising the hotel and the bus tickets. That was very kind.'

'My pleasure,' said Bill. He glanced at the street and up at the moon. 'I'd best be going. It's late, and we both have to be up early. Keep an eye out the bus window as you go past Ashville. I'll be there waving.' He seemed unsure of what to do next, but then he leaned towards her, saying, 'I hope this isn't too rude,' before he kissed her gently on the cheek.

Eileen felt the blood run to her cheek again, but she replied, 'Not rude at all. Goodnight, Bill.'

'Goodnight, Eileen,' he said, turning slowly.

She waited on the footpath outside the hotel, her heart pounding as Bill returned to his motorbike. Mounted, engine kickstarted and clicked into gear, Bill circled onto the empty road, waved, and accelerated, taillight glowing as he rode into the night.

In the hotel bed, Eileen was wrapped in the scent of Bill's cologne, the lingering sensation of his kiss on her cheek and the touch of his rough, workman's hands in hers. His voice whispered to her and the sensations of riding pillion on his motorbike through the country nightscape tingled her body. She could hear her mother warning her to be wary of men, and Ruby's wisdom that a man did not complete anyone, and she had promised herself she would not wait for a Prince Charming, or expect the fairy tale to ever become real, but tonight he came riding his mechanical steed to carry her to the ball and there he swept her off her feet and stole her heart. Perhaps the dream could become real after all.

1953

"I wish I was going some place. I wish you were going some place. We could go together."
Kathie Bleeker

The last light traced a burnished edge along the horizon over Lake Alexandrina and January heat lingered like a warm hand on her shoulder as Eileen waited by the cream Ford ute, watching Bill approach with a rifle. The weapon fascinated her. She associated guns with soldiers, and guards on duty at the Repat. 'Have you been spotlighting before?' Bill asked in the purple twilight outside the shed.

'No,' Eileen replied.

'Then you're in for some fun,' he promised. He held out his hand to help Eileen into the ute tray beside John Robinson, a rake thin man with greasy and uncombed hair who was introduced to Eileen as Bill's friend. 'Lindsay will drive slowly, and Molly will hold the spotlight,' Bill explained, referring to the property owners in the ute cabin. 'It can get rough, so make sure you hold on,' he advised.

'We ready?' John queried.

'Ready?' Bill asked Eileen.

'Ready,' she replied.

John banged on the cabin roof and called, 'Crank her up!'

The headlights flicked on, the ute lurched forward, and Eileen lost her balance, but Bill steadied her, asking, 'Are you sure you don't want to sit in the cabin? You can squeeze between Lindsay and Molly.'

Regaining her balance and grip, Eileen said eagerly, 'No. This will be more fun.'

Lindsay stopped the ute at the house gate and Molly opened the passenger's door, but John leapt over the tray sill, yelling, 'It's all right, Missus Lloyd! I got this one!' He trotted to the gate, lifted the latch, swung the gate open and Lindsay drove through. John began closing the gate, until Molly yelled, 'Hold up!'

A black and white Border Collie ran through the opening and sat beside the ute, eyeing Bill expectantly. 'Chips is keen!' Bill said.

'Let him up,' Lindsay replied.

'Come on,' Bill urged. 'Up!'

Chips sprang, hooked his paws over the lip of the tray and scrambled aboard, tail wagging, pink tongue lolling happily, and Eileen bent to pat his head. 'Can't leave the chaser behind,' John noted, as he climbed into the tray. 'No show without Punch.'

'All aboard?' Lindsay called.

'Full steam ahead, cap'n!' John replied.

The ute dipped and rolled across the rough ground, headlights tracking across the yellow summer grass and patches of sandy earth as Lindsay braked and steered to avoid treacherous rabbit warrens and hardy yakka bushes that thrust rigid spears to the evening sky. In the tray, Bill lifted his .22 rifle and slid the bolt to load a bullet with precise efficiency. John did likewise. 'Next paddock over we'll start shooting,' Bill explained to Eileen. She felt adrenalin rising, watching the men transform into hunters, their eyes scouring the semi-dark countryside for their quarry, and she began to imagine a world with men at war, vigilant, wary, determined.

'There's one!' John yelled. Eileen stared along the headlight path and spotted a white tail bobbing erratically, weaving between grass clumps, before disappearing to the left.

'They're out and about,' Bill observed, turning to Eileen. 'We should bag a few tonight.'

Eileen was simultaneously excited by the hunt, curious as to what would happen when they did choose a target, and awed by the men's primitive mood, their simmering desire to shoot and kill. She understood their reasons. Rabbits were noxious pests. 'We're in the middle of the worst rabbit plague ever,' Lindsay Lloyd told her earlier in the afternoon, when Bill and she arrived at the farm on Bill's motorbike. 'Government released the myxomatosis virus two or three years ago to kill the rabbits, and it's done a pretty good job, but the little buggers are still causing damage. Stock starve because the bloody rabbits eat everything.'

'They reckon there were more than six hundred million rabbits in the country before they released the myxie,' Bill added in. 'That's more than seventy rabbits for every man, woman and child in Australia.'

'So that's why we hunt the little buggers,' Lindsay concluded. 'And we make a small income from selling their hides and meat.'

She understood the reasons, but not the lust to kill. *Why are we so different*? she wondered.

Lindsay halted at the next gate and waited for John to open it. Once through, John jumped back into the tray, but Lindsay and Molly climbed out of the cabin. Lindsay opened the bonnet and rigged wiring to the battery for the spotlight, which blinked into action, and Molly returned to the passenger's seat with the shining spotlight.

The second paddock was overgrown with mallee trees and bushes and yakkas, but Lindsay steered the ute expertly between obstacles while Molly scanned the landscape with the spotlight, searching for tell-tale white tails or long ears. John shuffled to the left side of the tray beside Bill, and they watched the sweep of the light as it threw the bush into stark light and shadow relief, while Eileen leaned against the ute's hood and let the warm night murmur in her ears.

'Got one!' John whispered harshly, tapping the hood. Lindsay eased the ute to a stop. 'Hold it steady, Missus Lloyd,' John ordered. He lifted his rifle and aimed. Eileen followed the line of John's rifle, but she couldn't see a rabbit in the pool of spotlight. Moths and insects swirled in the beam. She waited, muscles tensing, anticipating the report, but she still flinched and gasped when the rifle cracked. The rabbit bucked and flopped into the grass.

'Get it?' Bill asked.

'Think so,' John replied. Without prompting, Lindsay eased the ute forward until John could jump out. He retrieved his prize and proudly lifted the motley black and tan and white rabbit by its back legs, announcing, 'One!'

'So it begins!' Molly called from the cabin.

The fetid tang of damp fur, piss and blood tainted the air as John dropped his catch in the tray, odours reminding Eileen of darker moments in the wards, but she saw Chips was delighted by the event as he sniffed the carcass with methodical attention. 'Will he eat it?' Eileen asked, her nose wrinkling at the stench.

'Not like that,' Bill reassured her. 'He knows he'll get plenty to eat when we skin and gut them later.'

'Hold the light!' John whispered. He reloaded his rifle. 'There's another one. No, two. Steady, Missus Lloyd.'

The rabbits crouched on a low mound of bare earth twenty yards from the ute. One sat up, sniffing the air, ears upright, blinded by the sharp light. The other was hunched, creeping blindly towards the edge of the light. Both rifles cracked. The rabbit at the edge rolled over. The one sitting up cartwheeled backward and lay on the ground kicking. 'Fetch!' Bill ordered. Chips bounded out of the tray and loped towards the mound, took the first rabbit in his mouth, and trotted back to the ute, while John jogged out to collect the remaining rabbit. 'Up!' Bill ordered. Chips jumped into the ute and dropped the rabbit beside the first one.

'He's so clever!' Eileen exclaimed.

'He's a good dog,' Bill said. 'Works well with sheep and cattle too.'

'Did you train him?'

'Dad and I,' Bill said, as the ute lurched forward. 'Got him as a pup two years ago.'

Later in the evening, the moon scudding between clouds, thirty pair of rabbits loaded in the tray, Eileen's ears ringing with cracking gunfire and nostrils stinging to the stench of dead rabbits, Lindsay turned the Ford for home, and the moonlit ride across the paddocks and through the gates ended at the shed where they started. Molly ushered Eileen into the house while Bill, John and Lindsay unloaded the catch. 'We'll make hot black tea and have cake ready for the men when they come in,' Molly said. 'You can fill the kettle. I'll get the oven started.'

'What are the men doing now?' Eileen asked as they walked onto the veranda.

'They gut the rabbits, pair them, and hang them. The Rabbitoh truck will come by tomorrow to collect what we've caught,' Molly explained.

'Sometimes we take the haul into Meningie or Tailem Bend.' She held the door open for Eileen to enter the house.

'How long will it take?' Eileen asked.

'To get the rabbits ready? Thirty pair might take an hour, maybe less.' Molly closed the door and led Eileen into the kitchen. 'We've got plenty of time to make the tea. Let's have a round of cards first. Have you played Euchre?' Eileen shook her head. 'First lesson then,' Molly said as she picked up a card pack from the dresser. 'It's best as a game with pairs, but I'll teach you the basics, and another time we can play with four.'

Card game lesson over, as Eileen was filling the kettle, Pamela, Lindsay's dark-haired sister, the woman Bill introduced on Eileen's first visit to Ashville, emerged from the rear of the house, yawning. 'You should have come shooting,' Eileen said. 'It was fun.'

Pamela shook her head. 'I don't like that sort of thing.'

Molly placed a cake tin on the kitchen table, explaining, 'Pamela is soft when it comes to animals. She's good with them, looks after all the little ones, feeding and taking care, but she doesn't like killing them, do you Pamela?'

'Not if there's no need,' Pamela replied, as she opened the crockery cabinet and selected cups and saucers. 'They have feelings like we do.' Molly laughed good-naturedly. 'I guess they have feelings, but not like we do. God made us masters above the animals and provided them for our good.'

'He also made us responsible for caring for them,' Pamela replied. 'I do the caring part.'

'How's that kettle?' Molly asked.

Eileen sat with Molly and Pamela, and they talked about families and living on the farm, while they waited for the men to prepare the rabbits. 'I was born on a farm,' Molly explained, 'so I'm used to this life. It will be harder for a city girl like you to settle here.'

'Why?' Eileen asked.

'There are no city conveniences, no trams, no local shops, no electricity. It can get very lonely with the men working in the paddocks and you stuck in the house,' Molly said.

'Don't you help with the farm work?'

Molly laughed. 'I sometimes do more of it than Lindsay does. Pamela works with the men, don't you Pamela?' Pamela nodded shyly. 'She can mend fences, dig post holes, round up the sheep and shear and crutch them as good as any of the men.'

Eileen recognised Pamela had no interest in make-up or fashion or men. Jeans and a work shirt, curly brunette hair tied in a functional ponytail, fingernails cut short and solid boots were all Pamela wanted.

'There's always plenty to do,' Molly was saying. 'The usual things, like cooking and cleaning and looking after the house animals. They need to be done. And then there's the enjoyable things, like making clothes and knitting. I even find time for reading and doing crosswords between daily chores. You learn to make your own entertainment, Eileen. But we grew up to this, and we wouldn't have it any other way. You are going to find it very different from city living out here.'

'Bill's mother came from Adelaide,' Eileen said. 'She stayed.'

'True,' Molly agreed. 'But she had a job as well as family to look after. She taught at the Ashville school, up the road. We all went to school there, for a while, but I've heard the Government might be closing it down. It was opened way back in 1895, but the stone hall was only finished after the Great War. Some fine memories. I finished Grade Five. You?'

'Grade Seven,' Eileen replied. 'I liked school. I wish I could have stayed on, but I had to leave because my family needed me to work.'

'Same happened to me,' Molly said, 'although I was glad to be rid of it. Farms need everyone to do their bit. My older brothers helped Dad as soon as they were old enough. Mum had me helping her when she figured I knew enough not to need to go to school anymore.'

Eileen was about to reply, when the door opened and the men stomped in, wiping their feet on the door mat. 'Sorry,' Bill apologised to Eileen. 'It took longer than we thought. I better get you back to my grandmother's.'

'Hot cuppa first,' Molly ordered, 'and a slice of cake. It will keep you warm on that motorbike.'

Bill grinned and sat, saying, 'No arguing with Molly.'

Conversation skirted spotlighting, farm work and football, while the late supper was consumed, before Bill rose and said, 'We better get going.

May won't be happy with us sneaking in at midnight.' He moved behind Eileen's chair to shift it as she stood.

'Who's learning to be a proper gentleman?' Molly teased in a fake English accent.

'Leave the bloke alone,' Lindsay retorted. 'And don't get ideas I'm going to do the same.'

Late heat lingering in the night, Eileen pressed against Bill's back, arms wrapped around his waist, embracing his warmth and feeling the road and bike's vibrations shudder through him. She peered over his shoulder, wind ruffling her hair and stinging her eyes, and watched the AJS' headlight trace the bitumen towards Meningie. The engine burbled downhill and thumped and rattled along the long stretches, echoing across the surrounding sandhills and salt pans, and the lake glittered in the moonlight at the margins of the world. She was becoming accustomed to riding pillion behind Bill. He possessed an uncannily symbiotic relationship with the metal and oil and leather machinery bearing them along the narrow highway, and she felt safe, certain she was where she ought to be.

At May's cottage behind the Anglican manse and church, lying in her cotton slip with the bedclothes pulled aside because of the warm summer air, Eileen contemplated living in the country. The air was fresh, the scenery pleasant, and the animals were cute. People were kind and welcoming. The food was wholesome. Molly made it sound like farm work was hard, but she understood hard work as a nurse. The spotlighting adventure revealed a darker edge, a primal brutality to the lifestyle, but she rationalised the killing of rabbits as necessary, given what she learned about the rabbit plague and the cost to farmers. She heard conversations between country people about slaughtering farm animals for food and, while she now associated the meat she coveted during rationing with the doe-eyed calves and lambs she petted at the Lloyds' farm, she understood the necessity of the process to sustain people's lives. Choosing to live in the country meant relinquishing convenient aspects of city living to enjoy greater freedom and vitality and connection with nature. Connection appealed to her. She felt affinity for Bill's world. And she certainly felt more than an affinity with Bill. He was gentle and polite. He did not make demands or have expectations. He was Dudley and Ken and Mervyn bundled into one, without their pretensions: a gentle, kind and shy man. He was a future she longed for.

*

'What time is he meant to arrive?' Cooper asked impatiently. She lowered her cigarette and tried to make smoke rings as she exhaled. A bus trundled past, exhaust fumes mingling with the cigarette smoke.

'Now,' Eileen told her, eyes watering from the smoke. 'We're going to lunch at Auntie Chris' place.'

'Where's that?' Baxter asked.

'Sefton Park. Off Main North Road.'

'Is she married?' Cooper asked.

'Yes,' Eileen replied, exhaling smoke from her cigarette. 'Uncle Bob.'

'Already calling them Uncle and Auntie,' Cooper said, grinning. 'This must be serious.'

'It's pretty serious when you're spending every second weekend hopping on a bus and travelling two hours down to Meningie,' Baxter observed.

'That's a fine car!' Cooper declared as a black convertible stopped at the kerb and the driver hopped out.

'Bill!' Eileen exclaimed, and she ran to embrace him.

He kissed Eileen on the cheek, and whispered, 'Happy birthday.'

'Whose car is this?' she asked.

'You like it?'

'Yes,' she said, noting the shining black duco, red leather seats and white wall tyres. 'It's very sporty.'

'Nineteen-thirty-six Chevrolet coupe convertible with a straight-eight under the bonnet,' he smartly explained.

'It's yours?' Eileen asked, amazed.

'Paid cash to Smith's this morning. It's all mine,' he confirmed. 'Are you ready to go?'

'Home by six o'clock, Miss Bonney!' Cooper yelled. Cooper and Baxter blew kisses and pulled faces as they retreated towards the hospital gate.

'Bye, girls! Don't wait up for me!' Eileen shouted and waved.

With the sun on her face and the wind buffeting her hair, Eileen sat back to enjoy the drive. She watched houses and shops flash by, and she smiled at pedestrians and riders and drivers who stared at the black convertible, quietly pleased she was cruising through the city in a swanky car with a handsome young man.

Beyond the city centre and North Adelaide, and onto Main North Road, Bill turned onto a tree-lined street in Sefton Park, and he parked outside a tidy red brick and white masonry bungalow with a meticulous rose garden and trimmed lawn bounded by a white picket fence. A grey Wolseley sat in the driveway. Bill opened the car door for Eileen, and he took her arm to escort her to the porch and knocked on the white wooden door.

The woman who greeted them was stout and of similar height, and Eileen immediately recognised her family resemblance with Bill's father; the square facial line, aquiline nose, small eyes, although Chris' brown eyes were enlarged through thick lenses perched on her nose. Her dark brown hair was tied in an old-fashioned bun. 'My,' she said, assessing Eileen and Bill, 'you are quite the couple.' She invited them into the hallway bisecting the house and led them to the rear where a kitchen opened to the right and a laundry and door to the garden were on the left. 'Robert is in the shed, Bill,' Chris said. 'Be a dear and call him in for lunch please.' After Bill exited, Chris turned to Eileen. 'Well, I finally have the opportunity to meet you and, my goodness, you are every bit as beautiful as Bill said you are.'

Eileen blushed at the compliment, replying, 'Thank you.'

'Oh, don't be bashful. It's true,' Chris insisted. 'My brother thinks his son is a very lucky young man.' She lifted a white ceramic bowl of steaming roast vegetables from the side cabinet. 'Would you mind helping me to carry the food into the dining room?'

Eileen chose a crystal salad bowl and followed Chris along the hallway into a room where an elongated Blackwood oval dining table surrounded by eight high-back Blackwood chairs padded with green velvet dominated the centre. Blackwood cupboards flanked the table, the mirrored cabinets displaying crystal glassware and elegant china crockery. A patterned green rug adorned the floor beneath the table. Two photographs hung on the end wall, either side of the Georgian window; one recognisably Chris in her bridal gown, the other Eileen assumed was her husband, Robert, in his dark brown suit with a red carnation on his lapel. As she placed the salad bowl beside the vegetables in the table's centre, the back door opened and closed, and voices echoed up the hall.

'The men are in,' Chris announced. 'If you would like to wash your hands, the bathroom is the next door on the right before the kitchen. I'll fetch the meat.'

The meal was ample and satisfying, and conversation roamed around families and recent events. Bob mentioned the death of the Russian Communist leader, Stalin, to Bill, after Chris left the table to fetch dessert, but political matters were quickly brushed aside when Chris returned bearing a decorated cake with candles. Bill, Bob and Chris broke into a chorus of 'Happy birthday', ending with three cheers, and Chris said, 'Now blow out the candles.'

Bob chimed in, 'Best leave one to show you have a boyfriend.'

Eileen blew out the candles and Chris handed her a knife. 'Make a wish as you cut,' she instructed, 'but don't touch the plate with the knife or it will invalidate the wish.'

Sponge cake serves consumed, Bob produced a bottle of Penfolds port and poured a small glass for everyone to toast Eileen's birthday. Chris gathered the dishes from the table, refusing Eileen's offer to help by insisting her guests remain seated while she cleaned up, and she brought them an after-lunch cup of tea when she returned from the kitchen. Bob wanted to pursue further dialogue on the matter of Communism and trade unions in Australia, but Chris interrupted. 'The young people aren't interested in all that political nonsense, Robert. I think you can help me tidy up in the kitchen.' Robert shrugged to show his disappointment, and withdrew with Chris, leaving Bill and Eileen in the dining room.

'I hope you didn't mind the birthday celebration,' Bill said.

'I loved it,' Eileen reassured him. 'Your Uncle and Auntie are very kind.' Bill shifted in his chair to face Eileen, and his expression became solemn. He fossicked in his trouser pocket, slid off the chair onto one knee, and held a tiny black jewellery box towards her. 'This isn't going to come out right,' he began apologetically, and swallowed nervously. 'I visited your mother yesterday, so she knows what I'm about to say. I would like to ask you to marry me, Eileen.' He opened the box to reveal a silver ring with a head row of small diamonds.

Eileen glanced at the gift, and at the earnestness on Bill's face. His words echoed in her mind. She was astonished that he asked her mother for permission in advance. Tingling at her fingertips and toes, melting in her stomach, her face flushed, she hesitated to answer.

'I understand if you don't accept,' Bill said, 'but I've been offered a full-time job at Naranga Station, south of Meningie, starting in September, and I was hoping you would come with me, as my wife.'

'Oh, Bill,' Eileen gasped, elated. 'Yes! Yes, I would love to be your wife!'

Bill reached for her left hand, took the ring from its confinement, and slid it onto her finger. 'This was my grandmother's engagement ring. May was very proud to think you would receive it. It might need adjustment to fit properly.'

Eileen held out her hand to gaze at the ring. 'It fits exactly as it should,' she said, smiling. She raised her eyes to Bill, tears forming. 'I am so very, very happy.'

*

'Are you sure about this?' Clarice asked, looking sternly at Eileen. 'You and I both know this is not the first boy you've gotten engaged to, Girlie.'

Eileen forced her expression to be as sincere as she could muster to reply, 'I am very sure, Mum. Bill is a nice man, honest, hard-working, trustworthy, kind. I know he really loves me because he says so.'

'Men can say a lot of things,' Clarice warned. 'The easiest lie they tell us is that they love us. But they only say it so they can trick us into doing what they want us to do. I thought you had learned that by now, what with the way other men have treated you. I do not want my daughters making the same mistake I made.'

'Bill isn't like our father,' Eileen protested. 'He doesn't want to ruin my life. He wants to give me a better one, a life we can enjoy together.'

'He is taking you away from your family,' Clarice protested. 'Where is this Naranga Station?'

'Halfway between Meningie and Salt Creek. It's one of the biggest sheep stations in South Australia.'

'And what job will this young man be doing?'

'He will be a general farmhand. They want his mechanical skills.'

'And you?' Clarice asked. 'What will you do?'

'Bill says I can work as a kitchen hand, but he said the boss is also keen to have me because of my nursing background. People get sick on the station. Sometimes people get hurt. I can look after them.'

'And where will you live?'

'They have married couples' houses on the property,' Eileen replied. 'We will have a place of our own. It sounds wonderful.'

'It sounds too perfect,' Clarice said. 'Have you been there? Do you know what this Naranga is really like?'

'No,' Eileen admitted, 'but Bill and I are going there next month to see the boss and sign the work papers.'

'And the wedding?'

'August,' Eileen replied. 'It needs to be then because Bill starts working in September. And I will too.'

'You cannot jump in and out of marriage like you have with engagements, Girlie,' Clarice warned. 'Marriage is for life. It is ordained by God, sanctioned by the Church, and you cannot treat it like something you simply pick and choose to do.'

'That seems to be how Father treats it,' Eileen countered.

'Girlie Bonney, I will not have you talk about your father in that way.'

'But it's true!' Eileen protested. 'He doesn't respect your marriage.'

'He is still my husband and your father,' Clarice retorted, reddening in her face, 'and you will respect that. I asked you if you are ready to make that commitment before God.'

'Mum,' Eileen said earnestly, 'I'm ready. I love Bill, and he loves me. I know I'm ready because there have been other boys, so I know what will make me happy, and what won't. Bill makes me happy. He's polite, and gentle and sensitive, and he cares. I won't find anyone better than him. I know that in my heart.'

'And what about his illness? You told me he had a heart condition. You do not want to marry a lame duck.'

'A leaky valve,' Eileen said. 'It's a legacy from his Rheumatic Fever, but it's not life-threatening. And what about me with half a lung? He's taking a risk on a lame duck too.'

'You are hardly a lame duck,' Clarice replied. She paused and then took Eileen's hands in her own. 'If this is what you want, you know I am happy for you. I like the young man, too. It was nice of him to ask me for permission to marry you. That is a very pleasing sign of respect on his part. He seems generous of spirit and, it seems, he has a solid job.' She sighed and said, 'If this is what you truly want, you have my blessing, and my love.'

'Thank you, Mum,' Eileen said, and she hugged Clarice tightly. 'Thank you.'

Clarice pushed Eileen back to study her, until a smile broke across her features, and she said, 'Well, Girlie Bonney, why are we standing here? We have a wedding to organise, do we not?'

*

The motorcycles growled along the gravel road leading from the Prince's Highway to the farm gate, snarling engines slowing as the bikes reached the gate and turned to rattle over the cattle grid and onto the track leading to the old farmhouse. A grey car pursued the motorcycles. Away to the west, above Adelaide and the Mount Lofty Ranges, and south to the lakes and the Great Southern Ocean, brooding rain clouds threatened a big storm. Eileen waited at the farmhouse corrugated and pitch gate, watching the approaching procession. 'Looks like your family is arriving,' Henry, Bill's father noted. 'Bringing a storm with them too,' he added. He tilted his Akubra. 'A big storm.'

'You'll really like them,' Eileen said.

'I will make sure Churchill and the other horses are safe in the shed,' Henry said, turning away. 'Call me when there's a cuppa on the boil.'
Eileen waved enthusiastically as Peter and Lyla arrived on Peter's black BSA, and Bruce and Betty pulled in beside them, Betty hunched in the Norton sidecar wearing goggles and a leather flying cap. Ian, Judy and Josie waved from the windows of the Hillman, bouncing and rocking the car. Eileen opened the iron gate and ran to embrace Peter as he dismounted, and she moved from Peter to Lyla, to Bruce and Betty and everyone in

turn, laughing and smiling. 'Welcome to Malplyn!' she declared.

'Where's Bill?' Bruce inquired.

'On his way from Lloyd's.' As Eileen replied, she heard a faint engine and located a dark spot racing along the gravel road from the highway. 'Here he comes now.'

'Bloody hell!' Peter gasped as he tracked the motorcycle. 'How fast is he going?'

The Triumph Thunderbird throttled down through the gears as it neared the gate, and powered up the dirt track, before sliding to a stop beside the gathering. Bill switched off the engine, and said, 'Hello.'

Peter held out his hand to shake. 'If you don't mind me asking, how fast were you going?'

Bill ran his hand through his auburn hair before replying, 'Maybe ninety.'

Bruce whistled and held out his hand to shake, saying, 'Good to see you, Bill.' He gestured to his right, as Ian joined him, saying, 'My little brother, Ian.'

'And what about us?' Judy asked, pushing between Bruce and Ian.

'And our charming sisters,' Bruce said with a brief bow, 'Miriam Judith and Hirelle Josephine.'

Josie slapped Bruce's arm, saying, 'It's Josie,' and she gave a mock curtsy to Bill.

'Girlie's been telling us all about this farming hunk she's engaged to, but she's kept you away from us. Now I see why,' Judy remarked.

Bill shook hands with Judy and Josie, and then he flicked the Triumph's stand out to take the bike's weight and dismounted. 'The weather's looking pretty crook down in Adelaide,' he said. 'Lucky you came up this evening.'

'Well, we're up for an evening of fun,' said Peter. 'Worth the trip.'

'There's a dance at Ashville tomorrow night,' Eileen said.

'And that's why we came,' said Ian.

Bill kissed Eileen's cheek and asked, 'Where's Dad?'

'Stabling the horses,' Eileen replied.

'I'll go help him finish up.' Bill slid off his leather pilot's gloves.

'Mind if we tag along?' Peter asked.

'Don't mind at all,' Bill replied. 'This way,' and he led the three young men through the iron gate and past the house towards the cattle yards and stable.

'I'll show you around,' Eileen offered. To the women and she led them through the gate into a tiny iron-bound yard. 'Those are the cellars,' she said, indicating two peaked corrugated iron roofs with stone step entrances leading underground. 'The one on the left is where Henry keeps all his horse equipment and the meat safe.'

'Meat safe?' Josie repeated. 'No refrigerator?'

'No electricity,' Eileen said, turning to open a white wooden screen door into the house. 'Like during the war.'

'We had electricity,' Judy corrected.

Eileen ushered the women into the low-ceilinged lean-to kitchen. 'Wood stove, cupboards, no running water,' she continued. 'Wash house behind you.'

'Where does the water come from?' Betty asked, as she eyed the Singer wringer washtub in the wash house.

'Bucket from the underground rainwater tank,' Eileen explained. 'I'll show you where that is outside, but first come through here.'

They gathered at rectangular wooden table in a room with a small open fireplace and a faded blue curtained window, two doors leading to other spaces. 'Dining room,' Eileen said. 'Probably was used as the original kitchen when the stone house was hand-built last century by a brother and sister. This is an extension on the original two rooms they built. That's why the roof slopes down to the lean-to.'

'And why nothing is straight,' said Judy.

'It's a low ceiling,' Yvonne remarked. 'Even I can touch it.'

'Wally would hit his head on the door frames,' Josie added. 'He's growing so tall.'

'The room to the left is a bedroom,' Eileen continued. 'Through that door into the hallway are two more bedrooms, either side. Follow me.' She led them in single file down the short hall and through the back door onto a grassed space bordered by a lean-to corrugated iron shed. A conspicuous rustic iron edifice stood to the left. 'The dunny,' Eileen announced, pointing at the toilet.

'Oh, goodness me!' Lyla exclaimed. 'A long drop.'

'Not even that,' Eileen said. 'A wooden seat with a five-gallon tin that gets emptied when it's full.'

'And a million spiders, I'm guessing,' said Judy. 'I'm not having any of that!'

'Is that Bill's father?' Betty asked, pointing past another shed that opened into a wooden-posted stockyard to a solidly built man astride a tall chestnut horse. Bill, Bruce, Peter and Ian were shepherding two more horses into the yard.

'It is,' Eileen confirmed. 'Henry.'

'Magnificent horse,' Betty said.

'Churchill,' Eileen said. 'Named after you-know-who. Nineteen hands.'

'What does Henry do on this farm?' Josie asked, as they watched him dismount at the stockyard gate.

'He doesn't do much here,' Eileen said. 'He's a boundary rider for the Bowman family. They live on the lake shore, about four miles away, and they own the land all the way to the lake and south to that boundary of sandhills. Henry rides the boundaries and paddocks, making sure the stock is safe, and he mends fences and other jobs as needed.'

'And all this land is Henry's?' Lyla asked.

'No,' Eileen replied. 'He has a hundred and twenty acres. Two paddocks. All the land you see stretching north beyond the closest fence line belongs to the McFarlane family, and east of here is owned by the Mason family, all the way past Mason's Lookout. That's the biggest sandhill you can see.'

'You picked the wrong farmer's son,' Judy said, eyebrow raised.

'You're not going to live here, are you?' Josie asked.

'It's primitive,' added Judy. 'You wouldn't catch me living here.'

'No, of course we're not staying here,' Eileen said, grinning. 'Bill and I are going to a big sheep station, south of Meningie where we have a cottage of our own among the married workers.'

'I certainly hope they have electricity and flushing dunnies,' Lyla remarked. 'This is like living in the last century.'

'It is terribly rustic,' Betty said with mocking aloofness.

'And Henry lives here alone?' Lyla asked.

'He does,' Eileen said. 'His wife died more than thirteen years ago.'

'Must be lonely,' Lyla noted.

'Here comes trouble,' Judy announced, indicating the approaching men.

'And the dogs,' Josie added, seeing two black Kelpies and a black and white Border Collie trotting towards them. 'They're cute.'

'The Border Collie is Chips,' Eileen explained. 'He's a lovely dog. Very clever and very fast.'

'Named after Chips Rafferty?' Judy suggested.

'Indeed,' Eileen confirmed. 'Anyway, we better get the tea and cake organised.'

In the evening, fire crackling in the fireplace, meal shared, dishes cleaned and put away, the men and women huddled around the dining table, smoking and playing poker in the glow of the flickering kerosene lamp. A gust of wind howled around the stone walls and rattled the iron roof, the rain picked up intensity and everyone stopped talking, raising their eyes from their cards, swapping glances. Josie tightened her grip on Eileen's arm. 'Guess the storm found its way inland,' Bill remarked, lit cigarette drooping from the left side of his mouth. 'It usually comes across Lake Alexandrina, straight from the Southern Ocean.'

'Stronger winds than we expected,' Lyla noted.

'Another beer?' Peter asked, lifting the bottle.

'Just a top up,' Clive answered, pushing his glass towards Peter.

'Ladies?' Peter asked.

'Pass,' Lyla said, but Eileen pushed her glass forward, and Peter tilted the bottle towards it.

'You've got a taste for it, Girlie,' Clive remarked. 'Put some meat on those bones.'

'Anyone for a ciggie refresh?' Betty asked.

Thunder rumbled across the house, rattling the corrugated iron and boards, and Josie squeaked with alarm. 'We are definitely in for it,' Ian said. 'I will have another beer, then.'

'Who's turn?' Clive asked, looking around the table at everyone pressing close together in the tiny room, faces lit by the yellow lamp flame. 'I'm up,' said Bill.

'Where's Henry?' Josie asked.

'He goes to bed early,' Bill explained, as he swapped two cards. 'He will be up before sunrise and on his way to work before we get up.'

'What if it's still stormy in the morning?' Bruce asked.

'Someone has to check on the livestock and make sure the sheep are not in trouble anywhere around the property,' Bill replied. 'That's what Dad does, every kind of weather.'

'Has he always been a stockman?' Lyla asked, as she handed the lighter to Eileen.

'Yes,' Bill said.

'How come you didn't become one?' Lyla asked.

'I prefer wheels over legs,' Bill replied. 'My brother took on the horses.'

'Racehorses,' Bruce said with a sly wink. 'I should get to know your brother. He might have some favourable tips.'

'You and your gambling,' Betty said, poking Bruce's arm.

'I never bet what I can't afford to lose,' Bruce argued, as he laid down his cards, revealing three aces and two queens. He made a brief triumphant trumpet sound from the corner of his mouth, before stating, 'Case in point.' Everyone threw in their hands, while Bruce scraped the kitty of pennies towards himself. 'Going again?' he asked.

'I'm going to bed,' Lyla said.

'Me too,' Josie added, yawning.

'And me,' said Judy.

'I'll go another round,' Bill confirmed.

'Looks like the men are staying up,' Eileen said.

'Looks like the men are sleeping in here under the table,' Betty said. 'Come on, Lyla. You can share my bed and keep me warm.'

'Sisters in the other room,' said Eileen, and she took Judy and Josie's arms in hers. 'No sneaking into our rooms and keep the noise down.'

'Bossy Girlie,' Ian remarked. 'Are you sure you know what you're getting yourself in for, Bill?'

'He can't wait,' Eileen said, blowing a kiss to her fiancé.

'But he will have to tonight,' Judy said, as the women squeezed through the bedroom door. 'Goodnight boys.'

GIRLIE

*

Recalling the weekend on Henry's farm with her siblings and in-laws brought a smile to Eileen's lips while she waited for the tram on Goodwood Road in the cool, sunny morning. It was a weekend filled with riding and driving, and banter and laughter, the amusing card games in the middle of the Friday night storm, and the Saturday night dancing in Ashville was a whirl of energy and frivolity. Her little sister met a young man who worked in the Meningie Post Office, John Webb, and they danced together most of the night. Everyone teased Josie about her new beau and how short he was. 'Although height means nothing for horizontal dancing,' Bruce noted lewdly, eliciting gasps of false outrage and snorting giggles from his listeners. Judy also enjoyed the night, but she partnered with different men every dance, and showed no interest beyond politely flirtatious encounters. The men periodically disappeared outside to smoke and drink, but Eileen and her sisters chatted with the local women and many congratulated Eileen on her engagement to 'that handsome young man', the single ones revealing a tinge of envy in their voices.

Eileen boarded the tram and sat opposite a balding man in a grey suit who was focused on reading a newspaper, the front page splashed with photographs and articles covering Elizabeth the Second's coronation. The British world that created Australia was rapidly changing. Where there was an Empire before the Second World War with a King ruling subject nations throughout Asia, Australia and New Zealand included, there was now a Commonwealth ruled by a Queen, and countries like India, Burma and Sri Lanka were taking independent paths. The world she knew, the British world she learned about in school, was changing irrevocably. Ken's revelation about Australians having their own national identity instead of being British citizens, the influx of migrants from Europe speaking different languages, eating different food, and wearing different clothes, meant her British-oriented world was morphing into a melting pot of nations and creeds, and the hopes and fears of people who did not look to the English monarchy as their anchor, their pillar of culture and continuity. The changes underway, and those to come, were opportunities and threats to Australia. Eileen could not imagine Australians not speaking English, not eating English food, not wearing English or even American-inspired fashion. Wasn't that what the soldiers fought for in World War Two – to protect the English-speaking culture?

She sighed and shifted in her seat. She could not influence the changing political landscape. Politics was a distraction belonging to the rich and powerful who made the laws, acquired more wealth and paid themselves. People like herself did what they were legally expected to do: vote when required. In the end, she knew her vote was inconsequential. Politicians weren't interested in her life or her needs. Their interests lay in themselves, their families and their friends.

She marshalled her rambling thoughts. Her immediate world was changing even more rapidly. On August fifteenth, she was promising herself to one man, and changing her family name, like changing a garment, only the name change was far more permanent and mildly disappointing. Bonney had a friendly, familiar ring. It was her name, her family name, the name that tied her to her mother and brothers and sisters. Shillitoe was an awkward name, one she imagined having to spell out whenever someone asked. Bill said it was an old English name, her friends said it sounded more Welsh than English, but no one really knew its origin. *Why do women have to take their husband's family name*? she wondered. How much simpler would it be to keep her own name, her birth name, her identity? What she did like was the promise in the new name. Eileen Frances Shillitoe. That person did not yet exist. She could fashion Eileen Shillitoe into the person she wanted to be. Eileen Bonney was a child, a nurse, a young woman with an uncertain future and a messy past. Eileen Shillitoe could be someone new, a woman living in the country, a wife working with her husband to build a future. The new name led to a rebirth and a new life.

That potential new life, though, felt like the new world taking shape around her. She was leaving the city and her childhood world to move to a vastly different world in the Upper South-East of South Australia, a world roughly drawn, even on official maps, a place lacking milk and bread delivery vans, sewers and trams, a place of dusty dirt roads angling into the distant mallee, full of heat, flies and rabbits. Her family had fun on the farm and enjoyed exploring the gravel roads and travelling into Meningie, but they told her they believed she was choosing a difficult lifestyle by exchanging the emerging civilisation of electricity and cars for the archaic past. Only she wasn't choosing the changing world. Bill was the choice she was making. Something about him inspired her, captured her, made her believe whatever world he inhabited would be a world she would choose to embrace. He was gentle, attentive, interesting, vibrant.

The tram rattled and dinged from stop to stop, people boarding and disembarking, until Eileen reached the Goodwood precinct. She alighted and walked briskly to the bridal shop where Josie and Judy were waiting. 'Are you ready?' Judy asked.

Eileen took her sister's arm, replying, 'Ready as I'll ever be,' and they entered the shop.

A short, stylishly dressed woman, black hair foisted in a bun, rouge deep brown on her cheeks, intercepted the trio as they approached the counter, and asked in a pseudo-educated voice, 'May I be of assistance, ladies?'

Eileen replied, 'I'm getting married.'

'Congratulations!' the woman responded cheerily. 'A good reason to be here, then. When is the big day?'

'August fifteen,' Eileen replied.

'Excellent,' the woman said. 'That means we have ample time to select and create a beautiful dress.' She introduced herself as Mabel Chandler and led the young women to a table laden with open books. 'These are photographs and drawings and patterns of the gorgeous gowns we make for our brides. Please take your time to look through what we've made or can offer. What colour scheme are we seeking to compliment the bridal dress?'

'Powder blue,' Eileen replied.

'Something blue,' Mabel mused. 'Very appropriate. For the bridesmaids?'

'For one,' Eileen said. 'The other will wear pink.' She nodded to Josie and Judy.

'May I suggest the corsage is also in blue. Is there a flower girl?'

'Robyn,' Eileen said.

'She should wear yellow,' Mabel suggested.

'No,' Eileen replied. 'She will wear pale blue.'

Mabel raised an eyebrow, but smiled demurely and said, 'Shall we look at the dresses?'

*

The nurses crowded Eileen, offering suggestions and analysing choices for the wedding. 'Something old?' asked Baxter.

'My wedding ring,' Eileen replied. 'It belonged to Bill's grandmother.'

'I thought that was the engagement ring?' Baxter questioned.

'Both,' Eileen confirmed. 'She wants me to have both rings.'

'Something new?' Cooper chimed in.

'My dress, of course.'

'Something borrowed?' asked Langley.

'The wedding cars. My brothers are lending their cars.'

'Aren't you supposed to wear it?' Baxter argued.

'I don't have anything borrowed to wear.'

'Wait,' Cooper said. 'Wait here. I'll be back.' She rose from the bed and headed out of the room.

'Where is she going?' Eileen asked.

'Probably remembered she left her cigarette burning in her room,' Baxter replied.

'What about something blue?' Parsons asked.

'My corsage,' Eileen answered.

'And your sisters are the bridesmaids,' Baxter said. 'Groomsmen?'

'Bill's brother, Colin, and my brother, Peter. My big brother, Bruce, is giving me away.'

'Not your father?' Jennifer asked.

'I haven't seen him for ages.'

'That's disappointing,' said Langley.

'I'm back!' Cooper announced, coming through the door. She held a frilly white object in her hand which she passed to Eileen.

'What is it?' Eileen asked, rolling the elasticised lace in her hand.

'A garter, of course,' Cooper replied. 'You can borrow that.'

'I can't wear your garter,' Eileen protested, passing it back to Cooper.

'Of course you can,' Cooper said. 'Besides, it's not soiled. I've never worn it, so you don't need to worry.'

'What are you doing with a fancy garter?' Baxter asked. 'Can I look at it?'

Eileen handed the garter to Baxter as Cooper answered her. 'It was a gift from a sailor.'

Baxter held it up to evaluate and said, 'This is expensive material and embroidery. You must have done something very special to earn it.'

'Don't be revolting,' Cooper retorted, winking at the others. 'He gave it to me because he was madly in love with me.'

'Madly in lust with you, judging by this saucy piece of apparel,' Baxter said, as she handed it to Eileen. 'Let Bill go searching for that on your wedding night. I bet the sailor went searching for it.'

'I told you I never wore it,' Cooper said. 'Besides, if he did go searching for it, he would've found something far more interesting.'

'Oh, Cooper, really,' Baxter said, shaking her head.

'Eileen can think of us when Bill is removing the garter with his teeth,' Cooper added, and the young women burst into loud laughter and cries of disgust.

'What on earth is going on in here?' Sister Hersey asked, as she opened the door. 'There are other girls trying to settle down to sleep. A little decorum please.'

'Eileen's getting married,' Baxter said.

'Yes, I know,' Sister Hersey replied. 'And, with the cackling going on in here, I think most of the hospital knows.' She turned to Eileen. 'Nurse Bonney, a word please?'

Eileen rose from the bed, handed the garter to Cooper, and followed Hersey into the corridor. 'What is it?' she asked.

'You have a phone call on hold,' Hersey explained.

'Who is it?'

'He said his name is Dudley and you would know who he is.'

'Oh,' Eileen gasped, and her heart sank.

'Do you want to take the call?' Hersey asked.

'Yes,' Eileen said, gathering her emotions. 'I'll go down at once.'

Hersey touched Eileen's shoulder gently, and said, 'We're all very happy for you, Bonney.'

Eileen headed for the hospital telephone, full of trepidation, her mind racing with reasons why Dudley Wright would ring her, and she fumbled with the receiver. The line hummed as she pressed the receiver to her ear. 'Hello?' she tentatively asked.

'Eileen?' a familiar voice spoke.

'Yes. Speaking.'

'I need to see you.'

*

She knew in every fibre of her being she should not have agreed, and yet he held a residual and deep hook in her heart, and she had to meet him in the Botanic Gardens as he asked. The cold July wind gnawed at her cheeks, as if warning her she was making a bitter mistake, and thin grey clouds scattered soft, sad rain across the city. She avoided eye contact, as she walked along North Terrace, fearing strangers might peer into her heart and spy the turmoil within. The easiest path would have been to deny him, to hang up the phone, wordless, to have never left the Nurses' Quarters to take the call in the first place, but the easiest path was not the one she chose.

She passed through the sturdy ironwork gate onto the path into the Gardens where a solitary figure in a dark blue overcoat and matching Homburg under an open umbrella waited. Eileen slowed her pace as Dudley held out a hand, and she kept her hands in her pockets. 'Hello, Eileen,' he said. 'You can share the umbrella.'

'It's not that wet,' she replied. 'We can shelter under the trees.'

'I've missed you,' he said, when they stopped under a tree canopy by the path. 'I've wanted to see you again for a long time.'

'Dudley,' Eileen said, meeting his longing gaze, 'I'm getting married.'

'I know. I read the notice in *The Advertiser*.'

'Then why do you want to see me?'

'Remember the first time we came here?' Dudley asked.

'Yes,' Eileen replied coldly. 'Why do you want to see me now?'

Dudley paused before he said, 'To ask you not to marry this bloke.'

The unexpected request cut deep into Eileen's being, and she stammered as she asked, 'Why?'

'Because I love you, Eileen,' Dudley said emphatically. 'I've always loved you, and you know that I've always loved you. Deep in your heart, you know.'

'You're married,' she said bluntly. 'And before that you were engaged. You never told the truth, Dudley Wright. Not once. Not ever.'

'I made a mistake,' he pleaded. 'I don't love Carol, not like I love you. You have to believe me. I'm not lying.'

'We've been through this before, Mister Wright,' Eileen said, her tone taking on firmer formality. 'You are a married man, and your responsibility is to your wife. You should not be talking to me, especially like this.'

'Eileen,' Dudley pleaded. 'I want to set things right.'

'You should have set things right from the beginning, but you didn't,' Eileen asserted, her hands trembling. 'You played games with me while you were promised elsewhere. You broke my heart into a million pieces, Dudley Wright. You made me hate myself because I ran away instead of fighting for you. Except there was nothing to fight for, was there? You were always going to marry Carol. Always.' She hesitated, caught her breath and said, 'She is a more appropriate match for you, isn't she? Your family chose her, didn't they? Your sister warned me. You only wanted me as a plaything on the side to keep your life more interesting.'

'It wasn't like that,' Dudley protested. 'I thought I loved Carol, until I met you. Then I realised I didn't want to marry a girl like her, one that plays tennis and sips champagne, and has good friends over for afternoon tea on the patio overlooking the property. I want someone who enjoys having fun and dancing, and being free, someone who knows how to be alive.'

'Stop it, Dudley!' Eileen cried angrily. 'No more lies!'

'I'm not lying!' he declared.

'Not to me,' she said. 'To yourself. To Carol. To everyone else. Stop lying. Too many people are getting hurt. And I don't want to be one of those people anymore. I'm done here. I'm going home.' Dudley grabbed Eileen's arm to stop her, and she wheeled, her eyes aflame. 'Let go of my arm!'

'Please don't marry this bloke,' he pleaded.

'His name is Bill, and I am marrying him because I love him!' Eileen stated fiercely. 'Now, take your hand off my arm, or I'll call the police.' She met his gaze and held it, until he released her arm. 'Thank you,' she said. 'Goodbye.' She turned and strode fiercely towards the Botanic Gardens gate onto North Terrace, refusing to look back, controlling her urge to collapse in anguish, fighting the surging pain in her breast, salty tears blurring the cold, grey world.

*

'Have you heard the news?' Baxter said, bursting into the ward, waving a copy of *The News*. 'It's over!'

Eileen looked up from the bed where she was washing a patient's arm as she prepared to reapply a bandage. 'Read it out,' urged Bert Manning, the patient in the first bed on the ward.

Baxter lifted the paper and read aloud, '"The Truce is signed. Fighting will end in Korea tonight." It says it will be over at ten-thirty tonight!'

A ragged and calm 'Hooray!' rose from several lips. 'Thank God someone has shown common sense,' said Jack Mitchell, whose arm Eileen was bathing.

'You would think,' Eileen said, gently towelling Jack's arm, 'they would have learned from the big war, but they haven't. How many wars have we had since the end of the Second World War?'

'Just this one,' Jack said.

'And wars in India, and the Middle East, and Indo China, to name others,' Eileen said. 'People are fighting all over the world. It's like everyone stopped fighting against Hitler and Hirohito and started fighting each other.'

'You sound like one of them pacifists,' said Jack.

'Maybe I am one of them pacifists,' Eileen replied, as she wrapped a fresh bandage on his arm. 'Maybe I don't like seeing young men like you getting killed or wounded.'

'Maybe young blokes like me hope they'll be looked after by a beautiful sheila like you,' he said.

'Fresh!' Eileen said, tightening and sealing the bandage, 'and I don't mean the cotton on your arm.' She held out her left hand, so Jack could see her engagement ring. 'You're a handsome man, Jack, but you're a few months too late.'

'Tell him you've changed your mind,' Jack said, as Eileen tidied up, and the men in adjacent beds laughed. 'Tell him you made a mistake and you've met a better bloke.'

Eileen turned, dropped the dirty bandaging and scissors in the waste as she passed the nurses station, and walked briskly from the ward, stumbling into a run at the door. Outside, in the brittle late July sunlight, she leaned against the brick wall and bent forward, wrapping her face in her hands as tears streaked her cheeks.

'Bonney?' a familiar voice called, and footsteps echoed on the concrete. 'Are you all right?' Eileen straightened, hastily wiping away her tears, sniffling and looking forlornly at Baxter. 'What's wrong, Bonney?'

'Am I doing the right thing?'

'What on earth do you mean?' Baxter asked, startled by the unexpected question. 'Doing what right thing?'

'Marrying Bill,' Eileen said. She looked down shamefully at her shoes.

'Eileen Bonney!' Baxter said. 'What the bloody hell brought this on?'

'I saw Dudley on the weekend,' Eileen confessed.

'Dudley?' Baxter queried, perplexed, and then understanding dawned. 'Not that married bloke who kept chasing you before you went to Heidelberg?' When Eileen didn't answer, Baxter asked, 'Oh, good God, Bonney, why?'

'He rang and asked to meet me.'

'Then you should have bloody well said no to him.'

'I nearly did, but then I thought, if I confronted him and had it out, I would feel better and be free of him.'

'Did you tell him you were marrying Bill?'

'He already knew. That's why he wanted to see me – to talk me out of marrying Bill,' Eileen said, and sniffed.

Baxter handed her an embroidered handkerchief. 'But you told him you were marrying Bill, anyway. Right?'

'Yes,' Eileen said, and wiped her nose. 'I told him to go home to his wife, and that I never want to see him again.'

'Good!' Baxter asserted. 'Then you did the right thing. What's all this nonsense about not doing the right thing? You love Bill, don't you?'

'Of course I love him.'

'Then everything is all right, isn't it?' Baxter asked rhetorically.

'What's going on?' Cooper asked, as she rounded the corner of the building.

Baxter quickly explained the cause to Cooper, who put a gentle hand on Eileen's shoulder. 'Buck up, girl,' she said. 'You're having a silly moment because getting married is terrifying. It's all right to be a little afraid.'

'How do you know what it's like?' Eileen asked.

Cooper smiled wanly. 'I was married once.' Eileen's surprise made Cooper smile wider. 'That's right, Bonney. We all have secrets.'

'I thought you only got engaged?'

'That was the first time,' Cooper said.

'When did you get married?' Eileen asked.

'When you were away. I married a bloke who was an orderly on Ward Eight. Tom Parkinson. Nice enough bloke, but he wanted someone to be his mum, and that's not me. And he figured it was his right to shag someone else, if he wanted, and I thought otherwise.'

'What happened?'

'I left him,' Cooper said. 'I moved back into the Nurses' Quarters after six months. Told him to shack up with his other women.'

'What did he do?'

'Oh, he tried to get me to go back to him. He threatened me, and then he begged me, and then he kept coming into my ward and interrupting work.'

'I remember that,' said Baxter. 'It wasn't nice.'

'No,' said Cooper. 'He was a mongrel. When I first reported him to Matron, not much happened, but when he started marching into the ward and yelling at me in front of the patients, Matron had the guards remove him, and she ordered him to stay away from our ward. In the end, he quit the Repat and, last I heard, he was living in Port Pirie and drinking himself rotten. Not that I care.'

'That must have been terrible,' Eileen said.

'It turned out all right,' Cooper said. 'I wasn't meant to be married. I like being by myself.'

'What if Bill is like Tom?' Eileen asked.

Cooper pulled a cigarette packet from her pocket and offered a cigarette to Eileen and Baxter before she retrieved one for herself. As they lit up, Cooper said, 'I doubt Bill will be anything like Tom. From what I've seen and heard from you, he's a nice man.'

'My mother said you don't know someone until you share the same house with them,' Baxter said, 'and you'll discover that soon enough. No marriage is perfect, Bonney. You both have to work at it.'

'You're right,' Eileen agreed. 'Bill is every bit the man I want to marry.'

'So, no more of Mister I-think-I'm-too-good-for-anyone-but-myself Wright,' Baxter said. 'And no more silly thoughts.'

'Thank you,' Eileen said. 'Thank you to both of you.'

'Everything organised?' Cooper asked between puffs.

'Yes,' Eileen told her. 'Less than a fortnight.' She leaned against the wall and drew back on her cigarette. *I know what I want*, she pondered, imagining she was addressing an image of Dudley. *I know who I am.*

*

Eileen shuddered at the icy touch of material as she slipped into her white lace over tulle wedding gown. The Saturday morning temperature was bitter. 'Definitely chilly,' Judy remarked, glancing at a tiny yellow wall Fahrenheit thermometer. 'Forty-six degrees.' She slid the zip along its channel to the nape of Eileen's neck.

'Brrrr,' Eileen shivered. She turned her head towards Robyn, her blond, blue-eyed flower girl in a powder blue dress, who was watching Eileen's preparation, and asked, 'Are you warm enough?'

'Yes, thank you,' Robyn politely replied. 'You look very pretty.'

'Thank you,' Eileen said. 'So do you.' She touched Robyn's rosy cheek before turning to her sisters. 'Well?'

'Snug fit,' Josie observed, standing back to admire her sister. 'You look gorgeous, Girlie.'

'Makeup all right?' Eileen asked.

'Perfect,' Judy confirmed.

Eileen peered into the broad dressing table mirror, searching for imperfections, fighting a rush of nerves. Her life had come to this morning, this moment. She wanted it to be perfect.

'Car's here!' Josie announced.

'Time for the veil,' Judy urged, lifting a mass of thin white lace. 'Sit down and we'll put it on.'

'I don't want to be the bride who arrived late.'

'You won't be if you sit still and let us do our job,' Judy remonstrated.

'Can you tell them we're almost ready?' Eileen asked anxiously.

'Sit still,' Judy ordered. She positioned the comb in Eileen's hair to hold her single tier, layered veil, while Josie left the room to tell Bruce they were almost ready.

'Why am I so nervous?' Eileen asked.

'I thought that would be obvious,' Judy replied. 'Keep still.'

The journey along Anzac Highway and West Terrace in Bruce's car seemed to be in slow motion and familiar landmarks drifted by as if she was seeing them for the last time, as if the next time she would see them the world would be different because she would no longer be Eileen Bonney. The world was changing. She willed it to change by choosing to marry Bill. She was leaving her childhood, her nursing life, her travels, and the men she ran from who wanted her to change when she wasn't ready to change. But now she was ready. Now it was time to change.

Eileen peered out the rear window at the black car bearing her sisters and the flower girl to her wedding destination, and the driver, her brother Clive, gave her the thumbs up. She smiled and looked ahead at the city panorama. As often as she tried to imagine this day, chased it in her dreams, pictured the pageantry and joy, the reality, the moment of now, thrilled and terrified her. There was no going back, no running away. This wasn't taking a train to Melbourne, or sailing to Devonport, or catching a bus to Hobart, or flying back to Adelaide from Whyalla in a DC3. This trip was one way. Marriage was forever. Her mother told her so. 'Your father will always be my husband, Girlie. Circumstances don't change the facts in God's eyes.' Despite all that Donald did to Clarice, his infidelities, his wastrel ways with money, his long absences, his indifferences, she still called him her husband, even defended him when anyone spoke ill of him, took his advice with the children, let him sleep in a garage behind her unit when he was homeless. Eileen struggled to reconcile the idea of commitment despite cruelty. Marriage seemed to be the greatest risk a woman could take; putting her trust, her life in the hands of a man for the sake of love. She prayed she wasn't misplacing her trust. 'I've made my choice,' she whispered. She was excited, full of hope: and she was terrified.

The stone tower of Holy Trinity church rose into view, and the clock face showed they were arriving on time. The priest outlined the church's history from its foundation in 1838 when they were at the wedding rehearsal, but all Eileen could remember as the car slowed to a stop was that a clock designed by Vulliamy was installed in the original tower. She peered up, wondering if the clock she could see was the original.

'Are you ready?' Bruce asked, from the driver's seat. Judy and Josie stood on the pavement by the rear passenger door.

Eileen steeled her nerves while she waited for Bruce to open her door. She gathered her veil and dress, and alighted, aware of a small group gathered outside the church on North Terrace. 'How do I look?' she asked Judy.

'Like a bride should look,' Judy replied.

'You look beautiful,' Josie assured her.

'Come on, Girlie,' Bruce said, linking his arm through hers. 'Time to give you away.'

Eileen clung to her big brother as they approached the arched wooden door. Bruce was her rock. Bruce was strong, reliable. It should have been her father walking her into the church, but he was a man of sand, unstable and too easily washed away. She looked to where Judy was organising Robyn to lead the way inside, and, for a moment, watching Robyn, Eileen remembered another little girl, the poor child Anthea in Minda Home, and she felt a pang of sorrow for that child. But the past was past. She could not change what had been. No one could. The church doorway led to the future. She was choosing to move forward, to leave the shadows of the past where they belonged.

Eileen searched the faces on the steps, glimpsing colleagues from the

Repatriation hospital who waved and blew kisses. In the narthex, as the organist broke into the opening chords of Mendelssohn's "Wedding March", her heart raced, and she tightened her grip on Bruce's arm. Joyful faces turned to greet her. She looked up.

At the end of the aisle, before the altar, Bill waited in his black suit, white shirt, and grey tie, flanked by his brother Colin and Eileen's brother, Peter. The broad grin lighting Bill's face thrilled Eileen. She walked steadily to him, drew alongside and, when Bruce released her arm, her nerves jangled, no longer with trepidation but expectation. She looked up at Father Geoffrey's grey bearded face, framed by the church's canonical icons and sculptures, and he smiled beneficently, assuring her all was well and right.

*

'To Bill and Eileen!' Colin proclaimed, flourishing his beer glass dramatically.

'To Bill and Eileen!' the reception crowd echoed, raising their glasses. People rattled cutlery against their glasses, so Bill leaned towards Eileen and kissed her gently on the lips to the delight and cheers of the assembly.

As Eileen resumed her seat at the bridal table, Colin leaned in from her left to say, 'My brother is a very lucky man.'

'He is, indeed!' Judy called from Bill's right. She winked at Eileen, and told her, 'Girlie, we've finished loading the presents into the car. We're ready to leave when you are.'

'A few more minutes,' Bill requested.

Squeezing her husband's hand, Eileen looked to the end of the bridal table where her mother sat with Bill's father. Henry was speaking, and Clarice was attentive, but Eileen could see her mother was exhausted from the day's long proceedings, so she rose and squatted at her mother's side, and asked, 'Are you all right?'

'Never happier,' Clarice replied, patting her daughter's hand. 'You look absolutely radiant, Girlie.'

'Thank you,' Eileen replied. She leaned in to kiss her mother's cheek. 'Thank you for being our mother.'

'My son worships you!' Henry declared. 'Today's the happiest I think I've ever seen him. He was so nervous this morning I thought he was going to burst.'

'Have you enjoyed the day?' Eileen asked.

'Thank you, yes,' Henry replied. 'It's been wonderful.'

'I have to call you Dad from now on,' Eileen said, and she leaned forward to kiss Henry on the cheek, conscious of his stubble and soapy aftershave. A tiny part inside her heart cried that the man she kissed was not her father. Bruce and Clive let him know the date and time of the wedding, but for whatever reasons he chose not to attend. A man of sand. Eileen straightened and smiled at Bill who was chatting with Bruce. Josie stood beside John, waggling her fingers in a childish wave, and Eileen grinned before stepping back from the reverie. Her whole family was celebrating her wedding, everyone except her father, and they were laughing and gay, as happy as she remembered them from childhood. Did they fully understand what this night meant for them, and for her? She was leaving. She entered Holy Trinity as Eileen Bonney, nervously embracing metamorphosis, but now she was someone quite new, a young woman making a fresh beginning, forging a future with Bill, a future away from Adelaide, away from the shadow of family, away from her past. But this time she wasn't running away. She was choosing to move on. She was choosing her pathway. There would be no returning, for better or for worse. And she was happier than she imagined possible.

Speeches finished, cake cut, band swinging and dancers swirling, raucous yelling and heavy drinking underway, Eileen whispered in Bill's ear, who nodded and spoke to Colin, who stood and yelled, 'Ladies and gentlemen!' He repeated the call and waited for the noise to subside before he announced, 'On behalf of Mister and Missus Shillitoe-' Cheers rose – 'I would like to thank all of you for celebrating this special day with them, and for your wonderful wishes and gifts. However, my big brother is feeling tired-' Pitying groans echoed around the room – 'and he has a long drive home before he can properly welcome his wife to her new bed.' Lusty cheers and raucous whistles erupted. Colin waited patiently for the hubbub to settle. 'Please rise and form an arch to steer the newlyweds through the door and into their new lives together.'

GIRLIE

Bruce, John, Clive, Peter, Ian and Wally coordinated the crowd into pairs to join hands and raise an archway, and Bill led Eileen through, surrounded by cheerful faces and laughter, and cries of 'Best wishes!' and 'Congratulations!'

Josie met Eileen in the hotel foyer and produced Eileen's winter overcoat, saying, 'It's freezing out there, Girlie. Put this on.'

Judy hugged Eileen. 'You look a dream,' she said. 'That man better look after my big sister or there will be hell to pay.'

Her brothers took their turns to embrace Eileen and wish her well, before Clive enfolded her. 'Thank you for everything,' she said. 'I wish Father had seen this.'

'He did,' Clive said.

'How?' Eileen asked, bewildered.

'The old man was watching from up on Waymouth Street bridge,' Clive told her.

'How do you know that?'

'I spoke to him after the wedding.'

'Why didn't he come down?' Eileen asked.

'You know him,' Clive said. 'He's not called the Elusive One for nothing. The old bastard has too many reasons for not being here.' He shrugged. 'Take care, Girlie. It won't be the same with you living so far away. Now, excuse me. I have to talk to your bloke. Time to give him some manly advice before you set off.'

Family and friends swirled around Eileen, their breaths puffing clouds into the night as they wished her well and made her promise to write or call or visit. She hugged Baxter and Cooper and other Repat colleagues. 'No more bed pans and soiled sheets,' Baxter said.

'Only cleaning up after one man, now,' Cooper added, and laughed. 'And that will be more than enough.'

'I'll visit when I come to town,' Eileen said.

'Sure you will,' Baxter said, cocking an eyebrow.

'I will!' Eileen promised.

'I think you're wanted elsewhere,' Cooper said, nodding past Eileen's shoulder.

Bill leaned into the group, to say, 'Ladies, we have to go.' He reached for Eileen's hand and led her through the crisp night air to the Chevrolet. He opened the door and ushered Eileen into the seat before scooting to the driver's side and climbing in, rubbing his hands together to drive out the cold. 'Ready, Missus Shillitoe?' he asked.

'Ready, Mister Shillitoe,' Eileen replied.

They pulled away from the kerb, Eileen waving at the people crowded under the streetlights, and drove from North Adelaide along King William Street through the illuminated late-night city, their faces glowing in the streetlights and headlights. 'What advice were my brothers giving you?' Eileen asked when they passed through Victoria Square.

Bill grinned. 'Car advice,' he replied.

'You were talking about cars?'

'What else would we talk about?' he asked.

'Are you happy?' Eileen asked.

'Never been happier,' Bill replied.

Eileen settled into the leather seat as they headed for Glen Osmond Road and the tollgate at the base of the climb to Mount Lofty. She pulled her coat close to keep out the chill, and reached for Bill's hand, seeing him grin in the patchy light at her affectionate touch. 'Warm enough?' he asked.

'Getting there,' she replied.

'Here comes the Devil's Elbow,' Bill warned. He shifted down gears to turn the Chev through the tight hairpin that announced the steep, winding climb to Eagle-on-the-Hill and the V8 engine growled as if it enjoyed the climbing challenge.

Eileen peered over Bill's shoulder at the glittering city lights flickering between hill spurs and trees, and she noticed an oddity glinting on the fringes of the car's lights, spinning motes disappearing even as the light caught them. She stared along the tracking headlights, before she said, 'Bill. Look.'

'Snow,' he replied, hearing Eileen's awe. 'It's snow.'

'Pull over!' she urged. 'I want to get out in it!'

'It's freezing,' he cautioned.

'I don't care!' she insisted. 'Pull over!'

Bill slowed the Chevrolet and pulled onto the roadside shoulder, applying the park brake before he switched off the engine, and they sat in silent fascination, watching the swirling, drifting white specks in the dull headlights. Eileen opened her door and climbed out and gazed up into the dark. Wet crystals touched and melted on her cheeks and forehead and hands. She stuck out her tongue to catch more flakes, relishing their butterfly sensation.

Bill joined her and asked, 'Have you ever seen snow?'

'From a distance, in Tasmania,' Eileen replied. 'I always wanted to touch it and be in it. Now I am.'

'It's melting before it hits the ground.'

'Not all of it,' Eileen corrected, pointing to a growing white skin coating the road and the verge.

Headlights arced across the hillside and a car idled slowly past, the passenger calling from the window, 'Everything all right?'

'We're fine!' Bill yelled, waving the car on.

More headlights appeared over the crest from the opposite direction, and a lorry rumbled past, windscreen wipers slapping slowly across the glass as the driver concentrated on the descent. Eileen waved to the driver, smiling as she remembered how often she waved at boys walking or riding past her old home on The Broadway. It had a been a long, fascinating, sometimes painful journey to this day and this moment. She had Baxter and Cooper to thank. And Ruby. Bruce. Her siblings, each in their own way. Her mother. Even her father. Girlie Bonney searched for and found Eileen Shillitoe, even though she never knew what the latter individual might be until now. Her life was changed, her world coated with a thin white and pure veneer. She shivered.

Bill stood behind Eileen and enfolded her in his arms, and his warmth radiated through her back. 'You're cold,' he whispered. 'We better get in the car.'

'One more minute,' Eileen pleaded, watching the snow settle on the roadside and bitumen. 'Right now,' she said quietly, joy thrilling through her, 'the world couldn't be more perfect.'

GIRLIE

Author's Note:

What began as an attempt to write a biography of my mother's formative years morphed into a proto-novel because of the need to 'fill the gaps' in her many stories, and at one point I almost decided to shift the entire project into a creative novel with all names changed and heightened drama, but in the end I settled on the hybrid outcome you have here.

The core of this tale was borne out of years of hearing fragments of my mother's life stories, rummaging through her extensive collection of photographs, and a series of interviews with my mother in the latter years of her life, and after her death with several of her relatives – Bruce Bonney, Ian and Vi Bonney, Judy Jeffries, Josie Webb, and Wally and Margaret Bonney – whose input was invaluable.

The key events in the story were real moments in Eileen's life, but most of the minor events are fictitious, or at least created from snippets of shared stories that were not detailed. Similarly, while the family characters are based on real people, as far as I could glean from interviews, most of the characters are fictional, and must not be seen as portrayals of actual people living or dead.

The background world and local historic details from 1944-1953 were carefully researched to give Eileen's story context.

This is a collage of an ordinary young woman's coming of age in the 1940s and early 1950s, a time when Australian social mores and expectations were very different, and the impact and aftermath of a World War and austerity threw many ordinary Australian lives into disarray. Not all heroes achieve greatness and thrive in challenging times. Some simply survive.

ABOUT THE AUTHOR

Tony Shillitoe's professional writing career was launched with the Andrakis fantasy trilogy: *Guardians*, *Kingmaker* and *Dragonlords* (Pan Macmillan. Tony subsequently published two more fantasy series – The Ashuak Chronicles trilogy and the Dreaming in Amber quartet (HarperCollins Voyager) – and also published young adult novels; *Joy Ride* (Wakefield Press), *Caught in the Headlights* (HarperCollins) and *The Need* (Amazon Kindle). He has short stories in a variety of anthologies and magazines, and he has self-published two anthologies – *Tales of the Dragon* and *The Red Heart* (Amazon Kindle).

Tony's fantasy novels, *The Last Wizard* and *Blood* (Ashuak Chronicles), were shortlisted for the Aurealis Best Fantasy Novel awards in 1995 and 2002 respectively. *Caught in the Headlights* was listed as a Notable Book for Older Readers in the 2003 Children's Book Council Awards and appeared on several Premier's Reading Lists.

Tony has an extensive education career across State, Private and International schools and organisations. He co-designed and delivered courses in the Adelaide TAFE Professional Writing courses from 1995-2000, which included mentoring writers.

Tony is currently working on multiple new projects in several genre.

www.ingramcontent.com/pod-product-compliance
Lightning Source LLC
Chambersburg PA
CBHW021831220426
43663CB00005B/201